To. Joan
From: Beverly
   With love

# 742
# Heart-Warming Poems

A Treasury of Verses, Classic and Colloquial, to Inspire, to Bless,
to Comfort and Entertain, by Over 310 Authors

Compiled and Edited by
## John R. Rice

## Sword of the Lord Publishers
### Murfreesboro, Tennessee

**B. McCALL BARBOUR**
28 GEORGE IV BRIDGE
EDINBURGH EH1 1ES, SCOTLAND

742 HEART-WARMING POEMS
COPYRIGHT, 1964, BY SWORD OF THE LORD PUBLISHERS

**ISBN 0-87398-758-6**


Second Printing, November, 1969
Third Printing, May, 1972
Fourth Printing, 1973
Fifth Printing, 1975
Sixth Printing, 1976
Seventh Printing, 1978
Eighth Printing, 1980
Ninth Printing, 1981

Printed in the United States of America

ACKNOWLEDGMENTS...

The publisher wishes to give grateful thanks to the following for permission to reprint these copyrighted poems and other selections:

"Conscience and Remorse," "He Had His Dream," "The Debt," by Paul Laurence Dunbar. Reprinted by permission of DODD, MEAD & COMPANY from The Complete Poems of Paul Laurence Dunbar.

"The Cup," "And So I Love," "Rest in His Love," "Prayer Without Words," "Trusting," "Wayfarers," "Enough," all by Martha Snell Nicholson. Used by permission of MOODY PRESS, Moody Bible Institute, Chicago 60610, Illinois.

"Christ in Paradise," by William Marion Runyan, from The Waiting Drummer, published by FLEMING H. REVELL COMPANY.

"Out of the Depths," by Father Ryan, from The Bible of the Expositor and the Evangelist, published by UNION GOSPEL PRESS.

"Then Jesus Came," by Oswald J. Smith, copyrighted by RODEHEAVER COMPANY and used by permission.

"Still, Still With Thee," by Harriet Beecher Stowe. Reprinted by permission of HOUGHTON MIFFLIN COMPANY, Boston, Massachusetts.

"By Faith," by Margaret Clarkson, from Clear Shining After Rain; "His Way," by Maude E. Cramer; "Occupied," by Lois Reynolds Carpenter. Used by permission of the SUNDAY SCHOOL TIMES, Philadelphia, Pennsylvania.

"Bereaved," by James Whitcomb Riley, from The Complete Poetical Works of James Whitcomb Riley, copyright 1937, reprinted by permission of THE BOBBS-MERRILL CO., INC., Indianapolis, Indiana.

"Thanksgiving," "Himself," "Resting," "A Prayer for a New Year," by A. B. Simpson:

By permission of CHRISTIAN PUBLICA-, TIONS, INC., Harrisburg, Pennsylvania.

All the poems by Annie Johnson Flint are copyrighted and reproduced by permission of EVANGELICAL PUBLISHERS, Toronto.

"Accepted" and "In Pain," by Margaret Clarkson, copyrighted by His Magazine, 1519 North Astor, Chicago 10, Illinois.

"My Gift," by Avis Christiansen, copyright 1962 by SINGSPIRATION, INC. All rights reserved. Used by permission.

"There Was a Miracle Performed," "When He Makes His Presence Known," "I Need the Shadows," and "The Lovely Land," copyright 1955 by Paul Hutchens in Manna in Music, No. 3. Used by permission of author.

"The Sisters," from the Poetry of Father Tabb. Used by permission of copyright holders, DODD, MEAD & COMPANY, New York, New York.

Poems by Lillie Buffum and Herbert Buffum, Jr., are used by permission. Copyrighted in Lilies From the Valley, by Lillie Buffum.

"Should You Go First," by Albert Rowswell, from Rosy Reflections. Copyrighted.

"Winding Road Ahead," "Thank God for the Bible," by Dr. James M. Gray, "The Blessed Dead" and "By Life or by Death," both by Dr. Will H. Houghton, used by permission of MOODY PRESS, Moody Bible Institute, Chicago 60610, Illinois.

Our sincere appreciation to the following authors for the use of their poems in this book:

Margaret Clarkson, Russell Stellwagon, Dr. Eugene M. Harrison, Mr. Burdette S. Gillilan for the use of the two poems by his father, Strickland Gillilan, Mrs. Leo R. Goodwin, Bill Harvey, L. O. Engelmann, Russell V. Jensen, Mrs. Lorie C. Gooding,

Paul Hutchens, R. W. Hart for "The Best Friend of All," by Ruby McKenzie; all poems by J. Danson Smith of Scotland used by his permission; Ezra M. Coppin; "Follow Me," copyrighted 1953 by Ira F. Stanphill. Used by permission.

Earnest effort has been made to secure permission from authors and owners for the use of their material. Any errors or omissions that may have possibly been made are unintentional and will be corrected in future printings if notification is sent to the publisher, Sword of the Lord.

# CONTENTS

The Complete Index of Authors, the Title Index, and the First Line
Index will be found in the back of the book.

# INTRODUCTION

What a rich store of treasures we have found for you in the poems assembled here! Here are masterpieces from Alfred Tennyson, William Wordsworth, Elizabeth Barrett Browning, Lord Byron, William Wadsworth Longfellow, John Greenleaf Whittier, Harriet Beecher Stowe, Henry van Dyke and Paul Laurence Dunbar.

Here are the best poems of Christian poets, Horatius Bonar, John Oxenham, Annie Johnson Flint, Martha Snell Nicholson and Margaret Clarkson. Among the sweetest are many of those blessed verses of J. Danson Smith of Great Britain.

Here are poems from Frances Ridley Havergal, Fanny J. Crosby, Grace Noll Crowell.

Here are new poems by new writers that add richly to Christian literature. For example, "Uriah" by Bill Harvey, Number 708; see if it does not have as much dramatic literary beauty on a scriptural theme, and richer spiritual insight even than Lord Byron's classic, "Vision of Belshazzar," Number 713. There are several other delightful poems by this devoted gospel singer.

"God-Omniscient," Number 122, by the late, tragic Jack Shuler seems to me powerful, classic, permanent literature. For Christmas poems we hope you will like "Jesus, Baby Jesus," Number 128, and "Christmas Angels," Number 126 by this compiler.

The colloquial poems of Lillie Buffum, wife of a famous song writer, are very sweet. We are glad to introduce poems by Shel Helsley, by Missionaries Russell Stellwagon, Fred Jarvis and L. O. Engelmann, along with scores of other writers. Hundreds of these poems are not available in any other book.

Here are Christian poems for use in pulpit, on platform and in classroom. Here are others not directly Christian, but inspiring, comforting and character-building, as well as entertaining. May a thousand preachers, teachers and writers find them helpful.

We beg the readers--do enjoy these poems! See the pages and pages of indexes at the back of the book. Read them over and find any poem here either by the title, by the first line or by the author. These three indexes at the back will prove specially helpful, we think.

We suggest that you read some poems every day. Read them aloud for your own best enjoyment and for the family. Here is rich, cultural value, spiritual refreshment, new courage in trials, new comfort in sorrow, old truth newly expressed that will bless afresh. Teach some poems to children, memorize some for your own heart enrichment. Truth is sweetened by poetic phrasing, is remembered better by rhyme and meter.

The compiling of these poems has been a joy. My editorial assistant, Miss Viola Walden, with three or four valued helpers has done weeks of splendid, hard work in getting permission, in copying, correcting, in layout and proofreading. God bless them! My grateful thanks to writers and publishers who have so generously given permission for use of copyrighted or original material.

The Bible commands us to "...be filled with the Spirit; Speaking to yourselves in psalms and hymns and spiritual songs, singing and making melody in your heart to the Lord" (Eph. 5:18, 19). May these poems help us so to delight in heart melody!

*John R Rice*

September 1, 1964

# BIBLE

## 1. THANK GOD FOR THE BIBLE

Oh, how we thank Thee, our God, for the Bible,
  Whose truth doth each century clearer reveal!
The fountain of wisdom and source of all knowledge,
  The court of humanity's final appeal.

Oh, here Thou revealest that Thou art our Father,
  The hand that hath fashioned and caused us to be;
Oh, "resident forces," "electrons," and "atoms"
  Could never have made or have loved us like Thee!

Oh, how can we thank Thee, our God, for the Bible,
  The Gospel's glad story!  Nor else had we known
Of sinners redeemed and made meet for Thy glory,
  Of sinners redeemed who shall sit on Thy throne!

Then glory and honor, dominion and power,
  Ascribe to the Trinity again and again;
To Father and Son, and the blest Holy Spirit,
  Forever and ever and ever--Amen!

                                   James M. Gray

## 2. THE BIBLE

We search the world for truth.  We cull
The good, the true, the beautiful,
From graven stone and written scroll,
And all old flower fields of the soul;
And, weary seekers of the best,
We come back laden from our quest,
To find that all the sages said
Is in the Book our mothers read.

                    John Greenleaf Whittier

## 3. THE BOOK OF BOOKS

Within this ample volume lies
The mystery of mysteries.
Happiest they of human race
To whom their God has given grace
To read, to fear, to hope, to pray,
To lift the latch, to force the way;
But better had they ne'er been born
That read to doubt or read to scorn.

                    Sir Walter Scott,
                    1771-1832

## 4. O THOU WORD OF GOD

Blessed inspired Word of God,
  Message sent from Heaven,
Filled with mercy, words that show
  Way to sins forgiven.

Ev'ry word of God is pure,
  Ev'ry word e'erlasting,
Coming from the mouth of God,
  Secret of all blessing.

Tried by millions, dungeon proved,
  Saints have found it precious;
Its unchanging promises
  Satisfy and bless us.

Jesus is the hero of
  All Its glory pages;
Christ the Lamb gives those who trust
  Life through endless ages.

O Thou Word of God, Holy Bible,
Show me the way to God; reveal His
                    precious Son;
O Thou Word of God, Holy Bible,
Shine in this darken'd heart of mine.

                    John R. Rice

## 5.  THE BIBLE

Where childhood needs a standard
   Or youth a beacon light,
Where sorrow sighs for comfort
   Or weakness longs for might,
Bring forth the Holy Bible--
   The Bible! Here it stands!
Resolving all life's problems
   And meeting its demands.

Though sophistry conceal it,
   The Bible! There it stands!
Though Pharisees profane it,
   Its influence expands.
It fills the world with fragrance
   Whose sweetness never cloys;
It lifts our eyes to Heaven,
   It heightens human joys.

Despised and torn in pieces,
   By infidels decried,
With thunderbolts of hatred
   The haughty cynics pride--
All these have railed against it
   In this and other lands;
Yet dynasties have fallen,
   And still the Bible stands!

To Paradise a highway,
   The Bible! There it stands!
Its promises unfailing,
   Nor grievous its commands.
It points man to his Saviour,
   The Lover of his soul;
Salvation is its watchword,
   Eternity its goal!

               James M. Gray

## 6.  GREATEST RICHES

This precious Book I'd rather own
   Than all the golden gems
That e'er in monarchs' coffers shone,
   Or on their diadems.
And were the seas one chrysolite,
   This earth a golden ball,
And gems were all the stars of night,
   This Book were worth them all.

Ah, no, the soul ne'er found relief
   In glittering hoards of wealth;

Gems dazzle not the eye of grief;
   God cannot purchase health.
But here a blessed balm appears
   For every human woe,
And they that seek that Book in tears--
   Their tears shall cease to flow.

              Author Unknown

## 7.  WHAT IS HOME WITHOUT A BIBLE

What is home without a Bible?
   'Tis a place where day is night,
For o'er life's beclouded pathway
   Heaven can shed no kindly light.

What is home without a Bible?
   'Tis a place where daily bread
For the body is provided,
   But the soul is never fed.

What is home without a Bible?
   'Tis a vessel on the sea,
Compass lost and rudder broken,
   Drifting, drifting, aimlessly.

Lost--the Bible!  Lost--its teachings!
   Lost--its help each day in seven:
Lost--to live by!  Lost--to die by!
   Lost?  What's lost?  The way to Heaven.

             Author Unknown

## 8.  THE BIBLE'S PEDIGREE

The Bible is, we plainly see;
Then it must have a pedigree.
It either is a Book divine,
Or men to make it did combine.
Suppose the latter, then they must
Either be wicked men or just;
Take either case and you will see
A proof of its divinity.

If wicked men composed this Book,
Surely their senses they forsook;
For they the righteous man defend,
And curse the bad from end to end.
If righteous, then they change their name,
For they the authorship disclaim,
And often say, "Thus saith the Lord,"
And testify, "It is His Word."
If it be not, they tell a lie
And all their righteousness deny.

             Author Unknown

## 9. RESTING

Resting on the faithfulness of Christ our Lord,
Resting on the fulness of His own sure Word,
Resting on His wisdom, on His love and power,
Resting on His covenant from hour to hour.
Resting in the fortress while the foe is nigh,
Resting in the lifeboat while the waves roll high,
Resting in His chariot for the swift, glad race,
Resting, always resting, in His boundless grace.

Frances Ridley Havergal


## 10. THE SPIRIT'S LIGHT

The Spirit breathes upon the Word,
  And brings the truth to sight;
Precepts and promises afford
  A sanctifying light.

A glory gilds the sacred page
  Majestic like the sun;
It gives a light to every age--
  It gives, but borrows none.

William Cowper


## 11. IT MUST BE FROM GOD

The Holy Bible must have been
Inspired of God and not of men.
I could not if I would, believe
That good men wrote it to deceive,
And bad men could not if they would,
And surely would not if they could,
Proceed to write a book so good.
And certainly no crazy man
Could e'er conceive its wondrous plan.
And pray, what other kinds of men
Than do these three groups comprehend?
Hence it must be that God inspired
The Word which souls of prophets fired.

Author Unknown


## 12. GOD'S UNCHANGING WORD

For feelings come and feelings go,
  And feelings are deceiving;
My warrant is the Word of God,
  Naught else is worth believing.

Though all my heart should feel condemned
  For want of some sweet token,
There is One greater than my heart
  Whose Word cannot be broken.

I'll trust in God's unchanging Word
  Till soul and body sever:
For, though all things shall pass away,
  His Word shall stand forever.

Martin Luther

# CHARACTER

## 13. TRUE GREATNESS

Were I so tall to reach the pole,
Or grasp the ocean with my span,
I must be measured by my soul:
The mind's the standard of the man.

Isaac Watts

## 14. THE CALL FOR MEN

Bring me men to match my mountains,
   Bring me men to match my plains;
Men with empires in their purpose,
   And new eras in their brains.
Bring me men to match my prairies,
   Men to match your inland seas;
Men whose thoughts shall prove a highway
   Up to ample destinies;
Pioneers to clear thought's marshlands
   And to cleanse old error's fen;
Bring me men to match my mountains--
   Bring me men.

Bring me men to match my forests,
   Strong to fight the storm and blast,
Branching toward the skyey future
   Rooted in the fertile past;
Bring me men to match my valleys,
   Tolerant of sun and snow,
Men out of whose fruitful purpose
   Time's consummate blooms shall grow;
Men to tame the tigerish instincts
   Of the lair, and cave, and den,
Cleanse the dragon, slime of nature--
   Bring me men.

Bring me men to match my rivers,
   Continent cleavers, flowing free;
Drawn by the eternal gladness
   To be mingled with the sea;
Men of oceanic impulse,
   Men whose moral currents sweep
Toward the wide-infolding ocean
   Of the undiscovered deep;
Men who feel the strong pulsation
   Of the central sea, and then
Time their current to its earth throb--
   Bring me men.

Sam Walter Foss

## 15. WHILE THE DAYS ARE GOING BY

There are lonely hearts to cherish
   While the days are going by;
There are weary souls who perish,
   While the days are going by.
If a smile we can renew,
As our journey we pursue,
Oh, the good that we may do,
   While the days are going by.

There's no time for idle scorning,
   While the days are going by;
Let your face be like the morning,
   While the days are going by.
Oh, the world is full of sighs,
Full of sad and weeping eyes;
Help your fallen brothers rise,
   While the days are going by.

All the loving links that bind us
   While the days are going by;
One by one we leave behind us,
   While the days are going by;
But the seeds of good we sow,
Both in shade and shine will grow,
And will keep our hearts aglow,
   While the days are going by.

George Cooper

## 16. CHRISTIAN PARADOX

It is in loving--not in being loved,--
   The heart is blest;
It is in giving--not in seeking gifts,--
   We find our quest.

If thou art hungry, lacking heavenly food,--
   Give hope and cheer.
If thou art sad and wouldst be comforted,--
   Stay sorrow's tear.

Whatever be thy longing and thy need,--
   That do thou give;
So shall thy soul be fed, and thou indeed,
   Shalt truly live.

Author Unknown

17. HE HAD HIS DREAM

He had his dream, and all through life,
Worked up to it through toil and strife.
Afloat fore'er before his eyes,
It colored for him all his skies:
  The storm-cloud dark
  Above his bark,
The calm and listless vault of blue
Took on its hopeful hue,
It tinctured every passing beam--
  He had his dream.

He labored hard and failed at last,
His sails too weak to bear the blast,
The raging tempests tore away
And sent his beating bark astray.
  But what cared he
  For wind or sea!
He said, "The tempest will be short,
My bark will come to port."
He saw through every cloud a gleam--
  He had his dream.

Paul Laurence Dunbar
1872-1906

18. I MUST GO ON

I must go on: my hand is put unto the plough;
The wind blows cold; the sluggard leaves the sod unturned;
Nor cares that in the time of harvest he must beg.
But I have seen a Ploughman, spite of wind and snow,
Plough an unbending furrow to the end;
And, ceaseless in His toil, break up the fallow ground.
And through the mist and murk of unpropitious days
Lay up in store the summer's golden harvest joy.
That Ploughman is the Master of my soul:
Therefore, in spite of storm and stress, like Him,
I must go on.

I must fight on: I have in conscience drawn the sword.
The fight is hard: the armed Ephraimites may flee
And fill the streets of Gath and Askelon with mirth;
But I have seen a Warrior take the field alone,
Unsheath His sword against infernal foes,
And, with undaunted soul, cut through the serried ranks
And, though forsaken of the men He came to save,
Pour out His blood to win for them the victor's crown.
That Warrior is the Captain of my soul.
And I, though I should stand alone, like Him,--
I must fight on!

And I must love: my heart is longer not my own.
The world allures, and fickle hearts may turn aside,
Nor care that ashes mark the place of yester's flame:
But I have seen a Lover, spite of scorn and hate,
Love through an agony of blood and tears;
And, ceaseless in His love for e'en His enemies,
Lay down His life, forsaken of the earth and sky,
And, rising, win a bride, and ring the marriage bells!
That Lover is the Lover of my soul;
And I, unto the endless end, like Him,
I too must love.

T. T. Shields

## 19. NOT UNDERSTOOD

Not understood, we move along asunder;
　　Our paths grow wider as the seasons creep:
Along the years we marvel, and we wonder
　　Why life is life; and then we fall asleep--
　　　　Not understood.

Not understood, we gather false impressions,
　　And hug them closer as the years go by,
Till virtues often seem to us transgressions;
　　And thus men rise and fall, and live and die--
　　　　Not understood.

Not understood! How trifles often change us!
　　The thoughtless sentence, or the fancied slight
Destroys long years of friendship, and estranges,
　　And on our souls there falls a freezing blight--
　　　　Not understood.

How many cheerless, lonely hearts are aching
　　For lack of sympathy! Ah, day by day,
How many cheerless, lonely hearts are breaking!
　　How many noble spirits pass away--
　　　　Not understood.

O God! that men could see a little clearer,
　　Or judge less harshly when they cannot see!
O God! that men would draw a little nearer
　　One another, then they'd be nearer Thee--
　　　　And understood.

Thomas Bracken

## 20. THE FEW

The easy roads are crowded
　　And the level roads are jammed;
The pleasant little rivers
　　With the driftingfolk are crammed.

But off yonder where it's rocky
　　Where you get a better view,
You will find the ranks are thinning
　　And the travelers are few.

But the steeps that call for courage
　　And the task that's hard to do,
In the end result in glory
　　For the never wavering few.

Author Unknown

## 21. THREE GATES

If I am tempted to reveal
　　A tale someone to me has told
About another, let it pass,
　　Before I speak, three gates of gold.

Three narrow gates: First, is it true?
　　Then, is it needful? In my mind
Give truthful answer, and the next
　　Is last and narrowest, Is it kind?

And if, to reach my lips at last,
　　It passes through these gateways, three,
Then I may tell the tale, nor fear
　　What the result of speech may be.

Author Unknown

## 22.    THE LAMENT OF THE DEAD SEA

When ages ago
This stream first did flow
From Lebanon's mountainous height,
My banks, robed in green,
Presented a scene
The Creator's heart to delight.

The stream I drank up,
Nor shared e'en a sup,
I kept all the water it gave;
No outlet did flow
To parched lands below
The Jordan in me found its grave.

I still found no peace,
Greed knows no surcease,
And saltness my soul did corrode.
A thirst never ceasing,
A thirst e'er increasing,
Just that was the doom Greed bestowed.

My banks are all bare,
No flowers grow there,
No fish in my waters can live.
The regions around
With deserts abound,
Not life, but destruction, I give.

What chance to repent?
I'm doomed to lament!
Remorse, not repentance, my creed.
In every clime
Till ending of time
I stand as the symbol of Greed.

Eugene M. Harrison

*(Written during his pilgrimage in Palestine. As he brooded over the salty sea and the surrounding scene of desolation, it seemed that the Dead Sea spoke to him in terms of the above lament.)*

## 23.    I AM HABIT

It is mighty hard to shake me;
In my brawny arms I take thee;
I can either make or break thee;
    I am Habit!

Through each day I slowly mold thee;
Soon my tight'ning chains enfold thee;
Then it is with ease I hold thee;
    Thus is Habit!

I can be both good and vile;
I can e'en be worth your while,
Or the cause of your bitter cry;
    I am Habit!

Oft I've proved myself a pleasure;
Proved myself a priceless treasure,
Or a menace past all measure;
    Thus is Habit!

Harmless though I sometimes seem, yet
My strange force is like a magnet;
Like a great and greedy dragnet;
    I am Habit!

Though you sometimes fear or doubt me
No one yet has lived without me;
I am present all about thee;
    Thus is Habit!

Choose me well when you are starting
Seldom is an easy parting;
I'm a devil or a darling!
    I am Habit!

Robert E. Sly

## 24.    THE LAST WORD

Creep into thy narrow bed,
Creep, and let no more be said!
Vain thy onset! all stands fast.
Thou thyself must break at last.

Let the long contention cease!
Geese are swans, and swans are geese,
Let them have it how they will!
Thou art tired; best be still.

They out-talked thee, hissed thee, tore thee?
Better man fared thus before thee;
Fired their ringing shot and passed,
Hotly charged--and sank at last.

Charge once more, then, and be dumb!
Let the victors, when they come,
When the forts of folly fall,
Find thy body by the wall!

Matthew Arnold
1822-1888

## 25. TO A TEACHER

Into your hands I give today
The fairest jewel of my heart, my daughter,
Asking that in my stead you'll be
To her, in these next years, a father.

Keep her from harm, and ever guide
Her steps and e'en her inmost thoughts aright,
Knowing that her mishap would be,
Now and until eternity, my blight.

Once she was small, and trusting held,
As in the village paths we went, my hand;
Now she will leave, and wisdom seek,
No longer small, yet still too weak to stand.

From this day forth, for long you'll be
Guide of her heart, the measure of true worth,
Her mother, father, God, her friend,
Angel, and all that's really good on earth.

See then the greatness of my trust
Ev'n as the Saviour gave to my poor dust, this heart,
Asking that, having done your best,
You'll send me back enriched, my girl.

L. O. Engelmann

## 26. WOUNDED BUT NOT SLAIN

I'm wounded now, but I'm not slain,
  I'm bruised and faint they say,
Just let me lie and bleed a while,
  I'll not be long this way.

My spirit's low, and my eyes flow,
  My heart is sad and sore,
But when my pen'ent tears are gone,
  I'll stand and fight some more.

I'll bind these wounds, I'll dry these tears,
  I'll close this bleeding vein,
I'll not lie here and weep and die,
  I'll rise and fight again.

'Twas yesterday, I bowed so low,
  Was weak from tears and pain,
Today I'm strong, my fears are gone,
  Today I fight again.

Author Unknown

## 27. BE THE BEST

If you can't be a pine on the top of a hill,
  Be a scrub in the valley, but be
The best little scrub by the side of the rill;
  Be a bush if you can't be a tree.

If you can't be a bush, be a bit of the grass,
  And some highway happier make;
If you can't be a muskie, then just be a bass,
  But the liveliest bass in the lake!

We can't all be captains, some have to be crew,
  There's something for all of us here.
There's big work to do, and there's lesser to do;
  And the task you must do is the near.

If you can't be a highway, then just be a trail;
  If you can't be a sun, be a star;
It isn't by size that you win or you fail--
  Be the best of whatever you are.

Douglas Malloch

### 28. THAT LITTLE CHAP O' MINE

To feel his little hand in mine, so clinging and so warm,
To know he thinks me strong enough to keep him safe from harm;
To see his simple faith in all that I can say or do,
It sort o' shames a fellow, but it makes him better too;
And I am trying hard to be the man he fancies me to be,
Because I have this chap at home who thinks the world o' me.
I would not disappoint his trust for anything on earth,
Nor let him know how little I just naturally am worth.
But after all, its easier, that brighter road to climb,
With the little hands behind me to push me all the time.
And I reckon I'm a better man than what I used to be
Because I have this chap at home who thinks the world o' me.

Author Unknown

### 29. TAKE TIME

Take time to work--it is the price of success.
Take time to think--it is the source of power.
Take time to play--it is the secret of perpetual youth.
Take time to read--it is the foundation of wisdom.
Take time to worship--it is the high way to reverence.
Take time to be friendly--it is the road to happiness.
Take time to dream--it is hitching our wagon to a star.
Take time to love and be loved--it is the privilege of the gods.
Take time to look around--it is too short a day to be selfish.
Take time to laugh--it is the music of the soul.

Selected

### 30. MY DAILY CREED

Let me be a little kinder,
Let me be a little blinder
To the faults of those about me;
Let me praise a little more;
Let me be, when I am weary,
Just a little bit more cheery;
Let me serve a little better
Those that I am striving for.

Let me be a little braver
When temptation bids me waver;
Let me strive a little harder
To be all that I should be;
Let me be a little meeker
With the brother that is weaker;
Let me think more of my neighbor
And a little less of me.

Author Unknown

### 31. BEST WORK YET UNDONE

With doubt and dismay you are smitten,
    You think there's no chance for you, son?
Why, the best books haven't been written,
    The best race hasn't been run,
The best score hasn't been made yet,
    The best song hasn't been sung,
The best tune hasn't been played yet;
    Cheer up, for the world is young!

No chance? Why, the world is just eager
    For things that you ought to create;
Its store of true wealth is still meager,
    Its needs are incessant and great;
Don't worry and fret, faint hearted,
    The chances have just begun;
For the best jobs haven't been started,
    The best work hasn't been done.

Berton Braley

## 32.  THE LEAK IN THE DIKE

The good dame looked from her cottage
  At the close of the pleasant day,
And cheerily called to her little son
  Outside the door at play:
"Come, Peter, come! I want you to go,
  While there is yet light to see,
To the hut of the blind old man who lives
  Across the dike, for me;
And take these cakes I made for him--
  They are hot and smoking yet;
You have time enough to go and come
  Before the sun is set."

Then the good-wife turned to her labor,
  Humming a simple song,
And thought of her husband, working hard
  At the sluices all day long;
And set the turf a-blazing,
  And brought the coarse, black bread;
That he might find a fire at night,
  And see the table spread.
And Peter left the brother,
  With whom all day he had played,
And the sister who had watched their sports
  In the willow's tender shade;

And told them they'd see him back before
  They saw a star in sight--
Though he wouldn't be afraid to go
  In the very darkest night!
For he was a brave, bright fellow,
  With eye and conscience clear;
He could do whatever a boy might do,
  And he had not learned to fear.
Why, he wouldn't have robbed a bird's nest,
  Nor brought a stork to harm,
Though never a law in Holland
  Had stood to stay his arm!

And now, with his face all glowing,
  And eyes as bright as the day
With the thoughts of his pleasant errand,
  He trudged along the way;
And soon his joyous prattle
  Made glad a lonesome place--
Alas! if only the blind old man
  Could have seen that happy face!
Yet he somehow caught the brightness
  Which his voice and presence lent;
And he felt the sunshine come and go
  As Peter came and went.

And now, as the day was sinking,
  And the winds began to rise,
The mother looked from her door again,
  Shading her anxious eyes,
And saw the shadows deepen,
  And birds to their homes come back,
But never a sign of Peter
  Along the level track.
But she said: "He will come at morning,
  So I need not fret or grieve--
Though it isn't like my boy at all
  To stay without my leave."

But where was the child delaying?
  On the homeward way was he,
And across the dike while the sun was up
  An hour above the sea.
He was stopping now to gather flowers;
  Now listening to the sound,
As the angry waters dashed themselves
  Against their narrow bound.
"Ah! well for us," said Peter,
  "That the gates are good and strong,
And my father tends them carefully,
  Or they would not hold you long!
You're a wicked sea," said Peter;
  "I know why you fret and chafe;
You would like to spoil our lands and homes;
  But our sluices keep you safe!"

But hark! through the noise of waters
  Comes a low, clear, trickling sound;
And the child's face pales with terror,
  And his blossoms drop to the ground.
He is up the bank in a moment,
  And, stealing through the sand,
He sees a stream not yet so large
  As his slender, childish hand.
'Tis a leak in the dike! He is but a boy,
  Unused to fearful scenes;
But, young as he is, he has learned to know
  The dreadful thing that means.
A leak in the dike! The stoutest heart
  Grows faint that cry to hear,
And the bravest man in all the land
  Turns white with mortal fear.
For he knows the smallest leak may grow
  To a flood in a single night;
And he knows the strength of the cruel sea
  When loosed in its angry might.

And the boy! He has seen the danger,
  And, shouting a wild alarm,

He forces back the weight of the sea
  With the strength of his single arm!
He listens for the joyful sound
  Of a footstep passing nigh;
And lays his ear to the ground, to catch
  The answer to his cry.
And he hears the rough winds blowing,
  And the waters rise and fall,
But never an answer comes to him,
  Save the echo of his call.
He sees no hope, no succor,
  His feeble voice is lost;
Yet what shall he do but watch and wait,
  Though he perish at his post!

So, faintly calling and crying
  Till the sun is under the sea;
Crying and moaning till the stars
  Come out for company;
He thinks of his brother and sister,
  Asleep in their safe, warm bed;
He thinks of his father and mother;
  Of himself as dying, and dead;
And of how, when the night is over,
  They must come and find him at last!
But he never thinks he can leave the place
  Where duty holds him fast.

The good dame in the cottage
  Is up and astir with the light,
For the thought of her little Peter
  Has been with her all the night.
And now she watches the pathway,
  As yester-eve she had done;
But what does she see so strange and black
  Against the rising sun?
Her neighbors are bearing between them
  Something straight to her door;
Her child is coming home, but not
  As he ever came before!

"He is dead!" she cries; "my darling!"
  And the startled father hears,
And comes and looks the way she looks,
  And fears the thing she fears:
Till a glad shout from the bearers
  Thrills the stricken man and wife--
"Give thanks, for your son has saved our land,
  And God has saved his life!"
So, there in the morning sunshine
  They knelt about the boy;
And every head was bared and bent
  In tearful, reverent joy.

'Tis many a year since then; but still,

When the sea roars like a flood,
  Their boys are taught what a boy can do
Who is brave and true and good.
For every man in that country
  Takes his son by the hand,
And tells him of little Peter,
  Whose courage saved the land.

They have many a valiant hero,
  Remembered through the years:
But never one whose name so oft
  Is named with loving tears.
And his deed shall be sung by the cradle,
  And told to the child on the knee,
So long as the dikes of Holland
  Divide the land from the sea!

                              Phoebe Cary

33.   SHALL I FEAR MAN

Shall I, for fear of feeble man,
The Spirit's course in me restrain?
Or, undismay'd in deed and word,
Be a true witness of my Lord?

Awed by a mortal's frown, shall I
Conceal the Word of God Most High!
How then before Thee shall I dare
To stand, or how Thine anger bear?

Shall I, to soothe th' unholy throng,
Soften Thy truth, or smooth my tongue,
To gain earth's gilded toys, or flee
The cross endured, my Lord, by Thee?

What then is he whose scorn I dread?
Whose wrath or hate makes me afraid?
A man! an heir of death! a slave
To sin! a bubble on the wave!

Yea, let men rage; since Thou wilt spread
Thy shadowing wings around my head:
Since in all pain Thy tender love
Will still my sure refreshment prove.

                    From Methodist Hymnal

*"Wherewithal shall a young man cleanse his way? by taking heed thereto according to thy word."--Ps. 119:9.*

## 34.   THE SPIDER AND THE FLY

"Will you walk into my parlor?" said the Spider to the Fly,
" 'Tis the prettiest little parlor that ever you did spy;
The way into my parlor is up a winding stair,
And I have many curious things to show when you are there."
"Oh no, no," said the little Fly, "to ask me is in vain;
For who goes up your winding stair can ne'er come down again."

"I'm sure you must be weary, dear, with soaring up so high;
Will you rest upon my little bed?" said the Spider to the Fly.
"There are pretty curtains drawn around, the sheets are fine and thin;
And if you like to rest awhile, I'll snugly tuck you in!"
"Oh no, no," said the little Fly, "for I've often heard it said
They never, never wake again, who sleep upon your bed!"

Said the cunning Spider to the Fly, "Dear friend, what can I do
To prove the warm affection I've always felt for you?
I have within my pantry, good store of all that's nice;
I'm sure you're very welcome--will you please to take a slice?"
"Oh no, no," said the little Fly, "kind sir, that cannot be,
I've heard what's in your pantry, and I do not wish to see!"

"Sweet creature," said the Spider, "you're witty and you're wise;
How handsome are your gauzy wings, how brilliant are your eyes!
I have a little looking-glass upon my parlor shelf;
If you'll step in one moment, dear, you shall behold yourself."
"I thank you, gentle sir," she said, "for what you're pleased to say,
And bidding you good-morning now, I'll call another day."

The Spider turned him round about, and went into his den,
For well he knew the silly Fly would soon come back again;
So he wove a subtle web in a little corner sly,
And set his table ready to dine upon the Fly.
Then he came out to his door again, and merrily did sing,
"Come hither, hither, pretty Fly, with the pearl and silver wing;
Your robes are green and purple, there's a crest upon your head;
Your eyes are like the diamond bright, but mine are dull as lead."

Alas, alas! how very soon this silly little Fly,
Hearing his wily, flattering words, came slowly flitting by;
With buzzing wings she hung aloft, then near and nearer drew,--
Thinking only of her brilliant eyes, and green and purple hue;
Thinking only of her crested head--poor foolish thing! At last,
Up jumped the cunning Spider, and fiercely held her fast.
He dragged her up his winding stair, into his dismal den
Within his little parlor--but she ne'er came out again!

And now, dear little children, who may this story read,
To idle, silly, flattering words, I pray you ne'er give heed;
Unto an evil counsellor close heart, and ear, and eye,
And take a lesson from this tale of the Spider and the Fly.

                                        Mary Howitt

## 35. "I SHALL NOT PASS AGAIN THIS WAY"

The bread that bringeth strength I want to give,
The water pure that bids the thirsty live:
I want to help the fainting day by day;
I'm sure I shall not pass again this way.
I want to give the oil of joy for tears,
The faith to conquer crowding doubts and fears,
Beauty for ashes may I give always;
I'm sure I shall not pass again this way.

I want to give good measure running o'er,
And into angry hearts I want to pour
The answer soft that turneth wrath away;
I'm sure I shall not pass again this way.
I want to give to others hope and faith,
I want to do all that the Master saith;
I want to live aright from day to day;
I'm sure I shall not pass again this way.

Selected

## 36. THE PIG WALKED AWAY

One evening in October
When I was far from sober
And dragging home a load with manly pride,
My feet began to stutter,
So I laid down in the gutter
And a pig came up and parked right by my side.
Then I warbled, 'It's fair weather
When good fellows get together,'
Till a lady passing by was heard to say,
"You can tell a man who boozes
By the company that he chooses"
Then the pig got up and slowly walked away.

Selected

## 37. TODAY

Today is ours--let's live it.
And love is strong--let's give it.
A song can help--let's sing it.
And peace is dear--let's bring it.

The past is gone--don't rue it.
Our work is here--let's do it.
The world is wrong--let's right it.
If evil comes--let's fight it.

The road is rough--let's clear it.
The future vast--don't fear it.
Is faith asleep?--let's wake it.
Today is free--let's take it.

Lydia L. Roberts

## 38. BETTER LOSE CLEAN THAN WIN FOUL

It is better to lose with a conscience clean
    Than to win with a trick unfair:
It is better to fail and to know you've been,
    Whatever the prize was, square:
Than to claim the joy of a far-off goal
    And the cheers of the standers-by,
And to know down deep in your inmost soul
    A cheat you must live and die.

Who wins by trick may take the prize,
    And at first he may think it sweet,

But many a day in the future lies
    When he'll wish he had met defeat.
For the man who lost shall be glad at heart,
    And walk with his head up high,
While his conqueror knows he must play
            the part
Of a cheat and a living lie.

Detroit Free Press

39.     BEGIN TODAY

Dream not too much of what you'll do tomorrow,
  How well you'll work another year;
Tomorrow's chance you do not need to borrow--
  Today is here.

Boast not too much of mountains you will master
  The while you linger in the vale below.
To dream is well, but plodding brings us faster
  To where we go.

Talk not too much about some new endeavor
  You mean to make a little later on.
Who idles now will idle on forever
  Till life is gone.

Swear not some day to break some habit's fetters,
  When this old year is dead and passed away;
If you have need of living wiser, better,
  Begin today!

                    Anonymous

40.   BOYS WORTH FORTY CENTS!

Your boy has learned to drink, I know,
  The habit has him fast;
A weakling he, to fall so low,
  And throw his life to waste.
But though drink wrecks him, do not cry,
  Its profits are immense;
These boys and girls come very high,
  For each brings forty cents!

Yes, forty cents for you and me,
  The same for every one;
Without this profit, what could we
  In these hard times have done?
So, foolish woman, dry your tears
  If you have any sense;
What if your boy drinks through the years;
  Don't you have forty cents?

Don't sit in sentimental gloom
  Bewailing his sad fate;
The drunkard dies, but in his room
  A hundred prospects wait.
Some silly temp'rance folks have tried
  With prohibition's fence
To save him from our liquor tide--
  Rob us of forty cents!

It matters not if drink takes health,
  Purity, morals, joy,
The state and nation must have wealth--
  What if it takes your boy?
Think what we get in revenue!
  It helps us all; and hence,
A recompense it is to you,
  For you have forty cents!

                    Lena S. Sanders

41.     DON'T TELL ME

Don't tell me what you will do
  When you have time to spare;
Tell me what you did today
  To ease a load of care.
Don't tell me what you will give
  When your ship comes in from the sea;
Tell me what you gave today
  A fettered soul to free.
Don't tell the dreams you have
  Of conquest still afar;
Don't say what you hope to be
  But tell me what you are.

                    Selected

## 42. LIFE'S MIRROR

There are loyal hearts, there are
      spirits brave,
  There are souls that are pure and true;
Then give to the world the best you have,
  And the best will come back to you.

Give love, and love to your life will flow,
  A strength in your utmost need;
Have faith, and a score of hearts will show
  Their faith in your word and deed.

Give truth, and your gift will be paid in kind,
  And honor will honor meet;
And a smile that is sweet will surely find
  A smile that is just as sweet.

Give sorrow and pity to those who mourn;
  You will gather in flowers again
The scattered seeds of your thought outborne,
  Though the sowing seemed but vain.

For life is the mirror of king and slave--
  'Tis just what we are and do;
Then give to the world the best you have,
  And the best will come back to you.

             Madeline Bridges,
             1844-1920

## 43. SOMEBODY'S MOTHER

The woman was old, and ragged, and gray,
And bent with the chill of the winter's day;
The street was wet with a recent snow,
And the woman's feet were aged and slow.
She stood at the crossing and waited long
Alone, uncared for, amid the throng
Of human beings who passed her by,
Nor heeded the glance of her anxious eye.

Down the street, with laughter and shout,
Glad in the freedom of school let out,
Came the boys, like a flock of sheep,
Hailing the snow piled white and deep;
Past the woman so old and gray
Hastened the children on their way,
Nor offered a helping hand to her,
So meek, so timid, afraid to stir
Lest the carriage wheels or the horses' feet
Should crowd her down in the slippery street.

At last one came of the merry troup,
The gayest laddie of all the group;
He paused beside her, and whispered low,
"I'll help you across, if you wish to go."
Her aged hands on his strong young arm
She placed, and so without hurt or harm,
He guided her trembling feet along,
Proud that his own were firm and strong;
Then back again to his friends he went,
His young heart happy and well content.

"She's somebody's mother, boys, you know,
For all she's old, and poor, and slow;
And I hope some fellow will lend a hand
To help my mother, you understand,
If ever so poor, and old, and gray,
When her own dear boy is far away."
And "somebody's mother" bowed her head
In her home that night, and the prayer
          she said
Was--"God be kind to the noble boy
Who is somebody's son, and pride, and joy."

            Author Unknown

*"Honour thy father and thy mother: that thy days may be long upon the land which the Lord thy God giveth thee."--Exod. 20:12.*

## 44. POISE

If you can keep your head when all about you
  Are losing theirs and blaming it on you;
If you can trust yourself when all men
      doubt you,
  But make allowance for their doubting, too;

If you can force your heart and brain and
      sinew
  To serve your term long after they
      are gone,
And so hold on when there is nothing in you
  Except the will which says to them,
      "Hold on!"

If you can fill the unforgiving minute
  With sixty seconds' worth of distance run,
Yours is the earth and everything that's in it,
  And--what is more--you'll be a man,
      my son!

            Rudyard Kipling

## 45.   FAITH

What if I say--
"The Bible is God's Holy Word,
Complete, inspired, without a flaw"--
But let its pages stay
Unread from day to day,
And fail to learn therefrom God's law?
What if I go not there to seek
The truth of which I glibly speak,
For guidance on this earthly way--
Does it matter what I say?

What if I say
That Jesus Christ is Lord Divine;
Yet fellow-pilgrims can behold
Naught of the Master's love in me,
No grace of kindly sympathy?
If I am of the Shepherd's fold,
Then shall I know the Shepherd's voice
And gladly make His way my choice.
We are saved by faith, yet faith is one
With life, like daylight and the sun.
Unless they flower in our deeds,
Dead, empty husks are all the creeds.
To call Christ, Lord, but strive not to obey,
Belies the homage that with words I pay.

Maud Frazer Jackson

## 46.   WHOM GOD CHOOSES

When God wants to drill a man,
And thrill a man, and skill a man,
When God wants to mold a man,
To play the noblest part;
When He yearns with all His heart
To create so great and bold a man
That all the world shall be amazed,
Watch His methods; watch His ways.
How He ruthlessly perfects
When He royally elects!
How He hammers him and hurts him,
And with mighty blows converts him
Into trial shapes of clay
Which only God understands;
While his tortured heart is crying,
And he lifts beseeching hands!
How He bends but never breaks
When his good He undertakes.
How He uses whom He chooses,
And with every purpose fuses--him;

But every act induces him
To try His splendor out...
God knows what He's about!

Selected

## 47.   COLUMBUS

Behind him lay the gray Azores,
  Behind the Gates of Hercules;
Before him not the ghost of shores,
  Before him only shoreless seas.
The good mate said: "Now must we pray,
  For lo! the very stars are gone.
Brave Admiral, speak, what shall I say?"
  "Why, say 'Sail on! sail on! and on!'"

"My men grow mutinous day by day;
  My men grow ghastly wan and weak."
The stout mate thought of home; a spray
  Of salt wave washed his swarthy cheek.
"What shall I say, brave Admiral, say,
  If we sight naught but seas at dawn?"
"Why, you shall say at break of day,
  'Sail on! sail on! sail on! and on!'"

They sailed and sailed, as winds might blow,
  Until at last the blanched mate said,
"Why, now not even God would know
  Should I and all my men fall dead.
These very winds forget their way,
  For God from these dread seas is gone.
Now speak, brave Admiral, speak and say"--
  He said: "Sail on! sail on! and on!"

They sailed. They sailed. Then spake
        the mate:
  "This mad sea shows his teeth tonight.
He curls his lip, he lies in wait,
  With lifted teeth, as if to bite!
Brave Admiral, say but one good word:
  What shall we do when hope is gone?"
The words leapt like a leaping sword:
  "Sail on! sail on! sail on! and on!"

Then, pale and worn, he kept his deck,
  And peered through darkness. Ah,
        that night
Of all dark nights! And then a speck--
  A light! a light! a light! a light!
It grew, a starlit flag unfurled!
  It grew to be Time's burst of dawn.
He gained a world; he gave that world
  Its grandest lesson: "On! sail on!"

Joaquin Miller

## 48. BUSYBODIES

Paul once wrote to Timothy, this truth he did declare
Of folks who went from house to house to peddle out their ware.
I think he called them busybodies, or something of the sort,
Or maybe it was "tattlers"--just to make it short.

Among the Thessalonians, he found there quite a few
Who really walked disorderly, and were busybodies too;
Classed with thieves and murderers, Peter then declares
That they are busybodies in other men's affairs.

They tell me folk are different, times have changed you know;
I find there are busybodies just everywhere I go.
The preacher and his family have to bear the brunt
And the humiliation of the busybodies' stunt.

They talk about the preacher--he can't, to save his life,
Buy a piece of furniture, or a garment for his wife
Without some busybody or tattler in the crowd
Gives out the information, "They're extravagant and proud."

The suit he chanced to purchase--the price was out of sight;
His hat and shoes too "nifty"; if he'd really done the right
He'd gone to Mrs. Tattler and asked for her advice.
She'd been so glad to give it, and settle on the price.

Then if the wife and children perchance get something new,
Why Mrs. Busybody just made the air turn blue.
"Where did they get the money to buy such lovely stuff?
My goodness, gracious, sister, their clothes were good enough."

What could we do without them--these busybodies? Say,
We'd have so little worry, we'd most forget to pray.
We wouldn't have a racket within the church domain;
The preacher and the people could live and dress the same.

I'm really thrilled about it, and will there ever be
A body of God's people so sanctified and free?
Whose words are golden apples in silver pictures rare--
They'd bring a blessing, and sunshine everywhere.

Lillie Buffum

## 49.  BEAUTIFUL GARMENTS

He would have us wear beautiful garments--
  Those which we may have through grace--
The robe of a tranquil spirit,
  The calm of a peaceful face;

The charm of a gentle manner,
  The lustre of heaven-lit eyes;

That robe of such sacred splendour,
  The spirit of sacrifice.

These, these, and yet other garments,
  All beautiful, bright and fair,
We may, by His grace, adorn us,
  And unto His glory wear.

J. Danson Smith

## 50.  FAR NOBLER

Far nobler the sword that is nicked and worn;
Far fairer the flag that is grimy and torn
Than when to the battle fresh they were borne.

He was tried and found true; he stood the test;
'Neath whirlwinds of doubt, when all the rest
Crouched down and submitted, he fought best.

There are wounds on his breast that can never be healed;
There are gashes that bleed and may never be sealed,
But, wounded and gashed, he won the field.

And others may dream in their easy chairs,
And point their white hands to the scars he bears;
But the palm and the laurel are his--not theirs.

Author Unknown

## 51.  BE TRUE!

Thou must be true thyself
  If thou the truth wouldst teach;
Thy soul must overflow if thou
  Another's soul wouldst reach!
It needs the overflow of heart
  To give the lips full speech.

Think truly, and thy thoughts
  Shall the world's famine feed;
Speak truly, and each word of thine
  Shall be a fruitful seed;
Live truly, and thy life shall be
  A great and noble creed.

Horatius Bonar,
1808-1889

## 52.  OUR CAN'TS AND CANS

If you would have some worthwhile plans
You've got to watch your can'ts and cans;
You can't aim low and then rise high;
You can't succeed if you don't try;
You can't go wrong and come out right;
You can't love sin and walk in light;
You can't throw time and means away,
And live sublime from day to day.

Selected

## 53.     WHY?

I saw a woman lying on a stair,
  Head down, flies crawling on her face
                and hair,
While lodgers came and went, nor looked
                at all.
  She was a masterpiece of Alcohol.

I saw an old man lying on a bed,
  Helpless for life, his weary old wife said,
His hip was broken in a needless fall--
  Achievement credited to Alcohol.

I saw a man in death's stark whiteness lie,
  A bullet through his heart.  I heard the cry
Of wife and children sensing hunger's thrall--
  Work of the all-efficient Alcohol.

I saw a lovely girl, clean-faced and fine,
  But foolish, plied by men with gin and wine.
Till self-respect had tottered to its fall.
  Another Magdalene.  Hail, Alcohol!

I saw these things--you may have seen
                them, too.
  The world is saturated with them through
                and through.
And there are those who claim it has
                a place--
  A drug that does that to the human race.

Clarence Edwin Flynn

### 54. HOW DID YOU DIE?

Did you tackle that trouble that came your way
    With a resolute heart and cheerful?
Or hide your face from the light of day
    With a craven soul and fearful?
Oh, a trouble's a ton, or a trouble's an ounce,
    Or a trouble is what you make it.
And it isn't the fact that you're hurt that counts,
    But only how did you take it?

You are beaten to earth? Well, well, what's that?
    Come up with a smiling face.
It's nothing against you to fall down flat,
    But to lie there--that's disgrace.
The harder you're thrown, why the higher you bounce;
    Be proud of your blackened eye!
It isn't the fact that you're licked that counts;
    It's how did you fight--and why?

And though you be done to the death, what then?
    If you battled the best you could;
If you played your part in the world of men,
    Why, the Critic will call it good.
Death comes with a crawl, or comes with a pounce,
    And whether he's slow or spry,
It isn't the fact that you're dead that counts,
    But only, how did you die?

E. V. Cooke

### 55.    KEEP KICKING

Two gay young frogs from inland bogs,
Had spent the night in drinking.
As morning broke and they awoke,
While still their eyes were blinking,
A farmer's pail came to the swale,
And caught them quick as winking.
'Ere they could gather scattered senses,
Or breathe a prayer for past offenses,
That granger grand, that guiltless man,
Had dumped them in the milkman's can.
They quickly find their breath will stop
Unless they swim upon the top.
They swim for life, they kick and swim
Until their weary eyes grow dim.
Their muscles ache, their breath grows short,
And gasping, speaks one weary sport,
"Say, old dear, I've had enough of life, no more
I'll try it. Sweet milk is not my diet."
"Tut tut, my lad," the other cries,

"A frog's not dead until he dies.
Let's keep on kicking, that's my plan.
We yet may see outside this can."
"No use, no use," faint heart replies,
Turns up his toes and gently dies.
Now the brave frog, undaunted still,
Kept kicking with a right good will,
Until with joy too great to utter
He found he'd churned a pound of butter.
And climbing upon this hunk of grease,
He floated to town with greatest ease.

Now the moral to the story is this:

When in your Christian life you find
You're weary of the toilsome grind,
Don't get discouraged and go down.
But struggle on, no murmur utter,
A few more kicks may bring the butter.

Author Unknown

# CHRIST, GOD

## 56.  JESUS, MY LORD

I'd rather get down at the feet of my Lord,
  And gather the crumbs as they fall,
Than sit as a guest at a sumptuous board,
  Where Jesus has not had a call.

I'd rather my body a temple should be,
  Where Jesus my Master would stay,
Than have all the wealth of the kingdoms,
      and see
  Him driven forever away.

I'd rather have Him for companion and friend,
  His Book for my counsel and guide,
Than walk in vain pleasure, and find at
      the end
  No refuge in which I may hide.

I want to leave all in His hands ev'ry day,
  To do as it seemeth Him best;
And self on the altar a sacrifice lay,
  And on His sweet promises rest.

Jesus, my Lord!  Jesus, my King!
  Down at Thy feet I fall;
Jesus, my Saviour, my Refuge, my Friend,
  Jesus, my Lord, my All.

                Amelia M. Starkweather

## 57.  PEACE ON EARTH

Here Peace alighted once,
  But could not find a home,
To Him who brought it, earth
  Could give no room.

Him and His peace man would not have,
  And in this Child of peace
Man saw no heavenly excellence,
  No grace, no comeliness.

Peace in that cradle lay,
  The Prince of Peace was there;
The fulness of His peace
  He brought with man to share.

                Horatius Bonar

## 58.  IN CHRIST

In Christ I have a pardon full
  From all the guilt of sin.
The fountain flowing from His wounds
  Keeps cleansing me within.

In Christ access to God is mine;
  He lives to intercede.
Before the Father's glorious throne
  He brings my slightest need.

In Christ I've found a calm repose.
  While in His arms I rest,
The circling storms can hold no threat,
  Nor mounting waves molest.

In Christ I have a "blessed hope"
  No earthly prize can dim.
The trumpet's sound shall call me up,
  Eternity with Him!

Nor have I aught but what He gives,
  And, bowing at His feet,
This joyous truth enthralls my soul--
  In Christ I am complete!

                Samuel W. McGarvey

## 59.   JESUS

Lonely?  No, not lonely
  With Jesus standing by;
His presence always cheers me,
  I know that He is nigh.

Friendless?  No, not friendless
  Since Jesus is my friend;
I change, but He remaineth
  True, faithful to the end.

Saddened?  No, not saddened
  By scenes of deepest woe;
I should be if I knew not
  That Jesus loves me so.

Tired?  No, not tired;
  While leaning on His breast
My soul has full enjoyment
  Of His eternal rest.

                Charlotte S. C. Panton

## 60.  GOD EVER CARES

God ever cares!  Not only in life's summer,
    When skies are bright and days are long and glad;
He cares as much when life is draped in winter,
    And heart doth feel bereft, and lone, and sad.

God ever cares!  His heart is ever tender;
    His love doth never fail nor show decay;
The loves of earth, though strong and deep, may perish--
    But His shall never, never pass away.

God ever cares!  And thus when life is lonely,
    When blessings one time prized are growing dim, --
The heart may find a sweet and sunny shelter, --
    A refuge and a resting place in Him.

God ever cares!  And time can never change Him; --
    His nature is to care, and love, and bless;
And drearest, darkest, emptiest days afford Him
    But means to make more sweet His own caress.

                    J. Danson Smith

## 61.  JESUS DIED FOR SINNERS

Born without a bed in a stable,
    Wrapped in swaddling clothes in the hay;
Others had no room for the Saviour,
    There the Baby first saw the day.
Leaving golden streets, God and angels,
    For the straw on which Jesus lay.

Foxes have their holes, safe for sleeping,
    Birdlings peep secure in their nests;
But the Son of man, homeless, lonely,
    For His weary head had no rest.
Nazarene despised and rejected,
    Poverty was His and distress.

Weeping on the mount o'er the city,
    With compassion moved for the throng;
Seeking for the lost sheep astraying,
    Helping sick and well, weak and strong.
Shedding tears of grief for us sinners,
    Paying with His blood for our wrongs.

Sweating bloody sweat in the garden,
    Beaten before Pilate and tried;
With a crown of thorns, robed in scarlet,
    Nailed upon a cross where He died;
Hanging between thieves, naked, thirsting,
    Christ my Lord was thus crucified.

Now He's gone above with the Father,
    His high priestly pleading to do;
Ever for His own interceding,
    Then He'll come and take us Home too.
Ev'ry knee shall bow to the Saviour,
    Him we'll praise eternity through.

Jesus died for sinners,
    Pouring out His soul.
Those who take and trust Him
    Shall be fully whole.

                    John R. Rice

## 62.  CHRIST

He is a Path, if any be misled;
    He is a Robe, if any naked be;
If any chance to hunger, He is Bread;
    If any be a bondman, He is Free;
If any be but weak, how strong is He!
    To dead men Life He is, to sick men Health;
To blind men Sight, and to the needy Wealth;
    A Pleasure without loss, a Treasure without
        stealth.

                    Giles Fletcher, Leaves of Gold

## 63. "I AM THAT I AM"

*Exod. 3:14*

I Am the "Way" for the Traveler, John 14:6
I Am the "Truth" if distressed, John 14:6
I Am the "Life" for the Dying, John 14:6
I Am the "Bread," and the "Rest," Heb. 4:9--Matt. 6:48

I Am the "Rock" for the fainting, Exod. 17:6
I Am the "Pillar" by day, Exod. 14:19
I Am the "Light" for the groping, John 1:7
I Am the "Bush" by the way, Exod. 3:2

I Am the "Lion of Judah," Rev. 5:5
I Am the "Branch" (Isa. 11:1) and the "Vine," John 15:1
I Am the "Friend at Midnight," Luke 11:5
I Am the "Captain Divine," Joshua 5:14

I Am the "Prince of Peace," Isa. 9:6
I Am the "Wonderful One," Isa. 9:6
I Am the "Father Eternal," Isa. 9:6
I Am the "Well-Beloved Son," Matt. 3:17

I Am the "Coming Bridegroom," Matt. 25:6
I Am the "Manna" (Exod. 16:15), the "Rod," Exod. 4:2
I Am the "Corn of Wheat," John 12:24
I Am the "Word of God," John 1:1

I Am the "Door to the Sheepfold," John 10:7
I Am the "Shepherd There," John 10:11
I Am the "Morning Star," Rev. 22:16
I Am the "Lily" so fair, Song of Sol. 2:1

I Am the "Rose of Sharon," Song of Sol. 2:1
I Am the "Fisher of Men," Mark 1:17
I Am the "God Almighty," Rev. 1:8
I Am the "Beginning--the End," Rev. 1:8

I Am the "First" and the "Last," Rev. 1:11
"Alpha," "Omega" am I, Rev. 1:8
I Am the "King of kings," Rev. 17:14
I Am "He who lives on High," Rev. 21

I Am the "Lamb of God," John 1:29
I Am the "Saviour of Men," Luke 2:11
I Am the "Faithful Witness," Rev. 1:5
"The Creator" (Col. 1:16) and the "Amen," Rev. 3:4.

Louise Appleby Boyle

## 64. THE WASHERWOMAN'S FRIEND

In a very humble cot,
In a rather quiet spot,
In the suds and in the soap
Worked a woman full of hope,
Working, singing all alone
In a sort of undertone,
"With a Saviour for a friend,
He will keep me to the end."

Sometimes happening along,
I have heard the semi-song,
And I often used to smile,
More in sympathy than in guile;
But I never said a word
In regard to what I heard,
As she sang about her Friend,
Who would keep her to the end.

Not in sorrow nor in glee,
Working all day long was she,
As her children, three or four,
Played around her on the floor;
But in monotones the song
She was humming all day long,
"With a Saviour for a friend,
He will keep me to the end."

Just a trifle lonesome she,
Just as poor as poor could be;
But her spirits always rose
Like the bubbles in the clothes,
And though widowed and alone,
Cheered her with the monotone
Of a Saviour and a Friend,
Who would keep her to the end.

I have seen her rub and scrub
On the washboard in the tub,
While the baby, sopped in suds,
Rolled and tumbled in the duds,
Or was paddling in the pools
With old scissors stuck in spools,
She was humming of her Friend,
Who would keep her to the end.

Human hopes and human creeds
Have their roots in human needs,
And I would not wish to strip
From that washerwoman's lip
Any song that she can sing,
Any hope that song can bring,
For the woman had a Friend,
Who did keep her to the end. --Author Unknown

## 65. FAIREST LORD JESUS

Fairest Lord Jesus! Ruler of all nature!
O, Thou of God and man the Son!
Thee will I cherish, Thee will I honor,
Thou, my soul's glory, joy, and crown!

Fair are the meadows, fairer still the woodlands,
Robed in the blooming garb of spring;
Jesus is fairer, Jesus is purer,
Who makes the woeful heart to sing!

Fair is the sunshine, fairer still the moonlight,
And all the twinkling, starry host;
Jesus shines brighter, Jesus shines purer
Than all the angels Heaven can boast!

Anonymous

## 66. JESUS DRINKS THE BITTER CUP

Jesus drinks the bitter cup,
The winepress treads alone;
Tears the graves and mountains up,
By His expiring groan;
Lo! The powers of Heaven He shakes;
Nature in convulsions lies;
Earth's profoundest centre quakes;
The Jehovah dies!

Oh, my God, He dies for me,
I feel the mortal smart!
See Him hanging on the tree, --
A sight that breaks my heart!
Oh that all to Thee might turn!
Sinners, ye may love Him too;
Look on Him ye pierc'd, and mourn
For One who bled for you.

Weep o'er your desire and hope,
With tears of humblest love:
Sing, for Jesus is gone up,
And reigns enthron'd above:
Lives our Head, to die no more;
Power is all to Jesus given;
Worshipp'd as He was before,
The Immortal King of Heaven.

John Wesley
(From a Collection of Hymns--1779)

## 67.    THE CRUCIFIXION

Oh! How dreary, how distressing,
Bosom rending, soul oppressing,
  Was that awesome moment when
Christ, the perfect Lamb, was offered
And redemption's price was proffered
  For mankind enslaved to sin!

When the evil one--unchained--
On the Guileless, the Unstained,
  In his rage, his fury fell;
When the Christ for His elected
Bowed His head despised, rejected,
  Bearing all the pangs of Hell!

When from all His own absented
He in sore distress lamented
  In Gethsemane's dark night;
When the Easter moon ascending
On my Lord in sorrow bending
  Cast its sad, its somber light!

When that veriest of traitors
To his plotting instigators
  With a kiss betrayed his Lord,
When the rabble pressed around Him,
The defenseless One, and bound Him
  At the point of spear and sword!

When Sanhedrin in derision
Cast its infamous decision,
  Spat upon Him, at Him sneered,
Him, the Judge of all creation,
Whom with humble veneration
  Father Abraham revered!

When that craven, Pontius Pilate,
Durst condemn the One Inviolate
  While he set a felon free;
When upon the rabble's urging
He delivered Him to scourging
  And to death upon the tree!

When the thorn-crowned Son of David,
Robed in scorn by these depraved
  From the inner court was led,
There to bear the taunts of Jewry,
Hear their cries for blood, their fury
  Poured upon His sacred head!

When the Lamb of God most holy
'Neath His cross ascended slowly
  To the hill of Golgotha,
Plodding through that weary distance

Reft of every friend's assistance
  'Neath my sin's anathema!

When that bitter draught was given
And the brutal nails were driven
  Through His lived hands and feet;
And they lifted Him, the glorious,
Twixt the base, the mal-notorious,
  All man's whetted scorn to meet!

When that one, his venom nursing,
Turned on Him with bitter cursing
  For His patient, voiceless woe;
When in deep self-abnegation
He forgave the fulmination
  Of the multitude below;

When the Man without transgression
In whom sin ne'er found expression
  With heartbroken agony,
Cried in utter desolation,
"God! O God of my salvation,
  Why hast Thou forsaken Me?"

Deck your eyes, ye high spectators,
Angel hosts, His venerators,
  Be forever mystified!
Hear, O earth, with mortal terror,
Hear it sinners--steeped in error--
  How for you His soul is tried!

Know ye that in His affliction
Lies your hope, your benediction,
  Lies your claim to rest on high!
Though it fill your soul with sadness
Yet make room for joy, for gladness,
  Your redemption draweth nigh!

He the Crucified, the Smitten,
He the Bruised, the Serpent-bitten
  Is the Conqueror of Hell;
Is the Founder of creation,
Is the Bringer of salvation,
  Is the God of Israel!

Yea, all people, come beholding
Time's long mystery unfolding;
  Sons of men, observe with fear!
'Tis God's Word here vindicated.
'Tis God's will here demonstrated,
  God's decree enacted here!

For the guilt of His elected,
Lost in sin, to death subjected,

God His only Son doth ban,
In the selfsame moment showing
All His wrath at evildoing
    And His love for fallen man.

He, the Just, for sin's infraction
Needs must have full satisfaction
    But the blood makes sinners free.
Truth and grace here meet together,
Peace and justice kiss each other
    As foretold in prophecy.

Hence the Word was born of Mary,
Heaven-sent on earth to tarry,
    Root and branch of David's line!
Came to serve us, came to suffer,
Came Himself for us to offer,
    Came upon the cross to pine!

There He hung, reproached, derided!
There His raiment was divided
    'Mongst the mocking soldiery!
There endured He grief unspoken,
There His loving heart was broken
    By man's thankless perfidy!

Ah! What woes His woes engender
In those women, meek and tender
    Who from far partake His pain!
Ah! What tears! What bitter weeping,
For the Shepherd in whose keeping,
    They confided has been slain!

At the cross stood Jesus' mother,
Without son now, and a shudder
    Of despair transfixed her soul!
Oh, ye heavens! Did e'er anguish
Such as made that mother languish
    Over human bosom roll?

Oh! How dreary, how distressing,
Bosom-rending, soul-oppressing,
    Was that terrifying hour,
When the Son poured out His being,
Shed His lifeblood for the freeing
    Of mankind from Satan's power!

Stand in awe! The earth is quaking!
Rocks are rending! Saints awaking!
    CHRIST, THE MIGHTY SAVIOUR DIES!
Lo, the veil within the Temple
Tears in twain as an ensample
    Of re-opened Paradise!

Golgotha, thou saw'st that wonder,
How the Sun of suns went under,
    How the day was turned to night!
But that night will soon be lifted
And when all the clouds are rifted
    Then our hopes will turn to sight!

Lo! Fulfilled is every token,
Every word by prophet spoken,
    Justice has been satisfied!
All our hideous wounds are healed,
All our sordid sin concealed,
    Satan's dream has been denied!

Ah! The cross shall be my glory!
All my song and all my story,
    "Christ has borne the curse for me!"
Christ has paid for my transgression!
Christ has placed me in possession
    Of the Father's clemency!

Blessed all on Him believing!
Blessed all His grace receiving!
    Holy Spirit, Heavenly Dove,
Oh, inspire my soul to singing,
Oh, inspire my heart to bring
    Him my whole, my perfect love!

Praise--O Zion--praise Jehovah!!
Earth and all, sing "Hallelujah"
    With a new song's swelling tide!
PRAISE HIM--CONQUEROR OF EVIL!
PRAISE HIM--SAVIOUR OF HIS PEOPLE!
    PRAISE YOUR KING--THE CRUCIFIED!

                                    Dewey Westra

## 68.   HE DIED FOR ME!

Was it FOR ME He bowed His head,
Upon the cross, and freely shed
His precious blood--that crimson tide,
Was it FOR ME the Saviour died?

It was FOR ME...Yes all FOR ME...
O love of God...so great, so free...
O wondrous love...I'll shout and sing...
He died FOR ME...my Lord and King!

                                    J. Danson Smith

## 69.   IF I GAINED THE WORLD

If I gained the world, but lost the Saviour,
    Were my life worth living for a day?
Could my yearning heart find rest and comfort
    In the things that soon must pass away?
If I gained the world, but lost the Saviour,
    Would my gain be worth the lifelong strife?
Are all earthly pleasures worth comparing
    For a moment with a Christ-filled life?

Had I wealth and love in fullest measure,
    And a name revered both far and near,
Yet no hope beyond, no harbor waiting,
    Where my storm-tossed vessel I could steer;
If I gained the world, but lost the Saviour,
    Who endured the cross and died for me,
Could then all the world afford a refuge,
    Whither, in my anguish, I might flee?

O what emptiness!--without the Saviour
    'Mid the sins and sorrows here below!
And eternity, how dark without Him!--
    Only night and tears and endless woe!
What, though I might live without the Saviour,
    When I come to die, how would it be?
O to face the valley's gloom without Him!
    And without Him all eternity!

O the joy of having all in Jesus!
    What a balm the broken heart to heal!
Ne'er a sin so great, but He'll forgive it,
    Nor a sorrow that He does not feel!
If I have but Jesus, only Jesus,--
    Nothing else in all the world beside--
O then everything is mine in Jesus;
    For my needs and more He will provide.

                    Anna Olander
                    From the Swedish


## 70.   HE LIVES

The triune God conceived a plan
To pay the debt for ev'ry man
    Regardless of the cost.
He sent His only Son to die,
That we may reign with Him on high
    And thus redeemed the lost.

Christ Jesus struggled up a hill.
It was His Father's sovereign will
    To rend the veil in twain.

The cross, the cross, how large it loomed;
But without blood, the world was doomed,
    And life had been in vain.

How can we now but stand in awe,
In knowing Christ fulfilled the law
    Because our sins He bore.
He rose triumphant over death;
What God required has all been met.
    He lives forevermore!

                    Tom Johnson

## 71.  ALL FOR SINNERS

What Thou, my Lord, hast suffered,
  Was all for sinners' gain:
Mine, mine was the transgression,
  But Thine the deadly pain:
Lo, here I fall, my Saviour!
  'Tis I deserved Thy place;
Look on me with Thy favor,
  Vouchsafe to me Thy grace.

What language shall I borrow
  To thank Thee, dearest Friend,
For this, Thy dying sorrow,
  Thy pity without end?
Lord, make me Thine forever,
  Nor let me faithless prove:

Oh, let me never, never,
  Abuse such dying love.

Bernard of Clairvaux
Trans. by Jas. W. Alexander

## 72.  MY CUP

O Christ, what burdens bowed Thy head,
  Our load was laid on Thee;
Thou stoodest in the sinner's stead,
  Didst bear all ill for me.

Death and the curse were in our cup,
  O Christ, 'twas full for Thee,
But Thou hast drained the last dark drop,
  'Tis empty now for me.

Author Unknown

## 73.  THE NAME ABOVE EVERY NAME

*"I am the Almighty God [El Shaddai]."—Gen. 17:1.*
*"I am the Lord that healeth thee [Jehovah Ropheka]."*
*—Exod. 15:26.*

Oh what is Jehovah El Shaddai to me?
My Lord, God and Saviour, Immanuel, He;
My Prophet, Priest, Sacrifice, Altar and Lamb;
Judge, Advocate, Surety and Witness, I AM;
My Peace and my Life, my Truth and my Way;
My Leader, my Teacher, my Hope and my Stay;
Redeemer and Ransom, Atonement and Friend;
He's Alpha, Omega, Beginning and End.

Yea, more is Jehovah El Shaddai beside--
Avenger and Shepherd, and Keeper and Guide;
My Horn of Salvation, my Captain in war;
My Dayspring, my Sun, and my Bright Morning Star;
My Wonderful, Counsellor, Wisdom and Light;
My Shadow by day, and my Beacon by night;
Pearl, Ornament, Diadem, Treasure untold;
My Strength and my Sun, in Him I behold.

All this is Jehovah Ropheka and more--
My Bread and my Water, my Dwelling, my Door;
My Branch and my Vine, my Lily and Rose;
Rock, Hiding Place, Refuge, Shield, Covert, Repose;
My sure Resurrection, my Glory above;
My King in His beauty, my Bridegroom, my Love;
My all and in all in Christ Jesus I see,
For God hath made Him to be all things to me.

Now say to Thy soul, "What is He to thee?"

John H. Sammis

### 74. JESUS LOVES ME

Jesus is such a Saviour,
  Jesus is such a Friend.
Never forsakes nor leaves me,
  Nor fails my needs to send.
Jesus who died to save me,
  Jesus who sought for me,
Now with His love surrounds me,
  Oh, what a Friend is He!

Now in His love I glory,
  Rest and rejoice in Him.
Blood-bought and dear to Jesus,
  My joy is full within.
Nothing then, I'm persuaded,
  Can take me from His hand,
Nor height nor depth, nor powers,
  Satan, nor self, nor man.

Why should you slight the Saviour?
  Why turn from Him away?
Where will you find forgiveness,
  Loving care, night and day?

Nobody else could save you,
  Nobody else could pay
Sin's debt for poor, lost sinners,
  He would be yours today.

What can I do for Jesus?
  How may I Him repay?
Oh, to tell all the story,
  Of His salvation's way.
Never a theme for singing,
  Never a truth for praise
As Jesus' love for sinners,
  I'll sing it all my days.

Jesus loves me,
Yes, Jesus loves me;
For me He died,
And the crimson tide
Proves that He loves me,
That Jesus loves me;
So sing it again,
That Jesus loves me.

            John R. Rice

### 75. WHEN HE MAKES HIS PRESENCE KNOWN

Without His peace, my life is like a winter's day,
  The chilling winds of doubt my heart dismay;
But when my blessed Saviour makes His presence known,
  My doubts dissolve--He drives them all away.

Without His love, my life is like a wilted flower,
  With parched and withered leaves, athirst for rain;
But when my blessed Saviour makes His presence known,
  His love revives my drooping heart again.

Without His rest, my life is like a stormy sea--
  My fragile vessel tossing on its waves;
But when I see Him walk the crests that threaten me,
  I take from Him the rest my spirit craves.

Without His pow'r, I fight as one that beats the air,
  I have no strength temptation to defeat,
But when I let the Holy Spirit take control,
  My triumph over sin is made complete.

Without my Saviour's life infusing all my own,
  I'm like a barren tree or worthless vine;
But when within, His life is flowing full and free,
  The Spirit bears in me His fruit divine.

            Paul Hutchens

## 76.  CRUCIFY OR IGNORE?

When Jesus came to Golgotha
  They hanged Him on a tree;
They drove great nails through hands and feet
  And made a Calvary;
They crowned Him with a crown of thorns,
  Red were His wounds and deep,
For those were crude and cruel days
  And human flesh was cheap.

When Jesus came to our town,
  They simply passed Him by;
They did not hurt a hair of Him,
  They did not watch Him die;
For men had grown more tender,
  They would not cast a stone;
They only passed Him on the street
  And left Him there alone.

Still Jesus cried, "Forgive them
  For they know not what they do";
He prays that prayer for us tonight,
  For you and you and you;
We pass Him by and leave Him there,
  Without an eye to see,
And crucify our Lord afresh,
  As He prays for Calvary.

      Author Unknown

## 77.  JESUS ON THE CROSS

Jesus on the cross is hung!
  O look, my soul, and see.
The hands so oft outstretched in love
  Are pinioned to a tree.
O brand my hands and body, Lord,
  With marks of agony.

Jesus on the cross is hung!
  How rich is mercy there.
A crown of glory laid aside,
  A crown of thorns to wear.
When foes shall weave my thorny crown,
  Its shame I'll gladly bear.

Jesus on the cross is hung!
  O hungry soul, draw near.
The heart that throbbed with love divine
  Is pierced with cruel spear.
May burdens pierce this heart of mine
  And start the burning tear.

      Eugene M. Harrison

## 78.  HOW SWEET THE NAME OF JESUS SOUNDS

How sweet the name of Jesus sounds
  In a believer's ear!
It soothes his sorrows, heals his wounds,
  And drives away his fear.

It makes the wounded spirit whole,
  And calms the troubled breast;
'Tis manna to the hungry soul,
  And, to the weary, rest.

Dear name!  The rock on which I build,
  My shield and hiding place.
My never-failing treas'ry, filled
  With boundless stores of grace.

Till then I would Thy love proclaim
  With ev'ry fleeting breath;
And may the music of Thy name
  Refresh my soul in death.

      John Newton, 1779

## 79. JESUS KNOWS

*(Hebrews 4: 14-16)*

He knows the thorny way
  The bodily distress;
He knows these tents decay,
  And He stays by to bless.
We're cheered along meanwhile
  By His unclouded smile--
    Jesus knows!

He knows the pains and aches,
  The sight that's growing dim,
Account of all He takes
  For we belong to Him.
The trembling knees He'll hold,
  His arms do us enfold--
    Jesus knows!

He knows the hidden grief,
  The solitude He feels;
He gives us sweet relief;
  Joy afterward it yields.
Blessing for us ensured--
    Jesus knows!

      Author Unknown

## 80. O JESUS, JESUS

O Jesus, Jesus, dearest Lord!
  Forgive me if I say,
For very love, Thy sacred name
  A thousand times a day.

I love Thee so I know not how
  My transports to control;
Thy love is like a burning fire
  Within my very soul.

For Thou to me art all in all;
  My honor and my wealth;
My heart's desire, my body's strength,
  My soul's eternal health.

Burn, burn, O love, within my heart,
  Burn fiercely night and day,
Till all the dross of earthly loves
  Is burned, and burned away.

O light in darkness, joy in grief,
  O Heav'n begun on earth;
Jesus my love, my treasure, who
  Can tell what Thou art worth?

What limit is there to this love?
  Thy flight, where wilt Thou stay?
On, on! our Lord is sweeter far
  Today than yesterday.

            F. W. Faber

## 81. "REMEMBER CALVARY"

When Christians meet and talk of Him
  And tears oft' fill their eyes,
Their hearts well up and overflow
  At His great sacrifice.
Some looking on may wonder why,
  But praised be God, I see,
Before He left He told us to
  Remember Calvary.

Before He left He blessed the loaf,
  He blessed the chalice too;
"This is My flesh," they heard Him say,
  "The blood I shed for you.
Oft' as you will, do eat and drink,
  And so remember Me;
Yes, in this way from loving hearts
  Remember Calvary."

Then soldiers nailed Him to a cross,
  A tomb became His bed,
But death could not its prisoner hold,
  He rose up from the dead!
When leaving for His Home above,
  He gave us this decree:
"Tell all men that I died for them;
  Remember Calvary."

Oft' times life's trials are so great,
  Its joys are so few,
My heart is filled with this world's cares,
  So much of work to do;
But then there comes within my heart
  A voice, 'tis His own plea,
"My parting words, they were for you,
  'Remember Calvary.'"

And so I go to Jesus' cross
  And see Him die again,
I see Him suffer there for me,
  For me He bears such pain;
My heart is drawn once more to Him,
  This world means nought to me;
Oh, I'm so glad for His last words,
  "Remember Calvary."

Someday He's coming back again,
  I long for His return,
With eager eyes I upward gaze,
  For Him my heart doth yearn;
But 'til He comes I'll do His will
  And serve Him faithfully,
And tell the world my Saviour said,
  "Remember Calvary."

            Russell Stellwagon

## 82. THE MESSIAH

Foretold by the prophets, longed for by men,
  Heralded by angels, ministered by them;
Followed by thousands as earth's path
            He trod,
  Wonderful Counselor, the Mighty God!

Forsaken, rejected, He took my place;
  Bearing my sin, my blame, and disgrace.
So much He loved me, a creature of sod,
  This Wonderful Counselor, the
            Mighty God!

            Margaret Wendel

### 83. THEY TELL ME...

They tell me
That some have heard the mighty chariot wheels
Roar in the distance; that the world's salt tears
Are cleaving their last furrows in her cheeks.
It may be so. I know not. Oft the ear
Attent and eager for some coming friend,
Construes each breeze among the vocal boughs
Into the tokens of his wished approach.
But this I know: He liveth and shall stand
Upon this earth; and round Him, thick as waves
That laugh at noon with light, uncounted hosts of His redeemed.
O, dawn, Millennial day! Come blessed morn!
Appear, Desire of Nations! Rend Thy heavens,
And stand revealed upon Thy chosen hill.

Dean Alford

### 84. HE LOVES YOU STILL

He loves you still, how long His love has waited,
    As in your sinful way you wander'd on.
You wounded Him, ah yes! you crucified Him;
    But still He loves and seeks the erring one.

The prodigal in far-off country wasted his
    Means in sin, and shamed his father's name.
Nor to his senses came until forsaken;
    Then wretched, hungry to his father came.

How can such love be spurned without regretting?
    'Twill surely end in punishment and pain.
The loving Saviour then will stand in judgment.
    And all earth's sins and pleasures end in vain.

He loves you still, but storms of wrath are gath'ring,
    His love cannot excuse determined sin.
The loving heart of Christ your sin has broken.
    Oh, turn today for mercy; let Him in.

Such love is mine! I take Him as my Saviour,
    And all my sins He buried and forgave.
Remember them? Ah no, they are forgotten.
    And now He's mine, my guilty soul is saved.

He loves so long, He loves so well,
    He loves you more than tongue can tell;
He loves so long, He loves so well;
    He died to save your soul from Hell.

John R. Rice

85.    WONDERFUL SAVIOUR

Jesus has loved me--wonderful Saviour!
　Jesus has loved me, I cannot tell **why;**
Came He to rescue sinners all worthless,
　My heart He conquered--for Him I
　　　　　would die.

Jesus has saved me--wonderful Saviour!
　Jesus has saved me, I cannot tell **how;**
All that I know is, He was my ransom,
　Dying on Calvary with thorns on His brow.

Jesus will lead me--wonderful Saviour!
　Jesus will lead me, I cannot tell **where;**
But I will follow, thro' joy or sorrow,
　Sunshine or tempest, sweet peace or
　　　　　despair.

Jesus will crown me--wonderful Saviour!
　Jesus will crown me, I cannot tell **when;**
White throne of splendor hail I with gladness,
　Crowned 'mid the plaudits of angels
　　　　　and men.

　　　　　J. Wakefield MacGill

86.    THE MIGHTY WONDERS
　　　　　OF HIS NAME

If I should take my scroll, and pen,
With all the eloquence of men,
The things that in my heart abide,
Since I've known Him, the Crucified,
A world of books could not contain
The mighty wonders of His name.

If I could speak with angel power
Till men would listen, hour on hour,
To stories of the Saviour's love
And glories of the Home above,
The best I'd speak could not explain
The mighty wonders of His name.

If I could sing till men would see
The face of God instead of me,
And bow themselves unto the ground,
And turn from sin the world around;
My song would never half make plain
The mighty wonders of His name!

　　　　　Shel Helsley

87.  JESUS IS ALL I NEED

　I need Jesus ev'ry day,
　　Toil and burden plague my way,
　Need forgiveness, need His guiding,
　Need His wisdom, His providing.
　　So I always need my Jesus.

　Once I thought I had no need,
　　Felt so strong, a broken reed!
　Loved my sin, but then self failed me,
　Overwhelmed with sin and failure,
　　So I turned at last to Jesus!

　Now His Spirit comforts, guides,
　　His strong angels watch beside.
　All His wealth is mine when needing,
　All His mercy for my pleading,
　　How could I live without Jesus.

　Now with outstretched hand He pleads,
　　Offers love for sinner's needs.
　All their sins can be forgiven,
　Justified, they wait for Heaven;
　　Ev'ry soul so needs the Saviour.

　Jesus is all I need,
　　Jesus is all I need,
　All I need to cure sin's sickness,
　All I need for wants and weakness,
　All I need for joy and witness,
　　Jesus Christ is all I need!

　　　　　John R. Rice

88.  GOD LOVES YOU

"God loves you!" Truly, that sounds good!
　Three words--expressed in half a breath--
Yet words not fully understood,
　Nor can be, not this side of death.

But when believed then life grows sweet,
　And shadows lose their sombre gloom;
"God loves you"--let me them repeat,
　Then e'en the grave shall be no tomb.

Did not God empty Heaven above
　When Christ His Son He sent to die?
Who trusts in that redeeming love
　Shall live through all eternity.

　　　　　J. Danson Smith

## 89. PERHAPS TODAY

Perhaps today the clouds will part asunder,
  Reveal a glory brighter than the sun,
And we shall view with transport, joy and wonder,
  The hope of earth and Heaven's beloved One.

Perhaps today the world's last taunt shall grieve us,
  And Satan, foiled, his final dart shall cast,
And all our flesh's frailties shall leave us,
  And disappointment evermore be past.

Perhaps today from weary beds of anguish
  God's suffering saints shall breathe their final sigh,
In glory rise, no more on earth to languish,
  To meet their great Deliv'rer in the sky.

Perhaps today the trump of God resounding,
  Shall wake the sleepers from their beds of clay,
And we with them our longed-for Lord surrounding,
  Shall see His glorious face--perhaps today!

Author Unknown

## 90. IN MEMORY OF TWO SONS

Somewhere upon a battlefield,
  In a war of bygone years,
One of our nation's brave sons fell,
  And brought a mother's tears;
An unsung hero of our land
  Died so we might be free,
I'd like to take his hand in mine,
  Say, "Thanks, you died for me,
Though some may soon forget, by one
  You shall remembered be."

Somewhere upon a lonely hill,
  On a rugged cross of wood,
Another Son laid down His life--
  The precious Son of God;
Somewhere in Heaven up above
  It brought a Father's tears,
And so He knows that mother's heart,
  Oh yes, He knows and cares,
Did He not soothe her deepest grief,
  And calm her anxious fears?

And through the death of His dear Son,
  By the sacrifice He made,
Our freedom from all sin was won,
  The debt was fully paid;
I'd like to take His hand in mine,
  Say, "Christ, you died for me,

I thank you for your suffering
  Upon the cruel tree,
Though others may perhaps forget,
  I give my all to Thee."

Russell Stellwagon

## 91. HE IS NEAR!

I know not in what watch He comes
  Or at what hour He may appear,
Whether at midnight or at morn,
  Or in what season of the year;
  I only know that He is near.

The centuries have gone and come,
  Dark centuries of absence drear;
I dare not chide the long delay,
  Nor ask when I His voice shall hear;
  I only know that He is near.

I do not think it can be long
  Till in His glory He appear;
And yet I dare not name the day,
  Nor fix the solemn Advent year;
  I only know that He is near.

Horatius Bonar

## 92.   "CONCERNING HIMSELF"

### (Luke 24:27)

| | |
|---|---|
| Chosen men of God had spoken, | II Peter 1:20,21 |
| O'er the years the Word had come, | Hebrews 1:1 |
| Holy Writ cannot be broken, | John 10:35 |
| In God's time--the Promised One. | Acts 13:23 |
| | |
| Generations rising, falling, | Psalm 105:8 |
| Waiting, hoping they might see, | Luke 2:25 |
| Him, for whom their hearts were calling, | Romans 10:10 |
| Lord of all eternity. | Psalm 90:2 |
| | |
| Prophet after Moses' pattern, | Deuteronomy 18:15 |
| Priest like Aaron, only pure, | Hebrews 4:14-16 |
| King like David, but not earthen, | John 8:23 |
| For this Kingdom shall endure. | Isaiah 9:7 |
| | |
| Surely such a mighty ruler | Proverbs 23:11 |
| Must with pomp and splendor come, | Isaiah 53:2 |
| Few envisioned His appearing | Luke 19:43,44 |
| With a stable for His home. | Luke 2:12 |
| | |
| Just as Scripture had foretold it | Isaiah 42:9 |
| Lo, a Virgin shall conceive, | Isaiah 7:14 |
| Child is born and Son is given, | Isaiah 9:6 |
| Who would this report believe? | Isaiah 53:1 |
| | |
| Grew in stature, rose in favor, | Luke 2:52 |
| Hailed by Zacharias' son, | Luke 1:67-76 |
| Lamb of God, repent and follow, | John 1:29 |
| Signs and wonders being done. | Matthew 11:2-6 |
| | |
| But beyond His life and teachings, | I Corinthians 15:3 |
| To this end the Christ was born, | I John 3:8 |
| That He give His life a ransom, | Matthew 20:28 |
| Pardon, hope, for all who mourn. | Isaiah 61:1-3 |
| | |
| To the cross our Lord was taken, | Matthew 27:31 |
| In the tomb His body lay, | Matthew 27:57-60 |
| Then in triumph He did waken, | Acts 1:3 |
| Death to Life, O glorious day! | Revelation 1:18 |
| | |
| For the cleansing blood, we're thankful, | I John 1:7 |
| To a risen Christ we pray, | I Timothy 2:5 |
| Help us heed thy Great Commission, | Matthew 28:19,20 |
| Preach this Gospel every day. | Romans 1:16 |

Shel Helsley

## 93. ON THEE MY HEART IS RESTING

On Thee my heart is resting:
  Ah! this is rest indeed!
What else, Almighty Saviour,
  Can a poor sinner need?
Thy light is all my wisdom,
  Thy love is all my stay;
Our Father's Home in glory
  Draws nearer every day.

Great is my guilt, but greater
  The mercy Thou dost give;
Thyself, a spotless offering,
  Hast died that I should live.
With Thee my soul unfettered
  Has risen from the dust;
Thy blood is all my treasure;
  Thy Word is all my trust.

Through me, Thou gentle Master
  Thy purposes fulfill:
I yield myself forever
  To Thy most holy will.
What though I be but weakness
  My strength is not in me;
The poorest of Thy people
  Has all things, having Thee.

When clouds are darkest round me,
  Thou, Lord, art then most near,
My drooping faith to quicken,
  My weary soul to cheer.
Safe nestling in Thy bosom,
  I gaze upon Thy face.
In vain my foes would drive me
  From Thee, my hiding-place.

'Tis Thou hast made me happy;
  'Tis Thou hast set me free.
To whom shall I give glory
  Forever but to Thee!
Of earthly love and blessing
  Should every stream run dry,
Thy grace shall still be with me--
  Thy grace to live and die!

                Theodore Monod

## 94. PERFECT PEACE

Like a river glorious is God's perfect peace;
Over all victorious in its bright increase;
Perfect, yet it floweth fuller every day,
Perfect, yet it groweth deeper all the way.

Hidden in the hollow of His blessed hand,
Never foe can follow, never traitor stand;
Not a surge of worry, not a shade of care,
Not a blast of hurry touch the spirit there.

Every joy or trial falleth from above,
Traced upon our dial by the Sun of Love,
We may trust Him fully, all for us to do;
They who trust Him wholly find Him wholly true.

                Frances Ridley Havergal

## 95. A QUIET HEART

Quiet, Lord, my froward heart:
  Make me teachable and mild;
Upright, simple, free from art;
  Make me as a weanèd child,
From distrust and envy free,
  Pleased with all that pleaseth Thee.

What Thou shalt today provide
  Let me as a child receive;
What tomorrow may betide
  Calmly to Thy wisdom leave.
'Tis enough that Thou wilt care:
  Why should I the burthen bear?

As a little child relies
  On a care beyond his own;
Knows he's neither strong nor wise,
  Fears to stir a step alone;
Let me thus with Thee abide,
  As my Father, Guard and Guide.

                John Newton

"Wherefore God also hath highly exalted him, and given him a name which is above every name: That at the name of Jesus every knee should bow, of things in heaven, and things in earth, and things under the earth; And that every tongue should confess that Jesus Christ is Lord, to the glory of God the Father."
--Phil. 2:9-11.

## 96. THE STRANGER AT THE DOOR

Behold a stranger at the door;
He gently knocks--has knocked before;
Has waited long, is waiting still;
You treat no other friend so ill.

Oh lovely attitude,--He stands
With melting heart and open hands;
Oh matchless kindness, and He shows
This matchless kindness to His foes.

But will He prove a Friend indeed?
He will,--the very Friend you need:
The Friend of sinners? Yes, 'tis He,
With garments dyed on Calvary.

Rise, touched with gratitude divine;
Turn out His enemy and thine;
That soul-destroying monster, Sin,
And let the heavenly Stranger in.

Admit Him ere His anger burn,--
His feet, departed, ne'er return;
Admit Him, or the hour's at hand,
You'll at His door rejected stand.

O let the dear Saviour come in,
He'll cleanse the heart from sin;
O keep Him no more out at the door,
But let the dear Saviour come in.

T. C. O'Kane

## 97. CHRIST ALONE

Strange, fantastic claims abound;
    You may hear them all around,
Some have visions, trances, dreams,
    Others--cunning, subtile schemes;
Golden plates or "bluish flame,"
    "Cosmic rays"--they're all the same;
One thing common do they share:
    (You can tell them anywhere);
Works or money you must pay
    Else "no help for you" they say.

But when from these frauds we turn,
    When for truth and right we yearn;
God will tell you in His Word
    That your faintest prayer is heard;
And you'll know there's only one
    Who can save "beneath the sun."
All the rest--impostors be--
    Christ alone can set you free.

He made claims as well. We're sure
    His credentials still endure.

No impostor raised the dead,
    Made the crippled strong instead,
Stilled a storm and calmed a sea,
    Set a demon captive free,
Cleansed the leper from his stain,
    Gave his life and rose again.
Only one will qualify
    To redeem and justify.
Christ alone can save from sin,
    Trust Him now and enter in.

Shel Helsley

## 98. CHRIST

Christ for sickness, Christ for health,
Christ for poverty, Christ for wealth,
Christ for joy, Christ for sorrow,
Christ today, and Christ tomorrow;
Christ my Life, and Christ my Light,
Christ for morning, noon and night;
Christ when all around gives way,
Christ my everlasting stay;
Christ my rest, Christ my food,
Christ above my highest good;
Christ my well beloved, my Friend,
Christ my pleasure without end;
Christ my Saviour, Christ my Lord,
Christ my portion, Christ my God;
Christ my Shepherd, I His sheep,
Christ himself my soul doth keep;
Christ my Leader, Christ my Peace,
Christ hath brought my soul's release,
Christ my Righteousness divine,
Christ for me, for He is mine;
Christ my Wisdom, Christ my Meat,
Christ restores my wand'ring feet,
Christ my Advocate and Priest,
Christ who ne'er forgets the least;
Christ my Teacher, Christ my Guide,
Christ my Rock, in Christ I hide;
Christ the everlasting Bread,
Christ His precious blood hath shed;
Christ hath brought us near to God,
Christ the everlasting Word,
Christ my Master, Christ my Head,
Christ who for my sins hath bled;
Christ my Glory, Christ my Crown,
Christ the Plant of great Renown,
Christ my Comforter on high,
Christ my Hope draws ever nigh.

H. W. S.

## 99. CHRIST IN PARADISE

*Luke 23:39-43*

See, Father, I have brought with Me
  This trophy rare;
We both were hanging on a tree--
  I heard his prayer;
And since for sinners there I bled,
  For him the crimson stream was shed.

I heard that cry--"Remember me!"
  My soul it stung.
Too piteous his agony,
  As there we hung.
My word I pledged within a trice--
"Today. . .with Me in Paradise!"

The first fruits of My dying there
  To Thee I yield;
O Father, what the harvest rare
  From that world field!
This malefactor, first to come,
Leads all the ransomed sinners Home!

William Marion Runyan

## 100. LOOKING UNTO JESUS

*Hebrews 12: 1, 2*

Because He set before me
  The way that I should take,
I look up to the Father
  And pray for Jesus' sake:
"Help me to run with patience
  And lay aside the weight,
The sin which does beset me,
  And win the race by faith."
I'm looking unto Jesus,
  Who for me did endure
The cross of shame and sorrow,
  To give me life secure.
Please do not look to others,
  No matter what they are,
Your race will surely suffer
  And get behind by far,
It's Jesus, only Jesus,
  Example of the race,
Our steps in His forever,
  Till we shall see His face.

Adele C. Jorg

## 101. 'TIS JESUS IN MY HEART

I woke up this morning with joy in my heart;
  Such peace within my soul!
My sins are forgiven, my heart is at rest,
  Since Jesus took control!

A glad day it was when I opened my heart,
  Invited Jesus therein.
And oh, how He blest me and made me God's child,
  And gave me Heav'n within.

Then come all you sinners your way ends in death,
  But Jesus died for sin,
His blood paid the debt, and He ransomed your soul.
  Oh, take the Saviour in.

Oh, what a Redeemer and oh, what a Friend!
  He's always by my side.
He comforts and keeps me and guides all my way.
  His joy within abides!

'Tis Jesus! 'Tis Jesus! He now is in my heart.
  'Tis Jesus who saved me and keeps me each day,
  'Tis Jesus in my heart!

John R. Rice

### 102. THREE WORDS OF THE MASTER

Three little words from the Master,
  Three words from His lips divine,
Wrought miracles rare, could
          accomplish more
Than science could do through the years
    of time.

Just three little words, "Peace, be still"--
  As simple as they could be,
But when they left the Master's lips
  They calmed the storm on Galilee.

Just three short words, "Who touched me?"--
  As He jostled the anxious throng.
He knew that virtue had gone from Him,
  And a woman was made strong.

Just three words, "Lazarus, come forth"
  So easily written or said--
But when the Saviour spoke those words
  There was power in them to raise the dead.

Three final words, "It is finished"
  When Jesus was crucified.
The veil rent in twain, the earth trembled
  The moment the Saviour died.

Three glorious words, "HE IS RISEN"
  Like joybells eternal, they ring;
He is risen with hope for all mankind,
  And life everlasting, to bring.

                    Lillie Buffum

### 103. AMAZING GRACE

Amazing Grace--that in the past--
Back in eternities so vast,
The Father God His Son should slay--
The sin of unborn man to pay:
And in that act included me--
I wonder much--how could it be.

Amazing Grace--that He the Son,
The blessed and Eternal One,
Should leave at length the hallowed bliss
Of Heaven's unsullied righteousness
And come to earth and take the place
Of every man of Adam's race.

Well might angelic hosts have wept
When Christ to God His promise kept;
And heavenly choirs had ceased to sing
At sight of Christ's dark suffering.
'Tis all, indeed, too deep to trace;
We can but say--"Amazing Grace."

                    J. Danson Smith

### 104. "COME, SEE THE PLACE"

He laid aside His princely robes
  And came to earth one day,
A darling, helpless, little Babe
  Upon a bed of hay.
It was earth's first Christmas morn--
"Come, see the place"--where Christ
              was born.

He came of lowly parentage
  As poor as poor could be,
The Lord of lords--the King of kings,
  The Man of Galilee.
He healed the sick--He raised the dead,
Yet--had no place to lay His head.

And then in dark Gethsemane
  Forsaken and alone,
He knelt in silent agony
  Beside a cold, hard stone.
'Twas there the Saviour was betrayed--
"Come, see the place"--where Jesus prayed.

Upon Mount Calvary's rugged brow
  He paid the debt for me;
He bowed His precious head and died
  Upon the cruel tree.
They pierced His hands and pierced
              His side--
"Come, see the place"--where Jesus died.

They took Him from the rugged cross
  And laid Him in the tomb;
They thought and felt quite satisfied
  That they had sealed His doom.
But angels rolled the stone away--
"Come, see the place"--where Jesus lay!

One day the clouds bore Him away
  Back to His Father's throne,
And all the blest angelic host
  Gave Him a welcome home.
His former glory He regains--
"Come, see the place"--where Jesus reigns!

                    Lillie Buffum

### 105. IF CHRIST HAD HAD A DOG...

I wonder if Christ had a little black dog
  All curly and woolly like mine;
With two silky ears, and a nose round and wet,
  And eyes brown and tender that shine.

I'm afraid that He hadn't, because I have read
  How He prayed in the garden alone,
For all of His friends and disciples had fled,
  Even Peter, the one called a "stone."

And oh, I am sure that that little black dog,
  With a heart so tender and warm,
Would never have left Him to suffer alone,
  But, creeping right under His arm,

Would have licked those dear fingers in agony clasped,
  And counting all favors but loss,
When they took Him away, would have trotted behind
  And followed Him quite to the cross!

                    Elizabeth Gardner Reynolds


### 106. HE DIES: HE LIVES!

He dies! the Friend of sinners dies!
  Lo! Salem's daughters weep around;
A solemn darkness veils the skies,
  A sudden trembling shakes the ground.
Come, saints, and drop a tear or two
  For Him who groan'd beneath your load:
He shed a thousand drops for you--
  A thousand drops of richer blood.

Here's love and grief beyond degree:
  The Lord of glory dies for man!
But lo! what sudden joys we see;
  Jesus, the dead, revives again.
The rising God forsakes the tomb;
  (In vain the tomb forbids His rise);
Cherubic legions guard Him Home,
  And shout Him welcome to the skies.

Break off your tears, ye saints, and tell
  How high your great Deliv'rer reigns;
Sing how He spoil'd the hosts of Hell,
  And led the monster Death in chains:
Say, Live forever, wondrous King!
  Born to redeem, and strong to save;
Then ask the monster, where's thy sting?
  And, where's thy vict'ry, boasting grave?

                    Old Methodist Hymn


### 107. WONDERFUL JESUS

Wonderful Jesus, wonderful King;
Through all the ages His praises I'll sing;
Born in a manger, humble and meek,
Loving the sinner He came here to seek.
Dying on Calv'ry, bearing the shame,
Suff'ring for me there, He took all my blame;
Wonderful Jesus, wonderful King,
Through all the ages, His praises I'll sing.

Wonderful Saviour, all highest Lord,
Ruler of Heaven revealed in the Word;
Coming from Heaven, leaving His throne,
Seeking the lost and redeeming His own.
Oh how I love Him, wonderful Friend,
Saving and keeping, so true to the end.
Wonderful Saviour, all highest Lord,
Ruler of Heaven revealed in the Word.

Wonderful Jesus, wonderful Friend,
I'll ever serve Him until time shall end;
Came once in meekness, Saviour of men,
Some day in glory He'll come back again.
From David's throne He'll rule o'er the land,
Smiting all evil, with almighty hand.
Wonderful Jesus, wonderful Friend,
I'll ever serve Him until life shall end.

                    L. O. Engelmann

## 108. JESUS, THE VERY THOUGHT OF THEE

Jesus, the very thought of Thee
  With sweetness fills my breast;
But sweeter far Thy face to see,
  And in Thy presence rest.

Nor voice can sing, nor heart can frame,
  Nor can the memory find
A sweeter sound than Thy blest name,
  O Saviour of mankind!

O Hope of every contrite heart!
  O Joy of all the meek!
To those who fall, how kind Thou art!
  How good to those who seek!

But what to those who find? Ah! this
  Nor tongue nor pen can show;
The love of Jesus, what it is,
  None but His loved ones know.

Jesus, our only joy be Thou,
  As Thou our prize wilt be;
In Thee be all our glory now,
  And through eternity.

        Bernard of Clairvaux;
        Trans. by Edward Caswall

## 109. LAID ON JESUS

I lay my sins on Jesus,
  The spotless Lamb of God;
He bears them all and frees us
  From the accursed load:
I bring my guilt to Jesus,
  To wash my crimson stains
White in His blood most precious,
  Till not a stain remains.

I lay my wants on Jesus;
  All fullness dwells in Him;
He healeth my diseases,
  He doth my soul redeem:
I lay my griefs on Jesus,
  My burdens and my cares;
He from them all releases,
  He all my sorrows shares.

I long to be like Jesus,
  Meek, loving, lowly, mild;
I long to be like Jesus,
  The Father's holy Child:
I long to be with Jesus
  Amid the heavenly throng,
To sing with saints His praises,
  And learn the angels' song.

        Horatius Bonar

## 110. NO VARIABLENESS

No variableness! With whom? Well, not with me;
My heart is fixed; and I would faithful be:
But yet, alas, I fail in constancy.

No variableness! With whom? Not e'en my friend--
The dearest one--on whom I might depend
Doth fail at times to rightly comprehend.

No variableness! With whom? With Him, my Lord!
It is the statement of His blessed Word:
And they who know Him best with this accord.

Thus unto Him, when shadowed or distressed,
With all that would my inner soul molest,
I'll go for pardon, comfort, peace, and rest.

And shall I find that He is just the same,
E'en though, perchance, I have to come with shame?
Ah, yes--unchanged! Thrice blessed be His name.

        J. Danson Smith

## 111. A CRADLE HYMN

Hush! my dear, lie still and slumber,
  Holy angels guard thy bed!
Heavenly blessings without number
  Gently falling on thy head.

Sleep, my babe; thy food and raiment,
  House and home, thy friends provide;
All without thy care or payment:
  All thy wants are well supplied.

How much better thou'rt attended
  Than the Son of God could be,
When from Heaven He descended
  And became a child like thee!

Soft and easy in thy cradle:
  Coarse and hard thy Saviour lay,
When His birthplace was a stable
  And His softest bed was hay.

Blessed babe! what glorious features--
  Spotless fair, divinely bright!
Must He dwell with brutal creatures?
  How could angels bear the sight?

Was there nothing but a manger
  Cursed sinners could afford,
To receive the heavenly Stranger?
  Did they thus affront their Lord?

Soft, my child: I did not chide thee,
  Though my song might sound too hard;
'Tis thy mother sits beside thee,
  And her arms shall be thy guard.

Yet to read the shameful story
  How the Jews abused their King,
How they served the Lord of Glory,
  Makes me angry while I sing.

See the kinder shepherds round Him,
  Telling wonders from the sky!
Where they sought Him, there they
          found Him,
  With His virgin mother by.

See the lovely Babe a-dressing;
  Lovely infant, how He smiled!
When He wept, the mother's blessing
  Soothed and hush'd the holy Child.

Lo, He slumbers in His manger,
  Where the horn'd oxen fed:

Peace, my darling; here's no danger,
  Here's no ox anear thy bed.

'Twas to save thee, child, from dying,
  Save my dear from burning flame,
Bitter groans and endless crying,
  That thy blest Redeemer came.

May'st thou live to know and fear Him,
  Trust and love Him all thy days;
Then go dwell forever near Him,
  See His face, and sing His praise!

                    Isaac Watts

## 112. HARD TO UNDERSTAND

That God has made the earth and skies,
Is not so hard to realize;
That He has caused the streams to flow,
Is something even children know;
That birds and bees, and flow'rs
          and trees,
And rugged hills, and velvet leas;
That winter winds, and summer rains,
And autumn leaves and grassy plains,
Are all the product of His hand,
The least of us could understand.
But how a man, who once was clay,
And then was fashioned in a day,
Could turn from God, who breathed
          on him,
And sink so pitifully in sin,
Is something difficult to see,
At least, beyond the mind of me.

But wait, I've one thing more to say,
And you'll agree with me, I pray.
Of all the crimes since time began;
Of all the wickedness of man,
The worst was done when Jesus died,
The Lord Incarnate, crucified.
The creature in rebellion bent,
Creator's body to be rent.
But matchless grace, supernal love,
That God could leave His Home above,
And suffer death, by those He made,
And deem their ransom price as PAID,
Is something none can comprehend,
Bless God, thank God, for such a Friend.

                    Shel Helsley

## 113.   IVORY PALACES

For three and thirty years they stood,
Empty and eloquent
Of Him Who laid His glory down,
And went, obedient,

To die for sins of you and me.
He must have turned His eyes
At times in homesick longing toward
His mansions in the skies.

I think the doors were never sealed,
But plainly left ajar,
And something of Him lingered there,
Though He had gone so far.

Perhaps the angels peered within
Each waiting, empty room,
And whispered of strange things, the cross,
Gethsemane, the tomb.

And sometimes God Himself went there
To think about that One
Who never had been far from Him,
His well beloved Son.

Now in His palaces the light
Shines out from every room,
And angels never cease their song,
"The Son of God is home!"

                    Martha Snell Nicholson

## 114.   THE WAY, THE TRUTH, THE LIFE

Without the Way, there can be no going;
Without the Truth, there can be no knowing;
Without the Life, there can be no growing.

Since Christ is the Way, we ought to
                    walk in Him;
Since Christ is the Truth, we ought to
                    trust in Him;
Since Christ is the Life, we ought to
                    live in Him.

Thou who art the Way, lead us;
Thou who art the Truth, teach us;
Thou who art the Life, continue to live in
                    us and love us.

                    Samuel Judson Porter

## 115.   IT MATTERS TO HIM

My child, I know thy sorrows,
Thine every grief I share;
I know how thou art tested,
And what is more, I care!

Think not I am indifferent
To what affecteth thee;
Thy weal and woe are matters
Of deep concern to Me.

But, child, I have a purpose
In all that I allow;
I ask thee then to trust Me,
Though all seems dark just now.

How often thou hast asked Me
To purge away the dross;
But this refining process
Involves for thee a cross!

There is no other pathway
If thou wouldst really be
Conformed unto the image
Of Him who died for thee.

Thou canst not be like Jesus
Till self is crucified;
And as a daily process
The cross must be applied.

                    Author Unknown

## 116.   A SUFFERING CHRIST

A suffering God upon the tree;
A suffering Christ who died for me;
A suffering Lord who cared for me
That I might live eternally.

A suffering God in love divine;
A suffering Christ life's treasure mine;
A suffering Lord in Him to find,
A tranquil heart--a peaceful mind.

A suffering God--a Father's heart;
A suffering Christ who ne'er forgot;
A suffering Lord to share my lot;
A suffering God!  Oh, staggering thought.

                    Edwin C. Swanson

### 117.  I LOVE THE DEAR SAVIOUR

I love the dear Saviour, the Father's full image,
Creator of all things, the Man who is God.
The End and Beginning, ordained to all homage,
"I Am" and Jehovah, Almighty my Rock.

I love the dear Saviour, who laid aside raiment
Of Deity's glory, a Babe and a Man.
A virgin His mother, His place as a servant,
And then on the cross paid my debt in God's plan.

I love the dear Saviour who died to redeem me,
Who ransom'd my soul from the torments of Hell;
Who bought me and saved me, and now lives within me,
How frail is my heart that I love Him so ill.

I love Thee, my Saviour,
Oh, teach me to love Thee:
Oh, praise, praise, praise!
The fairest, the lovely, my God, my blest Saviour,
Oh, praise, praise, praise!

John R. Rice

### 118.  JESUS EVER NEAR

He is near thee, ever near thee--
  He the never failing Friend.
Darkest night or sorest trouble
  Cannot hide the face of Him.
Greatest grief or loss or failure
  Need not ban His peace within.

Songs in pain and joy in sorrow
  With the Saviour now within.
All my need in want or plenty,
  All forgiveness for my sins--
Not a sparrow falls unnoticed,
  Dearer are His own to Him.

Ever near thee, soul rebellious,
  Though you scorn, reject His love,
Still He pleads and follows always
  With His Spirit, Heav'nly Dove.
See His Hands, His side all wounded,
  He would woo thee by His love.

He so near, the Man of Sorrows,
  He was tempted as thou art.
Never sinning, yet He pities
  All who stumble when they start.
Interceding, ever pleading
  For the meek and contrite heart.

John R. Rice

### 119.  THERE ALWAYS WILL BE GOD

They cannot shell His Temple
  Nor dynamite His throne;
They cannot bomb His city,
  Nor rob Him of His own.

They cannot take Him captive,
  Nor strike Him dead and blind,
Nor starve Him to surrender,
  Nor make Him change His mind.

They cannot cause Him panic,
  Nor cut off His supplies;
They cannot take His kingdom,
  Nor hurt Him with their lies.

Though all the world be shattered,
  His truth remains the same;
His righteous laws still potent,
  And Father still His name.

Though we face war and struggle,
  And feel their goad and rod,
We know above confusion,
  **There always will be God!**

H.  C. Ede

### 120. THE CROSS AND AFTER

O Cross of Calvary! What hast thou meant to men; since
    first thy baneful shadow fell across Golgotha's stern
    and rugged crest,
And on thee, bleeding, dying, hung the Christ? What bitter
    agony of soul was theirs, who, crushed by Roman power,
    long had hoped it had been He who Israel should redeem--
To see His hands--with healing in their touch, pierced through
    with cruel nails.
His noble brow all torn and bleeding 'neath the crown of
    thorns
His enemies in mockery had entwined,
While 'round Him surged the pitiless, jeering mob.

No wonder was it that the sky grew dark,
And graves were opened, and the earth did quake
And rocks were rent, and terror reigned supreme!
What hopes were crushed in that dread, tragic hour which
    marked the loneliness and dark despair of those disci-
    ples who had loved their Lord?

The night came on apace.
With reverent hands did Joseph of Arimathea gently lay
    the body of his Master in the tomb, and he and those few
    women following him found some poor ray of comfort in
    the thought that though their Lord no longer walked with
    them, His precious body in the tomb was safe from prow-
    ling beasts--
And human foes alike.
The great stone at the door scarce heavier seemed than their
    sad hearts, as, weary and forlorn, they homeward turned,
    and darkness of the night descended, like a pall, upon the
    scene.

The silence of that night was oft disturbed by smothered sobs
    of those whose pent-up grief had banished slumber,
While, methinks, a few, worn-out, grief-spent, exhausted,
    fell asleep
Dreamed of the tragedy of yesterday,
And weeping, even in their sleep, still moaned in accents
    piteous,
"The Cross! The Cross!"

### (PART II)

The Sabbath day is past.
The beams of dawn now gild the East, but bring no ray of hope
    to cheer the aching hearts of those who haste their blessed
    Lord's dead body to anoint.
And who should roll away the heavy stone, and break the seal
    by Pilate's order placed?
Ah me! What fear, bewilderment and joy, to find the stone by
    Angel hands removed!
What strange, incredible tale fell on their ears?

What wondrous words the waiting Angels spake--
"Why do ye seek the living 'mong the dead?
Fear not, for Christ is risen!  Come and see!"

Departing from the sepulcher, they ran to spread the glorious
        tidings,
"Christ is risen!"
And later, Christ appeared at various times, proving infallib-
        ly He was alive.
And forty ne'er-to-be-forgotten days
He talked with those who loved Him, of the things pertaining
        to the kingdom of their God,
Interpreting the meaning of the Cross.
And thus they learned how it behooved the Christ--all sinless
        as He was--to suffer death,
To make atonement for the sins of men,
Giving His life a ransom for mankind, that we, through Him,
        might have eternal life.
Then, having suffered all these things, to rise triumphant and
        victorious from the grave, and enter into
Glory, long foretold.

And as they understood the plan divine,
And thought, with clearer vision, of the Cross,
The bitterness and anguish of their souls were swallowed up
        in awe and reverent love.
And so with calm and strengthened faith serene,
Knowing the Comforter would come to them,
They saw their risen Lord ascend on high,
To dwell with God the Father evermore.

And ever since that time, the Cross has stood on Calvary's
        rugged crest through all the years,
Shedding a light effulgent and divine.
And brightly now and evermore shall gleam
That light to lead us Home.
And naught can harm, if we accept the atonement Jesus made.
We too can have the Comforter with us,
In panoply of love securely dwell,
And sing with all the countless hosts redeemed
And find our glory in the Cross!  The Cross!

                    Bessie F. Mason


121.    MYSTERY DIVINE

Ere God had built the mountains,
    Or raised the fruitful hills;
Before He filled the fountains
    That feed the running rills;
In Thee, from everlasting,
    The wonderful I Am
Found pleasures never wasting,
    And Wisdom is Thy name.

And couldst Thou be delighted
    With creatures such as we,
Who, when we saw Thee, slighted
    And nailed Thee to a tree?
Unfathomable wonder!
    And mystery divine!
The voice that speaks in thunder
    Says, "Sinner, I am thine!"

                    William Cowper

### 122.  GOD-OMNISCIENT

In the morning of the ages,
From the realm of outer-darkness
Peered the eye of
    God-omniscient,
Roving, scanning, piercing, probing
The eternal night, and finding
Naught save that which to be seen must
By some pow'r be first created.
But since now and then and always
Are as one to God-omniscient,
He beheld a vast creation
Passing thru the void of aeons;
For He was
 God-omniscient...

(...If you speak that word, the nothing
And the space and outer-darkness
Will start throbbing with creation!
...You must know that light brings shadow;
And that mountains form the valley;
And where life is, death comes stalking;
And that love can turn to hatred!)
 But He did it anyway...

Ageless and abysmal silence
Shrank before the voice that thundered
That one word--the word that made it:
All that is and ever will be.
And He smiled at worlds in orbit
And in smiling showed His pleasure--
Till a shadow crossed His thinking
That bowed down His head with sorrow,
For He was
 God-omniscient...

(...You have found it--found that Time-world
Out of tune midst constellations,
Haunted by the gruesome spectre
Of a terrifying day when
Man will cast the deepest shadow!
...Sigh and moan in lamentation;
Brood in awful contemplation
At the shadow of a cross!
At the skull-like hill where man will
Pierce Thy heart with unnamed torture
Never felt by Thee, immortal--
Thee who gave him breath and being!)
 But He did it anyway...

For, since God is God-omniscient
Time blends into the eternal;
And beyond the place of suff'ring
He beheld a host, pure, blood-washed,

Crowning Him in adoration
In that Kingdom of Tomorrow!
And their song was to His tribute
Who would mingle tears and blood drops
On a starlit cross of anguish
On a starlit hill called Calv'ry.
So He smiled the smile of triumph,
For He was
 God-omniscient...

(...If you do it, God-omniscient,
Choose that one world out of order
From the myriad fiery pinpoints
Weaving now their perfect pattern
On the sombre face of midnight;
You but do it ever knowing
That at length it will the sum be
Of Thy deepest woe and heartbreak!
...You'll regret it if you do it!)
 But He did it anyway...

For the end is the beginning
And the now is the forever
To the Mind all-comprehending;
So He held in hands creative
Cradle, grave of that one creature
He would make in His own image.
And a garden known as Eden
Blushed in beauty where He made it;
And the dust became the creature--
Dust that moved, and saw and heard Him:
Walking dust; and hands that touched Him--
Lo the man!  From dust he wakened
In the likeness of his Maker!
And they walked and talked together,
Sighed the sigh of love together
Down the shaded paths of Eden--
But the sigh came low and grief-wrought
From the heart of
 God-omniscient...

(...You have done it, God-omniscient!
You've a world and you've a creature
With a will to choose.  And choosing,
He will walk thru shadows rather
Than in light.  And in his choosing
He will barter life and spirit
Just to make your Calvary!

Let the stark ghost of this terror
Find abode within your thinking--
When you hear the sound of hammer
On the anvil forging nails!  And
When axe is laid to timber, with
Each blow you'll know the torture
Of that Roman rack of horror--

The dread cross awaiting Thee!
Thus you'll die a thousand deaths
Before the time!  Think and rescind, Thee!)
     But He did it anyway...

For the now and the forever
Are as one to Mind-omniscient;
And He saw the blood drops leading
Past the cross and on to glory--
Knew there'd be the place of prayer and
Grace thru faith, born of contrition;
Saw the crowning day, made bolder
By the backdrop of His suff'ring;
And He deemed it worth the heartbreak,
For He was
     God-omniscient...

(...Unleashed hate--unbridled fury,
In exchange for perfect Eden, you
Gave Him Gethsemane!
Dark Gethsemane--the blood-sweat
And the cup that overflows now
With all sin, past, now, and future--
Not His own, but yours, you rebel!
Stay your hand!--It is enough!--Why
Must you torture add to torture?
Would you smite the cheek of Jesus?
Stripe the aching back of Jesus?
Crown with thorns the brow of Jesus?
Spit upon the gentle Jesus?
Sneer, and jeer in scorn at Jesus?
...Mighty God--all this is nothing
When compared with what awaits Thee!
Yonder is the cross and mountain
Where the cup of wrath will spill to
Fix Thee to the cross of Calv'ry--
...With a word you made him!--now with
But a word you can destroy him!  Say
The word!--Don't go to Calv'ry!)
     But He did it anyway...

For the past can be forgotten
By the One who is omniscient;
All the past can be as never--
And the future is forever--
To the One who is omniscient.
And the past and present faded
In the light of the eternal;
And the future was a torch that
Lighted all the way His footsteps
Went--and marked the place where mortal
Sank to dust beneath the cross-piece
And eternal God, blood-blinded,
Staggered meekly to the summit
As a Lamb, born for the altar,

Walks in meekness to the slaughter.
Thus He walked, this
     God-omniscient...

(...Steel on steel!--Great God-omniscient,
How the sound rings thru the valley;
Steel on steel and nails that pierce Thee--
Must you moan and suffer so?
With what contrast blood is flowing
O'er Thy pale and whited body,
Dropping down from toes and elbows
To the dirt of Calvary!  Once you
Spoke a word!  But speak it
Once again and worlds will vanish;
And the rebel, too, will vanish; and
The heartbreak, too, will vanish!
Who, like Thee, omniscient, knows it?)
     But He did it anyway...

For omniscience knows no curtain
'Tween the here and the hereafter
And He gave His life, well knowing
He would take it up again!
For today is as tomorrow
And He knew that His tomorrow
Would know neither pain nor sorrow--
Man, you rebel, how He loved you!
How He pitied you and loved you!
Neither now nor the forevers
Could portray how much He loved you
When He bore that cross to Calv'ry...
     Yet He did it anyway,
Knowing all the while He'd win you--
You who've owned Him Lord and Saviour--
For He was
     God-omniscient!

                                    Jack Shuler


## 123.  ALL THE WAY MY SAVIOUR LEADS ME

All the way my Saviour leads me;
     What have I to ask beside?
Can I doubt His tender mercy,
     Who through life has been my Guide?
Heavenly peace, divinest comfort,
     Here by faith in Him to dwell!
For I know, whate'er befall me,
     Jesus doeth all things well.

All the way my Saviour leads me,
     Cheers each winding path I tread,
Gives me grace for every trial,

Feeds me with the living bread.
Though my weary steps may falter,
    And my soul athirst may be,
Gushing from the Rock before me,
    Lo! a spring of joy I see.

All the way my Saviour leads me;
    Oh, the fullness of His love!
Perfect rest to me is promised
    In my Father's house above.
When my spirit, clothed immortal,
    Wings its flight to realms of day,
This my song through endless ages;
    Jesus led me all the way.

Fanny Crosby
1820-1915

### 124. ANYWHERE WITH JESUS

Anywhere with Jesus I can safely go;
Anywhere He leads me in this world below;
Anywhere without Him dearest joys would fade;
Anywhere with Jesus I am not afraid.

Anywhere with Jesus I need fear no ill,
Tho' temptations gather round my pathway still;
He Himself was tempted that He might help me;
Anywhere with Jesus I may victor be.

Anywhere with Jesus I am not alone;
Other friends may fail me, He is still my own;
Tho' His hand may lead me over dreary ways,
Anywhere with Jesus is a house of praise.

Anywhere with Jesus over land and sea,
Telling souls in darkness of salvation free;
Ready as He summons me to go or stay,
Anywhere with Jesus when He points the way.

Anywhere with Jesus I can go to sleep,
When the dark'ning shadows round about me creep;
Knowing I shall waken, never more to roam,
Anywhere with Jesus will be home, sweet home.

Anywhere! Anywhere!
Fear I cannot know;
Anywhere with Jesus
I can safely go.

D. B. Towner

### 125. HE'LL NEVER LET YOU DOWN

He'll never let you down who lean on Jesus.
    He never disappoints a trusting soul.
For ages long the sad and brokenhearted
    Have trusted Him to make them fully whole.

I've tried Him many years, in many burdens;
    I needed Him, and found He fails me not.
How blessed, sweet to take Him ev'ry
                    problem,
    And ask for help and guidance for my lot.

I came to Him, a child, and took salvation.
    For many years I've tried Him ev'ry day.
But never have I found He left me hungry
    Or friendless, walking on a lonely way.

In fiery furnace some have found the Saviour
    Was walking with them, left them not alone.
No smell of fire was found upon their
                    garments,
    And they rejoiced, their faithful
                    faces shone.

He's ever near the penitent who seek Him;
    He answers those who come with all
                    their heart.
To Jesus come for help and for forgiveness;
    He'll never let you down who choose
                    His part.

John R. Rice

# CHRISTMAS

### 126. CHRISTMAS ANGELS

I thought I heard the angels
  As they talked of Jesus' birth:
One said, "Look, I see the shepherds
  In the fields, soon to the earth
I'll announce the gladdest tidings
  Ever heard in that world's dearth."

"Wasn't Mary glad?" said Gabriel
  "When I hailed the choice God made.
She should bear God's one begotten
  Prophesied, the mother-maid!"
"All my soul doth magnify Him,
  God my Saviour," so she said.

"God sent me to tell the wise men
  Through a star," another said.
"They had read the Prophet Daniel;
  Thus to seek the King were led.
I must warn of Herod's plan to
  Kill the baby in His bed."

Gabriel told how Zacharias
  Heard from him John would be born,
Then how troubled Joseph trembled
  On his bed distressed, forlorn,
Till he gladly heard that Mary
  Still was pure, and took her home.

Then a flutter--what assembling,
  To announce the Saviour's birth.
"Let me tell it!" "Oh, I want to,"
  Eager faces, holy mirth.
"Could we have a part," they pleaded
  "To tell men of peace on earth?"

'Twas agreed that every angel
  Should the mighty chorus swell
First the good news, one declaring,
  Then the "Peace on earth" as well
Chanted by the million voices.
  All the sky God's glory held.

Was a tear of sweet compassion
  On an angel's holy face?
"How afraid were poor lost sinners
  When we came to tell God's grace!
Oh, they need our blessed Jesus,
  All of Adam's fallen race!"

"Come my darlings," to the cherubs
  Gabriel called, "take up your harps.

Sing with gladness of the Saviour,
  Sing of hope in world so dark."
But one cherub said, "I can't sing:
  When will Jesus tune my harp?"

Well, the angels have our Jesus;
  They'll return some millions strong
When with Jesus we are raptured,
  When He reigns they'll come along.
They are servants pure and watchful
  Of redeemed ones--so our song.

Oh, the holy angels watching
  All encamped about the saints;
Little children, aged, poor ones
  Need not fear nor fret nor faint.
Christmas angels, ever near us
  God's sweet care with no complaint.

John R. Rice

### 127. CHRISTMAS

No sheep in the folds,
No Star in the West,
No Babe lulled to sleep
On His young mother's breast.
But sheep of God's flock
Straying far from His love,
And a glorified Man
Interceding above.

No gold and no myrrh,
No sweet frankincense,
But the gift of the heart
When the sinner repents.
No music on earth
From the angelic bands;
But the praise and prayer
Of the saved of all lands.

Apart from the Christ--
No joy at His birth,
Though merry and gay
All the feasting on earth;
The candles burn out,
And the feasting is done,
But the Glory of Heaven
Shines forth in God's Son.

Betty Scott Stam
Yang Chow, China, 1931

## 128. JESUS, BABY JESUS

Jesus, Baby Jesus, of a virgin mother born,
Laid in manger cradle, wrapped in swaddling clothes and warm.
Birth cry in a darkened stable, in the inn no room,
Jesus, Baby Jesus, Son of God, to share earth's gloom.

Jesus, how the angels with delight the story told,
Told to Mary, Joseph and the shepherds at their fold.
Full of light, the heavens, as they chanted "Peace on earth!"
Jesus, Baby Jesus, what glad news, a Saviour's birth!

Wise men came to see Him, having seen His star afar,
Brought their gifts of precious gold and frankincense and myrrh.
Herod heard, was troubled, could not kill the Holy Child.
Jesus, Baby Jesus, King and Priest, and Saviour mild.

Jesus, Baby Jesus, Son of God and Son of man,
Tempted, poor and suff'ring, no one knows us as He can!
Holy, righteous, blameless, fitting sacrifice complete.
By His blood atonement, God and sinners in Him meet.

Jesus, Baby Jesus, there's a cross along the way.
Born to die for sinners, born for crucifixion day!

John R. Rice

## 129. IN BETHLEHEM

'Twas night in little Bethlehem,
  All calm and clear and mild,
And tenderly, with voice and touch,
  A mother soothed her child;
"Sleep, little one, the day is done,
  Why do you wake so long?"
"Oh, mother dear, I seem to hear
  A wondrous angel song."
"Not so, my son, my precious one,
  'Twas but the wind you heard,
Or drowsy call of dreaming bird,
Or osiers by the streamlet stirred
  Beneath the hillside trees;
Some bleating lamb that's gone astray,
Or traveller singing on his way
  His weariness to ease.
Rest, little son, till night is done,
  And gloomy darkness flees."
Yet while she spoke the shepherds ran
  In haste the road along,
To find the Mother and the Babe,
  For they had heard the song.

"Rest, little son, the night's begun,
  Why do you toss and sigh?"
"A brighter star than others are,
  O'er yon low roof hangs nigh."
"Not so, my son, my darling one,
  I see no gleaming star
That shines more bright than others are;
'Tis but a lamp that burns afar,
  Or glow-worm's wandering spark;
Some shepherd's watch-fire in the night,
Or traveller's torch that blazes bright
  To cheer him through the dark.
Sleep, little son, till night is done,
  And upward springs the lark."
Yet, while she spoke, three kings had come,
  Three kings who rode from far,
To lay their gifts at Jesus' feet,
  For they had seen the star.

And so today, beside our way,
  The heavenly portents throng,
Yet some there be who never see
  The Star, nor hear the Song.

Annie Johnson Flint

## 130. HIS NAME AT THE TOP

I had the nicest Christmas list,
  The longest one in town,
Till Daddy looked at it and said,
  "You'll have to cut it down."

I knew that what he said was true
  Beyond the faintest doubt,
But was amazed to hear him say,
  "You've left your best Friend out."

And so I scanned my list again,
  And said, "Oh, that's not true!"
But Daddy said, "His name's not there,
  That Friend who died for you."

And then I clearly understood,
  'Twas Jesus that he meant;
For Him who should come first of all
  I hadn't planned a cent!

I'd made a Christmas birthday list,
  And left the Saviour out!
But, oh, it didn't take me long
  To change the list about.

And though I've had to drop some names
  Of folks I like a lot,
My Lord must have the most--because
  His name is at the top!

Author Unknown
Baptist Bible Tribune

## 131.    WISDOM OF THE WISE MEN

Plodding through the desert, wise men from afar;
Not a soul to guide them, nothing but a star;
Many folk to mock them for their silly care;
"What are stars to follow through the empty air?"

Plodding through the desert, seeking for a King,
Fools of common legend, fancies all a-wing;
There are mighty monarchs in the Eastern lands;
Why pursue another, toiling o'er the sands?

Plodding through the desert, scorning gain and ease,
What is this you carry in your treasuries?
What of royal favour do you hope to gain
With your precious presents and your plodding pain?

Gold is fit donation for a mighty throne,
But the myrrh and incense, who would care to own?
Myrrh--a stern reminder man is for the sod;
Incense, for the worship of a holy God.

Plodding through the desert with this royal gold,
Know you not of Herod, jealous, crafty, bold?
Herod holds the sceptre in a mighty town.
His a cruel temper; he will strike you down.

Plodding through the desert, those sagacious men,
Glimpsing King and kingdom past our mortal ken.
Glory, glory, glory, hid from common eyes;
'Mid the mob of mockers, they alone were wise.

Amos R. Wells

## 132. CHRISTMAS MEANS REMEMBERING

Remembering
    Thee, Christ of God, whose humble birth
      Led to the meaner cross, that we
    Might know the joy and holy mirth
      Of sin's pow'r shattered, life to be--
      Christmas means remembering.

Remembering
    You, who by precious ties of heart
      Are bound to us in tender thought
    The family circle, friends apart,
      And the whole "house of faith,"
          blood-bought--
      Christmas means remembering.

Remembering
    Those suff'ring hunger, want, and fear
      Yet loved by Him as much as we.
    From war-torn world the call comes,
          clear,
      "In giving, ye have giv'n to Me."
      Christmas means remembering.

Remembering
    The millions yet to whom the star
      Of Bethlehem has never shone,
    Who sit in darkness, sin, despair,
      Without our God, our hope, alone--
      Christmas means remembering.

Remembering
    The promise sure--He comes again!
      Our day of loving labor wanes;
    To live for self is life in vain,
      We "occupy" till Jesus reigns.
      Christmas means remembering.

                    F. E. J.

## 133. OUR FATHER DID

That Christmas Day, if you were God,
And that were your Son on that stable sod,
Wrapped for death with its sin-cursed sting,
Would you have made the angels sing?
Would you have sent a lovely star
To guide the wise men from afar,
While weaklings did what haters bid?
...Our loving Heavenly Father did.

              Paul Rader

## 134. THE STAR OF BETHLEHEM

    Not to the king the Star,
      Flaming in light afar;
Not to the king on his throne apart,
With fear and hate in his evil heart,
Speaking smoothly with lying ruse
To find the new-born King of the Jews;
    Not to the king the flame,
      The light and the glory came.

    Not to the seers the Star,
      Shedding its beams afar;
Not to the seers with their downbent looks,
Poring over their ancient books,
Searching where and pondering when,
He should be born who is Saviour of men;
    Not to the seers the flame,
      The light and the glory came.

    Not to the sword the Star,
      Glowing and bright afar;
Not to the sword that sought where He lay,
Callous and cruel and eager to slay;
Never were bearers of swords so led
Where helpless and innocent blood was shed;
    Not to the sword the flame,
      The light and the glory came.

    But to the wise the Star,
      Lighting their path afar;
Unto the wise who truly sought,
With reverent worship and loving thought.
These to the Child the Star could bring,
To lay their gifts at the feet of the King;
    Unto the wise the flame,
      The light and the glory came.

              Annie Johnson Flint

## 135. A BED IN MY HEART

Ah, dearest Jesus, holy Child,
Make Thee a bed, soft, undefiled,
    Within my heart, that it may be
    A quiet chamber kept for Thee.
My heart for very joy doth leap,
My lips no more can silence keep.
    I too must sing, with joyful tongue,
    That sweetest ancient cradle song,
Glory to God in highest Heaven,
Who unto man His Son hath given,
    While angels sing with pious mirth,
    A glad New Year to all the earth.

              Martin Luther

136. THE CHILD OF THE MAID

On Christmas Day the Child was born,
On Christmas Day in the morning;--

    --To tread the long way, lone and lorn,
    --To wear the bitter crown of thorn,
    --To break the heart by man's sin torn,
    --To die at last the Death of Scorn.

For this the Child of the Maid was born,
On Christmas Day in the morning.
But that first day when He was born,
Among the cattle and the corn,
The sweet Maid-Mother wondering,
And sweetly, deeply, pondering
The words that in her heart did ring,
Unto her newborn King did sing--

"My Baby, my Baby,
My own little Son,
Whence come You,
Where go You,
My own little One?
Whence come You?
And now, unto me all alone
That wonder of wonders is properly known.
Where go You?
Ah, that now, 'tis only He knows,
Who sweetly on us, Dear, such favor bestows.
In us, Dear, this day is some great work
        begun,--
Ah me, little Son dear, I would it were done!
I wonder...I wonder...
And--wish--it--were--done!

"O little, little feet, dears,
So curly, curly sweet!--
How will it be with You, dears,
When all Your work's complete?
O little, little hands, dears,
That creep about my breast!--
What great things You will do, dears,
Before You lie at rest!
O softest little head, Dear,
It shall have crown of gold,
For It shall have great honor
Before the world grows old!
O sweet, white, soft round body,
It shall sit upon a throne!
My little One, my little One,
Thou art the Highest Son!
All this the angel told me,
And so I'm sure it's true,
For he told me who was coming--
And that sweet thing is YOU."

On Christmas Day the Child was born,
On Christmas Day in the morning;--

    --He trod the long way, lone and lorn,
    --He wore the bitter crown of thorn,
    --His hands and feet and heart were torn,
    --He died at last the Death of Scorn.

But through His coming Death was slain,
That you and I might live again,
For this the Child of the Maid was born,
On Christmas Day in the morning.

           John Oxenham

*"For unto us a child is born, unto us a son is given."--Isa. 9:6.*

137.    CHRISTMAS

It's a hard old row that I have to hoe,
  With the coming of Christmastime,
For my income's small, and I need it all,
  I've a place for the last thin dime.
And I used to fret, and I do it yet,
  At the cost of the children's tree.
And I'd sigh and say that the Christmas day
  Brought nothing but debts for me.

But on that glad night, when the snow
        lays white,
  And the last "good-night" has been said,
And the tree is trimmed, and the lights
        are dimmed
  And I stand by the children's bed;
I've never a thought of the toys I've bought,
  For the heart in my selfish breast
Dissolves like the snow, when the south
        winds blow--
  I'm glad that I've done my best.

For I know my wealth is my children's health,
  And a home where their laughter rings--
That I've treasure there that I would not share
  For the gold of a hundred kings.
And I breathe a prayer on the Christmas air,
  For the man who must walk alone--
Who on all this earth, with its Yuletide mirth,
  Has no one to call His own.

           Author Unknown

138. THE MOST "WONDERFUL" DAY OF THE YEAR

God has brought us once more to this wonderful day,
    The most wonderful day in the year;
When the prophets of old in the Scriptures foretold
    That a wonderful Child would appear.


'Twas a wonderful thing that so holy a God
    Should consider His creatures at all;
When the first man He made His command disobeyed,
    And spoiled His great work at the Fall.


But in wonderful mercy, foreseeing that Fall,
    God ordained in the ages before
That the Son of His love should come down from above,
    And His perfect creation restore.


In the fullness of time that most wonderful Child--
    Although born of a woman indeed--
Came to live among men, but beyond angels' ken--
    In two natures, as God had decreed.


From His earliest days He was found in God's ways,
    As a youth to the Temple He sped;
Little children He blest, to the weary gave rest,
    But had nowhere to lay His own head!


Oh! what shall be said of the work that He did
    When He hung upon Calvary's tree?
Where He died all alone, for our sins to atone,
    Out of pity for you and for me!


But alas!  It is not a more wonderful thing
    That so many for whom Jesus came
Never give Him their days, but they choose their own ways,
    And refuse to acknowledge His claim!


Yet this Christmas once more seems to knock at our door,
    To arouse us from slumber today;
Lest we love not the Lord, nor give heed to His Word,
    And our seasons of grace pass away.


Patient Lord, we would say, on this wonderful day,
    Thy most wonderful Name we adore;
We will give Thee our days, and we'll walk in Thy ways,
    And we'll live to Thy praise evermore.

                                        Sidney Collett

## 139. READY FOR CHRISTMAS

"Ready for Christmas," she said with a sigh,
As she gave a last touch to the gifts piled high,
Then wearily sat for a moment and read,
Till soon, very soon, she was nodding her head.

Then quietly spoke a voice in her dream,
"Ready for Christmas? What do you mean?
Ready for Christmas when only last week
You wouldn't acknowledge your friend on the street.

"Ready for Christmas, while holding a grudge?
Perhaps you had better let God be the judge,
Why, how can the Christ-child come and abide
In the heart that is selfish and filled with pride?

"Ready for Christmas when only today
A beggar lad came and you turned him away
Without even a smile to show that you cared?
The little he asked--it could have been spared.

"Ready for Christmas? You've worked, it is true,
But just doing the thing that you wanted to do.
Ready for Christmas? Your circle's too small--
Why, you are not ready for Christmas at all!"

She awoke with a start and a cry of despair,
"There's so little time and I've still to prepare.
O Father, forgive me, I see what You mean,
To be ready means more than a house swept clean."

Yes, more than the giving of gifts and a tree,
It's the heart swept clean that He wants to see;
A heart that is free from bitterness, sin--
Ready for Christmas--and ready for HIM.

Alice Haneche Mortensen

## 140. THE PRINCE OF PEACE

To us a Child of hope is born,
To us a Son is given;
Him shall the tribes of earth obey,
Him, all the hosts of Heaven.

His name shall be the Prince of Peace,
Forevermore adored;
The Wonderful, the Counselor,
The great and mighty Lord.

His power, increasing, still shall spread;
His reign no end shall know;
Justice shall guard His throne above,
And peace abound below.

To us a Child of hope is born,
To us a Son is given;
The Wonderful, the Counselor,
The mighty Lord of Heaven.

Author Unknown

## 141. GOD'S CHRISTMAS GIFT

The festive spirit fills the air,
And people's hearts are gay,
There're trees and lights and lots of toys,
'Twill soon be Christmas day;
So much is said of Santa Claus
And of the gifts he gives,
So little said of God's dear Son
Whose own birthday it is.

Wild merriment is on every hand,
They drink and dance and curse,
They must forget what Christmas is,
Why Jesus came to earth;
If He should speak at Christmastime,
I'm sure that He would say,
"I'd rather you My birth not keep
Than do it in this way."

E'en as it was one bygone night
In far-off Bethlehem,
When Jesus in a manger lay,
No room within the inn;
Today He's shut outside men's hearts,
Hearts filled with sin and wrong.
They care not that with nail-pierced hand
He's knocked there, oh, so long.

They give their presents to their friends,
Receive gifts from each one,
Neglecting God's great Christmas gift--
He gave His only Son
To die upon the awful cross
And pay our debt of sin,
To open wide the gates of Heaven
And let us enter in.

The gift's still waiting at the tree,
So few His Word believe,
Though offered freely to all men,
They will not Christ receive;
The tree is just a cross of wood,
Unsightly to behold.
But oh, the gift the dear Lord gives
Is better far than gold.

There are no lights to light His tree,
No decorations fine,
No pretty tinsel, balls, and bells
That glitter, gleam, and shine;
And yet there're stains of His own blood
To ransom our whole race,
There's light to guide the wanderer home
That shines from His dear face.

Why should His gift rejected be?
How God must grieve today!
When He has paid so great a price,
Should Christ be turned away?
Oh! open now your heart's door wide,
Receive God's gift of love,
His joy and peace and grace He'll give,
Eternal life above.

                    Russell Stellwagon

## 142. CHRISTMAS BELLS

I heard the bells on Christmas day
Their old familiar carols play,
    And wild and sweet
    The words repeat,
Of "Peace on earth, good will to men!"

And thought how, as the day had come,
The belfries of all Christendom
    Had rolled along
    The unbroken song,
Of "Peace on earth, good will to men!"

Till ringing, singing on its way,
The world revolved from night to day,--
    A voice, a chime,
    A chant sublime,
Of "Peace on earth, good will to men!"

And in despair I bowed my head;
"There is no peace on earth," I said,
    "For hate is strong
    And mocks the song
Of peace on earth, good will to men!"

Then pealed the bells more loud and deep:
"God is not dead; nor doth He sleep!
    The wrong shall fail,
    The right prevail,
With peace on earth, good will to men!"

                Henry Wadsworth Longfellow,
                    1807-1882

*"Therefore the Lord himself shall give you a sign; Behold, a virgin shall conceive, and bear a son, and shall call his name Immanuel."*
*--Isa. 7:14.*

## 143. HIS POVERTY -- MY WEALTH

*For Him--"No room. . .in the inn."--Luke 2:7.*
*For us--"tidings of great joy. . . ."--Luke 2:10.*
*". . .though he was rich, yet for your sakes he*
*became poor, that ye through his poverty might*
*be rich."--II Cor. 8:9.*

I've traveled long
With a carol song,
To be with the loved of mine,
And the homing plane
Sped the high airlane
Bringing me to the holiday time,
To the joyfilled faces,
To the sweet embraces,
To love gifts and tinseled pine.

But the Christmas Child
Crossed the spaces wild,
Past the moon and the stars He made--
From eternal light
To the age-long night
Of the world, with glad tidings lade.
No room in the inn,
The Saviour from sin,
In a manger's straw, was laid.

No room for Him,
Blessed Saviour of men
Has the world. But in rapture I say,
"Come in, Lamb of God!
My Saviour, My God,
To my heart come Thou in and stay."
My peace by His pain,
His poorness all gain
To me, this Christmas Day.

John R. Rice

## 144. A SWEET CHRISTMAS

Why shouldn't this Christmas be sweeter
Than ever a Christmas before,
When Jesus is tenfold the dearer,
Outpouring His grace more and more?

Why shouldn't the future be brighter
With glad expectations each day?
Why shouldn't each burden seem lighter
With Jesus our King on the way?

Why shouldn't our vision be clearer,
His last blest command to obey,

While ever His coming draws nearer,
And millions in darkness still stray?

Oh, thus can this Christmas be sweeter
Than ever a Christmas before,
If souls that are dying are dearer,
And on them Christ's love we outpour.

Alice Reynolds Flower

## 145. THE CHRIST OF CHRISTMAS

The Christ of Christmas now behold,
The Christ of Christmas morn;
The One by prophets long foretold
In Bethlehem is born.
He is God's Son, Immanuel,
Our Saviour and our King;
Let every heart the tidings tell
And with the angels sing.

The shepherds rest beside the sheep
Upon Judean hill;
An angel choir disturbs their sleep
With songs that echo still.
To Bethlehem in early morn
The shepherds wend their way;
Their hearts rejoice, the Babe is born,
And sleeps upon the hay.

The wise men cross the deserts wild,
Their treasures rare to bring;
Beneath the star they find the Child,
A Babe and yet a King!
To worship Him and minister
As to a king of old,
They offer frankincense and myrrh
And treasures made of gold.

Rejoice! for Christmas comes again
Around the whole wide earth,
To spread abroad God's love to men
As seen in Jesus' birth.
While Christmas bells in gladness ring,
Ring out o'er land and sea,
Make Him your Saviour and your King,
To reign eternally.

The Christ of Christmas let us adore,
His praises let us sing,
And love and serve Him evermore,
This wonderful Saviour and King.

Eugene M. Harrison

### 146. THE VIRGIN MARY TO THE CHILD JESUS

Sleep! Sleep, mine HOLY ONE!
My flesh, my Lord!--what name? I do not know--
A name that seemeth not too high or low,
   Too far from me or Heaven.
My JESUS, that is best; that Name being given
By the majestic angel whose command
Was softly as a man's beseeching said,
When I and all the earth appeared to stand
   In the great overflow
Of light celestial from His wings and head!
   Sleep! Sleep, my SAVING ONE!

We sat among the stalls at Bethlehem,
The dumb kine from their fodder turning them,
   Softened their horned faces
   To almost human gazes
   Toward the Newly Born;
The simple shepherds from star-lit brooks
   Brought visionary looks,
As yet in their astonished hearing, rung
   The strange, sweet angel-tongue:
The magi of the East, in sandals worn,
   Knelt reverent, sweeping round,
With long pale beards, their gifts upon the ground,
   The incense, myrrh, and gold
These baby hands were impotent to hold.
So, let all earthlies and celestials wait
   Upon Thy royal state.
   Sleep! Sleep, my KINGLY ONE!

Elizabeth Barrett Browning

# CONSECRATION and SURRENDER

## 147.   STRONG SON OF GOD

Strong Son of God, immortal Love,
   Whom we, that have not seen Thy face,
   By faith, and faith alone, embrace,
Believing where we cannot prove;

Thine are these orbs of light and shade;
   Thou madest Life in man and brute;
   Thou madest Death; and, lo, Thy foot
Is on the skull which Thou hast made.

Thou wilt not leave us in the dust:
   Thou madest man, he knows not why,
   He thinks he was not made to die;
And Thou hast made him:  Thou art just.

Thou seemest human and divine,
   The highest, holiest manhood, Thou.
   Our wills are ours, we know not how;
Our wills are ours, to make them Thine.

Our little systems have their day;
   They have their day and cease to be;
   They are but broken lights of Thee,
And Thou, O Lord, art more than they.

We have but faith: we cannot know,
   For knowledge is of things we see;
   And yet we trust it comes from Thee,
A beam in darkness: let it grow.

Let knowledge grow from more to more,
   But more of reverence in us dwell;
   That mind and soul, according well,
May make one music as before,

But vaster.  We are fools and slight;
   We mock Thee when we do not fear:
   But help Thy foolish ones to bear;
Help Thy vain worlds to bear Thy light.

Forgive what seem'd my sin in me,
   What seem'd my worth since I began;
   For merit lives from man to man,
And not from man, O Lord, to Thee.

Forgive my grief for one removed,
   Thy creature, whom I found so fair.
   I trust he lives in Thee, and there
I find him worthier to be loved.

Forgive these wild and wandering cries,
   Confusions of a wasted youth;
   Forgive them where they fail in truth,
And in Thy wisdom make me wise.

       From "In Memoriam" Proem,
       Alfred Tennyson, 1809-1892

## 148.   "WHAT IS IN THY HAND?"

What hast thou in thy hand,
   Woman?  "One handful" more.
Go feed the prophet, and 'twill last
   Till famine days are o'er.

What hast thou in thy hand,
   Widow?  "A pot of oil."
Go pour it out, and find a store
   Of rich and priceless spoil.

What hast thou in thy hand,
   Mary?  Some "perfume rare."
Pour it upon His head; 'twill flow
   In fragrance everywhere.

And, Dorcas, what hast thou?
   "A needle and some thread."
Give them to God, they'll bless the poor,
   And bring thee from the dead.

What hast thou in thy hand,
   Widow?  "Two mites"--no more.
Give them to God, and they shall grow
   To be a mighty store.

What hast thou in thy hand,
   Mother?  "A baby's hand."
Train it for Him, so shall thy life
   Bear fruit in every land.

What hast thou in thy hand,
   Teacher?  "A child's young mind."
Teach it to live for God and man,
   So shalt thou bless mankind.

What hast thou in thy hand,
   Writer?  "A common pen."
Use it to write His messages
   Upon the hearts of men.

          Selected

## 149. TAKE UP THY CROSS

The Crucifixion Road is full of sorrows;
  The jeering voices added to the pain;
But take thy cross, O child of God, and follow,
  And shun not the reproach in Jesus' name.

Reproach there is defending, bold, the Bible.
  Reproach, with zeal and tears to seek the lost,
And shame to preach of sin and Hell and judgment;
  Reproach to seek God's pow'r at any cost.

I'm called unloving if I turn in sorrow
  From "learned" churchmen who reject the Word.
I'm mocked and shunned because I call not "brother"
  Those famed false friends of Christ who mock His blood.

The servant is not better than His master;
  The world that so hates Him should hate me too!
Outside the gate is now the place for Christians.
  Not crowns, but crosses fit disciples true.

I'll suffer, then, with all the saints and prophets.
  I'll walk the Calv'ry road, smile at the pain.
Then, when He reigns, O glory! What a prospect!
  His own who suffer with Him, too shall reign.

"Take up thy cross," said Jesus, and I will!
  Although discipleship be rugged still.
    But if He give me grace,
    I'll run this patient race,
Be crucified with Jesus as He wills.

                                          John R. Rice


## 150.   BY THY LIFE I LIVE

I love, my God, but with no love of mine,
  For I have none to give;
I love Thee, Lord, but all the love is Thine,
  For by Thy life I live.
I am as nothing, and rejoice to be
Emptied and lost and swallowed up in Thee.

Thou, Lord, alone art all Thy children need,
  And there is none beside;
From Thee the streams of blessedness
            proceed;
  In Thee the blest abide,
Fountain of life, and all-abounding grace,
Our source, our center, and our
            dwellingplace!

                Madame Jeanne Marie Guyon,
                      1648-1717


## 151.   LORD, I AM THINE

Lord, I am Thine, entirely Thine,
Purchased and saved by blood divine;
With full consent Thine I would be,
And own Thy sovereign right in me.

Thine would I live, Thine would I die,
Be Thine, thro' all eternity;
The vow is past beyond repeal.
And now I set the solemn seal.

Here, at the cross where flows the blood
That bought my guilty soul for God,
Thee, my new Master, now I call,
And consecrate to Thee my all.

                        Samuel Davies

## 152. FOLLOW ME

I traveled down a lonely road
And no one seemed to care;
The burden on my weary back
Had bowed me to despair;
I oft complained to Jesus
How folks were treating me.
And then I heard Him say so tenderly:

"My feet were also weary,
Upon the Calvary road;
The cross became so heavy,
I fell beneath the load.
Be faithful, weary pilgrim.
The morning I can see;
Just lift your cross and follow close to Me."

"I work so hard for Jesus,"
I often boast and say;
"I've sacrificed a lot of things
To walk the narrow way.
I gave up fame and fortune;
I'm worth a lot to Thee."
And then I hear Him gently say to me:

"I left the throne of glory
And counted it but loss;
My hands were nailed in anger
Upon a cruel cross.
But now we'll make the journey
With your hand safe in Mine;
So lift your cross and follow close to Me."

O Jesus, if I die upon
A foreign field some day,
'Twould be no more than love demands,
No less could I repay.
"No greater love hath mortal man
Than for a friend to die,"
These are the words He gently spoke to me.

"If just a cup of water
I place within your hand,
Then just a cup of water
Is all that I demand.
But if by death to living
They can Thy glory see;
I'll take my cross and follow close to Thee."

Ira Stanphill
*Copyright 1953 by Ira F. Stanphill*
*Used by permission.*

## 153. HIMSELF

Once it was the blessing,
 Now it is the Lord;
Once it was the feeling,
 Now it is His Word;
Once His gift I wanted,
 Now, the Giver own;
Once I sought for healing,
 Now Himself alone.

Once 'twas painful trying,
 Now 'tis perfect trust;
Once a half salvation,
 Now the uttermost;
Once 'twas ceaseless holding,
 Now He holds me fast;
Once 'twas constant drifting,
 Now my anchor's cast.

Once 'twas busy planning,
 Now 'tis trustful prayer;
Once 'twas anxious caring,
 Now He has the care;
Once 'twas what I wanted,
 Now what Jesus says;

Once 'twas constant asking,
 Now 'tis ceaseless praise.

Once it was my working,
 His it hence shall be;
Once I tried to use Him,
 Now He uses me;
Once the pow'r I wanted,
 Now the Mighty One;
Once for self I labored,
 Now for Him alone.

Once I hoped in Jesus,
 Now I know He's mine;
Once my lamps were dying,
 Now they brightly shine;
Once for death I waited,
 Now His coming hail;
And my hopes are anchored
 Safe within the veil.

All in all forever,
 Jesus will I sing;
Ev'rything in Jesus,
 And Jesus ev'rything.

A. B. Simpson

154.    SECRET OF FREEDOM

Make me a captive, Lord,
    And then I shall be free;
Force me to render up my sword,
    And I shall conqueror be.
I sink in life's alarms
    While by myself I stand;
Imprison me within Thine arms,
    And strong shall be my hand.

                George Matheson


155.    JESUS, LIKE THEE!

O Jesus, make me as Thou art,
    So sensitive to sin,
So I will grieve o'er all my faults
    And every wrong within;
That I may learn Thy holy way,
    And daily walk so near,
That always I may see Thy face,
    Nor Thy displeasure fear.

Lord, give me such compassion as
    Thou hast for hearts in pain,
So I may weep with those who weep
    Until they're glad again,
With sins forgiven, burdens gone
    By trusting, Lord, in Thee.
Oh, for a tender, loving heart
    Like Thine to beat in me!

Thou didst not shun the hate and shame,
    The spitting nor the thorns;
In Pilate's hall mid jeers and scourge
    Thy heart with love was torn.
Oh, may I suffer, Lord, for Thee,
    Like Thee to bear the shame,
That Christians who are true should bear
    Like Thee, and for Thy name.

To seek the lost, to save from Hell,
    Lord Jesus, Thou didst come
To earth in shame to die for us,
    That Heav'n may be our home.
Dear Jesus, may I too go out
    To win and save the lost--
Yes, go with tears and broken heart
    Like Thee, at any cost.

                John R. Rice


156.    MY GIFT

What can I give Him
Poor as I am;
If I were a shepherd,
I would give Him a lamb.
If I were a wise man,
I would do my part.
But what can I give Him?
I will give my heart.

                Christiana Rossetti


157.    VESSELS UNTO HONOR

Some "vessels" God appoints to fame,
Others are called to suffer shame,
In following the Lamb;
To bear the cross, and all it means,
Dwelling amid dark Calvary's scenes,
Suffering for Jesus' name.

God's choicest gems are little known,
The cross leads ever to the throne,
Through suffering we shall reign,
Then count it joy to bear the cross,
To suffer pain, and shame, and loss,
That we may glory gain.

The suffering saint alone can know,
The wond'rous grace Christ can bestow,
While passing through the fire.
The furnace may in heat increase,
But grace Divine shall never cease,
'Twill holier zeal inspire.

Christ took all to the marriage feast
To share the joy; greatest and least,
Were glad to follow there.
But into dark Gethsemane,
He only took the chosen three,
Such scenes so few can bear.

Today as in the days of old,
Out of the many, few are called,
This suffering life to share.
If counted worthy of our King,
To take our share of suffering,
Should we not gladly bear?

                H. E. Jessop

158.    BATTER MY HEART

Batter my heart, three person'd God; for, you
As yet but knocke, breathe, shine, and seeke to mend;
That I may rise, and stand, o'erthrow mee 'and bend
Your force, to breake, blowe, burn and make me new.
I, like an usurpt towne, to'another due,
Labour to'admit you, but oh, to no end,
Reason your viceroy in mee, mee should defend,
But is captiv'd, and proves weake or untrue.
Yet dearely 'I love you,' and would be lov'd faine,
But am bethroth'd unto your enemie,
Divorce mee, 'untie, or breake that knot againe,
Take mee to you, imprison mee, for I
Except you'enthrall mee, never shall be free,
Nor ever chast, except you ravish mee.

John Donne

159.    CROWDED OUT

Is Christ crowded out of your busy life
  With the toiling that each day brings?
    With the strain and stress
    Of the cares that press
  You've no time for the King of kings.

"No room in the inn" for the Christ-Child
        blest,
  "In a manger so low He lay";
    In the hearts of men
    O'er and o'er again,
  There's no room for Him still today.

"The foxes have holes and the birds
        have nests,"
  But nowhere for His head divine
    Had the Son of man,
    Should He come again
  Find a place in your heart and mine.

The hearts of the ones whom He died to save
  Is the home which He seeks today;
    By His life bought yet
    He is crowded out,
  And "away with Him," still they say.

There's coming a day in the great sometime
  If for Christ you have never room,
    You will knock and wait
    At the pearly gate,
  Crowded out there will be your doom.

Crowded out! crowded out!
  You've no time for His service, you say;
While for pleasure and business you always
        have time,
  Is Christ crowded out today?

Mrs. C. H. Morris

160.    KEEP GIVING

"Go break the needy sweet charity's bread
For giving is loving," the Angel said.
"And must I keep giving again and again?"
My angry and pitiless answer ran.
"Oh, no," said the Angel--piercing me
        through--
"Just give till the Master stops giving to you."

Selected

161.    THE SISTERS

The waves forever move;
The hills forever rest:
Yet each the heavens approve,
And Love alike hath blessed
A Martha's household care,
A Mary's cloistered prayer.

John Banister Tabb

## 162. "OUTSIDE THE CAMP"

*"Let us go forth therefore UNTO HIM without (outside)*
*the camp, bearing his reproach."—Heb. 13:13.*

This is the day! This is the hour!
To prove our God's almighty power;
To follow Him whate'er befall,
And answer gladly to His call--
  **To go "without the camp!"**

**Apart from those who doubt His Word,**
**From those who have denied your Lord!**
O Christian, hasten to His side,
Who for your sin was crucified--
  **And go "without the camp!"**

'Tis only now that we can bear
In His reproach, our little share.
He did not stop to count the cost
When going forth to save the lost--
  He went "without the camp!"

**And though you here may stand alone, --**
At that Great Day, upon His throne,
In robes of righteousness arrayed--
**What joy to know the choice you made--**
  To go "without the camp!"

Author Unknown

## 163. MORE HOLINESS GIVE ME

More holiness give me,
  More strivings within;
More patience in suff'ring,
  More sorrow for sin;
More faith in my Saviour,
  More sense of His care;
More joy in His service,
  More purpose in prayer.

More gratitude give me,
  More trust in the Lord;
More pride in His glory,
  More hope in His Word;
More tears for His sorrows,
  More pain at His grief;
More meekness in trial,
  More praise for relief.

More purity give me,
  More strength to o'ercome;
More freedom from earth-stains,
  More longings for Home;
More fit for the kingdom,
  More used would I be;
More blessed and holy,
  More, Saviour, like Thee.

P. P. Bliss, 1873

## 164. SOMETIME

Sometime, when all life's lessons have been learned,
  And sun and stars forevermore have set,
The things which our weak judgment here has spurned,
  The things o'er which we grieved with lashes wet,
Will flash before us out of life's dark night,
  As stars shine most in deeper tints of blue;
And we shall see how all God's plans were right,
  And how, what seemed reproof, was love most true.

And we shall see that while we frown and sigh,
  God's plans go on as best for you and me:
How, when we called, He heeded not our cry,
  Because His wisdom to the end could see.
And e'en as prudent parents disallow
  Too much of sweet to craving babyhood,
So God, perhaps, is keeping from us now
  Life's sweetest things because it seemeth good.

And if, sometimes, commingled with life's wine,
  We find the wormwood, and rebel and shrink,
Be sure a wiser hand than yours or mine
  Pours out this portion for our lips to drink.
And if some friend we love is lying low,

Where human kisses cannot reach his face,
Oh, do not blame the loving Father so,
But bear your sorrow with obedient grace.

And you shall shortly know that lengthened breath
Is not the sweetest gift God sends His friends;
And that sometimes the sable pall of death
Conceals the fairest boon His love can send.
If we could push ajar the gates of life,
And stand within, and all God's working see,
We might interpret all this doubt and strife,
And for each mystery find a key.

But not today. Then be content, poor heart!
God's plans, like lilies pure and white, unfold.
We must not tear the close-shut leaves apart--
Time will reveal the calyxes of gold.
And when, with toil all past, we reach the land
Where tired feet, with sandals loose, may rest,--
When we shall clearly know and understand,--
I think that we will say that "God knew best."

May Riley Smith

### 165.    JUDGMENT SEAT

When I stand at the judgment seat of Christ,
And He shows me His plan for me;
The plan of my life as it might have been,
Had He had His way and I see--

How I blocked Him' here and I checked
Him there;
And I would not yield my will--
Will there be grief in my Saviour's eyes--
Grief, though He loves me still?

He would have me rich, and I stand
there poor,
Stripped of all but His grace,
While memory runs like a hunted thing
Down the paths I cannot retrace.

Then my desolate heart will well nigh break,
With tears that I cannot shed;
I shall cover my face with my empty hands,
I shall there bow my uncrowned head.

Lord, of the years that are left to me,
I give them to Thy hand;
Take me and break me, mold me to
The pattern Thou hast planned.

Martha Snell Nicholson

### 166.    LET GO!

This world holds nothing so dear
That Christ cannot give us more:
His love, His peace, His joy--
Far more than heart could implore.
Our lives lose much He has for us
As we cling to our earthly ties:
In Him are pleasures forevermore,
Let go--for Christ satisfies!

Selected

### 167.    FIREWORDS

"O God, my words are cold:
The frosted frond of fern or feathery palm
Wrought on the whitened pane--
They are as near to fire as these my words;
Oh, that they were flames!" Thus did I cry,
And thus God answered me: "Thou shalt
have words,
But at this cost, that thou must first be burnt.
Not otherwise, and by no lighter touch,
Are firewords wrought."

Amy Carmichael

168.    SO DID I

I was caught within the center
  Of a milling frenzy mob,
That spat upon and ridiculed
  The unflinching Son of God;
I beheld them as they mocked Him
  And I heard their taunting cry;
As they jeered Him in their madness--
  As they did, so did I.

On His head with brutal fingers
  They did thrust a thorny crown,
And the maddened mob roared louder
  As the blood came trickling down.
With the lashes then they scourged Him
  While the mob cried, "Crucify,"
Dragging forth the heavy crosses--
  And as they did, so did I.

Through the crowded streets they led Him
  To a hill without the wall,
And the crowd that lately cheered Him
  Loudly scoffed now at His fall.
Then I heard the sound of hammers,
  And I watched the crosses rise
To a cry of hate full-fruited--
  And as they did, so did I.

Nearer to the cross and nearer
  Did I work my way apace,
'Til I reached the feet of Jesus
  And could look upon His face.
Then my lips forgot their mocking
  And I felt my hatred die;
When that thief beside sought pardon--
  As that thief did, so did I.

Then He healed my every heartache,
  With His blood purged out my sin;
Promised me a life eternal,
  Gave me perfect peace within.
On the path where earnest Christians
  Struggle daily to draw nigh,
To the perfect rest of Heaven--
  As they do, so shall I.

With my cross I'll follow Jesus;
  Let the mob do as it will--
Though it heap abuse upon me,
  In His steps I'll follow still.
Step by step I'll follow Jesus,
  Though the clouds bedim the sky,
And a martyr's death await me--
  Yet as they die, so can I.

But we wait till shout of triumph
  Marks the ending of the siege,
And the angel who recorded
  Blots the fatal final page.
Then the trumpet loud will signal
  And in the twinkling of an eye,
As the saved of earth go upward--
  As the saved go, so shall I.

Selected

169.  WAIT ON GOD

Each moment draw from earth away
  My heart, that lowly waits Thy call;
Speak to my inmost soul, and say,
  "I am thy Love, thy God, thy All!"
To feel Thy power, to hear Thy voice,
  To taste Thy love, be all my choice.

John Wesley

170.  THE PRUNED BRANCH

It is the branch that bears the fruit,
  That feels the knife,
To prune it for a larger growth
  A fuller life,

Though every budding twig be lopped,
  And every grace
Of swaying tendril, springing leaf
  Be lost a space.

Oh, thou whose life of joy seems reft,
  Of beauty shorn,
Whose aspirations lie in dust,
  All bruised and torn,

Rejoice, though each desire, each dream,
  Each hope of thine
Shall fall and fade, it is the hand
  Of love divine

That holds the knife, that cuts and breaks
  With tenderest touch,
That thou, whose life hast borne some fruit,
  May now bear much.

Annie Johnson Flint

171.    FIRST FOR GOD

First days for God,
Before thy life is molded,
And God is given
Second place--or none.
Give Him thy time,
And see His plan unfolded;
Find in thy years
Eternity begun.

First hours for God;
The day will not be wasted
If thou dost tarry
In His presence till
Strength from His strength
Is found for every burden,
Thou art encircled
By His holy will.

First thoughts for God,
Who giveth power for thinking;
Humble and contrite
Be thy will to learn.
He thought of thee
In living and in dying;
For thine affection
Does thy Saviour yearn.

So shalt thou seek
Him first, and be rewarded;
So shalt thou find
Himself thy great supply;
No day, nor hour,
Nor thought, without His blessing;
With Christ to live!
And so, with Him, to die!

Will H. Houghton

172.    JESUS HIMSELF

I do not ask Thee, Lord, for outward sign,
    For portents in the earth or flaming sky;
It is enough to know that Thou art mine,
    And not far off, but intimately nigh.

No burning bush I need to speak Thy name,
    Or call me forward to the newer task;
Give me a burning heart, with love aflame,
    Which sees Thee everywhere, is all I ask.

No pillar-cloud I seek to mark my way
    Through all the windings of the trackless years;
Thou art my Guide, by night as well as day,
    To choose my path, and hush my foolish fears.

I do not look for fiery cloven tongues,
    To tell for me the pentecostal hour;
The Father's promise for all time belongs
    To him who seeks the Spirit's quickening power.

I do not ask for voices from the sky;
    The thunder-peal I might not understand;
But let me hear Thy whisper, "It is I!
    Fear not the darkness, child, but take My hand!"

What can I ask but Thine own Self, dear Lord?
    Omniscience and omnipotence are Thine.
Let but my will with Thy sweet will accord,
    And all Thou hast, and all Thou art is mine!

Henry Burton

## 173. CREATE IN ME A CLEAN HEART

O Thou who walketh on the wings of wind
  Blow bare the secrets of my inmost heart,
And clear away unconscious sins I've sinned
  As well as conscious ones that wound and smart;
Make it a little sanctuary where
Thou wilt restore Thy chastened child in prayer.

Then like a wind-harp tune it up to praise
  So all its seasons shall like springtime be,
As when peach blossoms on the soft warm days
  Drift down pink petals and sweet odors free,
Or when fresh water-springs gush close to hand
By paths that otherwise were arid sand.

                    Grace W. Haight

## 174. LET YOURSELF ALONE

Vain and fruitless is the struggle
  Self to sanctify;
God alone can cleanse and keep you,
  Wherefore should you try?
Oh, the needless cares and conflicts
  You had never known,
If you'd learned the simple lesson--
  Let yourself alone.

Let your eyes keep looking upward;
  Cease to look within;
All your introspection cannot
  Cleanse a single sin.
You will find your best self-effort
  Vain, and worse than vain,
As the touch of soiled fingers
  Only leaves a stain.

Leave your rights and reputation
  In the Master's hand.
What though men misunderstand you,
  Jesus understands;
He can shield and vindicate you,
  Right your every wrong,
Turn the hate of men and devils
  Into joy and song.

It is life you need, not labor--
  Life that springs from Him;
If you'd have your cup run over,
  Fill it to the brim.
All the springs of power and blessing
  Flow from yonder throne;
If you'd have them fill and flood you,
  Let yourself alone.

              A. B. Simpson

## 175. I NEED THE SHADOWS

I need the shadows,
I would not dwell in constant jubilee;
I need the shadows,
From dull routine of sunlight, to be free;
I need to feel the smart of pain, abundant grace
     to entertain--
I need the shadows.

I need the shadows,
Lest I neglect to fellowship with Him;
I need the shadows,
For happiness alone, can faith bedim;
My heart requires a sense of loss that I may
     understand the cross--
I need the shadows.

I need the shadows--
The storm-tossed sea to cause my heart to fear;
I need the shadows,
That I His blessed "Peace, be still!" may hear;
As birds at twilight seek their nest, so shadows
     call my heart to rest--
I need the shadows.

I need the shadows,
Upon the path to Heaven's wonderland;
I need the shadows,
To feel the strength of His sustaining hand;
The trouble-shadows on the trail, like markers,
     say, "He cannot fail."
I need the shadows.

             Paul Hutchens

## 176.  GOD'S BEST

God has His best things for the few
  Who dare to stand the test;
God has His second choice for those
  Who will not have His best.
It is not always open ill
  That risks the Promised Rest;
The better often is the foe
  That keeps us from God's best.
Some seek the highest choice,
  But, when by trials pressed,
They shrink, they yield, they shun the cross
  And so they lose God's best.
Give me, O Lord, Thy highest choice,
  Let others take the rest;
Their good things have no charm for me,
  I want Thy very best.
I want in this short life of mine,
  As much as can be pressed
Of service true to God and man--
  Make me to be Thy best.

        A. B. Simpson

## 177.  OTHERS

Lord help me to live from day to day
  In such a self-forgetful way,
That even when I kneel to pray
  My prayer shall be for others.

Help me in all the work I do
  To ever be sincere and true;
And know that all I do for Thee
  Must needs be done for others.

Let self be crucified and slain,
  And buried deep and all in vain
May efforts be to rise again,
  Unless to live for others.

And when my work on earth is done,
  And my new work in Heaven begun,
May I forget the crown I won
  While thinking still of others.

Others, Lord, yes others,
  Let this my motto be,
Help me to live for others
  That I may live like Thee.

        Charles D. Meigs

## 178.  ABIDING

I have learned the wondrous secret
  Of abiding in the Lord;
I have found the strength and sweetness
  Of confiding in His Word.
I have tasted life's pure fountain,
  I am trusting in His blood;
I have lost myself in Jesus,
  I am sinking into God.

I am crucified with Jesus,
  And He lives and dwells with me;
I have ceased from all my struggling.
  'Tis no longer I but He.
All my will is yielded to Him,
  And His Spirit reigns within;
And His precious blood each moment,
  Keeps me cleansed and free from sin.

For my words, I take His wisdom;
  For my works, His Spirit's power,
For my ways, His ceaseless Presence
  Guides and guards me every hour.
Of my heart, He is the Portion,
  Of my joy, the boundless Spring;
Saviour, Sanctifier, Healer,
  Glorious Lord, and coming King!

        A. B. Simpson

## 179.  MY GIFT

I have not much to offer
  To Christ, my Lord and King;
No wealth, no might, no wisdom,
  No noble gift to bring.
"Five loaves and two small fishes?"
  But what alas are they
Among the throngs of hungry
  Who crowd life's troubled way?
"Five loaves and two small fishes?"
  Not much, dear heart, 'tis true;
But yield them to the Master
  And see what He can do!
Placed in His hands of mercy,
  Thy little will be much.
'Tis not thy gift that matters,
  But His almighty touch!

        Avis B. Christiansen

## 180. COMPULSION

GOD LAID HIS HAND UPON MY LIFE--
But Fear crept in!
I did not know what task His will might set,
Pride guarded well the portals that He met,
And swift Rebellion came to the key;
I went my way and heeded not His plea.

GOD LAID HIS HAND UPON MY LIFE--
But Pain crept in!
Upon a couch of sickness, racked and torn,
I laid with mind and heart and soul forlorn;
Again Rebellion voiced her protest wild:
No love would thus treat e'en a wayward
child.

GOD LAID HIS HAND UPON MY LIFE--
But Death crept in!
With anguished soul I gazed upon the sward
Where lay all I had worshipped and adored;
I walked in loneliness and grief each day,
But fierce Rebellion o'er my will held sway.

GOD LAID HIS HAND UPON MY LIFE--
But Need crept in!
For Fame and Wealth and all that life
held dear
Had crumbled in my path to ashes drear;
My longing heart cried out for rest
and peace;
Still arrogant Rebellion barred release.

GOD LAID HIS HAND UPON MY LIFE--
Then Love walked in!
I recognized His voice; I saw His face;
A calm and sweet assurance came apace;
Rebellion fled before His gracious mien
And like a tired child I crept within
His loving, waiting arms, and slept serene!
I slept; I waked!
And now
With His beloved hand upon my life
I walk--and work--and dwell with God!

Anne Catherine White

## 181. WHAT IT MEANS

It does not matter what it means, poor heart,
The dear Lord knows, to bear it is your part,
Nor think some strange thing happens unto you
Which He would not allow so, if He knew.

He does know. In His all-wise Fatherhood
He knows it and allows it for your good.
He is not hard, you do not think He is
When in the night you find your hand in His.

When it was light you sought to walk alone
And thought the strength He gave you all your own;
You did not ask what that last blessing meant--
Just smiled and took it, satisfied, content.

You thought he knew
And planned the sweet surprise which came to you.
Then do you, tried one, take life's sweet and good
Yet cannot trust His all-wise Fatherhood?

But think it makes mistakes whene'er it sends
Some hindrance which your eager haste offends?
You think it strange this trial, swift and keen,
And in your weakness ask, "What does it mean?"

I think the language of God's heart would read,
"I love My child, I note his slightest need,

I long to prosper him all his ways--
To give him quiet nights and peaceful days.

"But if I do, he'll lose himself from Me,
My outstretched hand he will not wait to see.
I'll place a hindering wall before his feet,
There he will wait, and there we two shall meet.

"I do it not in wrath for broken laws,
Or willful disobedience, but because
I want him nearer and I cannot wait
For him to come, for he might wander late.

"My child will wonder, will not understand
Still half in doubt he'll clasp My outstretched hand,
And when at last upon My heart he leans
He will have ceased to wonder what it means."

Annie Johnson Flint

### 182.    LET US GO ON

*"Therefore, leaving the . . . first principles . . . let us go on."—Heb. 6:1.*

Some of us stay at the cross,
    Some of us wait at the tomb,
Quickened and raised together with Christ,
    Yet lingering still in its gloom;
Some of us bide at the passover feast
    With Pentecost all unknown--
The triumphs of grace in the heavenly place
    That our Lord has made our own.

If the Christ who died had stopped at the cross
    His work had been incomplete,
If the Christ who was buried had stayed in the tomb
    He had only known defeat;
But the Way of the Cross never stops at the Cross,
    And the way of the Tomb leads on
To victorious grace in the heavenly place
    Where the risen Lord has gone.

So, let us go on with our Lord
    To the fulness of God He has brought,
Unsearchable riches of glory and good
    Exceeding our uttermost thought;
Let us grow up into Christ,
    Claiming His life and its powers,
The triumphs of grace in the heavenly place
    That our conquering Lord has made ours.

Annie Johnson Flint

## 183. CRUCIFIED AGAIN

I crucified my Lord today,
  And afterward, it dawned on me
That I could not have pierced Him more
  Than He was pierced at Calvary!

I failed to take my stand for Him;
  When sinners mocked and cursed His name,
I did not say one single word
  To let them know my dreadful shame.

I did not speak to one lost soul
  About my loving Lord this day,
Because I feared the ridicule,
  And let my pride stand in the way.

When I was asked to join in sin,
  I weakened with a careless nod.
And when I was asked about my Lord,
  I brushed it off, ashamed of God!

I drove a nail into the hand
  That long ago was pierced for me.
And I could not have pierced Him more
  Than He was pierced at Calvary!

                    Evelyn Taylor

## 184. LORD, SPEAK TO ME, THAT I MAY SPEAK

Lord, speak to me, that I may speak
  In living echoes of Thy tone;
As Thou hast sought, so let me seek
  Thy erring children lost and lone.

Oh teach me, Lord, that I may teach
  The precious things Thou dost impart;
And wing my words, that they may reach
  The hidden depths of many a heart.

Oh fill me with Thy fullness, Lord,
  Until my very heart o'erflow
In kindling thought and glowing word,
  Thy love to tell, Thy praise to show.

Oh use me, Lord, use even me,
  Just as Thou wilt, and when and where;
Until Thy blessed face I see,
  Thy rest, Thy joy, Thy glory share.

                    Frances Havergal,
                    1836-1879

## 185. ASHAMED OF JESUS

Jesus and shall it ever be
A mortal man ashamed of Thee!
Ashamed of Thee, whom angels praise,
Whose glories shine thro' endless days?

Ashamed of Jesus! sooner far
Let evening blush to own a star:
He sheds the beams of light divine
O'er this benighted soul of mine.

Ashamed of Jesus! that dear Friend
On whom my hopes of Heaven depend!
No; when I blush, be this my shame,
That I no more revere His name.

Ashamed of Jesus! yes, I may
When I've no guilt to wash away,
No tears to wipe, no good to crave,
No fears to quell, no soul to save.

Till then, nor is my boasting vain,
Till then I boast a Saviour slain;
And oh, may this my glory be,
That Christ is not ashamed of me.

                    Joseph Grigg, 1765

## 186. FREEDOM IN CHRIST

A little bird I am,
  Shut in from fields of air;
But in my cage I sit and sing
  To Him who placed me there;
    Well pleased a prisoner to be,
    Because, my God, it pleases Thee.

My cage confines me round;
  Abroad I cannot fly;
But though my wing is closely bound,
  My heart's at liberty.
    My prison walls cannot control
    The flight, the freedom of the soul.

Oh! it is good to soar,
  These bolts and bars above,
To Him whose purpose I adore,
  Whose providence I love;
    And in Thy mighty will to find
    The joy, the freedom of the mind.

                    Madam Guyon

## 187. AS HE WILLS

As He wills, my steps shall follow,
  As He leads, I'll take the way;
Murmur not, my heart, nor falter,
  Linger not, my feet, nor stay.

As He wills, yes, Jesus said it,
  Praying there, alone--alone--
In the darkness of the garden,
  Pleading at the Father's throne.

As He wills--it may mean sorrow;
  But His will is always best;
There the soul has calm assurance,
  And the heart has sweetest rest.

As He wills--there may be shadows
  In the path He marks for me,
But the sunshine of His presence
  Cheers me though I cannot see.

Though I cannot understand it,
  Why He thus has planned my way,
Yet I know all things are working
  For my good, each passing day.

Soon the clouds will break and scatter
  And the sun come beaming through,
Lighting up my soul with glory
  As I see His face anew.

Oh, the joy of trusting Jesus,
  Trusting where we cannot trace;
Leaning hard upon His promise,
  Proving His sufficient grace.

As He will till life is over,
  Till the gates swing open wide,
And I enter in triumphant
  To that home beyond the tide.

As He wills--through endless ages,
  Free from sorrow, pain and care,
Happy in His gracious presence,
  Heaven's joys to ever share.

                    Katie V. Hall


## 188. A LITTLE WHILE

A little while, and then the morning breaking
  Will see us safe at Home in Jesus' arms--
We'll shed our cares and wipe our tears of sorrow.
  A little while, then free from ev'ry harm.

A little while and fragrant o'er God's meadows
  We'll smell the flow'rs of Heaven's gardens fair.
The trees of life will shade our weary beings.
  A little while, no toil and labor there.

A little while, and tears of sad confession
  Will all be done, for sin will be no more.
Our happy hearts rejoice to see the Saviour--
  No more will grieve Him on that sinless shore.

A little while, to warn and win for Jesus--
  And then the night, when man can work no more!
Accounting then, to Jesus Christ our Saviour.
  A little while, to bring men to the door.

A little while, oh, may I live completely;
  A little while, sold out and not my own;
A little while, oh, Jesus, may I ever,
  Be wholly Thine until I reach my Home!

                    John R. Rice

### 189. THE LAND OF BEGINNING AGAIN

For each of us who have traveled the road
　　Of sorrow, misfortune and sin,
There's a wonderful place of courage and hope
　　Called the Land of Beginning Again!
There our mistakes, like lessons well learned,
　　May help us to set a new pace:
The thousand and one little faults that we have
　　Will depart in this wonderful place.

There hope, like a cloak that wraps us around,
　　Makes stronger our purpose to win.
And love, truth and faith are easily found
　　In this Land of Beginning Again.
Our own selfish thoughts we leave far behind
　　And give to each person his due:
Our promise we keep, and we do not forget
　　The things we intended to do!

No grudge in our heart, no malice, no strife,
　　No words that are ever unkind;
But a smile, and a laugh, and a loving hand-clasp
　　In the Land of Beginning we find.
The heartaches and griefs that discourage us so
　　When we try our poor lives to amend
Will pass away like a cloud from the sky
　　In this Land of Beginning Again.

Alice Chase Chinn

### 190. ONE THING I OF THE LORD DESIRE

One thing I of the Lord desire,
　　For all my way hath miry been:
Be it by water or by fire,
　　Oh make me clean!

If clearer vision Thou impart,
　　Grateful and glad my soul shall be;
But yet to have a purer heart
　　Is more to me.

Yea, only as the heart is clean
　　May larger vision yet be mine,
For mirrored in its depths are seen
　　The things divine.

I watch to shun the miry way,
　　And stanch the spring of guilty thought:
But, watch and wrestle as I may,
　　Pure I am not.

So wash Thou me without, within;
　　Or purge with fire, if that must be;
No matter how, if only sin
　　Die out in me.

Author Unknown

### 191. LORD, GIVE ME THESE

Of all the riches of Thy store,
If Thou dost grant me nothing more,
Lord, give me these:

A quiet mind, content, serene,
A loving heart, submissive, clean,
Lord, give me these.

And if Thou hast still more for me,
Then joy and gladness let them be,
But give me these.

Jo Beth Rice

## 192. THE PRAYER OF THE BURDENED HEART

THE HEAVENLY FLAME--O God,
Make this to be my heart's desire,
To feel Thy Spirit's quickening power,
And know His working every hour;
So thus to spread the Saviour's fame
          --exalt His name.

A GODLY ZEAL--O Lord!
Could I but catch the need of those
Whose souls are lost: eternal woes;
Who rush the bait the Devil throws:
To know and feel the pangs of Hell
          --ah, this is real.

THE YEARNING HEART--this, Lord,
Is but the least that I can do,
To show my love and zeal for You;
A heart that aches for others, too,
A soul from sin maintained apart
          --enthroned Thou art.

UNDYING LOVE--Thou Christ!
Was shown to me when on the cross,
Thy soul was made to bear the dross
Of sin's dark load--at what a cost,
To bring me peace from Heaven above
          --ah, this is love.

THIS VISION VAST--make mine;
That through this self: this frail, weak
         "ME,"
Christ, only Christ the world will see,
Till in my life or by my death,
By every tear, in every breath,
I keep His colors to the mast
          --then Home at last.

Ezra M. Coppin

## 193. JESUS, I MY CROSS HAVE TAKEN

Jesus, I my cross have taken,
  All to leave, and follow Thee;
Destitute, despised, forsaken,
  Thou from hence my all shalt be:
Perish ev'ry fond ambition,
  All I've sought, and hoped, or known;
Yet how rich is my condition,
  God and Heaven are still my own.

Let the world despise and leave me,
  They have left my Saviour, too;
Human hearts and looks deceive me,
  Thou art not, like man, untrue;
And while Thou shalt smile upon me,
  God of wisdom, love, and might,
Foes may hate, and friends may shun me,
  Show Thy face and all is bright.

Man may trouble and distress me,
  'Twill but drive me to Thy breast;
Life with trials hard may press me,
  Heaven will bring me sweeter rest.
Oh, 'tis not in grief to harm me,
  While Thy love is left to me;
Oh, 'twere not in joy to charm me,
  Were that joy unmixed with Thee.

Go then, earthly fame and treasure!
  Come disaster, scorn, and pain!
In Thy service, pain is pleasure;
  With Thy favor, loss is gain.
I have called Thee, Abba, Father;
  I have stayed my heart on Thee:
Storms may howl, and clouds may gather,
  All must work for good to me.

Henry F. Lyte, 1824

## 194. SELF OR CHRIST?

Oh, the bitter shame and sorrow
That a time could ever be
When I let the Saviour's pity
Plead in vain, and proudly answered,
  "All of self, and none of Thee!"

Yet He found me; I beheld Him
Bleeding on the accursed tree,
Heard Him pray, "Forgive them, Father!"
And my wistful heart said faintly,
  "Some of self and some of Thee!"

Day by day His tender mercy,
Healing, helping, full and free,
Sweet and strong, and, ah, so patient
Brought me lower, while I whispered,
  "Less of self, and more of Thee!"

Higher than the highest Heaven,
Deeper than the deepest sea,
Lord, Thy love at last hath conquered,
Grant me now my supplication--
  "None of self, and all of Thee!"

Theodore Monod

### 195.  I MUST DIE

I must die...
Not waiting 'til my hair is white,
Or falling in a battle fight,
Or sleeping on a final night,
But, daily.

Self must die...
All that self ever hoped to be;

Self dies hard, not easily;
In its place my Lord must see
A corpse.

I must die...
Clay I was and clay I'll be;
Let my Potter fashion me,
Then I'll be whatever He
Would wish.

Bill Harvey

### 196.   OUT OF TOUCH

Only a smile, yes, only a smile,
That a woman o'er burdened with grief
Expected from you; 'twould have given relief
For her heart ached sore the while;
But weary and cheerless she went away,
Because, as it happened, that very day
You were "out of touch" with your Lord.

Only a word, yes, only a word,
That the Spirit's small voice whispered, "Speak";
But the worker passed onward, unblessed and weak,
Whom you were meant to have stirred
To courage, devotion and love anew,
Because, when the message came to you,
You were "out of touch" with your Lord.

Only a note, yes, only a note,
For a friend in a distant land;
The Spirit said, "Write," but then you had planned
Some different work, and you thought
It mattered little, you did not know
'Twould have saved a soul from sin and woe;
You were "out of touch" with your Lord.

Only a song, yes, only a song,
That the Spirit said, "Sing tonight--
Thy voice is thy Master's by purchased right";
But you thought, " 'Mid this motley throng
I care not to sing of the City of Gold,"
And the heart that your words might have reached grew cold;
You were "out of touch" with your Lord.

Only a day, yes, only a day!
But, oh can you guess, my friend,
Where the influence reaches, and where it will end
Of the hours that you frittered away?
The Master's command is, "Abide in Me,"
And fruitless and vain will your service be,
If "out of touch" with your Lord.

Jean H. Watson

## 197. HIS YOKE IS EASY

The world deceives me; it offers peace and joy and rest,
But ever leaves me with hungry heart and second best;
I came to Jesus, and there I found it all I'd missed!

My soul was thirsty; I hewed me broken cisterns vain;
My heart was fainting; but all I found was failures' pain
Till I met Jesus, who watered me with Heaven's rain.

For songs in nighttime, for joy in pain and help in need,
My Saviour hears me, forgives my sins and guides my deeds;
I love to serve Him, and so I follow where He leads.

My life was empty of all that's good and true and clean;
Until I met Him, no peace my wicked heart had seen;
But all earth's tempests stirr'd up its sea of mire unclean.

A slave to Jesus, oh gladly would I ever be;
His labor joyful, reproach for Him is sweet to me;
Ten thousand blessings repay all pain I'll ever see.

His yoke is easy, His burden light;
His way is happy and always bright.
In this world's midnight, He is my light.
His yoke is easy, His burden light.

John R. Rice

## 198. HIS NAME ON ME

Write Thy name on my HEAD--
    That I may think for Thee;
Write Thy name on my LIPS--
    That I may speak for Thee;
Write Thy name on my FEET--
    That I may walk with and for Thee;
Write Thy name on my HANDS--
    That I may work with and for Thee;
Write Thy name on my EARS--
    That I may listen for Thee;
Write Thy name on my HEART--
    That I may love Thee;
Write Thy name on my SHOULDERS--
    That I may bear loads for Thee;
Write Thy name on my EYES--
    That I may see over Thee;
Write Thy name ALL OVER ME--
    That I may be wholly Thine--
        Always and everywhere.

B. H. Carroll

## 199. PURITY OF HEART

Blest are the pure in heart,
    For they shall see our God;
The secret of the Lord is theirs;
    Their soul is His abode.

Still to the lowly soul
    He doth Himself impart,
And for His temple and His throne
    Selects the pure in heart.

Lord, we Thy presence seek,
    May ours this blessing be;
Oh give the pure and lowly heart, --
    A temple meet for Thee.

To God, the Father, Son,
    And Spirit, One in Three,
Be glory, as it was, is now,
    And shall forever be.

Author Unknown

### 200. GOD-GIVEN THORNS

Strange gift indeed!--a thorn to prick,--
To pierce into the very quick;
To cause perpetual sense of pain;
Strange gift! And yet, 'twas given for gain.

Unwelcome,--yet it came to stay;
Nor could it e'en be prayed away.
It came to fill its God-planned place,--
A life-enriching means of grace.

And he who bore it, day by day,
Found Christ his power, his strength,
　　　　　his stay;
In weakness gloried, since thereby
The power of Christ might on him lie.

Oh much-tried saint, with fainting heart,
The thorn with its perpetual smart,
With all its wearing ceaseless pain
Can be thy means of priceless gain.

God's grace-thorns,--ah, what forms
　　　　　they take!
What piercing, smarting pain they make!
And yet, each one in love is sent,
And always just for blessing meant.

And so, whate'er thy thorn may be,
From GOD accept it willingly;
But reckon Christ,--His life--the power
To keep, in thy most trying hour.

And sure--thy life will richer grow;
HE grace sufficient will bestow:
And in Heav'n's morn thy joy 'twill be
That, by His thorn, He strengthened thee.

　　　　　J. Danson Smith

### 201. HIS WILL

My soul before Thee prostrate lies;
To Thee, her source, my spirit flies;
My wants I mourn, my chains I see;
Oh let Thy presence set me free.

Jesus, vouchsafe my heart and will
With Thy meek lowliness to fill;
No more her power let Nature boast,
But in Thy will may mine be lost.

　　　　　John Wesley

### 202. LET US DRAW NEAR

Let us draw near! The blood is spilt,
The Lamb has borne the sinner's guilt;
The atoning Sacrifice is made,
The righteous wrath of God is stayed--
　　　Let us draw near.

Let us draw near! The holy door
Stands opened wide forevermore;
No longer flaming angels guard
The gate by Jesus' hand unbarred--
　　　Let us draw near.

Let us draw near! O heart of stone,
Melt at the love to sinners shown!
The Holiest of all is thine--
O boundless love! O grace divine!
　　　Let us draw near!

Let us draw near, with hearts aglow,
In reverent stillness bowing low;
Before the Throne Love's emblems plead--
In simple faith, with all our need,
　　　Let us draw near!

　　　　　E. Margaret Clarkson

### 203. ALL MY HEART'S LOVE

What shall I give Him? What shall I render?
　How shall I repay my Lord's sacrifice?
Not all earth's riches, not all its treasure,
　But heart's devotion and love beyond price!

Oh, what investment; how much we cost Him!
　How much the Saviour has paid for His own!
Then what glad service, what heart allegiance
　May He expect from us for all He's done!

One day I'll see Him, Jesus, dear Saviour,
　See Him who bore all my sins on the tree.
His wounds and scars then ever reminding
　Of His atoning death, suff'ring for me.

Why should I murmur, hold back from sorrow,
　Dread to lose money or friends in His name?
Oh, I should welcome prison or scourging
　If I might thus have some part in His shame!

All my heart's love, all my fond dreams--
　Make them, Lord Jesus, only for Thee.
All that I am, all I could be--
　Take me, Lord Jesus, Thine e'er to be.

　　　　　John R. Rice

204.   WHEN I GET TO THE END OF THE WAY

The sands have been washed in the footprints
  Of the Stranger on Galilee's shore--
And the voice that subdued the rough billows
  Will be heard in Judea no more.
But the path of that lone Galilean
  With joy I will follow today;
And the toils of the road will seem nothing,
  When I get to the end of the way.

There are so many hills to climb upward,
  I often am longing for rest;
But He who appoints me my pathway,
  Knows just what is needful and best.
I know in His Word He hath promised
  That my strength "it shall be as my day;"
And the toils of the road will seem nothing,
  When I get to the end of the way.

He loves me too well to forsake me,
  Or give me a trial too much;
All His people have been dearly purchased,
  And Satan can never claim such.
By and by I shall see Him and praise Him,
  In the city of unending day;
And the toils of the road will seem nothing,
  When I get to the end of the way.

When the last feeble steps have been taken,
  And the gates of that city appear,
And the beautiful songs of the angels
  Float out on my listening ear;
When all that now seems so mysterious
  Will be bright and as clear as the day;
Then the toils of the road will seem nothing,
  When I get to the end of the way.

              Charles D. Tillman

# CONSOLATION and COMFORT

### 205. WHEN I AWAKE I AM STILL WITH THEE

Still, still, with Thee, when purple morning breaketh,
When the bird waketh and the shadows flee;
Fairer than morning, lovelier than the daylight,
Dawns the sweet consciousness, I am with Thee!

Alone with Thee, amid the mystic shadows,
The solemn hush of nature newly born;
Alone with Thee, in breathless adoration,
In the calm dew and freshness of the morn.

Still, still, with Thee, as to each new-born morning
A fresh and solemn splendor still is given,
So doth this blessed consciousness awakening,
Breathe, each day, nearness unto Thee and Heaven.

When sinks the soul, subdued by toil, to slumber,
Its closing eye looks up to Thee in prayer;
Sweet the repose beneath Thy wings o'ershading,
But sweeter still to wake and find Thee there.

So shall it be at last, in that bright morning
When the soul waketh and life's shadows flee;
Oh, in that hour, fairer than daylight dawning,
Shall rise the glorious thought, I am with Thee!

Harriet Beecher Stowe

### 206. GOOD CHEER

Ain't it fine today?
Sure, this world is full of trouble;
    I ain't said it ain't.
Lord, I've had enough and double
    Reason for complaint:
Rain and storm have come to fret me,
    Skies were often gray;
Thorns and brambles have beset me
    On the road--but, say--
    Ain't it fine today?

It's today that I am livin'--
    Not a month ago.
Havin', losin', takin', givin',
    As time wills it so.
Yesterday--a cloud of sorrow
    Fell across the way.
    It may rain--but, say--
    Ain't it fine today?

Selected

### 207. I KNOW NOT WHY

I know not why His hand is laid
    In chastening on my life,
Nor why it is my little world
    Is filled so full of strife.

I know not why, when faith looks up
    And seeks for rest from pain,
That o'er my sky fresh clouds arise
    And drench my path with rain.

I know not why my prayers so long
    By Him has been denied;
Nor why, while others' ships sail on,
    Mine should in port abide.

But I do know God is love,
    That He my burden shares,
And though I may not understand,
    I know, for me, He cares.

Grace Troy

## 208. DOES HE CARE?

What can it mean?  Is it aught to Him
That the days are long, and the nights are dim?
Can He be touched by the griefs I bear,
Which sadden the heart and whiten the hair?
About His throne are eternal calms,
And strong glad music of happy psalms,
And bliss unruffled by any strife--
How can HE care for **my** little life?

And yet, I want Him to care for me,
While I live in this world where sorrows be.
When the lights die down from the path I take;
When strength is feeble and friends forsake;
And love and music which once did bless,
Have left me to silence and loneliness;
Then my life-song changes to sobbing prayers,
And my heart cries out for a GOD WHO CARES.

When shadows hang o'er the whole day long,
And my spirit is bowed with shame and wrong,
And I am not good, and the bitter shade
Of conscious sin makes my soul afraid;
And the busy world has too much to do
To stay in its courses to help me through;
And I long for a Saviour--can it be
That the God of the universe CARES FOR ME?

Oh, wonderful story of deathless Love,
Each child is dear to that heart above!
He fights for me when I cannot fight;
He comforts me in the gloom of night;
He lifts the burden, for He is strong;
He stills the sigh and awakes the song;
The sorrows that bear me down HE shares,
And loves and pardons because HE CARES.

Let all who are sad take heart again;
We are not alone in our hours of pain;
Our Father looks from His throne above
To soothe and comfort us with His love.
He leaves us not when the storms are high,
And we have safety, for He is nigh;
Can that be trouble which He doth share?
Oh, rest in peace, for the Lord DOES CARE!

Hugh Miller

## 209.  "PEACE!  IT IS I"

Fierce was the wild billow,
　Dark was the night;
Oars labored heavily;
　Foam glimmered white.
Trembled the mariners,
　Peril was nigh;
Then said the God of Gods,
　"Peace!  It is I."

Ridge of the mountain wave,
　Lower thy crest.
Wail of the stormy wind,
　Be thou at rest.
Peril there none can be;
　Sorrow must fly
Where saith the Light of Life
　"Peace!  It is I."

Selected

## 210.  NEVER ALONE

*"I will never leave thee, nor forsake thee."*
*—Heb. 13:5.*

I'm never alone in the morning
　As I rise at the break of day,
As Jesus who watched through the darkness
　Says, "Lo, I am with you alway."

I'm never alone at my table,
　Though loved ones no longer I see;
For dearer than all who have vanished
　Is Jesus who breaks bread with me.

I'm never alone through the daylight,
　Though nothing but trials I see;
Though the furnace be seven times heated,
　The "form of the fourth" walks with me.

I'm never alone at the twilight
　When darkness around me doth creep;
And spectres press hard round my pillow,
　He watches and cares while I sleep.

I'm walking and talking with Jesus
　Each day as I journey along;
I'm never alone, Hallelujah!
　The joy of the Lord is my song.

Author Unknown

## 211.  WHEN WE SEE...

When we see the lilies
    Spinning in distress,
Taking thought to
    Manufacture loveliness;
When we see the birds all
    Building barns for store,
'Twill be time for us to worry--
    Not before!

Selected

## 212.  THE GOD OF COMFORT

I have been through the valley of weeping,
    The valley of sorrow and pain;
But the God of all comfort was with me,
    At hand to uphold and sustain.

As the earth needs the clouds and the
                        sunshine,
    Our souls need both sorrow and joy,
So He places us oft in the furnace,
    The dross from the gold to destroy.

When He leads through some valley of trouble
    His omnipotent hand we can trace;
For the trials and sorrows He sends us
    Are part of His lessons of grace.

Oft we shrink from the purging and pruning,
    Forgetting the husbandman knows
That the deeper the cutting and paring
    The richer the cluster that grows.

Well He knows that affliction is needed,
    He has a wise purpose in view;
And in the dark valley He whispers,
    "Hereafter thou shalt know what I do."

As we travel through life's shadowed valley,
    Fresh springs of His love ever rise,
And we learn that our sorrow and losses
    Are blessings just sent in disguise.

So we'll follow wherever He leads us,
    Let the path be dreary or bright,
For we've proved that our God can give
                        comfort,
    Or God can give songs in the night.

Author Unknown

## 213.  IN ALL THESE THINGS

God's promise is not freedom
    From trials in the race;
But power to transcend them
    Through His sufficing grace.

Not rest instead of labor,
    But in the labor rest;
Not calm instead of tempest,
    But calm when sore distressed.

Not light instead of darkness,
    Not joy instead of grief;
But brightness in the midnight,
    And in the woe, relief.

Not gain instead of losses,
    Not ease instead of pain;
But balm upon the anguish,
    And losses bringing gain.

Not strength instead of weakness,
    Not smile instead of tears;
Not peace instead of conflict,
    Not song instead of fears;

But weakness filled with power,
    And tears with radiance spread,
And peace amid the battle,
    And song e'er fears are fled.

Norman F. Douty

## 214.  SHADOWS

I cannot think that God has meant
For shadows to be fearsome things,
Else He would not have given us
The shadow of His wings;
Nor would His tall trees by the way
Trace out a cool, sweet place
Where weary travelers may pause
To find His soothing grace;
Nor would the shadows of the night
Enfold us in that tranquil rest
That falls upon the sleeping babe
Rocked at its mother's breast.
And though the shadows over life
May seem to creep apace,
Behind the darkest one of them
Is His assuring face.

Mrs. Claude Allen McKay

### 215. A WHITE PEARL SHONE

The cup is bitter, God--
  Take it away!
I cannot put it to my lips again!
  Have I not borne enough?
Some other day
  I'll bear this pain.
In vain my spirit cried,
  "Some other day."

But Calvary is not endured alone;
  And when the bitterness
  Was drained away--
There, within the cup,
  A white pearl shone!

Edna Fuchs

### 216. IF CHRIST WERE HERE TONIGHT

If Christ were here tonight and saw me tired
  And half afraid another step to take,
I think He'd know the thing my heart desired
  And ease that heart of all its throbbing ache.

If Christ were in this dull room of mine
  That gathers up so many shadows dim;
I am quite sure its narrow space would shine
  And kindle into glory, around Him.

If Christ were here, I might not pray so long,
  My prayer would have such little way to go
'Twould break into a burst of happy song,
  So would my joy and gladness overflow.

If Christ were here tonight, I'd touch the hem
  Of His fair, seamless robe, and stand complete
In wholeness and in whiteness; I, who stem
  Such waves of pain, to kneel at His dear feet.

If Christ were here tonight, I'd tell Him all
  The load I carry for the ones I love,
The blinded ones who grope and faint and fall,
  Following false guides, nor seeking Christ above.

If Christ were here! Ah, faithless soul and weak,
  Is not the Master ever close to thee?
Deaf is thine ear that canst not hear Him speak,
  Dim is thine eye, His face that cannot see.

Thy Christ is here and never far away,
  He entered with thee when thou camest in;
His strength was thine through all the busy day,
  He knew thy need, He kept thee pure from sin.

Thy blessed Christ is in thy little room,
  Nay, more, the Christ Himself is in thy heart;
Fear not, the dawn will scatter darkest gloom,
  And Heaven will be of thy rich life a part.

Margaret E. Sangster

217. CONSOLATION

Not dead--oh no, but borne beyond the
      shadows
  Into the full clear light;
Forever done with mist and cloud and tempest
  Where all is calm and bright.

Not even sleeping--called to glad awakening
  In Heaven's cloudless day:
Not still and moveless--stepped from earth's
      rough places
  To walk the King's highway.

Not silent--just passed out of earthly hearing
  To sing Heaven's sweet new song;
Not lonely--dearly loved and dearly loving
  Amid the white-robed throng.

But not forgetful--keeping fond remembrance
  Of dear ones left awhile;
And looking gladly to the bright reunion
  With handclasp and with smile.

Oh no, not dead, but past all fear of dying,
  And with all suffering o'er;
Say not that I am dead when JESUS calls me
  To live forevermore.

Marion E. C. Netherton

218. SECURITY

More secure is no one ever
Than the loved ones of the Saviour;
Not yon star, on high abiding,
Nor the bird in home-nest hiding.

God His own doth tend and nourish,
In His holy courts they flourish;
Like a father kind He spares them,
In His loving arms He bears them.

Neither life nor death can ever
From the Lord His children sever;
For His love and deep compassion
Comfort them in tribulation.

Little flock, to joy then yield thee!
Jacob's God will ever shield thee;
Rest secure with this Defender,
At His will all foes surrender.

What He takes or what He gives us
Shows the Father's love so precious;
We may trust His purpose wholly--
'Tis His children's welfare solely.

Lina Sandell

219. REMEMBRANCE...

I will remember--'tis good to remember--
  Years that are past, of God's goodness and grace;
To brood once again over memories tender;
  God's gracious dealings to grateful retrace.

Safely, indeed, hath His guiding hand led me,
  Through all life's highways and byways till now;
Richly, indeed, hath His bounteous hand fed me,
  Even in famine--though I knew not how.

Yea, in the sorrows which sometimes o'ertook me
  He was my succour, my strength and my stay:
And in calamities which sorely shook me
  He so supported, faith did not give way.

In such remembrance, reflection, recalling,
  Heart findeth confidence, mind grows serene;
Shall not His right hand, which kept me from falling,
  Be still as strong as in past it hath been?

J. Danson Smith

## 220. THERE WAS A MIRACLE PERFORMED

My eyes were blinded,
I could not see or love the Kingdom of
the Lord
Until, reminded
That faith could be restored by list'ning
to His Word;
To Him I turned my sightless eyes,
And caught a glimpse of Paradise;
I felt His touch--my heart was warmed,
And there was a miracle performed.

My life was aimless,
I had no lofty goal ambition to inspire,
My love was flameless,
I warmed myself by resolution's feeble fire;
To Christ I brought my listless will
And waited at His feet until
I felt His touch--my heart was warmed,
And there was a miracle performed.

My life was dreary,
I breathed a fearful, melancholy atmosphere;
My spirit weary,
Cried out for rest,--and lo, the Lord
Himself drew near;
His presence filled my heart with light
And put despair and fear to flight,
I felt His touch--my heart was warmed,
And there was a miracle performed.

So disappointed,
The prize my spirit sought receded from
my view;
But He anointed
My eyes and let me see that He in grace
foreknew
The gold I sought was only dross--
As every gain without the cross--
I felt His touch--my heart was warmed,
And there was a miracle performed.

My heart was yearning
For sympathy and love to stay my falling
tears;
But I was spurning
The love of God who every tortured
heart-cry hears;
My sorrows drove me to His Word,
I sensed the presence of my Lord,
I felt His touch--my heart was warmed,
And there was a miracle performed.

Paul Hutchens

## 221. WALK BESIDE ME

Walk beside me, blessed Jesus,
Thou who understanding sees us,
Only Thou who like us tempted
Can in pity love us, empty.
Walk beside me, Saviour dear.

Thou who knows my well of sorrow,
Give me hope of a tomorrow,
Where my tears of sad regretting
Are all dried in the forgetting,
Dry my tears then, Saviour dear.

Tempted as we, without sinning,
Such a High Priest understanding,
Oh, with boldness we are coming
To find help and mercy flowing,
Oh, uphold me, Saviour dear.

Some who walk beside will leave me,
Some will blame and not believe me,
O Thou always true Defender,
O Thou Friend of friendless sinner,
Stay beside me, Saviour dear.

Youth will grow grey hair and falter,
Health will fail and prospects alter,
O Thou Fount of life e'erlasting,
Bear me in Thy bosom resting,
Bear me ever, Saviour dear.

Walk beside me, never leave me,
Hold my hand, my Saviour dear.

John R. Rice

## 222. SAY IT NOW

If you have a tender message,
Or a loving word to say,
Don't wait till you forget it,
But whisper it today!

The tender word unspoken,
The letter never sent,
The long-forgotten messages,
The wealth of love unspent.

For these some hearts are breaking,
For these some loved ones wait,
Then give them what they're needing,
Before it is TOO LATE!

Author Unknown

## 223.  FAINT YET PURSUING

Be brave, dear friend!  God still has use for you,
Though head no longer wears its old-time hue;
Though strength grows feeble, and though sight may dim,
Thou hast a purpose and a place with Him.

Be brave, dear friend!  Nor 'neath the willow lie,
Nor 'neath the juniper request to die;
Let not thy courage nor thy strength go down,
Perchance for thee there waits a warrior's crown.

Faint not nor fear!  Thou still hast work to do,
Some noble task to finish or pursue;
Not till He calls to Heaven's sublime abode
Darest thou think to leave the pilgrim road.

Well, noble friend, be brave, be strong, be true!
Not yet is God's commission filled for you;
But, when shall come the end of life's long race,
How rich the welcome then to thine own place!

J. Danson Smith

## 224.  FOR THIS CRISIS

We must have Faith, for darkness is about us;
    There's light beyond, though we have lost our way.
Oh, falter not!  We'll find again the home path,
    And see the sunlight of a brighter day.

We must have Hope, for we are near despairing,
    And Hope will be an anchor to the soul;
Though stormy winds may roar their weird enchantment,
    Hope, radiant Hope, will help us find the goal.

We must have Love, and Love will lighten burdens;
    And Love will bring us cheer and banish care.
The greatest blessing life can ever bring us
    Is Love, which gives us strength to do and dare.

We must have God!  Without Him we are helpless!
    We've failed because we've tried to go alone--
And now in sorrow, care and tribulation,
    Come, seek the Lord, and bow before His throne.

The Light will come!  It never, never fails us!
    God ever lives--His promises are sure;
He holds the waves--the winds are in His fingers,
    In His blest care our future is secure!

Annie Agnes Smith

## 225. HE KEEPS THE KEY

Is there some problem in your life to solve,
  Some passage seeming full of mystery?
God knows, who brings the hidden things to light.
    He keeps the key.

Is there some door closed by the Father's hand
  Which widely opened you had hoped to see?
Trust God and wait--for when He shuts the door,
    He keeps the key.

Is there some earnest prayer unanswered yet,
  Or answered NOT as you had thought 'twould be?
God will make clear His purpose by-and-by.
    He keeps the key.

Have patience with your God, your patient God,
  All wise, all knowing, no long tarrier He;
And of the door of all thy future life
    He keeps the key.

Unfailing comfort, sweet and blessed rest,
  To know of EVERY door He keeps the key;
That He at last when just HE sees 'tis best,
    Will give it THEE.

Anonymous

## 226. WINGS OF THE MORNING

Though I take the wings of the morning
  And dwell by the farthest sea,
Even there, Lord, Thou art with me,
  And Thy right hand guideth me.

If I mount up with wings, as an eagle,
  And stand on the mountain peak,
Thy presence fills and thrills me,
  Lord, as Thy face I seek.

If I abide in the lowest depths,
  Burdened with grief and pain,
Even there, Lord, Thou art with me,
  To lift me up again.

In height or depth, my Father,
  In darkness or in light,
Thy matchless love surrounds me,
  O God of grace and might.

Mable Custis

## 227. " 'TIS I...FEAR NOT"

'Twas darkest night upon the lake:
The stout hearts of the men did quake;
They saw a spirit--so they said;
Their hearts were filled with awesome dread:
When, lo,--" 'Tis I, be of good cheer,"--
Composed their minds, dispelled their fear.

We, too, can dread some false alarm,
Which loudly speaks of coming harm;
Our hearts can cry with dark dismay
At sudden changes on life's way,
Until, perchance, His voice we hear--
" 'Tis I! Fear not! Be of good cheer!"

So oft He comes in strange disguise--
It seemeth so to mortal eyes;
To finite wisdom, human sense,
He, blessings, strangely doth dispense.
Thus dark enigmas--black as night--
Are changed when robed with Heav'n's
            clear light.

J. Danson Smith

### 228. HOW THE LORD SUSTAINS

*"Cast thy burden upon the Lord, and he shall sustain thee."—Ps. 55:22.*

CHRISTIAN, when thy way seems darkest,
  When thine eyes with tears are dim,
Straight to God thy Father hast'ning,
  Tell thy troubles all to Him.
Not to human ear confiding
  Thy sad tale of grief and care,
But before thy Father kneeling,
  Pour out all thy sorrows there.

Sympathy of friends may cheer thee
  When the fierce, wild storms have burst,
But God only can console thee
  When it breaks upon thee first.
Go with words, or tears, or silence,
  Only lay thee at His feet;
Thou shalt prove how great His pity,
  And His tenderness how sweet.

Think, too, thy divine Redeemer
  Knew as thou canst never know
All the deepest depths of suffering,
  All the weight of human woe;
And though now in glory seated
  He can hear thy feeblest cry,
Even hear the stifled sighing
  Of thy dumb heart's agony.

All thy griefs by Him are ordered;
  Needful is each one for thee;
Every tear by Him is counted,
  One too much there cannot be.
And if, whilst they fall so thickly,
  Thou canst own His way is right,
Then each bitter tear of anguish
  Precious is in Jesus' sight.

Far too well thy Saviour loves thee
  To allow thy life to be
One long, calm, unbroken summer,
  One unruffled, stormless sea.
He would have thee fondly nestling
  Closer to His loving breast;
He would have that world seem brighter,
  Where alone is perfect rest.

Though His wise and loving purpose
  Clearly yet thou mayest not see,
Still believe with faith unshaken,
  All will work for good to thee.
Therefore, when thy way is gloomy,
And thine eyes with tears are dim,
Straight to God thy Father hast'ning,
  Tell thy sorrows all to Him.

Author Unknown

### 229. OTHER THAN MINE
#### (Christ's Choice for Me)

*"... so are my ways higher than your ways, and my thoughts than your thoughts."—Isa. 55:9.*

I would have chosen a sunlit path,
  All strewn with roses fair,
With never a cloud to darken my way--
  Nor a shade of anxious care.
But He chose for me a better way--
  Not sunshine or roses sweet
But clouds o'er head and thorns below
  That cut and hurt my feet.
I have deep joys of another kind;
  My Rose of Sharon is He:
And as for sunshine--His lovely face
  Is perfect sunshine to me.

I would have chosen my life to be
  Active, tireless and strong;
A constant, ceaseless working for Him,
  Amid the needy throng.

But He chose for me a better lot--
  A life of frequent pain,
Of strength withheld when 'twas needed most,
  And loss instead of gain.
He gave me work of another kind,
  Far, far above my thought,
The work of interceding with Him
  For the souls that He had bought.

'Tis far, far better to let Him choose
  The way that we should take,
If only we thus leave our life with Him,
  He will guide without mistake.
We, in our blindness would never choose
  A pathway dark and rough,
And so we should never find in Him
  "The God who is enough";

In disappointment, trouble, and pain,
  We turn to the Changeless One,
And prove how faithful, loving and wise
  Is God's beloved Son.

Catherine S. Miller

## 230. FINDING GOD

I stand upon the mount of God
  With sunlight in my soul;
I hear the storms in vales beneath,
  I hear the thunders roll.

But I am calm with Thee, my God,
  Beneath these glorious skies;
And to the height on which I stand,
  No storms, nor clouds, can rise.

O, THIS is life! O, this is joy!
  My God, to find Thee so;
Thy face to see, Thy voice to hear,
  And all Thy love to know.

Horatius Bonar

## 231. RESTING

Once my hands were always trying,
  Trying hard to do my best;
Now my heart is sweetly trusting,
  And my soul is all at rest.

Once my brain was always planning,
  And my heart, with cares oppressed;
Now I trust the Lord to lead me,
  And my life is all at rest.

Once my life was full of effort,
  Now 'tis full of joy and zest;
Since I took His yoke upon me,
  Jesus gives to me His rest.

A. B. Simpson

## 232. HE STUBBED HIS TOE

Did you ever pass a youngster, who had been an' stubbed his toe,
And was sitting by the road side, just a crying soft an' low?
A holding of his dusty foot so hard and brown and bare,
An' trying to keep back from his eyes the tears that's gathering
    there?

You hear him sorter sobbin' like, and a snifflin' of his nose,
You stoop an' pat him on the head and try to ease his woes,
You treat him sorter kind like, and the first thing you know
He's up and off a smilin', clean forgot he stubbed his toe.

Along the road of human life, you'll find a fellow goin' slow,
And like as not he's some poor cuss, that's been an' stubbed
    his toe;
He was makin' swimmin' headway, until he bumped into a stone,
And his friends kept hurryin' on, and they left him here alone.

He ain't sobbin', he ain't snifflin', he's too old for sobs and cries,
But he's grievin' just as earnest, if it only comes in sighs,
And it does a lot of good sometimes to go a little slow,
And speak a word of kindness, to the guy that's stubbed his toe.

You can't tell yourself, and there ain't no way to know,
When it's going to come your turn to slip and stub your toe,
Today you're bright an' happy, in the world's sunlight and glow,
And tomorrow you're a freezin' and a trudgin' thru the snow.

The time you think you've got the world the tightest in your grip
Is the very time you'll find, you're the likeliest to slip,
And it's mighty comfortin', sometimes, I know,
To have a fellow stop, and help you, when you've been and
    stubbed your toe.

Author Unknown

### 233.    NO SHADOW OF TURNING

He fainteth not, nor is He ever weary,
    The Mighty One whose arm is strong to save;
He giveth strength to aid the fainting pilgrim,
    And to the weak, the courage to be brave.

He sleepeth not, His eyelids closing never;
    His children aye are kept within His sight;
The fallen one He lifts, and ever seeketh
    The straying feet to lead back to the light.

He faileth not; His faithfulness abideth;
    All others may, yet He is ever true;
His "fear nots" glow with comfort for the troubled;
    The faithful Guide will lead the journey through.

He changeth not, our Great High Priest forever;
    Within the veil for us He intercedes;
This is our hope, an anchor sure and steadfast,
    Fixed firm in Him who knoweth all our needs.

H. V. Andrews


### 234.   HE KNOWS

He knows it all--the winding path,
    The sky o'ercast and grey,
The steepness of the mountainside,
    The roughness of the way.

He knows it all--the haunting fear,
    The doubtings that distress,
The wond'rings and perplexities,
    And all the strain and stress.

He knows it all--each troubled thought,
    Each anxious wave of care,
And every burden, every grief,
    Or cross that thou dost bear.

He knows it all--thy weight of woe,
    Thine often tear-dimmed eye,
The stabbing pain, the slow, dull ache,
    And sorrow's broken cry.

He knows it all--but His to choose,
    And thine to take His choice!
He knows it all!  He planned it so!
    Then trust Him, and rejoice!

E. Margaret Clarkson


### 235. MY GRACE IS SUFFICIENT FOR THEE

When sin-stained, burdened and weary,
    From bondage I longed to be free,
Then came to my heart a sweet message:
    "My grace is sufficient for thee."

Though tempted and sadly discouraged,
    My soul to this refuge will flee,
And rest in the blessed assurance;
    "My grace is sufficient for thee."

My bark may be tossed by the tempest
    That sweeps o'er the turbulent sea--
A rainbow illumines the darkness:
    "My grace is sufficient for thee."

O Lord, I would press on with courage,
    Though rugged the pathway may be,
Sustained and upheld by the promise:
    "My grace is sufficient for thee."

Soon, soon the warfare will be over,
    My Lord face to face I shall see,
And prove, as I dwell in His presence:
    "My grace is sufficient for thee."

Author Unknown

## 236. ONE LITTLE HOUR

One little hour for watching with the Master,
  Eternal years to walk with Him in white;
One little hour to bravely meet disaster,
  Eternal years to reign with Him in light;

One little hour to suffer scorn and losses,
  Eternal years beyond earth's cruel frowns;
One little hour to carry heavy crosses,
  Eternal years to wear unfading crowns;

One little hour for weary toils and trials,
  Eternal years for calm and peaceful rest;
One little hour for patient self-denials,
  Eternal years of life where life is blest.

Then, souls, be brave and watch until
      the morrow;
  Awake, arise, your lamps of purpose trim.
Your Saviour speaks across the night
      of sorrow;
  Can ye not watch one little hour with Him?

Selected

## 237. REMEMBERED

*"Fear not. . .thou shalt not be forgotten of me."*
*--Isa. 44:2, 21. "Yea, they may forget, yet will*
*I not forget thee."--Isa. 49:15.*
*"Thus saith the Lord; I remember thee."--Jer. 2:2.*

Not forgotten, but remembered!
  Child of God, trust on with cheer!
Thy great Father's help is promised
  Every day throughout the year.
Not forsaken--but most precious
  Thou wilt ever to Him be;
Tenderly He whispers, "Fear not!
  I, the Lord, remember thee!"

Not forgotten, but remembered,
  Is the pledge of Love Divine!
He who loves and understands us,
  Best can plan thy path and mine.
His own Word cannot be broken,
  "As thy days thy strength shall be,"
He, Himself, the word hath spoken--
  "I, the Lord, remember thee!"

## 238. THE SYMPATHY OF CHRIST

*"In all their affliction he was afflicted."--Isa. 63:9.*

'Tis sweet to know--when we are tired,
      and pain
Lies on our hearts, and when we look in vain
For human comfort--that the heart Divine
Still understands these cares of yours
      and mine.
Not only understands, but day by day
Lives with us while we tread the
      earthly way--
Bears with us all our weariness, and feels
The shadow of the faintest cloud that steals
Across our sunshine--even learns again
The depths and bitterness of human pain.
There is no sorrow that He will not share--
No cross, no burden for our hearts to bear
Without His help--no care of ours too small
To cast on Jesus; let us tell Him all--
Lay at His feet the story of our woes,
And in His sympathy find sweet repose.

Author Unknown

## 239. BEREAVED

Let me come in where you sit weeping--aye,
Let me, who have not any child to die,
Weep with you for the little one whose love
  I have known nothing of.

The little arms that slowly, slowly loosed
Their pressure round your neck; the hands
      you used
To kiss--such arms--such hands I never knew.
  May I not weep with you?

Fain would I be of service--say something,
Between the tears, that would be comforting--
But ah! so sadder than yourselves am I,
  Who have no child to die.

James Whitcomb Riley

Not forgotten, but remembered--
  In His love for thee He planned,
Chosen, sealed, thy name engraven
  On His pierced and peerless hand.
When He calls thee, "Come up higher,"
  Thou shalt then His wonders see--
Wonders of His mighty promise--
  "I, the Lord, remember thee!"

L. C. Hasler

## 240. ARRIVED!

*"Absent from the body. . .present with the Lord" (II Cor. 5:8). "For I am in a strait betwixt two, having a desire to depart, and to be with Christ; which is far better" (Phil. 1:23).*

Oh, say, "She has arrived!"
　And not that, "She is gone!"
May ev'ry thought of her
　Be in the land of morn!

Arrived to hear Jesus' voice,
　And see His welcoming smile,
And then to greet again
　Those she has "lost a while!"

Arrived to tread no more
　The weary path of pain,
Nor feel the waning strength
　The body feels, again.

　　　　Selected.

## 241.　IF WE KNEW

If I knew that a word of mine,
A word not kind and true,
Might leave its trace
On a loved one's face,
I'd never speak harshly;
　　would you?

If I knew the light of a smile
Might linger the whole day through,
And lighten some heart
With a heavier part,
I wouldn't withhold it;
　　would you?

　　　　Anonymous

## 242. GOD'S CARE

Not a brooklet floweth
　Onward to the sea,
Not a sunbeam gloweth
　On its bosom free,
Not a seed unfoldeth
　To the glorious air,
But our Father holdeth
　It within His care.

Not a floweret fadeth,
　Not a star grows dim,
Not a cloud o'ershadeth,
　But 'tis marked by Him.
Dream not that thy gladness
　God doth fail to see;
Think not in thy sadness
　He forgetteth thee.

Not a tie is broken,
　Not a hope laid low,
Not a farewell spoken,
　But our God doth know.
Every hair is numbered,
　Every tear is weighed
In the changeless balance
　Wisest Love has made.

Power eternal resteth
　In His changeless hand;
Love immortal hasteth
　Swift at His command.
Faith can firmly trust Him
　In the darkest hour,
For the keys she holdeth
　To His love and power.

　　　　Author Unknown

## 243.　COMFORT

Though I cannot feel Thy hand, I know 'tis there,
　Thine ear bent down to catch my every prayer;
My Father's tender glance to strengthen me,
　When I in darkness grope unseeingly.

Thy Presence fills this humble place,
　Thine arms are round me in unseen embrace,
And oh, dear Father, though I cannot see,
　I know that Thou art here to comfort me.

　　　　Helen Pearl McDonald

## 244. THE LAND OF BEGINNING AGAIN

I wandered along in the shadowy way,
  With my soul sad and weary with pain,
In search of a land--a beautiful land--
  Called "The Land of Beginning Again."

I asked at an inn that stood hard by the road,
  And the keeper said never a word,
But pointed the way to the Mountains of Care,
  And The Valley of Hope Deferred.

I journeyed my feet to the Canyons of Toil,
  And down through the lowlands of grief;
I halted a moment and leant on my staff
  By the side of a rock, for relief.

A fellow wayfarer came near me and I
  Addressed myself to him and said:
"Canst tell me the way to Beginning Again?"
  He spake not, but pointed ahead.

I came to the place where the Shadows convene,
  Where the Past and the Present now stand
In solemn concourse, and where Memory lives
  With Grief, in a desolate land.

I asked of a travel-worn shade at my side,
  The way to Beginning Again;
He answered me not, but he pointed ahead,
  With a look of sad sorrow and pain.

"Shall I ever behold the fair land that I seek?"
  I mused, as I journeyed along.
Then heard I a whisper that thrilled me within,
  Like the notes of a wonderful song;

"This is The Land of Beginning Again;
  Behold how its beauties inspire!"
I looked and the morning was spreading its light,
  And filling the vale with its fire.

The shadows were gone, and the dark canyon road
  Was ablaze with a radiant light;
My sullen companions were vanished away,
  And gone were the fears of the night.

'Twas Christ that had whispered my sad soul within,
  With words like a wondrous refrain;
And lo, He had transformed the Present and Past
  To the Land of Beginning Again.

                    William Burton McCafferty

## 245. OUR GOD

*"For this God is our God for ever and ever: he will be our guide even unto death."—Ps. 48:14.*

God does not count the leaves upon the tree,
  Nor tabulate the brilliant, lavish spread
Of heaven's starry hosts. But, as for me,
  The very hairs are numbered on my head.

God does not count the sands upon the shore:
  Of every drop of rain since time began,
And all earth's blades of grass, He keeps
    no score--
  But numbers every secret thought of man.

God is so powerful that He could break
  The universe apart, or make it whole;
So personal that He would choose to take
  The road to Calvary--for every soul.

Helen Frazee-Bower

## 246. PASSING THROUGH

*"When thou passeth through the waters, they shall not overflow thee" (Isa. 43:2).*

"When thou passeth through the waters,"
  Deep the waves may be, and cold,
But Jehovah is our refuge
  And His promise is our hold;
For the Lord Himself hath said it,
  He the faithful God and true:
"When thou comest to the waters,
  Thou shalt **not go down**, but **through**."

Seas of sorrow, seas of trial,
  Bitterest anguish, fiercest pain,
Rolling surges of temptation
  Sweeping over heart and brain,
They shall never overflow us,
  For we know His Word is true;
All His waves and all His billows
  He will **lead us safely through**.

Threatening breakers of destruction,
  Doubt's insidious undertow,
Shall not sink us, shall not drag us
  Out to ocean depths of woe;
For His promise shall sustain us,
  Praise the Lord, whose word is true!
We shall not go down nor under,
  He hath said, "Thou **passest through**."

Annie Johnson Flint

## 247. AN OLD SAINT'S SOLILOQUY

God has been with me on life's long road,--
Easing its burdens and sharing its load;
Soothing its sorrows,--each cause for
    tears;--
God has been with me, through life's long
    years.

God still is with me, e'en now,--today,--
Bearing me gently o'er life's late way;
Tending and caring, with love unstayed;
Granting His comfort, His strength, His aid.

God will be with me, as on I go;
How long the road yet--just He doth know;
Trustful I journey--His hand holds mine:
Safe is my life in His care divine.

And when my journey is safely past,
When I the Father's House reach at last,--
Simple, but true, shall my song then be,
O'er all the love He bestowed on me.

Author Unknown

## 248. SLEEP

Sleep, little baby of mine;
Dear little heart, be at rest,
For Jesus, like you,
Was a baby once, too,
And slept on His own mother's breast.

Shut little sleepy blue eyes,
Night and the darkness are near--
But Jesus looks down
Through the shadows that frown,
And baby has nothing to fear.

Sleep, little baby of mine,
Soft on your pillow so white;
Jesus is here
To watch over you, dear,
And nothing can harm you tonight.

Oh, little darling of mine,
What can you know of the bliss,
The comfort I keep,
Awake and asleep,
Because I am certain of this.

Anonymous

### 249. LOSSES WILL TURN TO GAIN

Nothing can rest us, nothing bring us comfort,
    Save just the knowledge that God knows it all--
Knows all our grief, knows all our desolation,
    Yet bids us "COME," obedient to His call.

So in the twilight we will lay our sorrows
    Down at the feet of Him who promised "rest"
To all the tired ones, sad and heavy-laden,
    Weary with waiting and by care oppressed.

Unending love shall spur to brave endeavor,
    Strength will be given us to bear our pain,
And some day, somewhere, in the far-off future,
    Life's bitter losses will be turned to gain.

J. Danson Smith

### 250. NEVER FORGOTTEN

Years swiftly glide; friends pass away;
    And strength declines--like setting sun;
Familiar scenes change or decay
    When travelling days have long been run.

Although 'tis true, there is a "yet,"
    A blessed "yet" for you and me;
God says, "Yet will I not forget";
    How wondrous--in His mind to be!

And so, though years bring much that's
                    strange,
    And friends and loved ones pass away,
God still abides; He doth not change;
    He'll not forget. No! Never! Nay!

J. Danson Smith

### 251. WAYFARERS

There is no permanent calamity
    For any child of God;
Way-stations all, where we briefly stop
    Upon our homeward road.

Our pain and grief are only travel stains
    Which shall be wiped away,
Within the blessed warmth and light of Home,
    By God's own hand some day.

Martha Snell Nicholson

### 252. THE CUP

Another cup, dear Lord? And must
I drink this too?
Of late so much I've had
Of bitter brew!

"Trust Me, dear child; would I
Put to your lip
Or bid you drink a cup from which
I did not sip?

"Come, taste, and you will find
My balm can make
Like honey any draught that I
Ask you to take!"

Martha Snell Nicholson

### 253. BE COMFORTED

Be comforted! In God thy comfort lies!
    If He doth pain, He also would console;
The anodyne which soothes--just He supplies;
    He, He alone, the wounded can make whole.

The word is His! Nor will it mock nor fail!
    Be comforted! Let Him thy comfort be;
Balm for all pain, and light for loneliest vale,
    Himself the peace, the joy, the company.

J. Danson Smith

### 254. THE HUMAN TOUCH

*"Nevertheless God. . .comforted us by the coming of Titus" (II Cor. 7:5, 6).*

Out there in Macedonia in trouble and despair,
  Beset on every side with woes and burdened down with care,
God's messenger, the mighty Paul, was comfortless and lone:
  This comforter of other souls could claim none for his own.

But had our God forsaken him, whose love can ne'er forget?
  Could He who notes each sparrow's fall, allow this dire Kismet?
Ah no! Already on the way with consolation's balm,
  Was Titus, messenger of hope, the fears of Paul to calm.

Perhaps we know someone like Paul, disheartened by the way;
  Let us, like Titus, go to him and comfort him today.
For oft the man who knows God best, the man of faith and power
  Is longing for a human touch, amidst a trying hour!

Paul Hutchens

### 255. "WHEN THOU PASSEST THROUGH THE WATERS"

*Isaiah 43:2*

Is there any heart discouraged as it journeys on its way?
Does there seem to be more darkness than there is of sunny day?
Oh, it's hard to learn the lesson, as we pass beneath the rod,
That the sunshine and the shadows serve alike the will of God!
But there comes a word of promise, like the promise in the bow--
That, however deep the waters, they shall never overflow.

When the flesh is worn and weary, and the spirit is depressed,
And temptation sweeps upon it like a storm on ocean's breast,
There's a haven ever open for the tempest driven bird,
There's a shelter for the tempted in the promise of the Word;
For the standard of the Spirit shall be raised against the foe,
And, however deep the waters, they shall never overflow.

When a sorrow comes upon you that no other soul can share,
And the burden seems too heavy for the human heart to bear;
There is one whose grace can comfort, if you'll give to Him abode;
For the precious promise reaches to the depths of human woe,
That, however deep the waters, they shall never overflow.

When the sands of life are ebbing, and I near the Jordan's shore,
When I see its waters rising, and I hear its billows roar,
I will reach my hand to Jesus, in His bosom I shall hide,
And 'twill only be a moment till I reach the other side.
It is then the fullest meaning of the promise I shall know--
"When thou passest through the waters," they shall never overflow.

Author Unknown

## 256. THE WALL AND THE HEDGE

*"Hast thou not made an hedge about him. . .on*
*every side?"--Job 1:10.*
*"The devil may build a wall around you, but he*
*cannot roof you in."--Dan Crawford.*

The devil may wall you round
  But he cannot roof you in;
He may fetter your feet and tie your hands
And strive to hamper your soul with bands
  As his way has ever been;
But he cannot hide the face of God
  And the Lord shall be your Light,
And your eyes and your thoughts can rise to
        the sky,
Where His clouds and His winds and His birds
        go by,
  And His stars shine out at night.

The Devil may wall you round;
  He may rob you of all things dear,
He may bring his hardest and roughest stone
And think to cage you and keep you alone,
  But he may not press too near;
For the Lord has planted a hedge inside,
  And has made it strong and tall,
A hedge of living and growing green;
And ever it mounts and keeps between
  The trusting soul and the devil's wall.

The devil may wall you round,
  But the Lord's hand covers you--
And His hedge is a thick and a thorny hedge,
And the devil can find no entering wedge
  Nor get his finger through;
He may circle about you all day long,
  But he cannot work as he would,
For the will of the Lord restrains his hand,
And he cannot pass the Lord's command
  And his evil turns to good.

The devil may wall you round
  With his gray stones, row on row,
But the green of the hedge is fresh and fair,
And within its circle is space to spare,
  And room for your soul to grow;
The wall that shuts you in
  May be hard and high and stout,
But the Lord is sun and the Lord is dew
And His hedge is coolness and shade for you,
  And no wall can shut Him out.

                Annie Johnson Flint

## 257. ALL THINGS IN JESUS

I've found a joy in sorrow,
  A secret balm for pain;
A beautiful tomorrow
  Of sunshine after rain.
I've found a branch of healing
  Near every bitter spring;
A whispered promise stealing
  O'er every broken string.

I've found a glad hosanna
  For every woe and wail;
A handful of sweet manna
  When grapes of Eschol fail.
I've found a Rock of Ages
  When desert wells are dry;
And after weary stages,
  I've found an Elim nigh--

An Elim with its coolness,
  Its fountain and its shade;
A blessing in its fullness,
  When buds of promise fade.
O'er tears of soft contrition
  I've seen a rainbow light;
A glory and fruition
  So near--yet out of sight.

My Saviour, Thee possessing,
  I have the joy, the balm,
The healing, and the blessing,
  The sunshine and the psalm;
The promise for the fearful,
  The Elim for the faint,
The rainbow for the tearful,
  The glory for the saint.

              J. Danson Smith

## 258. CALM

There is a calm--the calm of sins forgiven
  Through knowing sin on Christ by God
          was laid;
Through looking to and resting on His merit,
  And knowing that our debt He fully paid.

And there's a calm about the unknown future;
  The earthly road; the fuller life above;
And things unknown--here, and in life's
       hereafter--
Vex not the soul who knows that God is Love.

              J. Danson Smith

### 259. NEW EVERY MORNING

Yea, "new every morning," though we may awake,
Our hearts with old sorrow beginning to ache;
With old work unfinished when night stayed our hand,
With new duties waiting, unknown and unplanned;
With old care still pressing, to fret and to vex,
With new problems rising, our minds to perplex;
In ways long familiar, in paths yet untrod,
Oh, new every morning the mercies of God!

His faithfulness fails not; it meets each new day
With guidance for every new step of the way;
New grace for new trials, new trust for old fears,
New patience for bearing the wrongs of the years,
New strength for new burdens, new courage for old,
New faith for whatever the day may unfold;
As fresh for each need as the dew on the sod;
Oh, new every morning the mercies of God!

                              Annie Johnson Flint

### 260. I KNOW

I know thy sorrow, child; I know it well,
Thou need'st not try with broken voice to tell.
Just let me lay thy head here on My breast,
And find here sweetest comfort, perfect rest!
Thou need'st not bear the burden, child,
                    thyself
I yearn to take it all upon Myself!

Then trust it all to Me, today--tomorrow--
Yes, e'en forever, for I know thy sorrow.
Long years I planned it all for thee,
Prepared it that thou might'st find need of Me;
Without it, child, thou would'st not come
                    to find

This place of comfort in this love of Mine.
Hadst thou no cross like this for Me to bear,
Thou would'st not feel the need of My
                    strong care,
But in thy weakness thou did'st come to Me,
And thus, through this, My plan, I have
                    won thee.
I know thy sorrow and I love thee more,
Because for such as thee I came and bore
The wrong, the shame, the pain of Calvary,
That I might comfort give to such as thee,
So, resting here, my child, thy hand in Mine,
Thy sorrow, to My care, today resign.

Dread not that some new care will come
                    tomorrow--
What does it matter--I know all thy sorrow.
And I will gladly take it all for thee,
If only thou wilt trust it all to Me;
Thou need'st not stir but in My love lie still.
And learn the sweetness of the Father's will.
That will was only planned for the best;
So, knowing this, lie still and sweetly rest--
Trust Me. The future shall not bring to thee
But that will bring thee closer still to Me.

                    Selected

# DEATH and HEAVEN

### 261. THE LITTLE ROBE OF WHITE

In a rosewood cradle a baby lay;
Its mother was stitching, stitching away
   On a little robe of white.
One foot on the rocker, she hoped to keep
Her frolicsome baby fast asleep,
   To finish her work that night.

In every stitch of the garment she wrought
That loving mother fastened a thought,
   Hopes for that little one;
And smiled on her babe with a happy pride,
As it slept in the cradle by her side,
   Till that little robe was done.

Then she folded up the cambric and lace,
And kissed her little one's chubby face
   That smiled in its infant glee.
She tossed it up and down in the air--
"How pretty you'll look, little babe, when
         you wear
   That new little robe," said she.

      *    *    *    *    *

In a rosewood coffin the baby lay;
Its mother had wept the night away,
   Watching its dying breath.
With it clasped to her breast, she
         prayed to keep
Her darling baby from going to sleep
   In the cold, cold arms of Death.

They buried the babe in the garment
         just wrought,
Whose every stitch held a hopeful thought,
   From that loving mother's sight.
On the marble stone she wrote with a tear:
"How many hopes lie buried here
   In the little robe of white."

      *    *    *    *    *

In the Saviour's arms a baby lay,
From its rosewood coffin far away,
   In the realms of love and light.
The angels a garment had folded about
Its little form which will never wear out--
   A seamless robe of white.

                    Author Unknown

## 262.  REGRET

*Sheltering Arms*

If I had known, oh, loyal heart,
  When, hand to hand, we said farewell,
How for all time our paths would part,
  What shadow o'er our friendship fell,
I should have clasped your hands so close
  In the warm pressure of my own
That memory still would keep its grasp--
    If I had known.

If I had known, when far and wide
  We loitered through the summer land,
What Presence wandered by our side,
  And o'er you stretched its awful hand,
I should have hushed my careless speech,
  To listen, dear, to every tone
That from your lips fell low and sweet--
    If I had known.

If I had known, when your kind eyes
  Met mine in parting, true and sad--
Eyes gravely tender, gently wise,
  And earnest, rather, more than glad--
How soon the lids would lie above,
  As cold and white as sculptured stone,
I should have treasured every glance--
    If I had known.

If I had known how, from the strife
  Of fears, hopes, passions, here below,
Unto a purer, higher life
  That you were called, oh! friend, to go,
I should have stayed my foolish tears,
  And hushed each idle sigh and moan,
To bid you last a long godspeed--
    If I had known.

If I had known to what strange place,
  What mystic, distant, silent shore,
You calmly turned your steadfast face,
  What time your footsteps left my door,
I should have forged a golden link
  To bind the hearts so constant grown,
And kept it constant ever there--
    If I had known.

If I had known that until Death
  Shall with his finger touch my brow,
And still the quickening of the breath
  That stirs with life's full meaning now,
So long my feet must tread the way
  Of our accustomed paths alone,

I should have prized your presence more--
    If I had known.

If I had known how soon for you
  Drew near the ending of the fight,
And on your vision, fair and new,
  Eternal peace dawned into sight,
I should have begged, as love's last gift,
  That you, before God's great white throne,
Would pray for your poor friend on earth--
    If I had known.

              Author Unknown

## 263.  AFTERWARDS

Light after darkness, gain after loss,
Strength after weakness, crown after cross;
Sweet after bitter, hope after fears,
Home after wandering, praise after tears.

Sheaves after sowing, sun after rain,
Sight after mystery, peace after pain;
Joy after sorrow, calm after blast,
Rest after weariness, sweet rest at last.

Near after distant, gleam after gloom,
Love after loneliness, life after tomb;
After long agony, rapture of bliss--
Right was the pathway leading to this.

          Frances R. Havergal

## 264.  I CANNOT THINK OF THEE
## WITH TEARS

Beloved!  I cannot wear for thee
  The sign of mourning as my dress,
For thou art keeping company
  With unimagined happiness;
The light of dayspring in thine eyes,
  Immortal health in every breath,
The splendor of thy summer skies--
  All tell me Christ hath banished death.

The coronation of thy King
  Awaits completion of the throng,
And all the choirs celestial bring
  Their tributes for the triumph song.
I have an invitation too,
  Which lights with hope our parted years,
And when I read its message through,
  I cannot think of thee with tears.

             C. C. White

### 265. REST

Beautiful toiler, thy work all done,
Beautiful soul into glory gone,
Beautiful life with its crown now won,
    God giveth thee rest.
Rest from all sorrows, and watching, and fears,
Rest from all possible sighing and tears,
Rest through God's endless, wonderful years--
    At home with the blest.

Beautiful spirit, free from all stain,
Ours the heartache, the sorrow and pain,
Thine is the glory and infinite gain--
    Thy slumber is sweet.
Peace on the brow and the eyelids so calm,
Peace in the heart, 'neath the white folded palm,
Peace dropping down like a wondrous balm
    From the head to the feet.

"It was so sudden," our white lips said,
"How we shall miss her, the beautiful dead,
Who take the place of the precious one fled;
    But God knoweth best.
We know He watches the sparrows that fall,
Hears the sad cry of the grieved hearts that call,
Friends, husband, children, He loveth them all--
    We can trust for the rest."

                Mary T. Lathrop

### 266. THERE IS A LAND

There is a land of pure delight,
  Where saints immortal reign;
Eternal day excludes the night,
  And pleasures banish pain;
There everlasting Spring abides,
  And never-whith'ring flowers;
Death, like a narrow sea, divides
  This heavenly land from ours.

Sweet fields beyond the swelling flood
  Stand dressed in living green;
So to the Jews old Canaan stood,
  While Jordan rolled between;
Could we but climb where Moses stood,
  And view the landscape o'er
Not Jordan's stream, nor death's cold flood
  Should fright us from the shore.

      Author Unknown

### 267. THE CELESTIAL CARAVAN

The caravan moves on and I am part
Of all the pilgrims, armed with holy chart,
Who seek a City bathed in crystal light
Which is our gleam by day, our fire by night.
We know our haven stands foursquare and tall
With jasper shining from each lifted wall,
And there shall be fair mansions for our rest
Within the jeweled City of our quest.
There shall be no more pain and no more
        tears
Within that white eternity of years,
And death shall pass away and blinding sorrow
Shall be forgotten on that promised morrow.
Come, comrade, fare across the earthly sod
To claim our high inheritance of God,
For it awaits, and through His guiding grace
We shall arrive and we shall see His face.

            Reid Crowell

268. OH, WHY SHOULD THE SPIRIT OF MORTAL BE PROUD?

*President Lincoln's favorite poem. He never tired of repeating
its suggestive lines.*

Oh! why should the spirit of mortal be proud?
Like a swift-fleeting meteor, a fast-flying cloud,
A flash of the lightning, a break of the wave,
Man passeth from life to his rest in the grave.

The leaves of the oak and the willow shall fade,
Be scattered around, and together be laid;
And the young and the old, and the low and the high
Shall moulder to dust and together shall die.

The peasant whose lot was to sow and to reap;
The herdsman who climbed with his goats up the steep;
The beggar who wandered in search of his bread,
Have faded away like the grass that we tread.

The saint who enjoyed the communion of Heaven;
The sinner who dared to remain unforgiven;
The wise and the foolish, the guilty and just,
Have quietly mingled their bones in the dust.

So the multitude goes, like the flowers, or the weed
That withers away to let others succeed;
So the multitude comes, even those we behold,
To repeat every tale that has often been told.

For we are the same our fathers have been;
We see the same sights our fathers have seen;
We drink the same stream and view the same sun,
And run the same course our fathers have run.

The infant a mother attended and loved;
The mother that infant's affection who proved;
The husband that mother and infant who blessed--
Each, all, are away to their dwellings of rest.

The maid on whose cheek, on whose brow, in whose eye,
Shone beauty and pleasure--her triumphs are by;
And the memory of those who loved her and praised
Are alike from the minds of the living erased.

The hand of the king that the sceptre hath borne;
The brow of the priest that the mitre hath worn;
The eye of the sage and the heart of the brave,
Are hidden and lost in the depth of the grave.

The thoughts we are thinking our fathers would think;
From the death we are shrinking our fathers would shrink;
To the life we are clinging they also would cling;
But it speeds from us all like a bird on the wing.

They loved, but the story we cannot unfold;
They scorned, but the heart of the haughty is cold;

They grieved, but no wail from their slumbers will come;
They joyed, but the tongue of their gladness is dumb.

They died, aye, they died--and we things that are now,
Who walk on the turf that lies over their brow,
Who make in their dwelling a transient abode,
Meet the things that they met on their pilgrimage road.

Yea, hope and despondency, pleasure and pain,
We mingle together in sunshine and rain;
And the smiles and the tears, the song and the dirge,
Still follow each other like surge upon surge.

'Tis the wink of an eye, 'tis the draught of a breath
From the blossom of health to the paleness of death,
From the gilded saloon to the bier and the shroud--
Oh! why should the spirit of mortal be proud?

William Knox


## 269. THE DAY IS DONE

The day is done, and the darkness
  Falls from the wings of Night,
As a feather is wafted downward
  From an eagle in his flight.

I see the lights of the village
  Gleam through the rain and the mist,
And a feeling of sadness comes o'er me
  That my soul cannot resist.

A feeling of sadness and longing,
  That is not akin to pain,
And resembles sorrow only
  As the mist resembles the rain.

Come, read to me some poem,
  Some simple and heartfelt lay,
That shall soothe this restless feeling,
  And banish the thoughts of day.

Such songs have power to quiet
  The restless pulse of care,
And come like the benediction
  That follows after prayer.

Then read from the treasured volume
  The poem of thy choice,
And lend to the rhyme of the poet
  The beauty of thy voice.

And the night shall be filled with music,

And the cares, that infest the day,
Shall fold their tents, like the Arabs,
  And as silently steal away.

Henry Wadsworth Longfellow,
1807-1882


## 270. THE EDEN ABOVE

We're bound for the land
  Of the pure and the holy,
The Home of the happy,
  The kingdom of love.
Ye wand'rers from God
  On the broad road of folly,
Oh, say, will you go
  To the Eden above?

Each saint has a mansion,
  Prepared and all furnished,
Ere from his small house
  He is summoned to move.
Its gates and its towers
  With glory are burnished,
Oh, say, will you go
  To the Eden above?

Author Unknown

## 271. HEAVEN

Since o'er Thy footstool, here below,
    Such radiant gems are strewn,
O! what magnificence must glow,
    My God, about Thy throne!
So brilliant here those drops of light--
There the full ocean rolls, how bright!

If night's blue curtain of the sky,
    With thousand stars enwrought,
Hung like a royal canopy,
    With glittering diamonds fraught--
Be, Lord, Thy temple's outer veil,
What splendor at the shrine must dwell.

The dazzling sun at noontide hour,
    Forth from his flaming vase,
Flinging o'er earth the golden shower,
    Till vale and mountain blaze--
But shows, O Lord! one beam of Thine:
What, then, the day where Thou dost shine?

Ah! how shall these dim eyes endure
    That noon of living rays?
Or how my spirit, so impure,
    Upon Thy glory gaze!
Anoint, O Lord, anoint my sight,
And robe me for that world of light.

                    W. A. Muhlenberg

*"For we know that if our earthly house of
this tabernacle were dissolved, we have
a building of God, an house not made with
hands, eternal in the heavens."--II Cor. 5:1.*

## 272. THE LIGHTS OF HOME

O the friends that now are waiting,
In the cloudless realms of day,
Who are calling me to follow
Where their steps have led the way;
They have laid aside their armor,
And their earthly course is run;
They have kept the faith with patience
And their crown of life is won.

They have laid aside their armor
For the robe of spotless white;
And with Jesus they are walking
Where the river sparkles bright.
We have labored here together,
We have labored side by side,
Just a little while before me
They have crossed the rolling tide.

On those dear familiar faces
There will be no trace of care;
Every sigh was hushed forever
At the palace gate so fair.
I shall see them, I shall know them,
I shall hear their song of love,
And we'll all sing hallelujah
In our Father's house above.

They are calling, gently calling,
Sweetly calling me to come,
And I'm looking through the shadows
For the blessed lights of Home.

                    Fanny J. Crosby

## 273. GOD'S ACRE

I like that ancient Saxon phrase which calls
    The burial-ground God's Acre! It is just;
It consecrates each grave within its walls,
    And breathes a benison o'er the sleeping dust.

God's Acre! Yes, that blessed name imparts
    Comfort to those who in the grave have sown
The seed that they had garnered in their hearts,
    Their bread of life, alas! no more their own.

Into its furrows shall we all be cast,
    In the sure faith that we shall rise again
At the great harvest, when the archangel's blast
    Shall winnow, like a fan, the chaff and grain.

Then shall the good stand in immortal bloom,
  In the fair gardens of that second birth;
And each bright blossom mingle its perfume
  With that of flowers which never bloomed on earth.

With thy rude plowshare, Death, turn up the sod,
  And spread the furrow for the seed we sow;
This is the field and Acre of our God,
  This is the place where human harvests grow!

               Henry Wadsworth Longfellow


## 274.  FULL SATISFACTION

Not here!  not here!  Not where the sparkling waters
  Fade into mocking sands as we draw near,
Where in the wilderness each footstep falters--
  "I shall be satisfied!"--but oh, not here!

Not here--where all the dreams of bliss deceive us,
  Where the worn spirit never gains its goal,
Where, haunted ever by the thoughts that grieve us,
  Across us floods of bitter memory roll.

There is a land where every pulse is thrilling
  With rapture earth's sojourners may not know,
Where Heaven's repose the weary heart is stilling,
  And peacefully life's time-tossed currents flow.

Far out of sight, while sorrows still enfold us,
  Lies the fair country where our hearts abide,
And of its bliss is nought more wondrous told us
  Than these few words, "I shall be satisfied."

"I shall be satisfied!"  The spirit's yearning
  For sweet companionship with kindred minds--
The silent love that here meets no returning--
  The inspiration which no language finds.

Shall they be satisfied?  The soul's vague longing--
  The aching void which nothing earthly fills?
Oh, what desires upon my heart are thronging,
  As I look upward to the heavenly hills!

Thither my weak and weary steps are tending--
  Saviour and Lord! with Thy frail child abide!
Guide me toward home, where, all my wanderings ending,
  I shall see Thee, "and shall be satisfied!"

               Anonymous

## 275.   'TWILL NOT BE LONG

'Twill not be long--this wearying commotion
   That marks its passage in the human breast
And, like the billows on the heaving ocean,
   That ever rock the cradle of unrest,
Will soon subside; the happy time is nearing,
   When bliss, not pain, shall have its rich increase;
E'en unto Thee the dove may now be steering
   With gracious message.  Wait, and hold thy peace;
         'Twill not be long!

The lamps go out; the stars give up their shining;
   The world is lost in darkness for awhile;
And foolish hearts give way to sad repining,
   And feel as though they ne'er again could smile.
Why murmur thus, the needful lesson scorning?
   Oh, read thy Teacher and His Word aright!
The world would have no greeting for the morning,
   If 'twere not for the darkness of the night;
         'Twill not be long!

'Twill not be long; the strife will soon be ended;
   The doubts, the fears, the agony, the pain,
Will seem but as the clouds that low descended
   To yield their pleasure to the parched plain.
The times of weakness and of sore temptations,
   Of bitter grief and agonizing cry;
These earthly cares and ceaseless tribulations
   Will bring a blissful harvest by-and-by--
         'Twill not be long!

'Twill not be long; the eye of faith, discerning
   The wondrous glory that shall be revealed,
Instructs the soul, that every day is learning
   The better wisdom which the world concealed.
And soon, aye, soon, there'll be an end of teaching,
   When mortal vision finds immortal sight,
And her true place the soul in gladness reaching,
   Beholds the glory of the Infinite--
         'Twill not be long!

" 'Twill not be long!" the heart goes on repeating;
   It is the burden of the mourner's song;
The work of grace in us He is completing,
   Who thus assures us--"It will not be long."
His rod and staff our fainting steps sustaining,
   Our hope and comfort every day will be;
And we may bear our cross as uncomplaining
   As He who leads us unto Calvary;
         'Twill not be long!

                              Anonymous

276. "SHOULD YOU GO FIRST"

Should you go first and I remain
   To walk the road alone,
I'll live in memory's garden, dear,
   With happy days we've known.
In Spring I'll wait for roses red
   When fades the lilacs blue,
In early Fall when brown leaves call
   I'll catch a glimpse of you.

Should you go first and I remain
   For battles to be fought,
Each thing you've touched along the way
   Will be a hallowed spot.
I'll hear your voice, I'll see your smile,
   Though blindly I may grope,
The memory of your helping hand
   Will buoy me on with hope.

Should you go first and I remain
   To finish with the scroll,
No length'ning shadows shall creep in
   To make this life seem droll.
We've known so much of happiness,
   We've had our cup of joy;
And memory is one gift of God
   That death cannot destroy.

Should you go first and I remain,
   One thing I'd have you do:
Walk slowly down the path of death,
   For soon I'll follow you.
I'll want to know each step you take
   That I may walk the same,
For someday down that lonely road
   You'll hear me call your name.

                    Albert Rowswell

277. WAKING

This mortal dies, --
But, in the moment when the light fails here,
The darkness opens, and the vision clear
Breaks on his eyes.
The vail is rent, --
On his enraptured gaze Heaven's glory breaks,
He was asleep, and in that moment wakes.

                    John Oxenham

278. NEXT TIME I'LL NOT BE LATE

There came a sad, sad message,
   Which said that 'You were gone';
My heart could not believe it,
   As the train rolled on and on.
I reached my destination,
   Too late to say 'good-bye!'
You had left on your 'vacation'
   For those 'mansions' in the sky.
I missed your smile of welcome,
   That twinkle in your eye,
Then, how I regretted,
   That I said that last good-bye.
'Come up a little higher,'
   You heard the angels say,
And they left the smile of Heaven
   Upon your face that day.
Your songs--you called your children,
   They are many, rich, and rare;
They've blest the many thousands,
   They sing them everywhere.
Your name--it is immortal;
   Your memory--we'll hold dear;
So while you sing with angels,
   We'll carry on down here.
I'll say "good-bye"--to only
   The cold and empty clay;
You always will be with me
   In spirit--every day.
So watch for me, beloved--
   Next time I'll not be late;
I promise I will meet you
   Inside the "Eastern Gate."

                    Lillie Buffum

279. AFRAID?

Why should I be afraid?
   It is not death to die.
'Tis but a step to glory
   And a mansion in the sky.

How can I be afraid?
   The Lord is with me still,
And loves me as He did that day
   He died upon the hill.

Afraid? Of what? No night's so dark
   It can His glory dim!
Afraid? Oh, no! Though Jordan roar
   I cross--dry shod--with Him.

                    Marian N. Daunecker

280.    ACROSS THE RIVER

When for me the silent oar
  Parts the Silent River,
And I stand upon the shore
  Of the strange Forever,
Shall I miss the loved and known?
Shall I vainly seek mine own?

Mid the crowd that comes to meet
  Spirits  sin-forgiven--
Listening to their echoing feet
  Down the streets of Heaven--
Shall I know a footstep near
That I listen, wait for, here?

Then will one approach the brink,
  With a hand extended?--
One whose thoughts I love to think
  Ere the veil was rended,
Saying, "Welcome! we have died,
And again are side by side."

Saying, "I will go with thee,
  That thou be not lonely,
To yon hills of mystery;
  I have waited only
Until now to climb with thee
Yonder hills of mystery."

Can the bonds that make us here
  Know ourselves immortal,
Drop away, the foliage sear,

At life's inner portal?
What is holiest below
Must forever live and grow.

I shall love the angels well,
  After I have found them,
In the mansions where they dwell,
  With the glory round them;
But at first, without surprise,
Let me look for human eyes.

Step by step our feet must go
  Up the holy mountain;
Drop by drop within us flow
  Life's unfailing fountain.
Angels sing with crowns that burn;
Shall we have a song to learn?

He who on our earthly path
  Bids us help each other--
Who His Well-beloved hath
  Made our Elder Brother--
Will but clasp the chain of love
Closer, when we meet above.

Therefore dread I not to go
  O'er the Silent River;
Death, thy hastening oar I know;
  Bear me, thou life giver,
Through the waters, to the shore
Where mine own have gone before.

                           Lucy Larcom

281.    NO FRIEND LIKE MUSIC

There is no whispering of any friend,
  No solace that can touch the quivering heart
In that lone hour when a sudden end
  Has captured laughter and there falls apart
A rainbow that has bridged a distant hill;
  When roses shatter on the stem, and dark
Crowds out the candle's shimmering flame and still
  The night creeps on with neither torch nor spark.

No friend like music when the last word's spoken,
  And pleading is a plea in vain;
No friend like music when the heart is broken,
  To mend its wings and give it flight again;
No friend like music, breaking chains and bars
  To let the soul march with the quiet stars!

                           Author Unknown

## 282. OH, THOSE SHINING FACES!

Oh, those shining faces,
   When we enter Gloryland!
Waiting at the portals,
   We will find our loved ones stand.
Ev'ry sorrow ended,
   Tears all dried, care ever past.
Oh, what praise and gladness,
   When we see our Lord at last!

Roses never fade there,
   Winter brings the saints no cold.
We will all be young then,
   Never tired, distressed, nor old.
Sinful self all conquered,
   Hateful sin and weakness gone.
Oh, we'll praise our Saviour,
   When we join redemption's song!

See the converts coming
   From the North, South, East and West!
See rewards for souls won,
   Reapers' joy and Heaven's rest.
There'll be pay for heartache;
   Those who suffered with Him, reign.
Hope becomes possession;
   Faith is sight and loss is gain!

Gates of pearl all gleaming;
   Jasper walls and streets of gold!
Trees of life all blooming
   By the river, we are told.
Then our mansions' beauty
   And the song of angels grand,
Face to face with Jesus--
   Oh, delightful Gloryland!

But to see Jesus! Jesus who saved me.
Just to see Jesus is Heaven at last!

                    John R. Rice

## 283. THE HILLSIDE CEMETERY

Here lie those people once so dear to me:
Where noisy birds now soften their loud calls,
The whispering winds move slowly through
                    the trees,
The lordly sun sends down his gentlest rays
Upon their resting place, for all is well.
They rest in peace.

                    Edna J. Stauffer

## 284. HE GIVETH HIS BELOVED SLEEP

When sets the weary sun,
   And the long day is done,
And starry orbs their solemn vigils keep;
   When bent with toil and care,
   We breathe our evening prayer,
God gently giveth His beloved sleep.

When by some slanderous tongue
   The heart is sharply stung,
And with the sense of cruel wrong we weep,
   How like some heavenly calm
   Comes down the soothing balm
What time He giveth His beloved sleep!

O sweet and blessed rest!
   With these sore burdens press'd,
To lose ourselves in slumber, long and deep,
   To drop our heavy load
   Beside the dusty road,
When He hath given His beloved sleep.

And on our closed eyes
   What visions may arise,
What sights of joy to make the spirit leap;
   What memories may return
   From out their golden urn,
If God but giveth His beloved sleep.

And when life's day shall close
   In death's last deep repose,
When the dark shadows o'er our eyelids creep;
   Let us not be afraid
   At this thick gathering shade,
For God so giveth His beloved sleep.

To sleep!--it is to wake
   When the fresh day shall break,
When the new sun climbs up the eastern steep;
   To wake with newborn powers
   Out from these darken'd hours,
For so He giveth His beloved sleep.

To die!--it is to rise
   To fairer, brighter skies,
Where Death no more shall his dread
                    harvest reap;
   To soar on angel wings
   Where life immortal springs,
For so He giveth His beloved sleep.

                    Anonymous

## 285.  THE HOUR OF DEATH

Leaves have their time to fall,
And flowers to wither at the north wind's breath,
    And stars to set--but all,
Thou hast all seasons for thine own, oh Death!

Day is for mortal care,
Eve for glad meetings round the joyous hearth,
    Night for the dreams of sleep, the voice of prayer--
But all for thee, thou mightiest of the earth.

The banquet hath its hour,
Its feverish hour of mirth, and song, and wine;
    There comes a day for grief's o'erwhelming power,
A time for softer tears--but all are thine.

Youth and the opening rose
May look like things too glorious for decay,
    And smile at thee--but thou art not of those
That wait the ripened bloom to seize their prey.

Leaves have their time to fall,
And flowers to wither at the north wind's breath,
    And stars to set--but all,
Thou hast all seasons for thine own, oh Death!

We know when moons shall wane,
When summer-birds from far shall cross the sea,
    When autumn's hue shall tinge the golden grain--
But who shall teach us when to look for thee?

Is it when spring's first gale
Comes forth to whisper where the violets lie?
    Is it when roses in our paths grow pale?--
They have one season--all are ours to die!

Thou art where billows foam,
Thou art where music melts upon the air;
    Thou art around us in our peaceful home,
And the world calls us forth--and thou art there.

Thou art where friend meets friend,
Beneath the shadow of the elm to rest--
    Thou art where foe meets foe, and trumpets rend
The skies, and swords beat down the princely crest.

Leaves have their time to fall,
And flowers to wither at the north wind's breath,
    And stars to set--but all,
Thou hast all seasons for thine own, oh Death!

Felicia Hemans

## 286. SHINE IN THE LIGHT OF GOD

I shine in the light of God;
  His likeness stamps my brow;
Through the Valley of Death my feet
      have trod,
  And I reign in Glory now!

No breaking heart is here;
  No keen and thrilling pain;
No wasted cheek where the frequent tear
  Hath rolled and left its stain.

O friends of mortal years,
  The trusted and the true,
Ye are watching still in the valley of tears,
  But I wait to welcome you.

Do I forget?  Oh no!
  For memory's golden chain
Shall bind **my** heart to the hearts below
  Till they meet to touch again.

Each link is strong and bright,
  And love's electric flame
Flows freely down, like a river of light,
  To the world from whence I came.

Do you mourn when another star
  Shines out from the glittering sky?
Do you weep when the raging voice of war
  And the storms of conflict die?

Then why should your tears run down,
  And your hearts be sorely riven,
For another gem in the Saviour's crown,
  And another soul in Heaven?

Author Unknown

## 287. GOD'S CITY FAIR

There is a river, the streams whereof
  Make glad God's City fair.
And trees of life all its banks adorn
  And fruit, each month, they bear.
Their leaves do heal all the pains and ills,
  There in God's City rare.

Ivory palaces, jasper walls,
  Pearl gates and streets of gold,
All gleaming bright in the light of God,
  And mansions, we are told
Prepared by Jesus for all His own
  In this Home of the soul.

Never a pain, nor a sigh nor tear
  But our God wipes away.
No death, no parting, no sad goodbys,
  For all things new are made.
And Christ, Beloved, Redeemer, King
  With us will be always.

Jesus is calling to all, Repent!
  Calling in mercy sweet,
Still off'ring all everlasting life,
  In Heaven loved ones greet.
A new heart yours and a home above,
  And ev'ry need He'll meet.

Precious the blood that Heaven's door opens.
  Great is the Saviour who pardons our sin.
Sweet is the Gospel that offers redemption,
  Marvelous Grace that will take sinners in!

John R. Rice

## 288. WAITING YONDER

They are not dead, those loved ones who have passed
  Beyond our vision for a little while.
They have but reached the Light while we still grope
  In darkness where we cannot see them smile.

\* \* \* \* \* \*

Then let us gird us once again with hope,
  And give them smile for smile the while we wait;
And loving, serving, when our Father calls,
  We'll go to find our dear ones wait us at the gate.

Author Unknown

289.   INTIMATIONS OF IMMORTALITY

Our birth is but a sleep and a forgetting;
The soul that rises with us, our life's star,
Hath had elsewhere its setting,
And cometh from afar.  Not in entire forgetfulness,
And not in utter nakedness,
But trailing clouds of glory, do we come from God, who is our home.
Heaven lies about us in our infancy!
Shades of the prison-house begin to close upon the growing boy;
But he beholds the light, and whence it flows, --
          He sees it in his joy.
The youth who daily farther from the east
          Must travel, still is nature's priest,
          And by the vision splendid
          Is on his way attended:
At length the man perceives it die away,
And fade into the light of common day.

          Oh joy! that in our embers
            Is something that doth live,
          That nature yet remembers
            What was so fugitive!
The thought of our past years in me doth breed
Perpetual benediction:  not, indeed,
For that which is most worthy to be blest, --
Delight and liberty, the simple creed
Of childhood, whether busy or at rest,
With new-fledged hope still fluttering in his breast, --
          Not for these I raise
          The song of thanks and praise;
          But for those obstinate questionings
          Of sense and outward things,
          Falling from us, vanishings,
          Blank misgivings of a creature
Moving about in worlds not realized,
High instincts before which our mortal nature
Did tremble like a guilty thing surprised, --
          But for those first affections,
          Those shadowy recollections,
          Which, be they what they may,
          Are yet the fountain-light of all our day,
          Are yet a master light of all our seeing,
            Upholds us, cherish, and have power to make
          Our noisy years seem moments in the being
          Of the eternal silence:  truths that awake,
            To perish never, --
Which neither listlessness, nor mad endeavor,
          Nor man, nor boy,
Nor all that is at enmity with joy,
Can utterly abolish or destroy!

          Hence in a season of calm weather,
            Though inland far we be,
Our souls have sight of that immortal sea

Which brought us hither, --
Can in a moment travel thither,
And see the children sport upon the shore,
And hear the mighty waters rolling evermore.

William Wordsworth


### 290. THE ROLL CALL

And now they stand
Beside a manly form, outstretched alone.
His helmet from his head had fallen. His hand
Still firmly grasped his keen but broken sword.
His face was white and cold, and, thinking he was gone,
They were just passing on, for time was precious,
When a faint sigh caught their attentive ears.
Life was still there, so bending down,
They whispered in his ears most earnestly,
Yet with that hush and gentleness with which
We ever speak to a departing soul--
"Brother! the blood of Jesus Christ, God's Son,
Cleanseth from every sin."

The pale lips moved,
And gently whispered "hush!" and then they closed,
And life again seemed gone.

But yet once more
They whispered those thrice blessed words, in hope
To point the parting soul to Christ and Heaven--
"Brother! The precious blood of Jesus Christ
Can cleanse from every sin."

Again the pale lips moved,
All else was still and motionless, for Death
Already had his fatal work half done;
But gathering up his quickly failing strength,
The dying soldier--dying victor--said:
"Hush! for the angels call the muster roll!
I wait to hear my name!"

They spoke no more.
What need to speak again? for now full well
They knew on whom his dying hopes were fixed,
And what his prospects were. So, hushed and still,
They, kneeling, watched.

And presently a smile,
As of most thrilling and intense delight,
Played for a moment on the soldier's face,
And with his one last breath he whispered, "Here!"

Author Unknown

### 291. RESIGNATION

There is no flock, however watched
      and tended,
  But one dead lamb is there!
There is no fireside howsoe'er defended,
  But has one vacant chair!

The air is full of farewells to the dying;
  And mournings for the dead;
The heart of Rachel, for her children crying,
  Will not be comforted!

Let us be patient! These severe afflictions
  Not from the ground arise,
But oftentimes celestial benedictions
  Assume this dark disguise.

We see but dimly through the mists
      and vapors;
  Amid these earthly damps
What seem to us but sad, funeral tapers
  May be Heaven's distant lamps.

There is no death! What seems so is
      transition;
  This life of mortal breath
Is but a suburb of the life Elysian,
  Whose portal we call Death.

She is not dead--the child of our affection--
  But gone unto that school
Where she no longer needs our poor
      protection,
  And Christ Himself doth rule.

In that great cloister's stillness and
      seclusion,
  By guardian angels led,
Safe from temptation, safe from sin's
      pollution,
  She lives, whom we call dead.

Day after day we think what she is doing
  In those bright realms of air;
Year after year, her tender steps pursuing,
  Behold her grown more fair.

Thus do we walk with her, and keep unbroken
  The bond which nature gives,
Thinking that our remembrance, though
      unspoken,
  May reach her where she lives.

Not as a child shall we again behold her;
  For when with raptures wild

In our embraces we again enfold her,
  She will not be a child;

But a fair maiden, in her Father's mansion,
  Clothed with celestial grace;
And beautiful with all the soul's expansion
  Shall we behold her face.

And though at times impetuous with emotion
  And anguish long suppressed,
The swelling heart heaves moaning like
      the ocean,
  That cannot be at rest--

We will be patient, and assuage the feeling
  We may not wholly stay;
By silence sanctifying, not concealing,
  The grief that must have way.

        Henry Wadsworth Longfellow

*"O death, where is thy sting? O grave, where is thy victory? The sting of death is sin; and the strength of sin is the law. But thanks be to God, which giveth us the victory through our Lord Jesus Christ."--1 Cor. 15:55-57.*

### 292. WHAT IS DEATH?

What is death? Oh! what is death?
  'Tis the snapping of the chain--
    'Tis the breaking of the bowl--
  "Tis relief from ev'ry pain--
    'Tis freedom to the soul--
  'Tis the setting of the sun
    To rise again tomorrow,
  A brighter course to run,
    Nor sink again to sorrow.
Such is death! Yes, such is death!

What is death? Oh! what is death?
  'Tis slumber to the weary--
    'Tis rest to the forlorn--
  'Tis shelter to the dreary--
    'Tis peace amid the storm--
  'Tis the entrance to our home--
    'Tis the passage to that God
  Who bids His children come,
    When their weary course is trod.
Such is death! Yes, such is death!

        Author Unknown

### 293.    THE BLESSED DEAD

*"And I heard a voice from heaven saying unto me, Write,*
*Blessed are the dead which die in the Lord from henceforth:*
*Yea, saith the Spirit, that they may rest from their labours;*
*and their works do follow them."--Rev. 14:13.*

The blessed dead!  Art sure the dead are blessed;
   "Unhappy dead," the world for ages cried;
Yet thou dost say that they are blessed in going--
   They live, yes, live--though some have said they died.

The blessed dead--a voice from Heaven said it.
   They happy are; believe it thou, and write;
They sleep not in the darkness of the valley,
   For them has dawned the day of longest light.

They died in Christ--these blessed ones now living,
   In Christ secure from here to yonder shore.
He took their place of judgment on Golgotha,
   To share His place with them forevermore.

Ah, blessed dead, how selfish we in weeping!
You risked your future on His good word keeping,
You risked your future on His good word keeping,
   Now, blessed dead, you gather home to God!

Will H. Houghton
read at grave of Rev. P. B. Chenault

### 294.    TRANSITION

*(A Christian's thought on death)*

If to die is to rise in power from the husk of the earth-sown wheat;
If to die is to rise in glory from the dust of the incomplete;
If Death fills the hand with fresh cunning, and fits it with perfect tool,
And grants to the mind full power for the tasks of its greatest school;
If Death gives new breath to the runner and wings to the imprisoned soul,
To mount with the song of the morning toward the limitless reach of its goal;
If to die is to throb with the ages of life that eternal abides,
And to thrill with inflowing currents of infinite Love's great tides;
If to die is to see with clear vision all mysteries revealed,
And away is swept the curtain from joys that are now concealed;
If Death is the end of all sorrow and crying and anxious care;
If Death gives fullness for longing, an answer to every prayer;
If to die is to greet all the martyrs and prophets and sages of old,
And to joyously meet by still waters the flock of our own little fold;
If to die is to join hosannas to a Risen, Reigning Lord,
And to feast with Him at His table on the bread and wine of His board;
If to die is to enter a City and be hailed as a child of its King--
O Grave, where soundeth thy triumph?
O Death, where hideth thy sting?

Author Unknown

295. HOMEWARD BOUND

*"So he bringeth them unto their desired haven."*
*—Ps. 107:30.*

I am homeward bound!  But I cannot tell
  If near may the haven be,
Or if many storms may beset my barque
  Ere I gain the Crystal Sea;
But I know that my Pilot is near at hand,
  And that is enough for me.

I am homeward bound!  And the sun sometimes
  Shines out from the golden west,
Till it almost seems like the gate of home
  And I think I am near my rest;
But if long or short may the voyage be
  Still my Pilot knoweth best.

And I know I shall reach the port at last--
  The haven where I would be,
Where the storms of life shall distress no more,
  And there, by the Crystal Sea,
The loved ones whose earthly voyage is o'er
  Are waiting to welcome me.

I am homeward bound!  'Twill be "Home, sweet home"!
  I shall see my Pilot's face;
Not a stranger there in a far-off land,--
  I shall feel His blest embrace;
And shall know more fully than e'er before
  All His sovereign love and grace.

          Rosa K. Russell

296. DEATH BE NOT PROUD

Death be not proud, though some have called thee
Mighty and dreadful, for, thou art not soe,
For, those, whom thou think'st, thou dost overthrow,
Die not, poore death, nor yet canst thou kill mee;
From rest and sleepe, which but thy pictures bee,
Much pleasure, then from thee, much more must flow,
And soonest our best men with thee doe goe,
Rest of their bones, and soules deliverie.
Thou art slave to Fate, Chance, kings, and desperate men,
And doth with poyson, warre, and sicknesse dwell
And poppie, or charmes can make us sleepe as well,
And better then thy stroake; why swell'st thou then?
One short sleepe past, wee wake eternally,
And death shall be no more, death, thou shalt die.

          John Donne

297.  NO SHADOWS THERE

No shadows There!  They joyfully behold Him!
    No cloud to dim their vision of His face!
No jarring note to mar the holy rapture,
    The perfect bliss of that most blessed place.

No burdens There!  These all are gone forever!
    No weary nights, no long or dragging days!
No sighing There, or secret, silent longings,--
    For all is now unutterable praise.

No conflicts There!  No evil hosts assailing!
    Such warfare past--forever made to cease;
No tempter's voice is heard within those portals;
    No foe lurks there to break the perfect peace.

No sorrows There!  no sadness and no weeping!
    Tears wiped away--all radiant now each face;
Music and song, in happy holy blending,
    Fill all the courts of that sweet resting place.

J. Danson Smith

298.    THRESHOLD OF HEAVEN

Do not ask me **not** to speak
About this journey I shall take.
'Tis but a step and then my eyes
Shall open to the great surprise
He has prepared.  Do you recall,
At Christmastime when we were small,
Our rapture and our eagerness,
And how we always tried to guess
What gifts our mother's hands had made?
Dear memories that will not fade!
Don't you remember, half our fun
Was in anticipation!
And then at last the opened door.
A breathless pause, a rush, and there
Beneath the tree our gifts were laid,
The gifts our mother's hands had made!

So at His threshold now I pause,
And ask you not to grieve because
I go into His other room.
Surely He would have me come
With eager wonder in my eyes
To see at last what rich surprise
The loving hands of our dear Lord
Made for His own.  Ear has not heard,

Eye has not seen, nor can the mind
Obscurely guess what we shall find
Beyond that opened door.  And so,
I pray that you will let me go,
Will loose love's last restraining bands.
A hush...a light...and lo, His hands
Have unveiled glory in a breath!
O gifts undreamed of,--brought by death!

Martha Snell Nicholson

299.    NOT DEAD

He is not dead--the child of our affection--
    But gone unto that school
Where he no longer needs our poor protection,
    And Christ Himself doth rule.

Day after day we think what he is doing
    In those bright realms of air;
Year after year, his tender steps pursuing,
    Behold him grown more fair.

Thus do we walk with him, and keep unbroken
    The bond which nature gives,
Thinking that our remembrance, though unspoken
    May reach him where he lives.

Henry Wadsworth Longfellow

300.   BEAUTIFUL ZION

Beautiful Zion, built above!
Beautiful city that I love!
Beautiful gates of pearly white!
Beautiful temple, God its light!

Beautiful trees, forever there!
Beautiful fruits they always bear!
Beautiful rivers gliding by!
Beautiful fountains never dry!

Beautiful light, without the sun!
Beautiful day revolving on!
Beautiful worlds on worlds untold!
Beautiful streets of shining gold!

Beautiful Heaven where all is light!
Beautiful angels clothed in white!
Beautiful songs that never tire!
Beautiful harps through all the choir!

Beautiful crowns on every brow!
Beautiful palms the conquerors show!
Beautiful robes the ransomed wear!
Beautiful all who enter there!

Beautiful throne for God the Lamb!
Beautiful seats at God's right hand!
Beautiful rest, all wanderings cease!
Beautiful home of perfect peace!

George Gill

301.   THE DESTRUCTION OF SENNACHERIB

*(Read Isaiah, chapters 36 and 37)*

The Assyrian came down like the wolf on the fold,
And his cohorts were gleaming in purple and gold;
And the sheen of their spears was like stars on the sea,
When the blue wave rolls nightly on deep Galilee.

Like the leaves of the forest when Summer is green,
That host with their banners at sunset were seen;
Like the leaves of the forest when Autumn hath blown,
That host on the morrow lay withered and strown.

For the Angel of Death spread his wings on the blast,
And breathed in the face of the foe as he passed;
And the eyes of the sleepers waxed deadly and chill,
And their hearts but once heaved, and for ever grew still!

And there lay the steed with his nostril all wide,
But through them there rolled not the breath of his pride;
And the foam of his gasping lay white on the turf,
And cold as the spray of the rock-beating surf.

And there lay the rider, distorted and pale,
With the dew on his brow, and the rust on his mail;
And the tents were all silent, the banners alone,
The lances unlifted, the trumpet unblown.

And the widows of Ashur are loud in their wail,
And the idols are broke in the temple of Baal;
And the might of the Gentile, unsmote by the sword,
Hath melted like snow in the glance of the Lord.

Lord Byron
1788-1824

302.   TELL MOTHER I'LL BE THERE

When I was but a little child, how well I recollect,
How I would grieve my mother with my folly and neglect;
And now that she has gone to Heaven I miss her tender care,
O Saviour, tell my mother I'll be there.

Though I was often wayward, she was always kind and good;
So patient, gentle, loving, when I acted rough and rude;
My childhood griefs and trials she would gladly with me share:
O Saviour, tell my mother I'll be there.

One day a message came to me, it bade me quickly come
If I would see my mother ere the Saviour took her home;
I promised her before she died, for Heaven to prepare;
O Saviour, tell my mother I'll be there.

Tell Mother I'll be there, in answer to her prayer,
This message, blessed Saviour, to her bear!
Tell Mother I'll be there, Heaven's joys with her to share,
Yes, tell my darling mother I'll be there.

                              Charles M. Fillmore


303.   WE'LL SEE CHRISTIANS AGAIN

The sun has gone to rest beneath the lake,
   And one by one the little stars awake;
But do not think because it slips from view,
   The sun has bid the earth a last adieu.
We say the sun has "gone to rest" when night
   Drops a veil that dims the mortal sight;
But it has risen on another world,
   The petals of its golden bloom unfurled,
And there the robin in the treetop sings,
And warmth and light awake all waiting things.

And so "at rest" is what we sometimes say
   Of that dear one who gently slipped away;
But he has simply vanished from the earth
   To find elsewhere a new and glorious birth;
Lost to our sight a little tearful while,
   His tender voice, his quick and eager smile.
But surely as the faithful, rising sun
   Returns to bless our eyes, so will this one
Be waiting when the dawn of dawns appears,
   So put away your sorrow and your tears,
And know that you will see him face to face,
Whose light already shines in that far place.

                              Lois Parrish

### 304. WHAT WILL IT BE?

*"Looking for that blessed hope."—Titus 2:13.*

*"I go to prepare a place for you. And if I go . . .*
*I will come again, and receive you unto myself.*
*—John 14:2, 3.*

What will it be to hear the voice of Jesus
   Calling His own to share His bliss above?
Called from the desert, from its cares and sorrows,
   Into the region of eternal love.

What will it be to see His face once marred,
   Now shining bright with glory, oh, so fair;
To see the look of love that greets His loved ones,
   Welcomed by Him, to share His fulness there?

What will it be?--oh, blessed, glorious portion;
   Hasten, O Lord, Thy coming. Come, Lord, come!
Thy love, Thy bliss, Thy glory, Lord, attract me
   To Thee, to scenes of joy, my hope, my Home.

E. Middleton

### 305. MY FIRST SWEETHEART

I used to bring her daisies, golden-rod and clover, too,
And I know she prized them higher than the sweetest rose that grew,
And it mattered not how withered all the simple blossoms were,
For she took them as the symbols of the love I bore for her.

Then I'd kiss her cheeks and tell her that when I became a man
I'd take her home to live with me, and then we'd sit and plan,
For the future happy days when, in some glorious southern clime,
She and I would make life one long dream of love and summertime.

No, I did not marry her, although I love her as of old;
And I know her love for me has never grown the least bit cold;
And the news that she is coming makes my heart grow light and glad,
For Mother was that old sweetheart--the first I ever had.

Russell "Punt" Batey

### 306. THE LOVELY LAND

I soon shall see the beauty of the Lovely Land--
   The country where the shining river flows--
The Paradise of love the Heavenly Father planned,
   The Lovely Land where Heaven's Garden grows.

I soon shall hear the music of the Lovely Land--
   The country where the singing river flows--
Redemption's anthem shall its euphony expand,
   The wonders of salvation to disclose.

I soon shall go to dwell within the Lovely Land--
  The country where the restful river flows--
No storm shall e'er destroy my homestead on that strand,
  No foe assail, no enemy depose.

I soon shall see my Saviour in the Lovely Land--
  The country where His peace forever flows--
Shall see His lovely face, shall touch His nail-scarred hand;
  One glimpse, my restless spirit will compose.

Paul Hutchens

## 307.   TO GREET YOU

We fain would send some word of warmest gladness--
  Some word of uplift, and of truest cheer;
For--myriad are the things and themes of sadness,
  Which come to meet us with each passing year.

'Tis good to dwell on things which cannot perish--
  Which cannot change, or fade, nor yet decay;
Those things which, deep within, we truly cherish,
  And which can never, never pass away.

The Lord our God--all-reaching and availing!
  The Peace of God--to keep both heart and mind!
The Power of God--sufficient and unfailing!
  The Grace of God--all wounds to soothe and bind!

The Presence here; the glad and sweet communion!
  The wondrous welcome--waiting over there!
The Father's House--and with those there what union!
  And endless joys which cannot here compare.

J. Danson Smith

## 308.   WHEN JESUS RECEIVES HIS OWN

I gaze upon yon everlasting arch
  Up which the bright stars wander as they shine;
And, as I mark them in their nightly march,
  I think how soon that journey shall be mine!

Not many more of life's slow passing hours,
  Shaded with sorrow's melancholy hue;
Oh, what a glad ascending shall be ours,
  Oh, what a pathway up yon starry blue!

A journey like Elijah's, swift and bright,
  Caught gently upward to an early crown,
In Heaven's own chariot of all blazing light,
  With death untasted and the grave unknown.

Oh joy! oh delight! should we go without dying!
  No sickness, no sadness, no dread, and no crying,
Caught up through the clouds with our Lord into glory,
  When Jesus receives "His own."

                              J. Danson Smith


### 309.    WE'LL MEET AGAIN

We'll meet again--the loved ones gone before us--
  In that bright realm--the land of light and love;
It may be that e'en now they're watching o'er us,
  And longing for the time we'll meet above.

We'll meet again--of that we may be certain,
  In that bright Home so wondrous and so fair,
Whose glories, veiled to us as by a curtain,
  Through God's redeeming grace we are to share.

We'll meet where neither sadnesses nor sorrows
  Shall for one moment rob the heart of joy;
Where there shall be no dark uncertain morrows,
  Or aught whatever to the bliss destroy.

Ah, yes, we'll meet again in that bright glory;
  How wondrous it will be to talk things o'er,
And to begin a fresh, but never-ending story
  Of life which shall endure forevermore.

                              J. Danson Smith


### 310.  WE'RE GOING HOME

We're going Home!  We're going Home!
No more o'er barren wastes to roam:
And if the way seem long we've trod,
We're going Home to Heaven and God.

What if the way be ofttimes rough--
We're going Home--that is enough!
How sweet the welcome that awaits
Our entry at Heaven's pearly gates.

What hallowed bliss within its walls!
What peaceful rest within its halls!
No sense of sin, no sound of strife,--
Just radiant, joyful, endless life.

What fellowship we then shall share!
How wonderful the frames we'll wear
In that dear realm--Heaven's Homing-place,
And all through Christ's redeeming grace.

                              J. Danson Smith

# DECISION

## 311. THE BUILDERS

All are architects of Fate,
  Working in these walls of Time;
Some with massive deeds and great,
  Some with ornaments of rhyme.

Nothing useless is, or low;
  Each thing in its place is best;
And what seems but idle show
  Strengthens and supports the rest.

For the structure that we raise,
  Time is with materials filled;
Our todays and yesterdays
  Are the blocks with which we build.

Truly shape and fashion these;
  Leave no yawning gaps between;
Think not, because no man sees,
  Such things will remain unseen.

In the elder days of art,
  Builders wrought with greatest care
Each minute and unseen part;
  For the gods see everywhere.

Let us do our work as well,
  Both the unseen and the seen;
Make the house, where gods may dwell,
  Beautiful, entire, and clean.

Else our lives are incomplete,
  Standing in these walls of Time,
Broken stairways, where the feet
  Stumble as they seek to climb.

Build today, then, strong and sure,
  With a firm and ample base;
And ascending and secure
  Shall tomorrow find its place.

Thus alone can we attain
  To those turrets, where the eye
Sees the world as one vast plain,
  And one boundless reach of sky.

Henry Wadsworth Longfellow
1807-1882

## 312. OPPORTUNITY

Master of human destinies am I.
Fame, love, and fortune on my footsteps wait,
Cities and fields I walk; I penetrate
Deserts and seas remote, and, passing by
Hovel, and mart, and palace, soon or late
I knock unbidden once at every gate!
If sleeping, wake--if feasting, rise before
I turn away. It is the hour of fate,
And they who follow me reach every state
Mortals desire, and conquer every foe
Save death; but those who doubt or hesitate,
Condemned to failure, penury and woe,
Seek me in vain and uselessly implore--
I answer not, and I return no more.

John James Ingalls
1833-1900

## 313. THE THREE CROSSES

Three crosses stood on Calvary's hill,
  Surrounded by a mob,
Two crosses bore two dying thieves,
  And one the Lamb of God.

Two crosses bore two dying thieves
  Who justly suffered shame;
The one cross bore God's sacrifice,
  The Lamb for sinners slain.

One thief received the dying Lamb,
  Repented of his sin;
The other thief refused to hear,
  And did not enter in.

B. F. Dotson

## 314. LEND A HAND

I am only one, but I am one;
I cannot do everything,
But I can do something.
What I can do I ought to do,
And what I ought to do
By God's grace I will do.

Edward Everett Hale

315.   LIFE'S COST

I could not at the first be born
But by another's bitter wailing pain;
Another's loss must be my sweetest gain;
And Love, only to win that I might be,
  Must wet her couch forlorn
With tears of blood and sweat of agony.

Since then I cannot live a week
But some fair thing must leave the daisied dells,
The joy of pastures, bubbling springs and wells,
And grassy murmurs of its peaceful days,
  To bleed in pain, and reek,
And die, for me to tread life's pleasant ways.

I cannot sure be warmed or lit
But men must crouch and toil in tortuous caves,
Bowed on themselves, while day and night in waves
Of blackness wash away their sunless lives;
  Or blasted and sore hit,
Dark life to darker death the miner drives.

Naked, I cannot clothed be
But worms must patient weave their satin shroud;
The sheep must shiver to the April cloud,
Yielding his one white coat to keep me warm;
  In shop and factory
For me must weary toiling millions swarm.

With gems I deck not brow or hand
But through the roaring dark of cruel seas
Some wretch with shivering breath and trembling knees
Goes headlong, while the sea-sharks dodge his quest;
  Then at my door he stands,
Naked, with bleeding ears and heaving chest.

I fall not on my knees and pray
But God must come from Heaven to fetch that sigh,
And pierced hands must take it back on high;
And through His broken heart and cloven side
  Love makes an open way
For me, who could not live but that He died.

O awful sweetest life of mine
That God and man both serve in blood and tears!
O prayers I breathe not but through other prayers!
O breath of life compact of others' sighs!
  With this dread gift divine
Ah, whither go?--what worthily devise?

If on myself I dare to spend
This dreadful thing, in pleasure lapped and reared,
What am I but a hideous idol smeared

With human blood, that with its carrion smile
  Alike to foe and friend
Maddens the wretch who perishes the while?

  I will away and find my God,
And what I dare not keep ask Him to take,
And taking Love's sweet sacrifice to make;
Then, like a wave the sorrow and the pain
  High Heaven with glory flood--
For them, for me, for all, a splendid gain.

                              Jane Ellice Hopkins


### 316.  SIMON PETER

I owned a little boat a while ago,
  And sailed a morning sea without a fear,
And whither any breeze might fairly blow,
  I steered my little craft afar or near,
Mine was the boat; and mine the air;
And mine the sea; nor mine a care.

My boat became my place of nightly toil,
  I sailed at sunset to the fishing ground.
At morn the boat was freighted with the spoil,
  That my all-conquering work and skill had found.
Mine was the boat; and mine the net;
And mine the skill and power to get.

One day there passed along the silent shore,
  While I my net was casting in the sea,
A man, who spake as never man before.
  I followed Him--new life began in me.
Mine was the boat, but His the voice;
And His the call, yet mine the choice.

Oh 'twas a fearful night out on the lake,
  And all my skill availed not at the helm,
Till Him asleep I wakened crying, "Take,
  Take Thou command; lest water overwhelm."
His was the boat; and His the sea;
And His the place o'er all and me.

Once from "HIS" boat He taught the curious throng,
  Then bade me let down nets out in the sea.
I murmured, but obeyed, nor was it long
  Before the catch amazed and humbled me.
"HIS" was the boat, and "HIS" the skill,
And "HIS" the catch, and "HIS" my will.

                              Author Unknown

317.   CONFESSION AND PEACE

No, not despairingly
  Come I to Thee;
No, not distrustingly
  Bend I the knee:
Sin hath gone over me,
Yet is this still my plea,
  Jesus hath died.

Ah! mine iniquity
  Crimson has been,
Infinite, infinite
  Sin upon sin;
Sin of not loving Thee,
Sin of not trusting Thee,
  Infinite sin.

Faithful and just art Thou,
  Forgiving all;
Loving and kind art Thou
  When poor ones call:
Lord, let the cleansing blood,
Blood of the Lamb of God,
  Pass o'er my soul.

Then all is peace and light
  This soul within:
Thus shall I walk with Thee,
  The loved Unseen;
Leaning on Thee, my God,
Guided along the road,
  Nothing between.

Horatius Bonar


318.   AS A MAN SOWETH

We must not hope to be mowers,
  And to gather the ripe gold ears,
Unless we have first been sowers
  And watered the furrows with tears.

It is not just as we take it,
  This mystical world of ours,
Life's field will yield as we make it
  A harvest of thorns or of flowers.

Johann W. von Goethe
1749-1832


319.   WHEN I HAVE TIME

When I have time, so many things I'll do
To make life happier and more fair
For those whose lives are crowded now with care;
I'll help to lift them from their low despair,
  When I have time.

When I have time, the friend I love so well
Shall know no more these weary, toiling days;
I'll lead her feet in pleasant paths always,
And cheer her heart with words of sweetest praise--
  When I have time.

When you have time, the friend you hold so dear
May be beyond the reach of all your sweet intent;
May never know that you so kindly meant
To fill her life with sweet content,
  When you had time.

Now is the time; ah, friend, no longer wait
To scatter loving smiles and words of cheer
To those around, whose lives are now so drear,
They may not need you in the coming years--
  Now is the time.

Miriam Brown

### 320. TWILIGHT DECISION

I gave my heart to Christ in life's cool evening,
    When on my wrinkled brow Time marked its toll;
At last, when silver dusk around me settled,
    I found that safe, sweet harbor for my soul.

The Holy Spirit rent the ebon curtain
    And tore asunder bonds I could not see;
The blindness, chains, and fetters sin had given
    Were gone--and I, at last, was wholly free.

O, wasted years! O, youth that could have served Him!
    O, bitter dregs of life that age must know!
But, blessed Saviour, Thou art now my refuge.
    I have yet time to love Thee e're I go.

                    Juanita Hale Shears


### 321. OPPORTUNITY

They do me wrong who say I come no more
    When once I knock and fail to find you in,
For every day I stand outside your door
    And bid you wake, and rise to fight and win.

Wail not for precious chances passed away,
    Weep not for golden ages on the wane!
Each night I burn the records of the day;
    At sunrise every soul is born again.

Laugh like a boy at splendors that have sped,
    To vanished joys be blind and deaf and dumb;
My judgments seal the dead past with its dead,
    But never bind a moment yet to come.

Tho' deep in mire, wring not your hands
            and weep;
    I lend my arm to all who say, "I can!"
No shamefaced outcast ever sank so deep
    But yet might rise and be again a man.

Dost thou behold thy lost youth all aghast?
    Dost reel from righteous retribution's blow?
Then turn from blotted archives of the past
    And find the future's pages white as snow.

Art thou a mourner? Rouse thee from thy spell;
    Art thou a sinner? Sins may be forgiven;
Each morning gives thee wings to flee
            from Hell,
Each night a star to guide thy feet to Heaven.

        Walter Malone


### 322. THE SUMMONS

Are you ready, dear friend, for the
            summons?
    Soon it may come to your door:
Remember 'tis only a heartbeat--
    A heartbeat to eternity's shore.
How oft' in the past you've determined
    Some day your sins to unload;
Yet still no nearer Heaven--
    Just nearer the end of the road.
A decision you now are making
    To continue the sinful way,
Or turn to a loving Saviour
    And live through eternal day.

To a friend I spoke of salvation
    And was shocked to hear him exclaim:
"All these years I've served the old Devil,
    I'll not deny him the few that remain!"
The Lord must have heard and decided
    No longer this soul needed breath;
A few days and he lay in his casket,
    Wrapt in the shroud of death.
Though years it may be in the coming,
    Or only a heartbeat away;
Are you ready, dear friend, for the
            summons
Should it come to your door today?

                    Floyd A. Cantwell

# ETERNAL VALUES

323.   THE VOICE IN THE TWILIGHT

I was sitting alone towards the twilight,
  With spirit troubled and vexed,
With thoughts that were morbid and gloomy,
  And faith that was sadly perplexed.

Some homely work I was doing
  For the child of my love and care,
Some stitches half wearily setting
  In the endless need of repair.

But my thoughts were about the "building,"
  The work some day to be tried:
And that only the gold and the silver
  And the precious stones should abide.

And remembering my own poor efforts,
  The wretched work I had done,
And even when trying most truly,
  The meagre success I had won.

"It is nothing but wood, hay and stubble,"
  I said, "it will all be burned,
This useless fruit of the talents
  One day to be returned.

"And I have so longed to serve Him,
  And sometimes I know I have tried,
But I'm sure when He sees such building
  He will never let it abide."

Just then, as I turned the garment,
  That no rent should be left behind,
My eye caught an odd little bungle
  Of mending and patchwork combined.

My heart grew suddenly tender,
  And something blinded my eyes,
With one of those sweet intuitions
  That sometimes make us so wise.

Dear child! she wanted to help me,
  I knew 'twas the best she could do,
But oh--what a botch she had made it--
  The gray mismatching the blue!

And yet--can you understand it?
  With a tender smile and a tear,
And a half-compassionate yearning,
  I felt she had grown more dear.

Then a sweet voice broke the silence,
  And the dear Lord said to me:
"Art thou tenderer for the little child,
  Than I am tender for thee?"

Then straightway I knew His meaning,
  So full of compassion and love,
And my faith came back to its Refuge
  Like the glad returning dove.

For I thought when the Master-Builder
  Comes down His temple to view,
To see what rents must be mended
  And what must be builded anew,

Perhaps, as He looks o'er the building,
  He will bring my work to the light,
And, seeing the marring and bungling,
  And how far it all is from right;

He will feel as I felt for my darling,
  And will say as I said for her:
"Dear child! she wanted to help Me,
  And love for Me was the spur.

"And for the true love that is in it,
  The work shall seem perfect as Mine,
And because it was willing service
  I will crown it with plaudit divine."

And there in the deepening twilight
  I seemed to be clasping a hand,
And to feel a great love constraining me
  Stronger than any command.

Then I knew by the thrill of sweetness,
  'Twas the hand of the Blessed One,
That would tenderly guide and hold me
  Till all the labor is done.

So my thoughts are nevermore gloomy,
  My faith is no longer dim;
But my heart is strong and restful,
  And mine eyes are unto Him.

                              Mrs. Herrick Johnson

324.    NO TIME FOR GOD

No time for God?
What fools we are to clutter up
Our lives with common things
And leave without heart's gate
The Lord of life and life itself--
Our God.

No time for God?
As soon to say no time
To eat or sleep or love or die.
Take time for God
Or you shall dwarf your soul,

And when the angel Death
Comes knocking at your door,
A poor, misshappen thing you'll be
To step into eternity.

No time for God?
Some day you'll lay aside
This mortal life and make your way
To worlds unknown,
And when you meet Him face to face,
Will He--should He
Have time for you?

Author Unknown

325.    KEEPING BOOKS

I've figured my blessings, I've counted my cares,
I've balanced the book of my daily affairs.

A column for credits, a column for debit,
A place for unkindness I cannot forget.

And yet there were pleasures along with the pain,
And seldom a loss but had some little gain.

I find I have more than I ever have known,
Astonished to note all the wealth that I own.

I've figured my blessings but little, I fear;
My cares I have counted each day and each year.

Forgotten the pleasure, the pain I have kept,
Forever in mind ev'ry moment I wept.

The loss I remember, the sorrow recall,
The happiness I hardly remember at all.

But now I have taken a balance at last,
The joys and griefs of the present and past.

I've figured my blessings, I've set them apart
In a book I am keeping, the book of my heart.

I need not set down all the trouble and care,
I find I had already written it there.

But I had forgotten the love that is mine...
It took a whole column, the hate but a line.

The joy always greater, the grief always less,
I'm really astonished at the wealth I possess.

From "Selah"

326.     BY LIFE OR BY DEATH

*(Philippians 1:20)*

*John and Betty Stam, two Moody Bible Institute gradu-*
*ates, were martyred in China, December 8, 1934. On Decem-*
*ber 6, John Stam wrote, "My wife, baby, and myself are to-*
*day in the hands of communists. All our possessions and*
*stores they have taken, but we praise God for peace in our*
*hearts and a meal tonight. God grant you wisdom in what*
*you do and us fortitude, courage, and peace of heart. He is*
*able, and a wonderful Friend in such a time." And in clos-*
*ing he said, "The Lord bless and guide you, and as for us,*
*may God be glorified, whether by life or death."*

So this is life, this world with all its pleasures,
    Struggles and tears, a smile, a frown, a sigh,
Friendship so true, and love of kin and neighbor?
    Sometimes 'tis hard to live--always, to die!

The world moves on, so rapidly the living,
    The forms of those who disappear replace,
And each one dreams that he will be enduring--
    How soon that one becomes the missing face!

In life or death--and life is surely flying,
    The crib and coffin carved from the selfsame tree.
In life or death--and death so soon is coming--
    Escape I cannot; there's no place to flee.

But Thou, O God, hast life that is eternal;
    That life is mine, a gift through Thy dear Son.
Help me to feel its flush and pulse supernal,
    Assurance of the morn when life is done.

Help me to know the values of these hours,
    Help me the folly of all waste to see;
Help me to trust the Christ who bore my sorrows,
    And thus to yield for life or death to Thee.

In all my days be glorified, Lord Jesus,
    In all my ways guide me with Thine own eyes;
Just when and as Thou wilt, use me, Lord Jesus,
    And then for me 'tis Christ, to live or die.

Will H. Houghton

327.   THE AWFUL NEED

O God, the awful need of those
Who feel no need of Thee,
Who wake and sleep and drink and eat
And toil and talk, while careless feet

Tread heedlessly the road that leads
    Unto eternity--
Keenly alive to earthly needs,
Yet feel no need of Thee.

Amy Carmichael

## 328.   A LITTLE

A little work, a little play
To keep us going--and
   So, good-day!

A little warmth, a little light
Of love's bestowing--and
   So, good-night!

A little fun, to match the sorrow
Of each day's growing--and
   So, good-morrow!

A little trust that when we die
We reap our sowing--and
   So, good-bye!

George du Maurier
1834-1896

## 329.   WHILE YOU LIVE

It's easy to talk of the money you'd spend
If you had a few dollars ahead;
But it's better to give a bit while you live--
Than a million--after you're dead!

Grenville Kleiser

## 330.   NOW

We shall do so much in the years to come,
   But what have we done today?
We shall give our gold in a princely sum,
   But what did we give today?
We shall lift the heart, and dry the tear;
We shall plant a hope, in place of fear,
We shall speak the words of love and cheer,
   But what have we done today?

We shall be so kind in the after while,
   But what have we been today?
We shall bring to each lonely life a smile,
   But what have we brought today?
We shall give to truth a grander birth,
And to steadfast faith a deeper worth;
We shall feed the hungering souls of earth,
   But whom have we fed today?

Waterman

## 331.   TOO BUSY

*"So teach us to number our days,*
*that we may apply our hearts unto*
*wisdom."--Ps. 90:12.*

Too busy to read the Bible,
   Too busy to wait and pray!
Too busy to speak out kindly
   To someone by the way!

Too busy to care and struggle,
   To think of the life to come!
Too busy building mansions,
   To plan for the heavenly Home.

Too busy to help a brother
   Who faces the winter blast!
Too busy to share his burden
   When self in the balance is cast.

Too busy for all that is holy
   On earth beneath the sky;
Too busy to serve the Master
   But--not too busy to die.

Author Unknown

## 332.   THE SONG OF HOPE

I hear it singing, sweetly singing,
Softly in an undertone;
Singing as if God had taught it,
"It is better farther on."

By night and day it sings the same song,
Sings it while I sit alone;
Sings it so the heart may hear it,
"It is better farther on."

It sits upon the grave and sings it--
Sings it when the heart would groan;
Sings it when the shadows darken,
"It is better farther on."

Farther on, yes, farther on,
It is better farther on;
What though life has many a sorrow,
Why should we new troubles borrow?
Faith can claim a bright tomorrow,
It is better farther on.

Author Unknown

### 333. LITTLE THINGS

Little drops of water,
  Little grains of sand,
Make the mighty ocean
  And the pleasant land.

Thus the little minutes
  Humble though they be,
Make the mighty ages
  Of eternity.

        Julia A. Fletcher Carney


### 334. A LITTLE TALK WITH JESUS

A little talk with Jesus,
  How it smooths the rugged road!
How it seems to help me onward,
  When I faint beneath my load;
When my heart is crushed with sorrow,
  And my eyes with tears are dim,
There is naught can yield me comfort
  Like a little talk with Him.

Ah, this is what I'm wanting,
  His lovely face to see;
And I'm not afraid to say it,
  I know He's wanting me.
He gave His life a ransom,
  To make me all His own,
And He'll ne'er forget His promise
  To me, His purchased one.

I cannot live without Him,
  Nor would I if I could;
He is my daily portion,
  My medicine and food.
He is altogether lovely;
  None can with Him compare;
Chiefest among ten thousand,
  And fairest of the fair.

So I'll wait a little longer,
  Till His appointed time,
And along the upward pathway
  My pilgrim feet shall climb.
There, in my Father's dwelling,
  Where many mansions be,
I shall sweetly talk with Jesus,
  And He will talk with me.

        William G. Fischer


### 335. THINGS THAT NEVER DIE

The pure, the bright, the beautiful
  That stirred our hearts in youth,
The impulses to wordless prayer,
  The streams of love and truth,
The longing after something lost,
  The spirit's yearning cry,
The striving after better hopes--
  These things can never die.

The timid hand stretched forth to aid
  A brother in his need;
A kindly word in grief's dark hour
  That proves a friend indeed;
The plea for mercy softly breathed,
  When justice threatens high,
The sorrow of a contrite heart--
  These things shall never die.

Let nothing pass, for every hand
  Must find some work to do,
Lose not a chance to waken love--
  Be firm and just and true.
So shall a light that cannot fade
  Beam on thee from on high,
And angel voices say to thee--
  "These things shall never die."

        Charles Dickens
        1812-1870


### 336. I WONDER

I wonder if ever a song was sung
  But the singer's heart sang sweeter!
I wonder if ever a rhyme was rung
  But the thought surpassed the meter!
I wonder if ever a sculptor wrought
'Til the cold stone echoed his ardent thought!
Or if ever a painter, with light and shade,
The dream of his inmost heart portrayed!

I wonder if ever a rose was found
  And there might not be a fairer!
Or if ever a glittering gem was ground,
  And we dreamed not of a rarer!
Ah! never on earth shall we find the best!
But it waits for us in the land of rest;
And a perfect thing we shall never behold
Till we pass the portal of shining gold.

        Anonymous

## 337. WISDOM

I took the best of my youth
  For pleasures all my own--
Forgetting I must some day reap
  The chaff that I had sown.

I took the best of every day,
  When mind was fresh and keen--
To do the special things I loved,
  The thing that would be seen.

My youth soon fled, and I, alone,
  Reaped sorrow for my pleasure;
The things I loved to do for show
  Proved but an empty treasure.

But when I gave my best to God,
  My life--the morning hour--
I found His pleasure was my own,
  His grace, my shining tower!

                    Mildred Allen Jeffery

## 338.   HE WAS NOT WILLING

"He was not willing that any should perish";
  Jesus enthroned in the glory above,
Saw our poor fallen world, pitied our sorrows,
  Poured out His life for us--wonderful love!
Perishing, perishing! Thronging our pathway,
  Hearts break with burdens too heavy to bear:
Jesus would save, but there's no one to tell them,
  No one to lift them from sin and despair.

"He was not willing that any should perish";
  Clothed in our flesh with its sorrow and pain,
Came He to seek the lost, comfort the mourner,
  Heal the heart broken by sorrow and shame.
Perishing, perishing! Harvest is passing,
  Reapers are few and the night draweth near:
Jesus is calling thee, haste to the reaping,
  Thou shalt have souls, precious souls for thy hire.

Plenty for pleasure, but little for Jesus;
  Time for the world, with its troubles and toys,
No time for Jesus' work, feeding the hungry,
  Lifting lost souls to eternity's joys.
Perishing, perishing! Hark! how they call us;
  "Bring us our Saviour, oh, tell us of Him!
We are so weary, so heavily laden,
  And with long weeping our eyes have grown dim."

"He was not willing that any should perish";
  Am I His follower, and can I live
Longer at ease with a soul going downward,
  Lost for the lack of the help I might give?
Perishing, perishing! Thou wast not willing;
  Master, forgive, and inspire us anew;
Banish our worldliness, help us to ever
  Live with eternity's values in view.

                    Lucy R. Meyer

339.   JESUS, KING OF PAIN

Lord Jesus, King of Pain,
   Thy subject I;
Thy right it is to reign:
   Oh, hear my cry,
And bid in me all longings cease
Save for Thy holy will's increase.

Thy right it is to reign
   O'er all Thine own;
Then, if Thy love send pain,
   Find there Thy throne,
And help me bear it unto Thee,
Who didst bear death and Hell for me.

Lord Jesus, King of Pain,
   My heart's Adored,
Teach me eternal gain
   Is Love's reward:
In Thee I hide me:  hold me still
Till pain work all Thy perfect will.

E. Margaret Clarkson


340.   PASS IT ON

Have you had a kindness shown?
   Pass it on.
'Twas not given for thee alone,
   Pass it on.
Let it travel down the years,
Let it wipe another's tears,
'Till in Heav'n the deed appears--
   Pass it on.

Did you hear the loving word?
   Pass it on--
Like the singing of a bird?
   Pass it on.
Let its music live and grow,
Let it cheer another's woe;
You have reaped what others sow--
   Pass it on.

'Twas the sunshine of a smile--
   Pass it on.
Staying but a little while!
   Pass it on.
April beam a little thing,
Still it wakes the flowers of spring,
Makes the silent birds to sing--
   Pass it on.

Have you found the heavenly light?
   Pass it on.
Souls are groping in the night,
   Daylight gone--
Hold thy lighted lamp on high,
Be a star in someone's sky,
He may live who else would die--
   Pass it on.

Be not selfish in thy greed,
   Pass it on.
Look upon thy brother's need,
   Pass it on.
Live for self, you live in vain;
Live for Christ, you live again;
Live for Him, with Him you reign--
   Pass it on.

Henry Burton
1840-1930


341.   TIME

Minutes past are minutes gone,
   Part of a past eternity.
Minutes future thou hath none,
   Their coming hath no certainty.
Minutes present are thine own,
   Be wise and use them for God alone.

Author Unknown


342.   SACRIFICE

Sacrifice?  The word is not for me--
Gladly I take my cross to follow Thee.
Could I be loath to yield my meager pittance,
When Thou dost offer Heaven's gold to me?
Let me obey Thee even unto death,
That to the far-flung fields Thy name be told.
Forsaking all?  What, Lord, could I forsake
That would not be repaid a thousandfold?
My life is Thine, Lord; never let me seek
To plan that life for which my Saviour died.
Thine, Lord, is the power to will and do--
That in my body Christ be magnified.
To know the excellency of Christ, my Lord,
What things were gain to me I count but loss;
Teach me the values of eternity--
To choose with Thee the pathway of the cross.

Elizabeth Howard Elliot

## 343. "ACCORDING TO THE PATTERN"

*(Hebrews 8:5)*

It is the common lot of man
For human skill to need a plan,
And so we labour, if we can,
    "According to the pattern."

For crochet, and for knitting, too,
The women like to have in view
Instructions, just to help them through,
    "According to the pattern."

And cooking is another art
Where recipes can play a part,
For mother likes to make a start
    "According to the pattern."

Men too have need of plans to aid
Their skill in every sort of trade,
For countless useful things are made
    "According to the pattern."

Can it be wise to daily build
The House of Life with toil unskilled?
It cannot stand unless fulfilled
    "According to the pattern."

The House is surely well begun
Whose plans ensure God's will is done,--
A Temple for the Holy One,
    "According to the pattern."

        C. C. White

## 345. THE LITTLE THINGS

He came a little sooner
  Than the other fellow did,
And stayed a little longer
  Than the other fellow would.
He worked a little harder,
  And he talked a little less,
He was never really hurried,
  And he showed but little stress,
For every little movement
  His efficiency expressed.
He saved a little money
  In a hundred little ways,
And banked a little extra

## 344. MARY AND MARTHA

*"Mary. . . sat at Jesus' feet and heard his word.
But Martha was cumbered about much serving."*--
        *Luke 10:39, 40.*

Martha was busy and hurried,
  Serving the Friend divine,
Cleansing the cups and the platters,
  Bringing the bread and the wine;
But Martha was careful and anxious,
  Fretted in thought and in word,
She had no time to be learning
  While she was serving the Lord,
For Martha was "cumbered" with serving,
  Martha was "troubled" with "things"--
Those that would pass with the using--
  She was forgetting her wings.

But Mary was quiet and peaceful,
  Learning to love and to live.
Mary was hearing His precepts,
  Mary was letting Him give--
Give of the riches eternal,
  Treasures of mind and of heart;
Learning the mind of the Master,
  Choosing the better part.

Do we ever labor at serving
  Till voices grow fretful and shrill,
Forgetting how to be loving,
  Forgetting how to be still?
Do we strive for "things" in possession,
  And toil for the perishing meat,
Neglecting the one thing needful--
  Sitting at Jesus' feet?

Service is good when He asks it,
  Labor is right in its place,
But there is one thing better--
  Looking up into His face;
There is so much He would tell us,
  Truths that are precious and deep;
This is the place where He wants us,
  These are the things we can keep.

        Annie Johnson Flint

When he got a little raise.
Of course, it's little wonder that
He murmurs with a smile,
As his dividends come regular--
  "Are the little things worth while?"

        Investor

346.    ONLY HEAVEN FREE

Earth gets its price for what earth gives us,
The beggar is taxed for a corner to die in,--
The priest has his fee who comes and shrives us,
We bargain for the graves we lie in.
At the Devil's booth are all things sold;
Each ounce of dross costs its ounce of gold.
For a cap and bells our lives we pay,--
Bubbles we buy with a whole soul's tasking;
'Tis only Heaven that's given away,--
'Tis God alone may be had for the asking!

James Russell  Lowell


347.    FAREWELL

My fairest child, I have no song to give you,
  No lark could pipe to skies so dull and gray,
Yet, ere we part, one lesson I can leave you
        For every day:

Be good, sweet maid, and let who will be clever;
  Do noble things, not dream them all day long;
And so make life, death, and that vast forever,
        One grand, sweet song.

Charles Kingsley

# FAITH, TRUST

## 348. REST OF THE WEARY

Rest of the weary, joy of the sad;
Hope of the dreary, light of the glad;
Home of the stranger, strength to the end;
Refuge from danger, Saviour and Friend.

Pillow where lying, love rests its head;
Peace of the dying, life of the dead;
Path of the lowly, prize at the end;
Bliss of the holy, Saviour and Friend.

When my feet stumble, to Thee I'll cry,
Crown of the humble, cross of the high;
When my steps wander, over me bend,
Truer and fonder, Saviour and Friend.

Thee still confessing, ever I'll raise
Unto Thee blessing, glory and praise;
All my endeavor, world without end,
Thine to be ever, Saviour and Friend.
                              Author Unknown

## 349. WINDING ROAD AHEAD

Life's highway doesn't always lie
    In smooth and sunny miles;
It often leads through rocks and hills,
    And dangerous defiles.
Sometimes dark mountains loom ahead,
    The winding trail seems dim;
But with us is our heavenly Guide,
    Full safe, we follow Him.
And when we've made our final mile
    And rounded our last bend,
We'll see the welcome lights of Home,
    And smile at journey's end.
                              Moody Monthly

## 350. HE LEADS

He leads us on by paths we did not know;
Upward He leads us though our steps be slow,
Though oft we faint and falter on the way,
Though storms and darkness oft obscure
            the day;
        Yet when the clouds are gone
        We know He leads us on.

He leads us on through all the unquiet years;
Past all our dreamland hopes, and doubts and fears;
He guides our steps, through all the tangled maze

## 351. PEACE

With eager heart and will on fire,
I strove to win my great desire.
"Peace shall be mine," I said; but life
Grew bitter in the barren strife.

My soul was weary, and my pride
Was wounded deep; to Heaven I cried,
"God grant me peace or I must die";
The dumb stars glittered no reply.

Broken at last, I bowed my head,
Forgetting all myself, and said,
"Whatever comes, His will be done";
And in that moment peace was won.
                              Henry van Dyke
                              1852-1933

## 352. NOT ALONE

I cannot do it alone;
    The waves run fast and high,
And the fogs close all around,
    The light goes out in the sky;
But I know that we two
    Shall win in the end,
        Jesus and I.

I could not guide it myself,
    My boat on life's wild sea;
There's One who sits by my side,
    Who pulls and steers with me.
And I know that we two
    Shall safe enter port,
        Jesus and I.
                              Selected

Of losses, sorrows, and o'er clouded days,
    We know His will is done;
And still He leads us on.
                              N. L. Zinzendorf

## 353. MY NEED

I need wide spaces in my heart
    Where Faith and I can go apart
    And grow serene.
Life gets so choked by busy living,
Kindness so lost in fussy giving
    That Love slips by unseen.
                              Anonymous

### 354. I WILL NOT BE AFRAID!

*"What time I am afraid, I will trust in thee."—Ps. 56:3.*
*"I will trust and not be afraid."—Isa. 12:2.*

I will trust Him, yea, I will trust,
  For He never hath failed me yet;
And never a day nor an hour,
  But mine uttermost need is met.
Though I dwell in the midst of foes,
  Yet there is my table spread,
And His presence wraps me round
  And His wings are over my head.
Father and Infinite God,
  My Refuge and Fortress Rock,
Where I hide from the tempest's wrath,
  And feel not the earthquake shock.
So I bide with a soul serene
  And a heart that is undismayed.
He is my Strength and my Shield;
  Of whom shall I be afraid?

I will not be afraid, for I know
  That He keepeth me safe from harm,
And He shall defend His own
  With a strong and a stretched-out arm.
Though I grope in perilous paths,
  In darkness and danger and doubt,
I know, as He brought me in,
  So He surely will bring me out.
For the God I serve today
  Is one with the God of old;
Still doth He guide my steps
  And still doth His hand uphold.
He giveth me rest from fear,
  For on Him my mind is stayed,
He is the Strength of my life;
  Of what shall I be afraid?

I will trust and not be afraid.
  I have seen, I have heard, I have known.
This mighty and terrible God
  Hath called me and made me His own.
"Dread not! Faint not!" He hath said,
  "For the battle belongs to Me.
Go forth with a song of praise,
  And My victory thou shalt see."
And where I go He will go,
  And He knoweth the way I take;
He is with me unto the end,
  And He will not fail nor forsake.
They that trust in the Lord
  Shall never be moved nor swayed.
"Fear not!" He hath said unto me,
  And why should I be afraid?

           Annie Johnson Flint

### 355. ACCEPTED

*"Accepted. . .in the Beloved."*

Unworthy? Yes, unworthy.
  What dost thou here?
Love's arms are wide to welcome
  And bring me near.

Unworthy? Yes, unworthy.
  How dare to pray?
The Holy Place is open--
  Love made a way.

Unworthy? Yes, unworthy.
  How hope for Heaven?
Hope for the poorest sinner
  By Love is given.

Unworthy? Yes, unworthy.
  Hast thou no fear?
Fear fleeth Love's pure presence,
  And love is here.

           E. Margaret Clarkson

### 356. BETTER THAN ALL

He was better to me than all my hopes;
  He was better than all my fears:
He made a bridge of my broken works,
  And a rainbow of my tears.
The billows that girded my sea-girt
    path
  But carried my Lord on their crest;
When I dwell on the days of my
    wilderness march
  I can lean on His love for the rest.

There is light for me on the
    trackless wild,
  As the wonders of old I trace--
When the God of the whole earth went
    before
  To search me a resting place.
Has He changed for me? Nay! He
    changeth not:
  He will bring me by some new way,
Through fire and blood and each
    crafty foe
  As safely as yesterday!

           J. Danson Smith

### 357. I WILL TRUST HIM

*"Though he slay me, yet will I trust in him."* —*Job 13:15.*

Anybody can trust Him when all goes well--
I'll trust Him when the stormy sea doth swell;
I'll trust Him when slander doth evil tell;
I'll trust Him to the very gates of Hell!

Anybody can trust Him when the sun shines--
I'll trust Him on sorrow's blackest confines;
I'll trust Him when sin its sweetest defines;
I'll trust Him when despair its worst outlines!

Anybody can trust Him with loved ones beside--
I'll trust Him when to me they are denied;
I'll trust Him when away they softly glide;
I'll trust Him whate'er doth me betide!

Anybody can trust Him when plenty abounds--
I'll trust Him when traced by poverty's hounds;
I'll trust Him when lean hunger's pinch confounds;
I'll trust Him until Gabriel's trumpet sounds!

Anybody can trust Him when sound and hale--
I'll trust Him when my life doth fade and fail;
I'll trust Him when pain brings its bitt'rest wail;
I'll trust Him e'en when death my cheeks doth pale!

R. W. L.

### 358. HER GLADNESS

My darling went
Unto the seaside long ago. Content,
I stayed at home, for oh, I was so glad
Of all the little outings that she had!
I knew she needed rest. I loved to stay
At home a while that she might go away.
"How beautiful the sea! How she enjoys
The music of the waves! No care annoys
Her pleasures," thought I; "Oh, it is so good
That she can rest a while. I wish she could
Stay till the autumn leaves are turning red."
"Stay longer, sister," all my letters said.
"If you are growing stronger every day,
I am so very glad to have you stay."

My darling went
To Heaven long ago. Am I content
To stay at home? Why can I not be glad
Of all the glories that she there has had?
She needed change. Why am I loath to stay
And do her work and let her go away?
The land is lovely where her feet have been;
Why do I not rejoice that she has seen

Its beauties first? That she will show to me
The City Beautiful? Is it so hard to be
Happy that she is happy? Hard to know
She learns so much each day that helps
           her so?
Why can I not each night and morning say,
"I am so glad that she is glad today"?

Author Unknown

### 359. CLIPPED WINGS

My days were once such shining things,
I seemed to feel I wore bright wings;
Came dark I had not known before,
And folded wings, too weak to soar.
Yet somehow, spite of grief and care,
There grew the sense that God was there.
'Twas strange He seemed not near to me
When hours were filled with laughter free!
Lord, didst Thou clip these wings of mine
To teach me how to lean on Thine?

Author Unknown

360.    MY HAND IN GOD'S

Each morning when I wake I say,
"I place my hand in God's today."
With faith and trust that by my side
He'll walk with me, my steps to guide.
He leads me with the tenderest care,
When paths are dark, and I despair.
No need for me to understand
If I but hold fast to His hand,

My hand in His; no surer way
To walk in safety through each day.
By His great bounty I am fed,
Warmed by His love, and comforted.
When at day's end I seek my rest,
And realize how much I'm blessed,
My thanks pour out to Him, and then
I place my hand in God's again.

Selected

361. WHEN THE BROOK DRIED

God knew when the widow's cruse was low
    And the meal was almost gone,
And He dried the brook where Elijah drank,
    And He sent His servant on,
That the handful of meal should not be spent,
    Or the little oil grow less,
And that, when the widow's son lay dead
    The prophet's prayer should bless.

Hath He dried the brook where thou long hast dwelt?
    Canst thou find no solace there?
Zarephath is ready if Cherith fail,
    With oil and meal to share.
Oh, tarry not, should He bid thee go,
    His messenger thou shalt be;
Thou shalt carry a blessing to those who wait,
    And a blessing waiteth thee.

Annie Johnson Flint

362.    PERFECT PEACE

Peace, perfect peace, with sorrows surging 'round?
On Jesus' bosom nought but calm is found.

Peace, perfect peace, with loved ones far away?
In Jesus' keeping we are safe, and they.

Peace, perfect peace, our future all unknown?
Jesus we know, and He is on the throne.

Peace, perfect peace, death shadowing us and ours?
Jesus has vanquished death and all its powers.

It is enough:  earth's struggles soon shall cease,
And Jesus calls us to Heaven's perfect peace.

Edward H. Bickersteth

363.     REST, WEARY SOUL!

Rest, weary soul!
The penalty is borne, the ransom paid,
For all thy sins full satisfaction made;
Strive not to do thyself what Christ has done;
Claim the free gift, and make the joy
                    thine own;
No more by pangs of guilt and fear distrest,
    Rest, sweetly rest!

Rest, weary heart,
From all thy silent griefs and secret pain,
Thy profitless regrets and longings vain;
Wisdom and love have ordered all the past,
All shall be blessedness and light at last;
Cast off the cares that have so long opprest;
    Rest, sweetly rest!

Rest, weary head!
Lie down to slumber in the peaceful tomb;
Light from above has broken through
                    its gloom:
Here, in the place where once thy
                    Saviour lay,
Where He shall wake thee on a future day,
Like a tired child upon its mother's breast,
    Rest, sweetly rest!

Rest, spirit free!
In the green pastures of the heavenly shore,
Where sin and sorrow can approach
                    no more,
With all the flock by the Good Shepherd fed,
Beside the streams of life eternal led,
Forever with thy God and Saviour blest,
    Rest, sweetly rest!

Anonymous


364.    TOMORROW

I have nothing to do with tomorrow,
    My Saviour will make that His care;
Should He fill it with trouble and sorrow
    He'll help me to suffer and bear.
I have nothing to do with tomorrow,
    Its burdens then why should I share?
Its grace and its faith I can't borrow,
    Then why should I borrow its care?

Selected


365.  TRUST IN GOD AND DO THE RIGHT

Courage, brother! do not stumble,
    Though thy path be dark as night;
There's a Star to guide the humble;
    Trust in God, and do the right.

Though the road be long and dreary,
    And the end be out of sight;
Foot it bravely, strong or weary,
    Trust in God, and do the right.

Perish policy and cunning;
    Perish all that fears the light;
Whether losing, whether winning,
    Trust in God, and do the right.

Shun all forms of guilty passion,
    Fiends can look like angels bright.
Heed no custom, school or fashion,
    Trust in God, and do the right.

Some will love thee, some will hate thee,
    Some will flatter, some will slight;
Cease from man, and look above thee--
    Trust in God, and do the right.

Simple rule, and safest guiding--
    Inward peace, and shining light--
Star upon our path abiding--
    Trust in God, and do the right.

N. M'Leod


366.  OF LILIES AND SPARROWS

I heard two sparrows chatting
    In a barren tree,
About a nest and baby birds,
    And faith returned to me.
If they can plan so gaily
    About their future home,
How can I doubt my Father's love,
    Which will supply my own?
I saw a lily, tall and fair
    Grow in a mud-hole, unafraid,
And I remembered Solomon, who
    Was never so arrayed.
For He has said He treasures us
    Far more than all these things,
And so I walk...clothed all in silk,
    While my spirit soars on wings.

Louise Appleby Boyle

### 367.   "FATHER, TAKE MY HAND"

The way is dark, my Father!  Cloud on cloud
Is gathering thickly o'er my head, and loud
The thunders roar above me.  See, I stand
Like one bewildered!  Father, take my hand,
   And through the gloom
   Lead safely home
    Thy child!

The day goes fast, my Father! and the night
Is drawing darkly down.  My faithless sight
Sees ghostly visions.  Fears, a spectral band,
Encompass me.  O Father! take my hand,
   And from the night
   Lead up to light
    Thy child!

The way is long, my Father! and my soul
Longs for the rest and quiet of the goal;
While yet I journey through this weary land,
Keep me from wandering.  Father, take my hand
   Quickly and straight
   Lead to Heaven's gate
    Thy child!

The path is rough, my Father!  Many a thorn
Has pierced me; and my weary feet, all torn
And bleeding, mark the way.  Yet Thy command
Bids me press forward.  Father, take my hand;
   Then safe and blest,
   Lead up to rest
    Thy child!

The throng is great, my Father!  Many a doubt
And fear and danger compass me about;
And foes oppress me sore.  I cannot stand
Or go alone.  O Father! take my hand,
   And through the throng
   Lead safe along
    Thy child!

The cross is heavy, Father!  I have borne
It long, and still do bear it.  Let my worn
And fainting spirit rise to that blest land
Where crowns are given.  Father, take my hand;
   And reaching down
   Lead to the crown
    Thy child!

      Henry N. Cobb

368. THE GRACIOUS ANSWER

The way is dark, My child! but leads to light.
I would not always have thee walk by sight.
My dealings now thou canst not understand.
I meant it so; but I will take thy hand,
   And through the gloom
   Lead safely home
    My child!

The day goes fast, My child! But is the night
Darker to Me than day? In Me is light!
Keep close to Me, and every spectral band
Of fears shall vanish. I will take thy hand,
   And through the night
   Lead up to light
    My child!

The way is long, My child! But it shall be
Not one step longer than is best for thee;
And thou shalt know, at last, when thou shalt stand
Safe at the goal, how I did take thy hand,
   And quick and straight
   Lead to Heaven's gate
    My child!

The path is rough, My child! But oh! how sweet
Will be the rest, for weary pilgrims meet,
When thou shalt reach the borders of that land
To which I lead thee, as I take thy hand,
   And safe and blest
   With Me shall rest
    My child!

The throng is great, My child! But at thy side
Thy Father walks: then be not terrified,
For I am with thee; will thy foes command
To let thee freely pass; will take thy hand,
   And through the throng
   Lead safe along
    My child!

The cross is heavy, child! Yet there was One
Who bore a heavier for thee; My Son,
My well-beloved. For Him bear thine; and stand
With Him at last; and, from thy Father's hand,
   Thy cross laid down
   Receive a crown,
    My child!

       Henry N. Cobb

### 369.  NOT SHORTENED!

*"The LORD'S hand is not shortened, that it cannot*
*save; neither his ear heavy, that it cannot hear."*
*—Isa. 59:1.*

"Not shortened!"  No!  His hand is never shortened--
    Although, at times, His coming shows delay;
Nor is His ear at any time e'er heavy,
    E'en if, to heed our cry, He strange doth stay.

"Not shortened!"  No!  His hand will ever save us;
    He nothing knows of problems or of task;
His powers remain forever all-availing
    To reach, and save, and lift--when we may ask.

"Not shortened!"  No!  No!  And so, if we are certain
    That naught on our part tends to keep Him back--
That nothing grieves Him over which He waiteth,
    Then, sure indeed, we nothing good shall lack.

"Not shortened!"  No!  Yet--sometimes He doth tarry;
    He sees, and knows--and sure, His hand will save;
But He doth love our feeble faith to strengthen--
    And we can honor Him by faith that's brave.

                                        J. Danson Smith

### 370.    HIS WAY

*"O Lord, I know that the way of man is not*
*in himself: it is not in man that walketh*
*to direct his steps."—Jer. 10: 23.*

God bade me go when I would stay
    ('Twas cool within the wood).
I did not know the reason why.
I heard a boulder crashing by
    Across the path where I had stood.

He bade me stay when I would go;
    "Thy will be done," I said.
They found one day at early dawn,
Across the way I would have gone,
    A serpent with a mangled head.

No more I ask the reason why,
    Although I may not see
The path ahead.  His way I go;
For though I know not, He doth know
    And He will choose safe paths for me.

                    Maude E. Cramer

### 371.    OH FOR A FAITH THAT
            WILL NOT SHRINK

Oh for a faith that will not shrink,
    Though pressed by ev'ry foe,
That will not tremble on the brink
    Of any earthly woe!

That will not murmur or complain
    Beneath the chastening rod,
But, in the hour of grief or pain,
    Will lean upon its God;

A faith that shines more bright and clear
    When tempests rage the while;
That seas of trouble cannot drown,
    Nor Satan's arts beguile;

Lord, give us such a faith as this,
    And then, whate'er may come,
We'll taste, e'en here, the hallowed bliss
    Of an eternal Home.

                            William H. Bathurst

## 372. THE PULL

A boy was flying his kite one day
Up out of sight, away, away.
It had soared till not a speck was seen,
Yet he stood there holding the string, serene.
"How do you know you have a kite?"
Asked a passerby as he saw the sight
Of the boy standing there gazing aloft,
His hair all ruffled by breezes soft.

"You had a kite, and you have a string,
But where is the kite? You see not a thing!
Maybe it's gone, blown far from here.
How do you know it's still up there?"
"I know it's there!" laughed the boy aloud,
His keen eyes fixed on a lacy cloud.
I don't have to see it; the wind is full
And my kite's up there--I feel the pull!"

And so it is in the Christian's life,
We've an anchor to windward against
        stress and strife.
Even though clouds obscure His face,
We need not doubt Him, we keep our place,
Serene and steady, we're not alone;
Up there is Jesus beside the throne.
We know He's there. Our hearts are full
Of confidence--we feel His pull!

Unseen He is by human eye,
And the scoffing skeptic is prone to cry:
"What do you hope for? It's all a dream--
A nebulous myth--no Christ you've seen!"
But we can serenely go on the while,
We don't have to see Him, we sense
        His smile!
And we'll see Him soon, for faith is full
Of peace and assurance; we feel His pull!

        Mary Burns Warmenhoven


## 373. "PUT HAND IN GOD'S HAND"

"I said to the man
At the gate of the new year,
'Give me a light that I
May tread safely into the unknown,'
And he replied, 'Go out into the darkness
And put your hand into the hand of God.
That shall be to you better than a light,
And safer than a known way.'"

        Selected


## 374. NEVER LONELY, NEVER FEARING

Never lonely, if the Saviour
  Walks beside me all the way;
Never feeling lost, unwanted,
  Darkest night or drearest day.

Never fearing! In the valley
  Of the shadow, fear no ill,
For He promised ne'er to leave me,
  And I know He never will.

Never wanting, for the Shepherd
  Leads me by the waters still;
All my needs His love providing,
  From His storehouse and His till.

Never stumbling, tho' my pathway
  Oft is stony, oft is rough.
But His angels' arms around me,
  Underneath me, hold me up.

Oh to doubt Him, to be fretful
  Were a sin I now confess;
Such a Saviour always with me,
  E'er to keep me and to bless.

Never lonely, never fearing,
  Never wanting, never sad.
Help me trust Thee, Lord to claim it;
  May Thy blessings make me glad.

        John R. Rice


## 375. I MUST HAVE GOD!

I must have God!
  I couldn't walk this thorny way
With stone beneath and cloud above,
  Or meet the struggle of each day
Without His love.

I must have God!
  I couldn't stand the hours at night,
Or troubled day with all its length,
  Or overlook what others say
Without His strength.

I must have God!
  I couldn't share the grief of those
Who need my help along life's way,
  Or comfort one in need of peace
Unless I pray.

        Wellington

## 376. FAITH AND HOPE

O don't be sorrowful, darling!
    Now, don't be sorrowful, pray;
For, taking the year together, my dear,
    There isn't more night than day.
It's rainy weather, my loved one;
    Time's wheels they heavily run,
But taking the year together, my dear,
    There isn't more cloud than sun.

We're old folks now, companion--
    Our heads they are growing gray;
But taking the year all round, my dear,
    You always will find the May.
We've had our May, my darling,
    And our roses, long ago;
And the time of the year is come, my dear,
    For the long dark nights, and the snow.

But God is God, my faithful,
    Of night as well as of day;
And we feel and know that we can go
    Wherever He leads the way.
Ay, God of night, my darling!
    Of the night of death so grim;
And the gate that from life leads out,
            good wife,
Is the gate that leads to Him.

                        Rembrandt Peale

## 377. HOW GENTLE

How gentle God's commands!
    How kind His precepts are!
Come, cast your burdens on the Lord,
    And trust His constant care.

Beneath His watchful eye
    His saints securely dwell;
That hand which bears all nature up
    Shall guard His children well.

Why should this anxious load
    Press down your weary mind?
Haste to your heavenly Father's throne,
    And sweet refreshment find.

His goodness stands approved,
    Unchanged from day to day:
I'll drop my burden at His feet,
    And bear a song away.

                        Author Unknown

## 378. TRUSTING, TRUSTING ALL THE TIME

Christ is near for all who seek.
He has saved and He will keep
    Souls entrusted to His love,
    He will keep till safe above.
So I'm trusting, trusting Jesus
    All the time.

Satan ever seeks my fall,
He accuses, tempts me, calls,
    But the Saviour, ever near,
    When I cry, will gladly hear.
So I'm trusting, trusting Jesus
    All the time.

Richly He supplies my needs,
Daily bread His children feeds.
    Sparrow fed and lily clothed,
    Better loved are we than those!
So I'm trusting, trusting Jesus
    All the time.

Trusting, trusting all the time,
All God's promises are mine;
    Trials, burdens, grief and loss,
    Are all carried to the cross.
So I'm trusting, trusting Jesus
    All the time.

Resting in Jesus,
Taking all my burdens
    Oh, my faith is small, but He
    Still is true to care for me.
So I'm trusting, trusting Jesus
    All the time.

                        John R. Rice

## 379. SEEING HIM WHO IS INVISIBLE

With my eyes upon the Saviour
    I can walk the sea of life
With its waves and billows 'round me,
    With its tempests, storms and strife.
Should I look upon another,
    Look at self or turn my gaze
On life's problems and temptations,
    I would sink beneath the waves,
Saviour, let me walk beside Thee,
    Let me feel my hand in Thine;
Let me know the joy of walking
    In Thy strength and not in mine.

                        John Sidebotham

### 380. HAVE FAITH IN GOD

Have faith in God, for He who reigns on high
Hath borne thy grief, and hears the suppliant's sigh;
Still to His arms, thine only refuge, fly,
        Have faith in God!

Fear not to call on Him, O soul distressed!
Thy sorrow's whisper woos thee to His breast;
He who is oftenest there is oftenest blest.
        Have faith in God!

Lean not on Egypt's reeds; slake not thy thirst
At earthly cisterns.  Seek the Kingdom first.
Though man and Satan fright thee with their worst,
        Have faith in God!

Go, tell Him all!  The sigh thy bosom heaves
Is heard in Heaven.  Strength and peace He gives,
Who gave Himself for thee.  Our Jesus lives;
        Have faith in God!

                              Anna Shipton

### 381. THE CONQUEROR

No matter how the storms may rage
Upon the sea of life,
No matter how the waves may beat,
No matter what the strife;
The Lord is just the same today
As when He walked the Sea,
And He can conquer every storm
That life may send to thee.

The waves are raging everywhere
And men are sore distressed,
But all they need is found in Him
Who giveth perfect rest;
So cast your care upon the Lord,
Whose strength will never fail;
He calms the waves for your frail bark,
His power will e'er prevail.

                Selected

### 382. BY FAITH

BY FAITH and not by sight,
  Saviour, I walk with Thee;
Lead Thou my feet aright;
  Choose Thou the path for me.

Choose Thou the path for me;
  I would not if I could;
For only Thou canst see
  My highest, heavenly good.

My highest, heavenly good
  Lies in Thy will alone,
Designed and understood
  By Love upon His Throne.

By Love upon His Throne
  My life is planned aright;
Secure in Christ alone
  I walk by faith, not sight.

                E. Margaret Clarkson

### 383. THE REASON WHY

Not until each loom is silent,
  And the shuttles cease to fly,
Will God unroll the pattern
  And explain the reason why.
The dark threads are as needful
  In the Weaver's skilful hand,
As the threads of gold and silver
  For the pattern which He planned.

                Selected

### 384.  HE ALSO SENDS THE RAIN

God's word came to Elijah
The third year saying, "Go
Reveal thyself to Ahab--
I'll send the rain;" and so,
When Ahab met Elijah,
This truth did God inspire:
Let god be God--who answers
By sending down the fire.

The fire came down from Heaven,
Consumed the sacrifice;
The Balaam prophets perished;
They paid a mighty price.
Then to Elijah's rescue
The Lord came once again;
He heard his prayer at Carmel,
And this time sent the rain.

It came in mighty torrents,
The Bible doth declare;
The heathen saw the answer
To old Elijah's prayer.
No doubt they'd mocked the prophet,
And asked him to explain
Why God sent down the fire,
When the country needed rain.

But God does first things always,
Just as they first should be;
He knows when we need trials,
And when the blessing see!
The great God of the heavens
Need never to explain;
He knows when fire is needed,
And when to send the rain.

Before a bush that's burning
The prophet stands in fear;
The voice of God is speaking,
And Moses lingers near.
His faith is mounting upward,
For God has made it plain
That He who sends the fire,
Will also send the rain.

Affliction of My people
I now do see and know;
I'll lead them to a country
Where milk and honey flow;
For trials precede blessings,
And power succeeds pain;
The God who sends the fire
Will also send the rain.

All blessings in the natural,
And blessings all Divine;
Grapes and lush pomegranates,
Honey and oil and wine.
Of course they fought some battles,
And giants too were slain--
The God who sent the fire
Will also send the rain.

There's Daniel 'mong the lions--
They could not raise a paw;
God's angel from Heaven
Then gave them all lockjaw.
It was the king, my brother,
That night who suffered pain,
While Daniel rested sweetly,
Enjoyed God's lovely rain.

The king arrived next morning,
And said with bated breath,
"O Daniel, is God able
To deliver thee from death?"
"O king, live forever;
My God has made it plain
That He who sends the fire
Will  also send the rain."

I see the Hebrew children--
They're walking through the flame.
The Son of man walks with them--
Oh , glory to His name!
The fire had lost its power;
They could not suffer pain;
It burned their bands asunder,
And set them free again.

They came from out that furnace
Without the smell of fire;
The Lord heard their petition,
And granted their desire.
He'll not forget us, brother,
So let's present our claim.
The God who sends the fire
Will also send the rain.

\* \* \* \* \* \* \* \* \*

The God of this old Bible
Is just the same today,
And He is doing business
The same old-fashioned way.
He's no respect for persons;
Our prayers are not in vain,
For if we suffer with Him,
We'll also with Him reign.

One thousand years with Jesus--
That will be glory then;
Some shall reign o'er five cities;
Some others over ten.
So keep filled with the Spirit;
Let me repeat again--
That He who sends the fire
Will also send the rain.

Lillie Buffum

## 385. HE CHOOSES FOR ME

Giver of every gift,
  Thy choice is best;
All-wise Eternal Love--
  In Thee I rest.

Yielding to Thy wise hand,
  Safe in Thy will--
Not asking why or how,
  Let me be still.

Looking on things unseen,
  By faith I see
Glory exceeding great
  Worketh for me.

Grace E. Troy

## 386. HE DIED--BUT LIVES!

I hear the words of love,
  I gaze upon the blood;
I see the mighty sacrifice,
  And I have peace with God.
'Tis everlasting peace,
  Sure as Jehovah's name;
'Tis stable as His steadfast throne,
  For evermore the same.

The clouds may go and come,
  And storms may sweep my sky,
This blood-sealed friendship changes not,
  The cross is ever nigh.
My love is ofttimes low,
  My joy still ebbs and flows;
But peace with Him remains the same.
  No change Jehovah knows.

## 387. THE LORD WILL PROVIDE

In some way or other the Lord will provide.
It may not be my way, it may not be thy way,
And yet in His own way the Lord will provide.

At some time or other the Lord will provide.
It may not be my time, it may not be thy time,
And yet in His own time the Lord will provide.

Despond, then, no longer; the Lord will provide.
And this be thy token--no word He hath spoken
Was ever yet broken.  The Lord will provide.

March on, then, right boldly; the sea shall divide;
The pathway made glorious, with shouting victorious,
We'll join in the chorus, "The Lord will provide."

Mary Ann W. Cook

*"Trust in the Lord with all thine heart;
and lean not unto thine own understanding.
In all thy ways acknowledge him, and he
shall direct thy paths."--Prov. 3:5,6.*

That which can shake the cross
  May shake the peace it gave,
Which tells me Christ has never died,
  Or never left the grave.
Till then my peace is sure,
  It will not, cannot yield;
Jesus, I know, has died and lives;
  On this firm rock I build.

I change, He changes not,
  The Christ can never die;
His love, not mine, the resting place,
  His truth, not mine, the tie.
The cross still stands unchanged.
  Though Heaven is now His home;
The mighty stone is rolled away,
  But yonder is His tomb.

And yonder is my peace,
  The grave of all my woes;
I know the Son of God has come,
  I know He died and rose.
I know He liveth now
  At God's right hand above;
I know the throne on which He sits,
  I know His truth and love.

Horatius Bonar

### 389. "GOD'S BANK AIN'T BUSTED YET"

The bank had closed; my earthly gains had vanished from my hand;
I felt there was no sadder one than I in all the land.
My washer woman, too, had lost her little mite with mine,
But she was singing as she hung the clothes upon the line.
"How can you be so gay?" I asked. "Your loss--don't you regret?"
"Yes, ma'am, but what's the use to fret?
  God's bank ain't busted yet!"

I felt my burdens lighter grow, her faith I seemed to share;
In prayer I went to God's great throne, and laid my burdens there.
The sun burst from behind the clouds, in golden splendor set;
I thanked God for her simple words:
  "God's bank ain't busted yet!"

And now I draw rich dividends, more than my hand can hold,
Of faith and love and hope and trust and peace of mind untold.
I thank the Giver of it all, but still I can't forget
My washer woman's simple words:
  "God's bank ain't busted yet."

Oh, weary one upon life's road, when everything seems drear,
And losses loom on every side and skies seem not so clear,
Throw back your shoulders, lift your head, and cease to chafe and fret--
Your dividends will be declared--
  "God's bank ain't busted yet!"
                             -- Author Unknown

### 390. REST IN HIS CARE
*Matthew 6:34*

Help me to place in Thy hands today
  The thing that my heart most fears--
Tomorrow's anguish and bitter pain,
  Tomorrow's sorrow and tears.

Ease Thou my burden, and lighten my load,
  Until only today is left;
Soft comes His voice in the hush of my soul,
  "O broken heart, and bereft.

"My grace is sufficient for thee today;
  Pillow upon My breast
Thy weary head; in My circling arms
  Thou shalt find rest.

"Today I can meet thine every need,
  And today My love can fill
The echoing chambers of thy heart--
  Then rest thee, and be still."

Be still and trust--tomorrow's tears
  May all be wiped away
By God Himself. O grieving heart,
  Thy Lord may come today!
            Martha Snell Nicholson

### 391. THE UNFINISHED PRAYER

"Now I lay me--say it, darling,"
  "Lay me," lisped the tiny lips
Of my daughter, kneeling, bending,
  O'er her folded finger tips.

"Down to sleep." "To s'eep," she murmured;
  And the curly head bent low.
"I pray the Lord," I gently added--
  "You can say it all, I know."

"P'ay de Lord," the words came faintly--
  Fainter still, "my soul to teep."
Then the tired head fairly nodded,
  And my child was fast asleep.

But the dewy eyes half opened
  When I clasped her to my breast,
And the dear voice gently whispered--
  "Mamma, God knows all de yest."

Oh! the trusting, sweet confiding
  Of the child-heart! Would that I
Thus might trust my Heavenly Father,
  He who hears my feeblest cry!
            Thomas H. Ayers

392.    FAITH'S VICTORY

Today, Despair came knocking at my door.
I let her in just for a while.
Her tear-stained face held not one smile,
But when I cried, O Lord, I cannot stand
                             much more,
There came another knocking at my door.
I ran to open it, and there stood Faith
                             outside.
I let her in, and we sat down beside
Despair who quickly said, I must away,
For I have many more to see today.
And as she left, I felt such peace inside.

Today, Despair came knocking at my door,
And for a while I heard her every word.
But when my anguished heart cried, Help
                             me, Lord!
Faith came a-knocking at my door.
Her face serene and wise, brought peace
And caused my wondering why to cease.
Despair can never stay with Faith in sight.
Faith penetrates the gloom with heavenly
                             light.
'Tis true, Despair did come to visit me,
But Faith came too, and brought me victory.

                        Margaret P. Gray


393.    BLESSED BURDENS

It is good to be weary for so we seek rest,
And we find it at last, as we lean on His
                             breast.
It is well to be lonely for then we may prove
That this Saviour can fill every void with
                             His love.

It is good to be weak, so that then we may turn
To the Strong One for help and His mightiness
                             learn.
It is well if we find that the desert is drear,
It is then we are taught that our Home is
                             not here.

It is good when our burdens are heavy to bear
If they send us to Him and drive us to prayer.
Every need is a boon, every sorrow is blest
When it leads us to put His great love to
                             the test.

                        J. Danson Smith


394.    TRUSTING

You ask how you learn to trust Him?
Dear child, you must just let go!

Let go of your frantic worry,
And the fears which plague you so;

Let go of each black tomorrow
Which you try to live today;

Let go of your fevered planning,
He knoweth all your way.

Fear not lest your slipping fingers
Let go of your Saviour too, --

Trusting is only knowing
He'll not let go of **you**!

                        Martha Snell Nicholson


395.    RESTING IN CHRIST

Are you resting in the Saviour?
    Are you trusting in His blood?
Do you shun all human labor
    As a ground of peace with God?
Is the cross of Christ your glory?
    Can you say, "For me He died"?
Is your only song and story
    Jesus Christ, the Crucified?

Then, if such is your condition,
    If to Christ you now belong,
How exalted your position,
    And how glad should be your song!
He has found us, we have found Him;
    Let us magnify His grace,
Till in Heaven we gather round Him,
    And behold Him face to face.

Is the Rock your sure foundation?
    And is Christ your Corner Stone?
Is He all your soul's salvation?
    Do you trust in Him alone?
Can you sing the song of Heaven--
    Of the Lamb that once was slain,
As a guilty one forgiven,
    As a sinner born again?

                        from Words of Peace

396.    MY TRUST

Upon a life I did not live,
    Upon a death I did not die,
Upon Another's life, Another's death,
    I stake my whole eternity.

Not on the tears which I have shed,
    Not on the sorrows I have known,
Another's tears, Another's griefs,
    On them I rest, on them alone.

Not what these hands have done
    Can save the guilty soul;
Not what this toiling flesh has borne
    Can make the spirit whole.

Thy blood alone, Lord Jesus,
    Can cleanse my soul from sin;
Thy Word alone, O Lamb of God,
    Can give me peace within!

                    Author Unknown


397. IF WE COULD SEE BEYOND TODAY

If we could see beyond today
    As God can see,
If all the clouds should roll away,
    The shadows flee;
O'er present griefs we would not fret,
Each sorrow we would soon forget,
For many joys are waiting yet
    For you and me.

If we could know beyond today
    As God doth know,
Why dearest treasures pass away,
    And tears must flow;
And why the darkness leads to light,
Why dreary days will soon grow bright,
Some day life's wrong will be made right,
    Faith tells us so.

If we could see, if we could know
    We often say,
But God in love a veil doth throw
    Across our way.
We cannot see what lies before,
And so we cling to Him the more,
He leads us till this life is o'er,
    Trust and obey.

                    Norman J. Clayton


398.    TRUST

We can trust God, O friends, in any sorrow,
    And in our hours of suffering and pain.
We can have faith that after lengthened
                    darkness
    His hand will light the lamp of hope again.

He understands, He knows, He cares, He
                    loves us,
    And any suffering, any grief that stays
Is somehow for our good and for His glory,
    If we but bear it bravely through the days.

It is not that He lacks the healing power
    To turn at once and bid our anguish cease;
He watches, waits, until we learn its meaning
    Before He gives the blessed boon of peace.

He knows who He can trust with pain and
                    sorrow,
    And we can trust Him for a bright
                    tomorrow.

                    Grace Noll Crowell


399.    RESTING IN HIS PROMISE

All my sins were laid on Jesus;
    On the cross my debt He paid.
Then He cried out, "It is finished!"
    Ere He in the tomb was laid.

Now there is no condemnation;
    Not a blot my record bears.
For my sins the blood all covers,
    Jesus' righteous robe I wear.

I have taken life eternal;
    I am now a son of God.
Of God's nature now partaker,
    Now no fear of judgment's rod.

"I will never leave, forsake thee,"
    None can take me from His hand.
So the Saviour's promise claiming,
    Now I live in Beulah Land.

Resting sweetly in His promise,
    Rest my soul on what He said.
Trusting fully, wholly trusting,
    In the price my Saviour paid.

                    John R. Rice

## 400. HE NEVER FAILETH

*"Jesus Christ the same yesterday,
and to day, and for ever."—Heb.
13:8.*

O thou of little faith,
   God has not failed thee yet;
When all looks dark and gloomy,
   Thou dost so soon forget--
Forget that He has led thee,
   And gently cleared thy way;
On clouds has poured His sunshine,
   And turned thy night to day.
And if He's helped thee hitherto,
   He will not fail thee now;
How it must wound His loving heart
   To see thy anxious brow!
O doubt not any longer,
   To Him commit thy way,
Whom in the past thou trusted,
   And is "the same...to day."

          Selected

## 401. TOO TIRED TO TRUST

"I'm too tired to trust, and too tired to pray!"
Said one as the overtaxed strength gave way;
"The one conscious thought by my mind possessed
Is, oh, could I just drop it all and rest!
But will God forgive me, do you suppose,
If I go to sleep as a baby goes,
Without even asking Him if I may,
Without even trying to trust or pray?"

Will God forgive you?  Why, just think, dear heart,
While language to you was an unknown art,
Did a mother deny you needed rest,
Or refuse to pillow you on her breast?
Oh, no, but she cradled you in her arms,
Then guarded your slumber against alarms;
And how quick was her mother-love to see
The unconscious yearnings awake in thee!

When you've grown too weary to trust or pray,
When overwrought nature has given way,
Then just drop it all, and give up to rest,
As you used to do on a mother's breast.
He knows all about it--the dear Lord knows,
So just go to sleep as a baby goes,
Without even asking Him if you may;
God knows when His child is too tired to pray.

He judges not solely by uttered prayer;
He knows when the yearnings of love are there;
He knows you do pray, He knows you do trust,
And He knows the limits of poor weak dust--
Oh, the wonderful sympathy of Christ
For His chosen one in that midnight tryst,
When He bade them sleep on and take their rest,
While on Him the guilt of the whole world pressed!
You've given your life up to Him to keep?
Then don't be afraid to go right to sleep.

          Anna J. Grannis

### 402. CALM ASSURANCE

Great peace have they, and quiet, calm assurance,
    Who love God's law, and on it daily feed;
They have a strength, a power and an endurance
    Which strangely nerves them in the hour of need.

Deep peace have they whose whole imagination,
    Whose mind and thought on God are constant stayed;
How free they are from fevered agitation,
    And nothing seems to make their soul afraid.

God's peace it is--which passeth understanding--
    Keeps heart and mind where lives are lived in prayer;
And troubles which confront, howe'er commanding,
    Drive not the soul thus kept to dire despair.

And so--in troubled days may this assurance,
    This calm assurance, keep your heart and mine;
We need no power of special, strong endurance,
    Enough--His peace--His wondrous peace divine.

                                J. Danson Smith

### 403. "WE WALK BY FAITH"

Surely the time will come at last
    When I can walk by sight!
So seldom have I clearly seen
    That all God's ways are right;
I've been content, sometimes, to trust
    What waits me round the bend:
'Tis natural I should long to see
    The journey's aim and end.

Suppose, my friend, your lack of sight
    Hides you from greater fears!
For they who trust no Father's love
    Walk lonely through the years.
'Tis surely better in the dark
    To clasp His guiding hand,
Knowing, although you cannot see,
    Your Father has command.

You will not reach the longed-for place
    Where sense out-measures trust,
For we are blinded by our sight--
    Frail children of the dust.
If you but leave the choice to Him
    He will not let you roam,
For He would have you walk by faith
    Throughout the journey Home.

                    C. C. White

### 404. GOD KNOWS

God knows, not I, the devious way
    Wherein my faltering feet must tread,
Before, into the light of day,
    My steps from out this gloom are led;
And since my Lord the path doth see,
    What matter if 'tis hid from me?

God knows, not I, how sweet accord
    Shall grow at length from out this crash
Of earthly discords, which have jarred
    On soul and sense. I hear the clash,
Yet feel and know that on His ear
Breaks harmony, full, deep, and clear.

God knows, not I, why, when I'd fain
    Have walked in pastures green and fair,
The path He pointed me hath lain
    Through rocky deserts, bleak and bare.
I blindly trust, since 'tis His will;
This way lies safety, that way ill.

His perfect plan I cannot grasp;
    Yet I can trust Love infinite,
And with my feeble fingers clasp
    The Hand that leads me to the light.
My soul upon His errand goes;
The end I know not; but God knows.

                    Author Unknown

## 405. "WHY FRET?"

"Why fret thee, soul,
For things beyond thy small control?
But do thy part, and thou shalt see
Heaven will take charge of them and thee.
Sow then thy seed, and wait in peace
The Lord's increase."

Author Unknown

## 406. DON'T WORRY

--Just do your best,
--And leave the rest
--To Him who gave you
--Life, --
--And Zeal and Labor, --
--And the Joy of Strife, --
--And Zest of Love, --
And all that lifts your soul above
The lower things.

Life's truest harvest is in what we would,
And strive our best for
Not most in what we could.
The things we count supreme
Stand, haply, not so high
In God's esteem
As How and Why.

All-seeing Sight
Cleaves through the husk of things,
Right to the Roots and Springs, --
Sees all things whole,
And measures less the body than the soul.
All-righteous Right
Will weigh men's motives,
Not their deeds alone.
End and Beginning unto Him are one;
And would for could shall oft, perchance,
                    atone.

Motives are seeds,
From which at times spring deeds
Not equal to the soul's outreaching hope.
Strive for the stars!
Count nought well done but best!
Then, with brave patience, leave the rest
To Him who knows.
He'll judge you justly ere the record close.

John Oxenham

## 407. WILL HE SLIGHT THY FAINT CRYING?

Sparrow, He guardeth thee;
Never a flight but thy wings He upholdeth;
Never a night but thy rest He enfoldeth;
    Safely He guardeth thee.

Lily, He robeth thee;
Though thou must fade, by the Summer
                    bemoaned,
Thou art arrayed, fair as monarch enthroned,
    Spotless, He robeth thee.

Hear, thou of little faith:
Sparrow and lily are soulless and dying;
Deathless art thou, will He slight thy
                    faint crying?
    Trust, thou of little faith!

Robert Gilbert Welsh

## 408. ENOUGH

I'm tired dear, in mind and heart.
I do not know
What further tasks He has for me
Before I go.

How strange that He should take the strong
And leave the weak
To walk alone, and work; and yet
I do not seek

To know His reasons, for HE knows.
I only pray,
"Show me Thy path, give me Thy strength,
Just for today."

Martha Snell Nicholson

## 409. STRENGTH IN WEAKNESS

I could not do without Thee,
    I cannot stand alone,
I have no strength or goodness,
    No wisdom of my own;
But Thou, beloved Saviour,
    Art all in all to me!
And perfect strength in weakness
    Is theirs who lean on Thee!

F. R. Havergal

## 410. THE FAITH OF LITTLE DAVID

For forty days he challenged,
  The Israel armies defied,
That mighty giant Goliath,
  "Send me a man," he cried.
But none accepts the challenge
  From out God's army then
Till little David came on the scene--
  The least of all of them.

His brothers were so embarrassed,
  They severely taunted him,
But David said, "Is there no cause--
  Why shouldn't I enter in?
I slew a bear, and also a lion
  Not so very long ago;
In the name of the God of Israel
  I'll lay that giant low."

He refused Saul's heavy armor--
  That stripling of a lad.
The name of God was his defense--
  The best that could be had.
So, down to the brook he gathered
  Five stones so smooth and small,
For Goliath had four brothers--
  He prepared to slay all.

He ran to meet the giant
  With heart so brave and strong,
For he had this consolation:
  The battle will not be long.
But Goliath was so insulted:
  "Am I a dog?" said he,
"That you, a stripling of a lad,
  Should come to challenge me."

"I'll give your flesh to the fowls,"
  The mighty giant said.
But David returned the answer,
  "I'll feed them yours instead."
"You come to me," said David
  "With a mighty spear and sword,
But I am coming to you
  In the name of God the Lord."

So saying, he swung his weapon
  And lo the deed was done;
Of stones he had a plenty,
  But he needed only one.
Let's slay these mighty giants
  That challenge us on our way,
For the God who lived in David's time
  Is the God we serve today.

                        Lillie Buffum

## 411.  YET A LITTLE WHILE

"A little while" the darkness and the storm cloud,
  The deepening gloom--the chilly, starless night--
Then the unsullied blaze of Heaven's glory,
  The entering into everlasting light.

"A little while" the sorrow and the heart-pangs,
  The partings from the dear ones that we love--
And then the glad reunions and the greetings,
  The words of welcome in the Home above.

"A little while" to bear reproach and scoffing,
  The curling lip, the scornful look and word--
And then to reign on yonder Throne forever,
  With Him our risen and our glorious Lord.

"A little while" to tell that wondrous story,
  Of matchless love, of free, unbounded grace--
And then these tongues shall only sing His praises
  And worship Him in that most holy place.

"A little while" to walk just simply trusting,
  Knowing whate'er He sends is always best--

And then to learn the reasons "why" and "wherefore,"
Our heads forever pillowed on His breast.

"A little while" and praying days are over,
No wish unfilled, no want unsatisfied--
But every heart just full to overflowing,
With praise to Him who once for sinners died.

"A little while!" O haste that longed-for moment,
When we shall see Thee, Master, face to face,
And sing with rapture through the courts of Heaven,
The wonders of Thy matchless, sovereign grace.

M. E. Rae


### 412.    THIS MOMENT

He's helping me now--this moment,
  Though I may not see it or hear,
Perhaps by a friend far distant,
  Perhaps by a stranger near,
Perhaps by a spoken message,
  Perhaps by the printed word;
In ways that I know and know not,
  I have the help of the Lord.

He's keeping me now--this moment,
  However I need it most,
Perhaps by a single angel,
  Perhaps by a mighty host,
Perhaps by the chain that frets me,
  Or the walls that shut me in;
In ways that I know and know not,
  He keeps me from harm and sin.

He's guiding me now--this moment,
  In pathways easy or hard,
Perhaps by a door wide open,
  Perhaps by a door fast barred,
Perhaps by a joy withholden,
  Perhaps by a gladness given;
In ways that I know and know not,
  He's leading me up to Heaven.

He's using me now--this moment,
  And whether I go or stand,
Perhaps by a plan accomplished,
  Perhaps when He stays my hand,
Perhaps by a word in season,
  Perhaps by a silent prayer;
In ways that I know and know not,
  His labor of love I share.

Annie Johnson Flint


### 413.    FAITH

Someone asked Luther,
  "Do you feel that you have been forgiven?"
He answered, "No, but I'm as sure
  As there's a God in Heaven.

"For feelings come and feelings go,
  And feelings are deceiving.
My warrant is the Word of God--
  Naught else is worth believing.

"Though all my soul should feel condemned,
  For want of some sweet token,
There is One greater in my heart,
  Whose Word cannot be broken.

"I'll stand on His unchanging Word,
  Till soul and body sever,
For though all things shall pass away
  His Word shall stand forever."

Selected

# FRIENDSHIP

### 414.  DID YOU?

Did you give him a lift?  He's a brother of man,
And bearing about all the burden he can.
Did you give him a smile?  He was downcast and blue,
And a smile would have helped him to battle it through.

Did you give him your hand?  He was slipping downhill,
And the world, so I fancied, was using him ill.
Did you give him a word?  Did you show him the road,
Or did you just let him go on with his load?

Did you ask what it was--why the quivering lip?
Why the half suppressed sob, and the scalding tears drip?
Were you a brother of his when the time came of need?
Did you offer to help him, or didn't you heed?

Do you know what it means to be losing the fight?
When a lift just in time might set everything right?
Do you know what it means--just the clasp of a hand?
When a man's borne about all a man ought to stand?

                                        F. B. Gawell

*"A man that hath friends must shew himself
friendly: and there is a friend that sticketh
closer than a brother."--Prov. 18:24.*

### 415.  AROUND THE CORNER

Around the corner I have a friend,
In this great city that has no end;
Yet days go by and weeks rush on,
And before I know it a year has gone,
And I never see my old friend's face;
For life is a swift and terrible race.
He knows I like him just as well,
As in the days when I rang his bell
And he rang mine.  We were younger then;
But now we are busy, tired men--
Tired with playing a foolish game;
Tired with trying to make a name.
"Tomorrow," I say, "I'll call on Jim,
Just to show that I'm thinking of him."
But tomorrow comes--and tomorrow goes,
And the distance between us grows and grows.
Around the corner,--yet miles away.
"Here's a telegram, sir,"--Jim died today!
And that's what we get, and deserve in
              the end--
Around the corner, a vanished friend.

                    Author Unknown

### 416.  MORE THAN GOLD

Lord, make me worthy, this I pray,
Of all the friends along my way;
The old friends, Lord, "The tried and true"
Who can forgive the things I do
   And love me still.

I pray, dear Lord, I may prove just
And worthy of my new friends' trust--
These strangers who have been most kind,
Whose smiles have eased both heart
                    and mind,
   With honest skill.

Recalling this, I am aware
That ever kindly, I must share
My love with friends, the new, the old;
More precious than a kingdom's gold
   Is friendship's thrill.

                              Selected

## 417. THE VILLAGE BLACKSMITH

Under a spreading chestnut-tree
  The village smithy stands;
The smith, a mighty man is he,
  With large and sinewy hands;
And the muscles of his brawny arms
  Are strong as iron bands.

His hair is crisp and black and long;
  His face is like the tan;
His brow is wet with honest sweat--
  He earns whate'er he can.
And looks the whole world in the face,
  For he owes not any man.

Week in, week out, from morn till night,
  You can hear his bellows blow;
You can hear him swing his heavy sledge,
  With measured beat and slow,
Like a sexton ringing the village bell,
  When the evening sun is low.

And children coming home from school,
  Look in at the open door;
They love to see the flaming forge,
  And hear the bellows roar,
And catch the burning sparks that fly
  Like chaff from the threshing-floor.

He goes on Sunday to the church,
  And sits among his boys;
He hears the parson pray and preach;
  He hears his daughter's voice
Singing in the village choir,
  And it makes his heart rejoice.

It sounds to him like her mother's voice,
  Singing in Paradise!
He needs must think of her once more,
  How in the grave she lies;
And with his hard, rough hand he wipes
  A tear out of his eyes.

Toiling, rejoicing, sorrowing,
  Onward through life he goes;
Each morning sees some task begin,
  Each evening sees it close;
Something attempted, something done,
  Has earned a night's repose.

Thanks, thanks to thee, my worthy friend,
  For the lesson thou hast taught!
Thus at the flaming forge of life

Our fortunes must be wrought;
Thus on its sounding anvil shaped
  Each burning deed and thought!

Henry Wadsworth Longfellow


## 418. NO TIME LIKE THE OLD TIME

There is no time like the old time,
  When you and I were young,
When the buds of April blossomed
  And the birds of springtime sung;
The garden's brightest glories
  By summer suns are nursed;
But, oh, the sweet, sweet violets,
  The flowers that opened first!

There is no place like the old place,
  Where you and I were born;
Where we lifted first our eyelids
  On the splendors of the morn;
From the milk-white breast that warmed us,
  From the clinging arms that bore,
Where the dear eyes glistened o'er us,
  That will look on us no more.

There is no friend like the old friend,
  Who has shared our morning days;
No greeting like his welcome,
  No homage like his praise!
Fame is the scentless sunflower,
  With gaudy crown of gold;
But friendship is the breathing rose,
  With sweets in every fold.

There is no love like the old love,
  That we courted in our pride;
Though our leaves are falling, falling,
  And we're fading side by side,
There are blossoms all around us,
  With the colors of our dawn,
And we live in borrowed sunshine
  When the day-star is withdrawn.

There are no times like the old times;
  They shall never be forgot!
There is no place like the old place--
  Keep green the dear old spot!
There are no friends like our old friends,
  May Heaven prolong their lives;
There are no loves like our old loves--
  God bless our loving wives!

Oliver Wendell Holmes

### 419.   THE FRIENDS

I called him John; he called me Jim;
Nigh fifty years that I knowed him
An' he knowed me; an' he was square
An' honest all that time an' fair.
I'd pass him mornin's goin' down
Th' road or drivin' into town,
An' we'd look up th' same old way,
An' wave a hand an' smile, an' say:
 " 'Day, John!"
 " 'Day, Jim!"

I guess you don't real often see
Such kind of friends as him an' me;
Not much on talkin' big; but, say,
Th' kind of friends that stick an' stay.
Come rich, come poor, come rain,
   come shine,
 Whatever he had was mine,
 An' mine was his; an' we both knowed
It when we'd holler on th' road:
 "How, John!"
 "How, Jim!"

An' when I got hailed out one year
He dropped in on me with that queer
Big smile, upon his way to town,
An' laid two hundred dollars down
An' says: "No int'rest, understand:
Or no note!" An' he took my hand
An' squeezed it; an' he drew away
'Cause there wa'n't nothin' more to say:
 "S'long, John!"
 "S'long, Jim!"

An' when John's boy came courtin' Sue,
John smiled, an'--well, I smiled some, too,
As though things was a-comin' out
As if we'd fixed 'em, just about.
An' when Sue blushed an' told me--why,
I set an' chuckled on th' sly;
An' so did John--put out his hand--
No words but these, y' understand:
 "Shake, John!"
 "Shake, Jim!"

An' when Sue's mother died, John come
An' set with me; an' he was dumb
As fur as speech might be concerned;
But in them eyes of his there burned
A light of love an' sympathy
An' friendship you don't often see.
He took my hand in his that day

An' said--what else was there to say?--
 "H'lo, John!"
 "H'lo, Jim!"

Somehow, th' world ain't quite th' same
Today! Tho' trees is all aflame
With autumn, but there's somethin' gone--
Went out of life, I guess, with John.
He nodded that ol' grizzled head
Upon th' piller of his bed,
An' lifted up that helpin' hand
An' whispered: "Some time!--Understand?"
 " 'Bye, John!"
 " 'Bye, Jim!"

James W. Foley

### 420.   THANK GOD FOR YOU

Thank God for you, good friend of mine,
Seldom is friendship such as thine;
How very much I wish to be
As helpful as you've been to me--
 Thank God for you.

When I recall from time to time
How you inspired this heart of mine,
I find myself inclined to pray,
"God bless my friend this very day"--
 Thank God for you.

Of many prayer quests, one thou art
On whom I ask God to impart
Rich blessings from His storehouse rare,
And grant to you His gracious care--
 Thank God for you.

So often at the throne of grace
There comes a picture of your face,
And then instinctively I pray
That God may guide you all the way--
 Thank God for you.

Some day I hope with you to stand
Before the throne at God's right hand,
And say to you at journey's end,
Praise God, you've been to me a friend--
 Thank God for you.

Author Unknown

## 421. DOG'S LOGIC

I haven't any pedigree,
I'm just a common cur;
I can't do tricks like circus dogs,
My life is--loving her.

I sleep outside her door at night,
My nose against the crack.
Sometimes her footsteps come my way.
I sigh when they turn back.

We go for walks, and romp and play.
I carry sticks and stones
To make her laugh, and often I
Bring her my choicest bones.

Sometimes I soil her dainty dress
With my wet, muddy paws,
But I've stopped chasing neighbor's cats,
(The worthless things) because

She cannot bear to have things hurt.
How dreadfully she cried
That time I caught a baby bird,
And bit it, and it died!

I've often heard her say that life
Was learning how to love,
And those who've learned it best will reap
The most rewards above;

And so I hope that when I go
With her up to the gate,
I'll not be left alone outside,
To wait and wait and wait.

For don't you think, since all my life
Is just spent loving her,
They'll let me through the gate although
I'm just a common cur?

Martha Snell Nicholson

## 422. TOGETHER

Come share the road with me, my own,
  Through good and evil weather;
Two better speed than one alone,
  So let us go together.

Come share the road with me, my own,
  And where the black clouds gather
I'll share the load with thee, my son,
  And we'll press on together.

So make we all one company,
  Love's golden cord our tether
And come what may, we'll climb the way
  Together--aye, together.

John Oxenham

## 423. I PRAY FOR YOU

I pray for you and yet I do not frame
  In words the thousand wishes of my heart.
It is a prayer only to speak your name,
  To think of you when we are far apart.
God has not need of words. He hears our love,
  And though my lips are mute I bow my head
And know He leans to listen from above
  And understands the things that are not said.
For love is prayer--and so my prayers for you
  Mount upward unto Him eternally--
They are not many and they are not few.
  All are as one that ever seems to be.
Thus do I pray for you and cannot say
When I begin or when I cease to pray.

Mary Dixon Thayer

## 424. SHOULD YOU FEEL INCLINED TO CENSURE

Should you feel inclined to censure
  Faults you may in others view,
Ask you own heart, ere you venture,
  If that has not failings, too.
Let not friendly vows be broken;
  Rather strive a friend to gain;
Many a word in anger spoken
  Finds its passage home again.

Do not, then, in idle pleasure,
  Trifle with a brother's fame;
Guard it as a valued treasure,
  Sacred as your own good name.
Do not form opinions blindly;
  Hastiness to trouble tends;
Those of whom we thought unkindly,
  Oft become our warmest friends.

Selected

425.     FORGIVENESS

My heart was gall'd with bitter wrong,
   Revengeful feelings fired my blood,
I brooded hate with passion strong,
   While round my couch black demons stood.
Kind Morpheus wooed my eyes in vain,
   My burning brain conceived a plan;
Revenge! I cried, in bitter strain,
   But conscience whispered, "Be a man."

Forgive! a gentle spirit cried,
   I yielded to my nobler part,
Uprose and to my foe I hied,
   Forgave him freely from my heart.
The big tears from their fountain rose,
   He melted, vowed my friend to be,
That night I sank in sweet repose
   And dreamed that angels smiled on me.

                    Anonymous

426.     CO-OPERATION

Two tough old mules--say get this dope--
Were tied together with a piece of rope.
Said one to the other, "You come my way,
While I take a nibble of that new-mown hay."
"I won't," said the other. "You come with me--
I have some hay over this way, you see."
So they got nowhere, just pawed the dirt,
Pulling each way--how that rope did hurt!
Then faced they about, those stubborn mules,
And, said, "We're acting just like human fools.
Let's pull together--I'll go your way,
Then you come with me, and we'll both eat hay."
So they ate their hay, and liked it, too,
And said, "Let's be comrades, good and true."
As the sun went down, they were heard to bray,
"Ah, this is the end of a perfect day!"

                    Author Unknown

427.  THE FRIEND WHO JUST STANDS BY

When trouble comes your soul to try
You love the friend who just stands by.
Perhaps there's nothing he can do;
The thing is strictly up to you,
For there are troubles all your own,
And paths the soul must tread alone;
Times when love can't smooth the road,
Nor friendship lift the heavy load.

But just to feel you have a friend,
Who will stand by until the end;
Whose sympathy through all endures,
Whose warm handclasp is always yours,
It helps somehow to pull you through
Although there's nothing he can do;
And so with fervent heart we cry,
"God bless the friend who just stands by."

                    Selected

428.     A PRAYER

It is my joy in life to find
   At every turning of the road
The strong arm of a comrade kind
   To help me onward with my load.
And since I have not gold to give,
   And love alone must make amends,
My only prayer is, while I live--
   God make me worthy of my friends.

            Frank Dempster Sherman

# HOLY SPIRIT

### 429.    COME, HOLY SPIRIT

Power, mighty pow'r, Jesus promised from on high;
  Power, souls to win, souls to save from sin.
O Thou breath of God, come upon the hearts that cry,
  Witnessing to poor, lost men.

Then came Pentecost and the Holy Ghost was giv'n;
  And they all were filled, all empowered till
Multitudes were saved, turned to Christ and were forgiven;
  We too should be Spirit-filled.

Satan-blinded men must convicted be, awaked!
  More than human pow'r, for God's work this hour.
Unseen pow'rs of Hell shattered till men fear and quake,
  By the Spirit's mighty pow'r.

Naked, fruitless Christians--we toil without God's pow'r.
  Fields are wasting white, waiting for God's might.
O Thou Holy Spirit, come crumble Satan's tower,
  Souls we'll reap before the night.

Thirsty are our hearts, so we wait upon the Lord.
  Earnestly we plead, this our utmost need.
Then with God's anointing we'll carry men the Word,
  Sow abroad the fruitful seed.

Come, Holy Spirit, fill me;
I need Thee, I seek Thee;
Come, Holy Spirit, fill me;
  Lord, fill me with the Holy Ghost.

John R. Rice

### 430.  THE HOLY GHOST IS HERE

The Holy Ghost is here,
  Where saints in prayer agree:
As Jesus' parting gift He's near
  Each pleading company.

Not far away is He,
  To be by prayer brought nigh,
But here in present majesty
  As in His courts on high.

He dwells within our soul,
  An ever-welcome Guest:
He reigns with absolute control
  As monarch in the breast.

Our bodies are His shrine,
  And He the indwelling Lord:
All hail, Thou Comforter Divine,
  Be evermore adored!

Obedient to Thy will,
  We want to feel Thy power,
O Lord of Life, our hopes fulfill,
  And bless this hallowed hour.

C. H. Spurgeon

## 431. COME, HOLY GHOST

Lord God, the Holy Ghost,
  In this accepted hour,
As on the day of Pentecost
  Descend in all Thy power.

We meet with one accord
  In our appointed place,
And wait the promise of our Lord,
  The Spirit of all grace.

Like mighty rushing wind
  Upon the waves beneath,
Move with one impulse every mind,
  One soul, one feeling breathe.

James Montgomery

## 432. BREATHE ON ME, BREATH OF GOD

Breathe on me, Breath of God,
  Fill me with life anew,
That I may love what Thou dost love,
  And do what Thou wouldst do.

Breathe on me, Breath of God,
  Until my heart is pure,
Until with Thee I will one will,
  To do or to endure.

Breathe on me, Breath of God,
  Till I am wholly Thine,
Till all this earthly part of me
  Glows with Thy fire divine.

Breathe on me, Breath of God,
  So shall I never die,
But live with Thee the perfect life
  Of Thine eternity.

Edwin Hatch, 1885

## 433. POWER OF PENTECOST

Pow'r of Pentecost come on us,
  Come, convert and save the lost.
Melt the harden'd hearts of sinners.
  Come, God's Power, at any cost.

Deadened churches, defeated preachers!
  Hearts are cold and zeal is slack!

Holy Ghost of God come on us;
  God of Pentecost, come back!

Vain are nature's gifts and graces;
  Vain our labors, vain our words
If God's Spirit be not on us.
  Saving power is the Lord's.

Satan's power has men blinded,
  Born to darkness, born to sin,
We must free from chains of bondage,
  With God's pow'r must bring them in.

Tired of worldly form and trappings,
  Tired of fruitless labor, lost.
God have pity on Thy people,
  Pour out now Thy Holy Ghost!

We would tarry for enduement;
  We would pray with one accord.
Help us thirst for Thine outpouring,
  Make us bold to speak Thy Word.

Holy Spirit, O God the Spirit,
  Breathe upon a life so fruitless,
Fill this vessel frail and useless.
  Oh, empower all my witness.
Holy Spirit, breathe upon me!

John R. Rice

*"And be not drunk with wine, wherein is excess; but be filled with the Spirit."--Eph. 5:18.*

## 434. EYES, EARS AND HEART

Anoint mine eyes,
  O Holy Dove!
That I may prize
  This Book of love.

Unstop mine ears
  Made deaf by sin,
That I may hear
  Thy voice within.

Break my hard heart,
  Jesus, my Lord;
In the inmost part
  Hide thy sweet Word.

Robert M'Cheyne

### 435. COME, HOLY SPIRIT, HEAVENLY DOVE

Come, Holy Spirit, heavenly Dove,
    With all Thy quick'ning powers;
Kindle a flame of sacred love
    In these cold hearts of ours.

Look, how we grovel here below,
    Fond of these trifling toys:
Our souls can neither fly nor go
    To reach eternal joys.

In vain we tune our formal songs,
    In vain we strive to rise:
Hosannas languish on our tongues,
    And our devotion dies.

Dear Lord, and shall we ever live
    At this poor, dying rate?
Our love so faint, so cold, to Thee,
    And Thine to us so great?

Come, Holy Spirit, heavenly Dove,
    With all Thy quick'ning powers;
Come, shed abroad a Saviour's love,
    And that shall kindle ours.

Isaac Watts, 1707

# THE HOME

436.  JUST TO BE NEEDED

"She always seems so tied" is what friends say;
She never has a chance to get away.
Home, husband, children, duties great and small,
Keep her forever at their beck and call.
But she confides, with laughter in her eyes,
She never yet felt fretted by these ties.
"Just to be needed is more sweet," says she,
"Than any freedom in this world could be."

Mary Eversley

## 437. I REMEMBER, I REMEMBER

I remember, I remember
  The house where I was born,
The little window where the sun
  Came peeping in at morn.
He never came a wink too soon,
  Nor brought too long a day;
But now I often wish the night
  Had borne my breath away!

I remember, I remember
  The roses, red and white,
The violets and the lily-cups--
  Those flowers made of light!
The lilacs where the robin built,
  And where my brother set
The laburnum on his birthday--
  The tree is living yet!

I remember, I remember
  Where I was used to swing,
And thought the air must rush as fresh
  To swallows on the wing;
My spirit flew in feathers then
  That is so heavy now,
And summer pools could hardly cool
  The fever on my brow.

I remember, I remember
  The fir-trees dark and high;
I used to think their slender tops
  Were close against the sky.
It was a childish ignorance,
  But now 'tis little joy
To know I'm farther off from Heaven
  Than when I was a boy.

Thomas Hood

## 438.  A PRAYER FOR MOTHER

Lord Jesus, Thou hast known
  A mother's love and tender care;
And Thou wilt hear while, for my own
  Mother dear, I make this morning prayer.

Protect her life, I pray,
  Who gave the gift of life to me;
And may she know from day to day
  The deepening glow of joy that comes from Thee.

As once upon her breast,
  Fearless and well content, I lay
So let her heart on Thee at rest,
  Feel fears depart and troubles fade away.

Ah, hold her by the hand,
  As once her hand held mine,
And though she may not understand
  Life's winding way, lead her in peace divine.

I cannot pay my debt
  For all the love that she has given;
But Thou, love's Lord, will not forget
  Her due reward--bless her in earth and heaven.

Henry van Dyke

### 439. A WORTHY WOMAN

A worthy woman who can find?
For her price is far above rubies.

The heart of her husband trusteth in her,
And he shall have no lack of gain.

She doeth him good and not evil
All the days of her life.

She seeketh wool and flax,
And worketh willingly with her hands.

She is like the merchant-ships;
She bringeth her bread from afar.

She riseth also while it is yet night,
And giveth food to her household,
And their task to her maidens.

She considereth a field, and buyeth it;
With the fruit of her hands she planteth
a vineyard.

She girdeth her loins with strength,
And maketh strong her arms.

She perceiveth that her merchandise is
profitable:
Her lamp goeth not out by night.

She layeth her hands to the distaff,
And her hands hold the spindle.

She stretcheth out her hand to the poor;
Yea, she reacheth forth her hands to
the needy.

She is not afraid of the snow for her
household:
For all her household are clothed with
scarlet.

She maketh for herself carpets of tapestry;
Her clothing is fine linen and purple.

Her husband is known in the gates,
When he sitteth among the elders of the land.

She maketh linen garments and selleth them,
And delivereth girdles unto the merchant.

Strength and dignity are her clothing;
And she laugheth at the time to come.

She openeth her mouth with wisdom;
And the law of kindness is on her tongue.

She looketh well to the ways of her household,
And eateth not the bread of idleness.

Her children rise up, and call her blessed;
Her husband also, and he praiseth her,
saying:

Many daughters have done worthily,
But thou excellest them all.

Grace is deceitful, and beauty is vain;
But a woman that feareth Jehovah, she shall
be praised.

Give her of the fruit of her hands;
And let her works praise her in the gates.

Proverbs 31:10-31, A.R.V.

### 440. WHEN YOU AND I WERE YOUNG

I wandered today to the hill, Maggie,
To watch the scene below;
The creek and the creaking old mill,
Maggie, as we used to long ago.
The green grove is gone from the hill,
Maggie, where first the daisies sprung;
The creaking old mill is still, Maggie,
Since you and I were young.

A city so silent and lone, Maggie,
Where the young and the gay and the best,
In polished white mansions of stone,
Maggie, have each found a place of rest,
Is built where the birds used to play, Maggie,
And join in the songs that were sung:
For we sang as gay as they, Maggie,
When you and I were young.

They say I am feeble with age, Maggie,
My steps are less sprightly than then,
My face is a well-written page,
Maggie, but time alone was the pen.
They say we are aged and gray, Maggie,
As sprays by the white breakers flung;
But to me you're as fair as you were, Maggie,
When you and I were young.

Geo. W. Johnson

## 441. THE EVENING PRAYER

All day the children's busy feet
  Had pattered to and fro;
And all the day their little hands
  Had been in mischief so,

That oft my patience had been tried;
  But tender, loving care
Had kept them through the day from harm,
  And safe from ev'ry snare.

But when the eventide had come,
  The children went upstairs,
And knelt beside their little beds,
  To say their wonted prayers.

With folded hands and rev'rent mien
  "Our Father," first they say,
Then, "Now I lay me down to sleep,"
  With childlike faith they pray.

With cheeks upon the pillow pressed,
  They give a kiss, and say,
"Good night; we love you, dear Mamma,
  You've been so kind today."

"Dood night; I love oo, too, Mamma,"
  And baby's eyelids close;
And tired feet and restless hands
  Enjoy the sweet repose.

The trouble and the weariness
  To me indeed seemed light,
Since love had thus my efforts crowned
  To guide their steps aright.

And as I picked the playthings up,
  And put the books away,
My heart gave grateful thanks to God,
  For His kind care all day.

                Author Unknown

## 442. THE BABY

Another little wave
  Upon the sea of life;
Another soul to save,
  Amid its toils and strife.

Two more little feet
  To walk the dusty road;
To choose where two paths meet--
  The narrow, or the broad.

Two more little hands
  To work for good or ill;
Two more little eyes,
  Another little will.

Another heart to love,
  Receiving love again;
And so the baby came,
  A thing of joy and pain.

                Anonymous

## 443. MY LITTLE WIFE

Our table is spread for two, tonight--
  No guests our bounty share;
The damask cloth is snowy white,
The services elegant and bright,
  Our china quaint and rare;
    My little wife presides,
    And perfect love abides.

The bread is sponge, the butter gold,
  The muffins nice and hot,
What though the winds without blow cold?
The walls a little world unfold,
  And the storm is soon forgot,
    In the fire-light's cheerful glow,
    Beams a paradise below.

A fairer picture who has seen?
  Soft lights and shadows blend;
The central figure of the scene,
She sits, my wife, my queen--
  Her head a little bent;
    And in her eyes of blue
    I read my bliss anew.

I watch her as she pours the tea,
  With quiet, gentle grace;
With fingers deft, and movements free,
She mixes in the cream for me,
  A bright smile on her face;
    And, as she sends it up,
    I pledge her in my cup.

Was ever man before so blest?
  I secretly reflect,
The passing thought she must have guessed,
For now dear lips on mine are pressed,
  An arm is round my neck.
    Dear treasure of my life--
    God bless her--little wife!

                Anonymous

### 444. FRUSTRATION

I wanted me a kitty, a pretty, yellow kitty,
   A fluffy, little kitty, that I could call my own.
And so I got a kitty, the cutest little kitty;
   I loved that little kitty, and made her all my own.
      She scratched me.

I wanted me a puppy, a shaggy, golden puppy,
   A frisky little puppy, to be my very own;
And so I got a puppy, the cutest little puppy,
   I loved that little puppy, and made him all my own.
      He bit me.

I wanted me a girlie, a pretty little girlie,
   A lovely, cuddly girlie, that I could call my own;
And so I got a girlie, a darling little girlie;
   I loved that little girlie, and made her all my own.
      She nagged me.

I wanted me a baby, a cuddly, little baby,
   A dimpled little baby, that I could call my own;
And so I got a baby, a cuddly, dimpled baby,
   A pretty little baby; he is my very own.
      He squalls all night.

I want to be a hermit, a lonely, bachelor hermit,
   A 'living on a mountain, all by myself alone.
But if I were a hermit, without a cat that scratches,
   Without a dog to bite me, without a wife to nag me,
Without a squalling baby, a 'living on a mountain, all by myself alone.
      Who'd love me?

               L. O. Engelmann

### 445. A BOY'S OPINION OF GRANDMOTHERS

Grandmas are awful nice folks--
   They beat all the aunts you can find:
They whisper quite softly to mammas
   To "let the boys have a good time!"

I'm sure I can't see it at all
   What ever a fellow would do
For apples and pennies and candy
   Without a grandma or two.

Grandmas have muffins for tea,
   And pies--a whole row--in the cellar,
And are apt, if they know it in time,
   To make chicken pie for a "feller."

And if he is bad now and then
   And makes a great racketing noise,

They only look over their specs
   And say, "Oh, boys will be boys!"

Quite often, as twilight comes on,
   Grandmas sing hymns very low
To themselves, as they rock by the fire,
   About Heaven, and when they shall go.

And then a boy, stopping to think,
   Will find a hot tear in his eye
To know what will come at the last--
   For grandmothers all have to die.

I wish they could stay here and pray,
   For a boy needs their prayers every night,
Some boys more than others, I s'pose,
   Such as I, need a wonderful sight.

               Author Unknown

### 446. WE'LL NEVER SAY GOODBYE

We say goodbye in parting
  With loved ones here below;
We always hope to meet again,
  As on our way we go.
But oft our hearts are grieving
  For those we never meet.
We'll say goodbye in sorrow
  Till we meet at Jesus' feet.

Our children leave the home nest
  For school or wedding bells;
Or country's call or mission field
  May take them far as well.
Now wedding bells are happy,
  And God's way always right.
And absent ones, we'll greet them
  In the City always bright.

We greet and part with dear ones;
  We say hello, goodbye;

And letters bind our fellowship;
  We miss them, though we try
To feel them always near us,
  And follow them with prayer.
But parting days are ended
  When we meet them in the air.

Oh happy, glad home-coming
  With Jesus in the sky:
For sometimes He seems far away,
  Though always if we try,
We find Him near to help us,
  His Spirit dwells within.
But only perfect union
  When we Heaven enter in.

We'll never say goodbye in Glory,
In the morning, over yonder;
We'll never say goodbye in Glory;
We'll never say goodbye up there.

John R. Rice

### 447. LEFT ALONE

It's the lonesomest house you ever saw,
  This big gray house where I stay;
I don't call it livin' at all, at all,
  Since my mother went away.

Four long weeks ago, an' it seems a year,
  "Gone home," so the preacher said,
An' I ache in my breast with wantin' her,
  An' my eyes are always red.

I stay out of doors till I'm almost froze,
  'Cause every corner and room
Seems empty enough to frighten a boy,
  And filled to the door with gloom.

I hate them to call me in to my meals,
  Sometimes I think I can't bear
To swallow a mouthful of anything,
  And see her not sittin' up there;

A-pourin' the tea an' passin' the things,
  An' laughin' to see me take
Two big lumps of sugar instead of one
  An' more than my share of cake.

"I'm 'most too big to be kissed," I used
    to say,
  But somehow I don't feel right

Crawlin' into bed as still as a mouse,
  Nobody saying "good-night";

An' tuckin' the clothes up under my chin,
  An' pushin' my hair back so--
Things a boy makes fun of before his chums,
  But things that he likes, you know.

There's no one to go to when things go wrong,
  She was always so safe and sure.
Why, not a trouble could tackle a boy
  That she couldn't up and cure!

There are lots of women, it seems to me,
  That wouldn't be missed so much--
Women whose boys are about all grown up,
  And old maid aunties, and such.

I can't make out for the life of me
  Why she should have to go,
An' her boy left here in this old gray house,
  A-needin' and wantin' her so.

I tell you, the lonesomest thing
  In this great big world today
Is a boy of ten whose heart is broke
  'Cause his mother is gone away.

Author Unknown

448.    MY MOTHER

Who fed me from her gentle breast
And hushed me in her arms to rest,
And on my cheek sweet kisses prest?
        My mother.

When sleep forsook my open eye,
Who was it sang sweet lullaby,
And rocked me that I should not cry?
        My mother.

Who sat and watched my infant head,
When sleeping on my cradle bed,
And tears of sweet affection shed?
        My mother.

When pain and sickness made me cry,
Who gazed upon my heavy eye,
And wept for fear that I should die?
        My mother.

Who dressed my doll in clothes so gay,
And taught me pretty how to play,
And minded all I had to say?
        My mother.

Who ran to help me when I fell,
And would some pretty story tell,
Or kiss the place to make it well?
        My mother.

Who taught my infant lips to pray,
To love God's holy Word and day,
And walk in wisdom's pleasant way?
        My mother.

And can I ever cease to be
Affectionate and kind to thee
Who wast so very kind to me--
        My mother.

Oh no, the thought I cannot bear;
And if God please my life to spare,
I hope I shall reward thy care,
        My mother.

When thou art feeble, old and gray,
My healthy arm shall be thy stay,
And I will soothe thy pains away,
        My mother.

And when I see thee hang thy head,
'Twill be my turn to watch thy bed,

And tears of sweet affection shed--
        My mother.

For God, who lives above the skies,
Would look with vengeance in His eyes
If I should ever dare despise
        My mother.
                            Jane Taylor


449.   "WRITE THEM A LETTER TONIGHT"

Don't go to the theatre, concert, or ball,
    But stay in your room tonight;
Deny yourself to the friends that call,
    And a good long letter write--
Write to the sad old folks at home,
    Who sit when the day is done,
With folded hands and downcast eyes,
    And think of the absent one.

Don't selfishly scribble "excuse my haste,
    I've scarcely the time to write,"
Lest their brooding thoughts go wandering
                        back
    To many a bygone night--
When they lost their needed sleep and rest,
    And every breath was a prayer--
That God would leave their delicate babe
    To their tender love and care.

Don't let them feel that you've no more need
    Of their love or counsel wise;
For the heart grows strongly sensitive
    When age has dimmed the eyes--
It might be well to let them believe
    You never forget them, quite;
That you deem it a pleasure, when far away,
    Long letters home to write.

Don't think that the young and giddy friends,
    Who make your pastime gay,
Have half the anxious thought for you
    That the old folks have today.
The duty of writing do not put off;
    Let sleep or pleasure wait,
Lest the letter for which they looked
                    and longed
    Be a day or an hour too late.

For the loving, sad old folks at home,
    With locks fast turning white,
Are longing to hear from the absent one--
    Write them a letter tonight.
                            Anonymous

## 450. WE LOVE OUR CHILDREN

We love our children when they're good,
  But when they're bad, in trouble,
For reasons barely understood
  We love them almost double.

We love our children when they want
  Affection and expect it,
And even more, those times they taunt
  Our loving and reject it.

We love them when they make us cry
  And when you'd think we daren't,
And no one knows the reason why,
  Except another parent.

Richard Armour


## 451. LITTLE BOY BLUE

The little toy dog is covered with dust,
  But sturdy and staunch he stands,
And the little tin soldier is red with rust,
  And his musket molds in his hands.

Time was when the little toy dog was new,
  And the soldier was passing fair;
And that was the time when our Little
          Boy Blue
Kissed them and put them there.

"Now don't you go till I come," he said,
  "And don't you make any noise!"
So, toddling off to his trundle bed,
  He dreamed of the pretty toys.

And as he was dreaming an angel song
  Wakened our Little Boy Blue--
Oh, the years are many, the years are long,
  But the little toy friends are true!

Aye, faithful to Little Boy Blue they stand
  Each in the same old place,
Awaiting the touch of a little hand,
  The smile of a little face.

And they wonder--as waiting these long
          years through
In the dust of their little chair--
What has become of our Little Boy Blue
  Since he kissed them and put them there.

Eugene Field


## 452. OLD GOLD MUD PIES

Down in the little back garden,
  Under a sunny sky,
We made mud pies together--
  My little sweetheart and I.
Stained was the little pink apron,
  Muddy the jacket blue,
As we stirred and mixed and tasted
  Out in the sun and dew.

Why do I dream of that garden,
  I who am old and wise?
Why am I longing, longing,
  For one of those old mud pies?
Oh, for the little pink apron!
  Oh, for the jacket blue!--
For the blessed faith of childhood
  When make-believes are true.

Author Unknown


## 453. THE DEAREST SPOT
OF EARTH IS HOME

The dearest spot of earth to me
  Is home, sweet home!
The fairy land I long to see
  Is home, sweet home!
There, how charmed the sense of hearing!
There, where love is so endearing!
All the world is not so cheering
  As home, sweet home!

        The dearest spot of earth to me
          Is home, sweet home!
        The fairy land I long to see
          Is home, sweet home!

I've taught my heart the way to prize
  My home, sweet home!
I've learned to look with lovers' eyes
  On home, sweet home!
There, where vows are truly plighted!
There, where hearts are so united!
All the world besides I've slighted
  For home, sweet home!

        The dearest spot of earth to me
          Is home, sweet home!
        The fairy land I long to see
          Is home, sweet home!

W. T. Wrighton

## 454. NOBODY KNOWS BUT MOTHER

They talk of a mother's toil and care,
 Of the tasks that her hands must do,
Of the furrows that creep o'er the brow once fair,
 Of the burdens and heartaches too.
But they know not the joy stitched in each little dress,
 The pattering footsteps that brighten and bless,
The thrill of a baby's loving caress--
 Ah, nobody knows but Mother.

They talk of her narrow and humble place,
 The monotonous life she leads,
While others are learning and growing apace,
 And doing such wonderful deeds.
But they know not the mystery deep that lies,
 Hidden away in a baby's eyes,
And every day brings a fresh surprise,
 That nobody sees but Mother.

There was never a task by the Father given,
 That brought not its blessing too,
And the life that liest the nearest Heaven,
 Was given, oh, Mother, to you.
The task is great, but the joy is sweet,
 The hours of prayer bring a faith complete,
And the highest wisdom our life can meet,
 Lies hid in the heart of a Mother.  --The Fireside

## 455. TWO LITTLE PAIRS OF BOOTS

Two little pairs of boots tonight,
 Before the fire are drying,
Two little pairs of tired feet
 In a trundle bed are lying;
The tracks they left upon the floor
 Make me feel much like sighing.

Those little boots with copper toes!
 They run the lifelong day,
And oftentimes I almost wish
 That they were miles away,
So tired am I to hear so oft
 Their heavy tramp at play.

They walked about the new-ploughed ground,
 Where mud in plenty lies;
They rolled it up in marbles round,
 And baked it into pies,
And then at night upon the floor,
 In every shape it dries.

Today I was disposed to scold,
 But when I see tonight,
These little boots before the fire,

With copper toes so bright,
I think how sad my heart would be
 To put them out of sight.

For in a trunk upstairs I've laid
 Two socks of white and blue;
If called to put those boots away,
 O God, what should I do?
I mourn that there are not tonight
 Three pairs, instead of two.

I mourn because I thought how nice
 My neighbor 'cross the way
Could keep her carpets all the year
 From getting worn and gray;
Yet well I know she'd smile to own
 Some little boots today.

We mothers weary get and worn,
 Over our load of care;
But how we speak of little ones,
 Let each of us beware;
For what would our fireside be at night
 If no little boots were there?

       R. T. Cross

### 456. MOTHER, ROCK ME TO SLEEP

Backward, turn backward, O Time, in your flight,
Make me a child again just for tonight!
Mother, come back from the echoless shore,
Take me again to your heart as of yore;
Kiss from my forehead the furrows of care,
Smooth the few silver threads out of my hair.
Over my slumbers your loving watch keep;
Rock me to sleep, Mother,--rock me to sleep.

Backward, flow backward, O Tide of the years;
I am so weary of toil and of tears,
Toil without recompense, tears all in vain,
Take them, and give me my childhood again;
I have grown weary of dust and decay,
Weary of flinging my soul-wealth away;
Weary of sowing for others to reap,
Rock me to sleep, Mother,--rock me to sleep.

Tired of the hollow, the base, the untrue,
Mother, oh Mother, my heart calls for you!
Many a summer the grass has grown green,
Blossomed and faded, our faces between.
Yet, with strong yearning and passionate pain,
Long I tonight for your presence again,
Come from the silence so long and so deep;
Rock me to sleep, Mother,--rock me to sleep.

Over my heart, in the days that are flown,
No love like mother-love ever has shone;
No other worship abides and endures,
Faithful, unselfish, and patient like yours;
None like a mother can charm away pain,
From the sick soul and the world-weary brain.
Slumber's soft calms o'er my heavy lids creep,
Rock me to sleep, Mother,--rock me to sleep.

Come let your brown hair, just lighted with gold,
Fall on your shoulders again as of old;
Let it drop over my forehead tonight,
Shading my faint eyes away from the light;
For with its sunny-edged shadows once more
Happily will throng the sweet vision of yore;
Lovingly, softly, its bright billows sweep;
Rock me to sleep, Mother,--rock me to sleep.

Mother, dear Mother, the years have been long
Since I last listened to your lullaby song;
Sing, then, and unto my soul it shall seem
Womanhood's years have been only a dream,
Clasped to your heart in a loving embrace
With your light lashes just sweeping my face,
Never hereafter to wake or to weep;
Rock me to sleep, Mother,--rock me to sleep.

                                        Elizabeth Akers Allen

457.                    MOTHERHOOD

## Two Sides of the Question

The One Side                                    The Other Side

It's such a waste of time to cook,
I'm just a walking cookery book,
I make and bake the morning through
The favorite pies and pudding, too.
And then, in half an hour, or less
My toil has gone to nothingness.
It's waste of time to dust the stairs,
To clean the brass, and polish chairs,
To sweep, and pick up bits of fluff,
For nothing's ever clean enough.
Five minutes after I have done,
Someone is sure to romp and run,
Kick out the stair-rods, flick the mats,
And slam the doors and scare the cats.
Some sticky hand is sure to press
The brasses from their sprightliness.
I tidy up, and do the dusting,
But all the while, my wings are rusting.
Then, washing day, it seems to me
Is just a waste of energy.
What use to stand before a tub
And soak and rinse, and blue and rub?
Next week the self-same garment's stain
Will come into my hands again.
It's such a waste of time to mend,
One has no sooner reached the end
Of last week's pile, then--need you ask it?
This week's fills up the mending basket.
The stockings which were hale and hearty
Return from each picnicking party
Weak and worn and wanly show
Great gaping holes in heel and toe,
While buttons have a cantankerous way
Of disappearing every day.
Sponging off the spots and ironing creases
Between it all I'm worn to pieces.
Woman, from cradle to grave
Is nothing but a galley slave.

I've done an angel's work today!
Yes, such an honor came my way.
Real angel's work! And, lest you doubt it,
I'm going to tell you all about it.
Well, first, I cooked. It was so nice
To plan the pies, stewed fruit, and rice.
God sent His angel once to make
Cakes for a poor wayfarer's sake.
But, just today He honored me,
And sent the task my way, you see.
Then, while I tidied up the place,
Gave every knob a radiant face
Back of my mind this thought would lurk,
That I was still at angel's work.
Putting away coats and dresses,
And moving small unsightlinesses.
For, oh! 'tis such a lovesome thing,
Just straightening out, and freshening.
And after that I washed a few
Small woolly garments, old, not new,
Things I had rubbed and rinsed before
Quite forty times, or even more.
And as I hung them on the line
I thought what God-like work was mine!
To cleanse--ah, me!--to wash out stains
Till not a single speck remains.
So, later in the day 'twas sweet
To sit and rest my tired feet
Mending the clothes, and plan out, too,
How to make old things into new.
For surely 'tis an angel's way
To put things right from day to day,
To find thin places, and repair
The glad rags and the sturdy wear.
Since wear and tear must surely be
On this side of Eternity,
I'm feeling very proud to say
I've done an angel's work today!

Author Unknown

458.      HOME

I turned an ancient poet's book,
  And found upon the page,
"Stone walls do not a prison make,
  Or iron bars a cage."
Yes, that is true, and something more
  You will find where'er you roam...

That marble floors and gilded walls
  Can never make a home.
But everywhere that love abides,
  And friendship is a guest,
Is surely home, and home, sweet home,
  For there the soul can rest.

Henry van Dyke

### 459. PARENTS OF TODAY

Oh, parents; have you stopped to think
  You hold a sacred place?
That child of yours; will he thank God
  You told him of God's grace?
Or will the future have to be,
  Where is my child today?
Because you had no thought of God,
  You lived for self your way.

You did not do things very bad,
  You had no time to pray.
You do have time for worldly things
  But none for God today.
You lead your child the way you go,
  For self at any cost;
Then find out when it is too late
  Your child and you are lost.

How comforting it is to know
  You taught your child to pray,
To read the blessed Word of God
  And live for God each day.

By word and life to love God's house
  For worship, prayer and praise,
Until you meet with all the saved
  For everlasting days.

How wonderful to fellowship
  With Christ the risen Lord,
With all the family saved by grace
  Rejoicing in God's Word.
For Mother sang each child to sleep
  With hymns of love and grace.
With joy they wait for Christ's return
  To meet Him face to face.

The man who has a Christian wife
  Has found a treasure rare,
A mother for his childrens' good
  Who nurtures them with prayer.
So Mother, if you know the Lord
  Live close to Him each day.
In every problem that you face
  Let Jesus lead the way.

                              Edward L. Crane


### 460. A HOUSE OR A HOME

The walls of a house may be builded of wood,
  Its foundations of brick or of stone;
But a genuine home is an exquisite thing
  For its builded of heartthrobs alone.

The price of a house may be reckoned at once,
  And paid with a handful of gold;
But the price of a home very few can compute,
  And that price they have never yet told.

The rooms of a house may be stately and grand,
  Their adornment a triumph of art;
But beauty of home is the final result
  Of the toil of an unselfish heart.

A house may be burned, may be sold or exchanged,
  Nor the loss of one's peace interfere;
But the loss of a home--how it crushes the heart!
  For our homes we all love and revere.

Of houses a man may possess many scores,
  Yet his poverty lead to despair;
But an honorable man, in a home of his own,
  Must be counted a true millionaire.

                        J. H. Sykes

## 461. LITTLE HATTIE'S CHAIR

The day that little Hattie died
  The house seemed strange and queer;
The furniture looked different,
  And everything was drear;
We children all would huddle close
  Upon the steps and try
To think of Heaven where she was,
  And then we all would cry.

Then Bobbie sneaked off by himself,
  And we hunted everywhere
Till Father found him in the yard
  In little Hattie's chair;
He was hid behind the lilac bush
  Where she would often play,
And his face was streaked with tears
  And he called, "Oh, keep away."

But Father kissed him on the head
  And lifted chair and all
And carried him into the house
  And on up through the hall;
Until he reached the attic door,
  And we kept following, too,
Because we wondered what it was
  That he was going to do.

He got a hammer and a nail
  And drove it 'way up high,
And said, "Now, children, you may kiss
  The little chair good-bye;
But you must never take it down
  And never sit on it"--
And there stood Mother, watching us--
  And we all cried a bit.

One Saturday when Bobbie was
  A-tracking to its lair,
A wild beast of the forest,
  He climbed the attic stair--
Quite softly in his stocking feet
  And peeped in through the door,
And there by little Hattie's chair
  Knelt Mother on the floor.

"O Jesus, spare the others--
  And make them pure and good,
Help me to train them carefully
  As a Christian mother should";
Then Bobbie tiptoed down the stairs
  And told us what he'd heard,
And we looked at one another
  But didn't speak a word.

That evening after Father came,
  And we got the songbooks out,
And took our turn in reading
  A Bible verse about;
He said he'd heard that we had been
  So very good all day,
But no one told him 'twas because
  Bobbie heard Mother pray.

Grace W. Haight

## 462. HIS NEW BROTHER

Say, I've got a little brother,
Never teased to have him, nother,
  But he's here;
They just went ahead and bought him,
And last week the doctor brought him;
  Wa'nt that queer?

When I heard the news from Molly,
Why! I thought at first 'twas jolly,
  'Cause, you see:
I s'posed I could go and get him,
An' then Mamma 'course she would let him
  Play with me.

But when I had once looked at him,
"Why," I says, "my sakes! is that him?
  Just that mite?"
They said, "Yes," and "ain't he cunnin'?"
  He's a sight.

He's so small, it's just amazin',
And you'd think that he was blazin',
  He's so red.
And his nose is like a berry,
And he's bald as Uncle Jerry
  On the head.

Why, he isn't worth a dollar;
All he does is cry and holler
  More and more;
Won't sit up, you can't arrange him;
I don't see why Pa don't change him
  At the store.

Now we've got to dress and feed him,
And we really didn't need him
  More'n a frog;
Why'd they buy a baby brother
When they know I'd good deal ruther
  Have a dog?

Author Unknown

## 463.   WITH DAD

Quite a long time ago I remember,
  Although just a towheaded lad,
That no matter where father was going
  I tagged right along with Dad.

I was never too busy with playthings
  Or games with the girls and the boys,
For when I'd see Dad starting somewhere,
  I'd forsake my companions and toys.

When I'd bounce out of bed in the morning
  And notice that maybe I had
Slept too late, I would do without breakfast
  Before I'd miss going with Dad.

And then late at night, although sleepy
  And tired, it would make my heart glad,
If he'd go to town on some pretext,
  And I could go out with my dad.

When it rained, and the street was a river,
  Then nothing could make me so sad
As the sight of him going without me;
  Oh, how lonely I felt without Dad.

Years have passed, and time brought its changes;
  With some of them good and some bad.
But there's one thing that time never altered--
  My ambition to travel with Dad.

Once again, a dark storm brought a river,
  And left my heart vacant and sad.
For he went on without me--but someday
  Again I'll be walking with Dad.

                    Herbert Buffum, Jr.

## 465.  NO BABY IN THE HOUSE

No baby in the house, I know,
  'Tis far too nice and clean.
No toys, by careless fingers strewn,
  Upon the floors are seen.
No finger-marks are on the panes,
  No scratches on the chairs;
No wooden men set up in rows,
  Or marshalled off in pairs;
No little stockings to be darned,
  All ragged at the toes;
No pile of mending to be done,
  Made up of baby-clothes;
No little troubles to be soothed;

## 464.   FORGOTTEN

A red carnation, did you say,
You wore upon last Mother's Day?
  And then forgot she was alone.
You never thought, perhaps, my dear,
That she'd be gone another year
  To her beloved eternal Home.

Of course you never meant to be
Quite so thoughtless of her, see;
  From day to day you'd just forget
A message might be sent some day
That Mother had just slipped away.
  Then comes the feeling of regret.

The letters that you did not write
She looked and longed for day and night--
  Just a message from her boy;
The things you could have done and said
To soothe her aching heart and head,
  And fill her soul with peace and joy.

It seems we ne'er appreciate
Until it really is too late
  The very dearest things on earth.
And who could love you more, my son,
Than your dear mother--she's the one--
  The one she is who gave you birth.

On Father's Day 'tis just as true
For Daddy--he's forgotten too;
  So busy with so many things--
No obligations, now, it seems
He's scarcely ever in their dreams.
  Neglect will bring a thousand stings.

So--don't neglect them while they're here
But try to fill their hearts with cheer;
  I'm very sure you'll not be sad.
When you wear the white carnation
You'll have no cause for condemnation;
  You always tried to make them glad.

                    Lillie Buffum

  No little hands to fold;
No grimy fingers to be washed;
  No stories to be told;
No tender kisses to be given;
  No nicknames, "Dove" and "Mouse;"
No merry frolics after tea--
  No baby in the house!

                    Clara G. Dolliver

## 466. DEDICATED

*"And when she could not longer hide him, she took for him an ark of bul-
rushes, and daubed it with slime and with pitch, and put the child therein;
and she laid it in the flags by the river's brink."*—Exod. 2:3.

To the river Nile to save her son
Hidden 'mongst reeds and rushes came one...
A praying mother of long ago...
Breath of God, on the rushes blow!

Faithful mothers with basket beds
Today send their children, prayer led,
Into this world of sin and woe,
Breath of God, on the rushes blow!

From my breast to the breast of the river of life
Goes my son...life of my life!
Pray I with the mother of Moses...Oh,
Breath of God, on the rushes blow!

Margaret Wendel

## 467. ONLY A DAD

Only a dad, with a tired face
Coming home from the daily race,
Bringing little of gold or fame,
To show how well he has played the game,
But great in his heart that his own rejoice
To see him coming, and to hear his voice.

Only a dad, with a brood of four,
One of ten million men or more,
Plodding along in the daily strife,
Bearing the whips and the scorns of life,
With never a whimper of pain or hate
For the sake of those who at home await.

Only a dad, neither rich nor proud,
Merely one of the searching crowd,
Toiling, striving, from day to day,
Facing whatever may come his way.
Silent, whenever the harsh condemn,
And bearing it all for the love of them.

Only a dad, but he gives his all
To smooth the way for his children small
To do, with courage stern and grim,
The deeds that his father did for him,
This is the line that for him I pen,
Only a dad, but the best of men.

Author Unknown

## 468. THE LIGHT OF OTHER DAYS

Oft in the stilly night,
  Ere slumber's chain has bound me,
Fond Memory brings the light
  Of other days around me:
    The smiles, the tears
    Of boyhood's years,
  The words of love then spoken;
    The eyes that shone
    Now dimm'd and gone,
  The cheerful hearts now broken!
Thus in the stilly night
  Ere slumber's chain has bound me,
Sad Memory brings the light
  Of other days around me.

When I remember all
  The friends so link'd together
I've seen around me fall
  Like leaves in wintry weather,
    I feel like one
    Who treads alone
  Some banquet hall deserted,
    Whose lights are fled,
    Whose garlands dead,
  And all but he departed!
Thus in the stilly night
  Ere slumber's chain has bound me,
Sad Memory brings the light
  Of other days around me.

Thomas Moore
1779-1852

### 469.     WHICH SHALL IT BE?

*A rich man who had no children proposed to his
poor neighbor, who had seven, to take one of
them, and promised, if the parents would consent,
that he would give them property enough to make
themselves and their other six children comfort-
able for life.*

Which shall it be?  Which shall it be?
I looked at John, John looked at me,
And when I found that I must speak,
My voice seemed strangely low and weak:
"Tell me again what Robert said;"
And then I, listening, bent my head--
        This is his letter:

        "I will give
A house and land while you shall live,
If, in return, from out your seven,
One child to me for aye is given."

I looked at John's old garments worn;
I thought of all that he had borne
Of poverty, and work, and care,
Which I, though willing, could not share;
I thought of seven young mouths to feed,
Of seven little children's need,
        And then of this.

        "Come, John," said I,
"We'll choose among them as they lie
Asleep."  So, walking hand in hand,
Dear John and I surveyed our band:
First to the cradle lightly stepped
Where Lilian, the baby, slept.
Softly the father stooped to lay
His rough hand down in a loving way,
When dream or whisper made her stir,
And huskily he said:  "Not her!"

We stooped beside the trundle bed,
And one long ray of twilight shed
Athwart the boyish faces there,
In sleep so beautiful and fair;
I saw on James' rough, red cheek
A tear undried.  Ere John could speak
"He's but a baby, too," said I,
And kissed him as we hurried by.
Pale, patient Robbie's angel face
Still in sleep bore suffering's trace,
"No, for a thousand crowns, not him!"
He whispered, while our eyes were dim.

Poor Dick! bad Dick! our wayward son--
Turbulent, restless, idle one--

Could he be spared?  Nay, He who gave
Bade us befriend him to the grave;
Only a mother's heart could be
Patient enough for such as he;
"And so," said John, "I would not dare
To take him from her bedside prayer."

Then stole we softly up above,
And knelt by Mary, child of love;
"Perhaps for her 'twould better be,"
I said to John.  Quite silently
He lifted up a curl that lay
Across her cheek in a wilful way,
And shook his head:  "Nay, love, not thee,"
The while my heart beat audibly.

Only one more, our eldest lad,
Trusty and truthful, good and glad,
So like his father.  "No, John, no!
I cannot, will not, let him go."
And so we wrote in courteous way,
We could not give one child away;
And afterward toil lighter seemed,
Thinking of that of which we dreamed,
Happy in truth that not one face
Was missed from its accustomed place;
Thankful to work for all the seven,
Trusting the rest to One in Heaven!

                    Ethel Lynn Beers

### 470.     HOME IS WHERE THERE'S
            ONE TO LOVE US

Home's not merely four square walls,
    Though with pictures hung and gilded;
Home is where Affection calls,
    Filled with shrines the Heart hath builded!
Home!--go watch the faithful dove,
    Sailing 'neath the heaven above us;
Home is where there's one to love!
    Home is where there's one to love us!

Home's not merely roof and room--
    It needs something to endear it;
Home is where the heart can bloom,
    Where there's some kind lip to cheer it!
What is home with none to meet,
    None to welcome, none to greet us?
Home is sweet--and only sweet--
    Where there's one we love to meet us!

                    Charles Swain

## 471. THE BAREFOOT BOY

Blessings on thee, little man,
Barefoot boy, with cheek of tan!
With thy turned-up pantaloons,
And thy merry whistled tunes;
With thy red lips, redder still
Kissed by strawberries on the hill;
With the sunshine on thy face,
Through thy torn brim's jaunty grace:
From my heart I give thee joy,--
I was once a barefoot boy!
Prince thou art,--the grown-up man
Only is republican.
Let the million-dollared ride!
Barefoot, trudging at his side,
Thou hast more than he can buy
In the reach of ear and eye--
Outward sunshine, inward joy:
Blessings on thee, barefoot boy!

O for boyhood's painless play,
Sleep that wakes in laughing day,
Health that mocks the doctor's rules,
Knowledge never learned of schools,
Of the wild bee's morning chase,
Of the wild-flower's time and place,
Flight of fowl and habitude
Of the tenants of the wood;
How the tortoise bears his shell,
How the woodchuck digs his cell,
And the ground-mole sinks his well;
How the robin feeds her young,
How the oriole's nest is hung;
Where the whitest lilies blow,
Where the freshest berries grow,
Where the groundnut trails its vine,
Where the wood-grape's clusters shine;
Of the black wasp's cunning way,
Mason of his walls of clay,
And the architectural plans
Of gray hornet artisans!--
For, eschewing books and tasks,
Nature answers all he asks;
Hand in hand with her he walks,
Face to face with her he talks,
Part and parcel of her joy,--
Blessings on the barefoot boy!

O for boyhood's time of June,
Crowding years in one brief moon,
When all things I heard or saw,
Me, their master, waited for.
I was rich in flowers and trees,
Humming-birds and honey-bees;

For my sport the squirrel played,
Plied the snouted mole his spade;
For my taste the blackberry cone
Purpled over hedge and stone;
Laughed the brook for my delight
Through the day and through the night,
Whispering at the garden wall,
Talked with me from fall to fall;
Mine the sand-rimmed pickerel pond,
Mine the walnut slopes beyond,
Mine, on bending orchard trees,
Apples of Hesperides!
Still as my horizon grew,
Larger grew my riches too;
All the world I saw or knew
Seemed a complex Chinese toy,
Fashioned for a barefoot boy!

O for festal dainties spread,
Like my bowl of milk and bread,--
Pewter spoon and bowl of wood,
On the door-stone, gray and rude!
O'er me, like a regal tent,
Cloudy-ribbed, the sunset bent,
Purple-curtained, fringed with gold,
Looped in many a wind-swung fold;
While for music came the play
Of the pied frogs' orchestra;
And, to light the noisy choir,
Lit the fly his lamp of fire.
I was monarch:  pomp and joy
Waited on the barefoot boy!

Cheerily, then, my little man,
Live and laugh, as boyhood can!
Though the flinty slopes be hard,
Stubble-speared the new-mown sward,
Every morn shall lead thee through
Fresh baptisms of the dew;
Every evening from thy feet
Shall the cool wind kiss the heat:
All too soon these feet must hide
In the prison cells of pride,
Lose the freedom of the sod,
Like a colt's for work be shod,
Made to tread the mills of toil,
Up and down in ceaseless moil:
Happy if their track be found
Never on forbidden ground,
Happy if they sink not in
Quick and treacherous sands of sin.
Ah! that thou couldst know thy joy,
Ere it passes, barefoot boy!

John Greenleaf Whittier

472.         BETSY AND I ARE OUT

Draw up the papers, lawyer, and make 'em good and stout;
Things at home are crossways, and Betsy and I are out.
We, who have worked together so long as man and wife,
Must pull in single harness the rest of our nat'ral life.

"What is the matter?" say you. I swan it's hard to tell!
Most of the years behind us we've passed by very well;
I have no other woman, she has no other man--
Only we've lived together as long as we ever can.

So I have talked with Betsy, and Betsy has talked with me,
So we've agreed together that we can't never agree;
Not that we've catched each other in any terrible crime;
We've been a-gathering this for years, a little at a time.

There was a stock of temper we both had for a start,
Though we never suspected 'twould take us two apart;
I had my various failings, bred in the flesh and bone;
And Betsy, like all good women, had a temper of her own.

First thing I remember whereon we disagreed
Was something concerning Heaven--a difference in our creed;
We arg'ed the thing at breakfast, we arg'ed the thing at tea,
And the more we arg'ed the question the more we didn't agree.

And the next that I remember was when we lost a cow;
She had kicked the bucket for certain, the question was only--How?
I held my own opinion, and Betsy another had;
And when we were done a-talkin', we both of us was mad.

And the next that I remember, it started in a joke;
But full for a week it lasted, and neither of us spoke.
And the next was when I scolded because she broke a bowl;
And she said I was mean and stingy, and hadn't any soul.

And so that bowl kept pourin' dissensions in our cup;
And so that blamed old cow was always a-comin' up;
And so that Heaven we arg'ed no nearer to us got,
But it gave us a taste of somethin' a thousand times as hot.

And so the thing kept workin', and all the self-same way:
Always somethin' to arg'e, and somethin' sharp to say;
And down on us came the neighbors, a couple dozen strong,
And lent their kindest service for to help the thing along.

And there has been days together--and many a weary week--
We was both of us cross and crabbed, and both too proud to speak;
And I have been thinkin' and thinkin', the whole of the winter and fall,
If I can't live kind with a woman, why, then, I won't at all.

And so I have talked with Betsy, and Betsy has talked with me,
And we have agreed together that we can't never agree;

And what is hers shall be hers, and what is mine shall be mine;
And I'll put it in the agreement, and take it to her to sign.

Write on the paper, lawyer--the very first paragraph--
Of all the farm and live-stock that she shall have her half;
For she has helped to earn it, through many a weary day:
And it's nothing more than justice that Betsy has her pay.

Give her the house and homestead: a man can thrive and roam,
But women are skeery critters, unless they have a home;
And I have always determined, and never failed to say,
That my wife never should want a home if I was taken away.

There is a little hard cash that's drawin' tol'rable pay:
Just a few thousand dollars laid by for a rainy day;
Safe in the hands of good men, and easy to get at;
Put in another clause there, and give her half of that.

Yes, I see you smile, Sir, at my givin' her so much;
Yes, divorces is cheap, Sir, but I take no stock in such!
True and fair I married her, when she was blithe and young;
And Betsy was al'ays good to me--exceptin' with her tongue.

Once, when I was young as you, and not so smart, perhaps,
For me she mittened a lawyer, and several other chaps;
And all of them fellers was flustered, and fairly taken down,
And I for a time was counted the luckiest man in town.

Once when I had a fever--I won't forget it soon--
I was hot as a basted turkey and crazy as a loon!
Never an hour went by me when she was out of sight--
She nursed me true and tender, and stuck to me day and night.

And if ever a house was tidy, and ever a kitchen clean,
Her house and kitchen was tidy as any I ever seen;
And I don't complain of Betsy, or any of her acts,
Exceptin' as when we've quarrelled, and twitted each other on facts.

So draw up the papers, lawyer; and I'll go home tonight,
And read the agreement to her, and see if it's all right;
And then, in the mornin', I'll sell to a tradin' man I know,
And kiss the child that was left to us, and out in the world I'll go.

And one thing put in the paper, that first to me didn't occur
That when I am dead at last she bring me back to her;
And lay me under the maples I planted years ago,
When she and I was happy; before we quarrelled so.

And when she dies I wish that she would be laid by me;
And, lyin' together in silence, perhaps we might agree;
And if ever we meet in Heaven, I wouldn't think it queer
If we loved each other the better for what we quarrelled here.

Will Carleton

473.          HOW BETSY AND I MADE UP

Give us your hand, Mr. Lawyer: how do you do today?
You drew up that paper--I s'pose you want your pay.
Don't cut down your figures; make it an X or a V;
For that 'ere written agreement was just the makin' of me!

Goin' home that evenin' I tell you I was blue,
Thinkin' of all my troubles, and what I was goin' to do;
And if my hosses hadn't been the steadiest team alive,
They'd 've tipped me over for certain; for I couldn't see where to
        drive.

No--for I was laborin' under a heavy load;
No--for I was travellin' an entirely different road;
For I was a'tracin' over the path of our lives ag'in,
And observin' where we missed the way, and where we might have
        been.

And many a corner we'd turned that just to a quarrel led,
When I ought to 've held my temper, and driven straight ahead;
And the more I thought it over the more these memories came,
And the more I struck the opinion that I was the most to blame.

And things I had long forgotten kept risin' in my mind,
Of little matters betwixt us, where Betsy was good and kind;
And these things flashed all through me, as you know things sometimes
        will
When a feller's alone in the darkness, and everything is still.

"But," says I, "we're too far along to take another track,
And when I put my hand to the plough I do not oft turn back;
And 'tain't an uncommon thing now for couples to smash in two;"
And so I set my teeth together, and vowed I'd see it through.

And when I come in sight o' the house 'twas some'at in the night,
And just as I turned a hill-top I see the kitchen light;
Which often a han'some pictur' to a hungry person makes,
But it don't interest a man so much that's goin' to pull up stakes.

And when I went in the house, the table was set for me--
As good a supper 's ever I saw, or ever want to see;
And I crammed the agreement down in my pocket as well as ever I
        could,
And fell to eatin' my victuals, which somehow didn't taste good.

And Betsy, she pretended to be lookin' all around the house;
But she watched my side coat-pocket like a cat would watch a mouse;
And then she went to foolin' a little with her cup,
And intently readin' a newspaper--a holdin' it wrong side up.

And when I'd done with my supper, I drawed the agreement out,
And give it to her without a word, for she knowed what 'twas about;
And then I hummed a little tune; but now and then a note
Got bu'sted by some animal that hopped up in my throat.

Then Betsy she went an' took her specks from off the mantelshelf,
And read the agreement over quite softly to herself;
Read it by little and little; for her eyes is gettin' old,
And lawyers' writin' ain't no point, especially when it's cold.

And after she'd read a little she give my arm a touch,
And kindly said she was afraid I was 'lowin' her too much;
But when she was through she went for me, her face a-streamin'
    with tears,
And kissed me for the first time in half-a-dozen years!

I don't know what you'll think, Sir--I didn't come to inquire--
But I picked up that agreement and stuffed it in the fire;
And I told her we'd bury the hatchet alongside of the cow;
And we struck an agreement never to have another row.

And I told her in the future I wouldn't speak cross nor rash
If half the crockery in the house was broken all to smash;
And she said in regards to Heaven, we'd try and prove its worth
By startin' a branch establishment, and runnin' it here on earth.

And so we sat a-talkin' three-quarters of the night,
And opened our hearts to each other until they both grew light;
And the days when I was winnin' her away from so many men
Was nothin' to that evenin' I courted her over again.

Next mornin' an ancient virgin took pains to call on us,
Her lamp all trimmed and a-burnin'--to kindle another fuss;
But when she went to pryin' 'round and openin' up old sores,
My Betsy rose politely, and showed her out-of-doors!

Since then I don't deny but we've had a word or two;
But we've got our eyes wide open now, and know just what to do
When one speaks cross the other just meets it with a laugh,
And the first one's ready to give up considerable more than half.

So make out your bill, Mr. Lawyer: don't stop short of an X;
Make it more if you want to, for I have got the checks!
I'm richer than a National Bank, with all its treasures told:
For I've got a wife at home now that's worth her weight in gold.

                         Will Carleton

474.     FAMILY PIE

One handful of forgiveness.
One heaping cupful of love.
A full pound of unselfishness,
Mix together smoothly with complete faith in God,
Add two tablespoons of wisdom,
One teaspoonful of good nature for flavor,
Then sprinkle generously with thoughtfulness.
This makes a wonderful family pie!

    The Log

### 475. MOTHER'S BOYS

Yes, I know there are stains on my carpet,
  The traces of small muddy boots;
And I see your fair tapestry glowing,
  All spotless with flowers and fruits.

And I know that my walls are disfigured
  With prints of small fingers and hands;
And that your own household most truly
  In immaculate purity stands.

And I know that my parlor is littered
  With many odd treasures and toys,
While your own is in daintiest order,
  Unharmed by the presence of boys.

And I know that my room is invaded
  Quite boldly all hours of the day;
While you sit in yours unmolested
  And dream the soft quiet away.

Yes, I know there are four little bedsides
  Where I must stand watchful each night,
While you may go out in your carriage,
  And flash in your dresses so bright.

Now, I think I'm a neat little woman;
  And I like my house orderly, too;
And I'm fond of all dainty belongings,
  Yet I would not change places with you.

No! keep your fair home with its order,
  Its freedom from bother and noise;
And keep your own fanciful leisure,
  But give me my four splendid boys.

                    Author Unknown


### 476. TO MOTHERS

Now I lay me down to sleep--
  Don't want to sleep, I want to think.
  I didn't mean to spill that ink;
I only meant to softly creep
  Under the desk an' be a bear--
  'Taint 'bout the spanking that I care.

'F she'd only let me 'splain and tell
  Just how it was an accident,
  An' that I never truly meant
An' never saw it 'til it fell.
  I feel a whole lot worse'n her;
  I'm sorry, an' I said I were.

I s'pose if I'd just cried a lot
  An' choked all up like sister does,
  An' acted sadder than I wuz,
An' sobbed 'bout the "naughty spot,"
  She'd said: "He shan't be whipped, he shan't,"
  An' kissed me--but, somehow, I can't.

But I don't think it's fair a bit,
  That when she talks and talks at you
  An' you wait patient till she's through,
An' start to tell your side of it,
  She says: "Now that'll do, my son,
  I've heard enough!"--'fore you've begun.

'F I should die before I wake--
  Maybe I ain't got any soul;
  Maybe there's only just a hole
Where 't ought to be--there's such an ache
  Down there somewhere! She seemed to think
  That I just loved to spill that ink!

                    Author Unknown


### 477. CHRIST'S PRESENCE IN THE HOUSE

Dear Friend, whose presence in the house,
  Whose gracious word benign,
Could once at Cana's wedding feast
  Turn water into wine,

Come visit us, and when dull work
  Grows weary, line on line,
Revive our souls, and make us see
  Life's water glow as wine.

Gay mirth shall deepen into joy,
  Earth's hopes shall grow divine,
When Jesus visits us, to turn
  Life's waters into wine.

The social talk, the evening fire,
  The homely household shrine,
Shall glow with angels' visits when
  The Lord pours out the wine.

For when self-seeking turns to love,
  Which knows not mine and thine,
The miracle is wrought,
  The water changed to wine.

                    James Freeman Clarke

## 478. LOVE LIGHTENS LABOR

A good wife rose from her bed one morn,
  And thought, with a nervous dread,
Of the piles of clothes to be washed,
          and more
  Than a dozen mouths to be fed.
"There's the meals to get for the men in
          the field,
  And the children to fix away
To school, and the milk to be skimmed and
          churned;
  And all to be done this day."

It had rained in the night, and all the wood
  Was wet as it could be;
There were puddings and pies to bake, besides
  A loaf of cake for tea.
And the day was hot, and her aching head
  Throbbed wearily as she said,
"If maidens but knew what good wives know,
  They would not be in haste to wed!"

"Jennie, what do you think I told Ben Brown?"
  Called the farmer from the well;
And a flush crept up to his bronzed brow,
  And his eyes half-bashfully fell:
"It was this," he said, and coming near
  He smiled, and stooping down,
Kissed her cheek--" 'twas this, that you were
          the best
  And the dearest wife in town!"

The farmer went back to the field, and the wife,
  In a smiling, absent way,
Sang snatches of tender little songs
  She'd not sung for many a day.
And the pain in her head was gone, and the
          clothes
  Were white as the foam of the sea;
Her bread was light, and her butter was sweet,
  And as golden as it could be.

"Just think," the children all called in
          a breath,
  "Tom Wood has run off to sea!
He wouldn't, I know, if he'd only had
  As happy a home as we."
The night came down, and the good wife
          smiled
  To herself, as she softly said:
" 'Tis so sweet to labor for those we love--
  It's not strange that maids will wed!"

Anonymous

## 479. BEHIND WITH HIS READING

Junior bit the meter man.
  Junior kicked the cook,
Junior's antisocial now
  (According to the book).

Junior smashed the clock and lamp.
  Junior hacked the tree
(Destructive trends and treated
  In chapters two and three).

Junior threw his milk at Mom.
  Junior screamed for more.
(Notes of self-assertiveness
  Are found in chapter four).

Junior tossed his shoes and socks
  Out into the rain.
(Negation, that, and normal--
  Disregard the stain).

Junior got in Grandpops room
  Tore up his fishing line.
That's to gain attention...
  (See page eighty-nine).

Grandpop seized a slipper and
  Yanked Junior 'cross his knee,
(Grandpop hasn't read a book
  Since 1893).

Selected

## 480. MOTHERS...AND...OTHERS

Others weary of the noise,
Mothers play with girls and boys;
Others scold because we fell,
Mothers kiss and make it well.
Others love us more or less
Mothers love with steadiness.
Others pardon, hating yet,
Mothers pardon and forget.
Others keep the ancient score,
Mothers never shut the door.
Others grow incredulous,
Mothers still believe in us.
Others throw their faith away,
Mothers pray, and pray, and pray.

Amos R. Wells

481. ME AN' PAP AN' MOTHER

When I was a little tike
  I set at th' table
'Tween my mother an' my pap;
  Et all I was able.
Pap  he fed me on one side,
  Mammy on th' other,
Tell ye we was chums, them days--
  Me an' Pap an' Mother.

Sundays we'd take great, long walks
  Through th' woods an' pasters;
Pap he al'ays packed a cane,
  Mother'n me picked asters.
Sometimes they's a sister 'long,
  Sometimes they's a brother;
But they al'ays was us three--
  Me an' Pap an' Mother.

Pap he didn't gabble much;
  Hel' his head down, thinkin'.
Didn't seem t' hear us talk,
  Nor th' cow-bells clinkin'.
Love-streaks all 'peared worried out
  'Bout one thing er nuther;
Didn't al'ays understand Pap--
  That's me an' Mother.

I got big an' went away;
  Left th' farm behind me.
Thinkin' o' that partin' yit
  Seems t' choke an' blind me.
'Course I'd be all safe an' good
  With m' married brother,
But we had to part, us three--
  Me an' Pap an' Mother.

Hurried back, one day; found Pap
  Changed, an' pale an' holler;
Seen right off he'd have t' go--
  Where we couldn't foller.
Lovin' streaks all showed up then--
  Ah, we loved each other!
Talked fast, jest t' keep back tears--
  Me an' Pap an' Mother.

Pap he's--dead; but Mother ain't;
  Soon will be, I reckon;
Claims already she can see
  Pap's forefinger beckon.
Life hain't long, I'll go myself
  One o' these days eruther.
Then we'll have good times agin,
  Me an' Pap an' Mother.

Purtier hills we'll have t' climb,
  Saunterin' 'long old fashion,
Hear th' wild birds singin' round;
  See th' river splashin'--
If God'd only let us three
  Be 'lone, like we'd ruther,
Heaven'd be a great ol' place
  For me an' Pap an' Mother.

Strickland W. Gillilan

482.    THE SPHERE OF WOMAN

They talk about a woman's sphere as though
  it had a limit;
There's not a place in earth or Heaven,
There's not a task to mankind given,
There's not a blessing or a woe,
There's not a whispered yes or no,
There's not a life, or death, or birth,
That has a feather's weight of worth--
  Without a woman in it.

C. E. Bowman

483.    HER MOTHER SPEAKS

She was so small so short a time ago;
  She lay against my heart, a baby thing,
And now I watch the lovely flush and glow
  Illumine her, that only love can bring.

They told me I would feel hot, jealous pain
  When first she turned to other arms
    from mine;
I have not found it so.  Not loss, but gain
  It is for me, she's found a love so fine.

I love him with a strange and tender love--
  This tall, sweet boy, whose laughing, clear
    young eyes
Saw dreams come true in her, and sought to prove
  Her not a child, but woman, woman wise.

They, love absorbed, I see her wholly his
  As he is hers until the end of time.
And yet--yet, I know that each one is
  In some way wholly, deeply, sweetly mine.

Author Unknown

484.    THE BABY'S SOLILOQUY

*Or I Wish My Mummy Didn't Smoke*

Dey say Dod made the babies;
  I dess that may be so,
But who den made the cigarette?
  Dat's what I'd like to know.
Dod sent me down from Heaven
  To lib with grown-up folk.
He gave me to my mummy, but
  I wish she didn't smoke.

I know my mummy loves me;
  She dresses me so nice,
And buys me lots of pretty things,
  No matter what the price.
My food is just the bestest
  That she can ever get.
But when she tries to feed me,
  She smoke a cigarette.

Once when my food was hottest,
  And Mummy tried to blow it,
She dropped some ashes in it--
  Course she didn't know it.
I fussed and fussed about it,
  I had to cough and choke;
I didn't like dem ashes
  And did I hate dat smoke!

I cry 'cause I'm a hurtin',
  My eyes dey smart so bad;
Den Mummy thinks I'm naughty,
  And goes and tells my dad.
Dey say my mom's a smoker--
  How could dat eber be?
It's the cigarette dat's a-smoking--
  She's just a sucker, don't you see?

When Mummy makes a dinner,
  Here comes a lot of folk;
And when dey's fru their eatin',
  Dey all begin to smoke.
Dere's not a window open
  And smoke is everywhere.
Den I wish I's back in Heaven--
  Dey don't have smoke up dere.

                    Lillie Buffum

# LOVE

## 485. TURNED INTO A BLESSING

*"The Lord thy God turned the curse into a blessing unto thee,
because the Lord thy God loved thee."—Deut. 23:5.*

(Genesis 41:52; Nehemiah 13:21; Genesis 1:20)

Turned into a blessing! What? The curse!
The thing which in itself could not be worse.
Turned into a blessing! Strange indeed, and so odd,
'Til we reflect 'twas by Almighty God.

Turned into a blessing! Not removed!
A richer, grander, sovereign work thus proved?
Not the withdrawing of an evil past--
But the transforming to a thing most blest!

Turned into a blessing! Can it be
That He who wrought for them can work for me?
Can take the thing so evil, and so strange,
And to a gem of blessing can it change?

Yes, into a blessing He can turn
The things which make us bleed, or which so burn;
Those evil things, which seem to so molest,
He can transform--to make us still more blest.

J. Danson Smith

## 486. AND SO I LOVE

When I was just a little child
I loved my mother so,
I liked to touch what she had touched.
And always tried to know

The things she loved the best of all
So I could love them too.
I made a secret list of them
Although she never knew.

And now that I am grown I love
My heavenly Father so,
And like a little child again
I humbly seek to know

The things which are most dear to Him,
So I may love them too,
And thus draw closer to His heart,
And so I love--the Jew!

Martha Snell Nicholson

## 487. KNOWLEDGE

I have heard it passeth knowledge,
  I believe what God hath said;
But the test is, do I prove it
  As my daily path I tread?

Is it merely that I think it,
  And accept what others say?
Does it fill my heart with singing,
  Is it in me day by day?

What is knowledge worth that's buried
  Like a jewel in the earth?
If we know God's love, our knowledge
  Must live in us--giving birth

To a love that feels for others,
  Looks upon them from God's side;
Lord, just keep me in that knowledge,
  Let me in Thy love abide!

From Evangelical Christian

488.   GOD LOVES ME

God loved,
And gave His Son
That I might ransomed be:
Christ loved,
And died that I
Might live eternally.

He loves me,
Loving on, He drew me
To His side;
For me,
Yes, all for me
My Lord was crucified.

Eva Gray


489.   TRUE LOVE

*Sonnet 116*

Let me not to the marriage of true minds
Admit impediments.  Love is not love
Which alters when it alteration finds,
Or bends with the remover to remove.
O, no! it is an ever-fixed mark,
That looks on tempests and is never shaken;
It is the star to every wandering bark,
Whose worth's unknown, although his height be taken.

Love's not Time's fool, though rosy lips and cheeks
Within his bending sickle's compass come;
Love alters not with his brief hours and weeks,
But bears it out even to the edge of doom.
    If this be error and upon me proved,
    I never writ, nor no man ever loved.

William Shakespeare
1564-1616


490.   EVER REMEMBERED

I want you to know you are ever remembered--
    The kindliest feelings encircle your name;
Though life's pressing claims may have silence engendered,
    Your place in remembrance remaineth the same.

I want you to know that, as busy thoughts travel
    On busiest days--as most surely they do--
Perhaps when some problem seems hard to unravel,
    My thoughts may instinctively travel to you.

And when at His footstool, untired, I would linger,
    And think of the many God-given as friends--
There comes 'gainst your name an invisible finger,
    And forthwith some word for you surely ascends.

J. Danson Smith

491.   IN SCHOOL-DAYS

Still sits the school-house by the road,
  A ragged beggar sunning;
Around it still the sumachs grow,
  And blackberry vines are running.

Within, the master's desk is seen,
  Deep scarred by raps official;
The warping floor, the battered seats,
  The jack-knife's carved initial;

The charcoal frescoes on its wall;
  Its door's worn sill, betraying
The feet that, creeping slow to school,
  Went storming out to playing!

Long years ago a winter sun
  Shone over it at setting;
Lit up its western window-panes,
  And low eaves' icy fretting.

It touched the tangled golden curls,
  And brown eyes full of grieving,
Of one who still her steps delayed
  When all the school were leaving.

For near her stood the little boy
  Her childish favor singled:

His cap pulled low upon a face
  Where pride and shame were mingled.

Pushing with restless feet the snow
  To right and left, he lingered;--
As restlessly her tiny hands
  The blue-checked apron fingered.

He saw her lift her eyes; he felt
  The soft hand's light caressing,
And heard the tremble of her voice,
  As if a fault confessing.

"I'm sorry that I spelt the word:
  I hate to go above you,
Because," --the brown eyes lower fell,--
  "Because, you see, I love you!"

Still memory to a gray-haired man
  That sweet child face is showing.
Dear girl:  the grasses on her grave
  Have forty years been growing!

He lives to learn, in life's hard school,
  How few who pass above him
Lament their triumph and his loss,
  Like her,--because they love him.

John Greenleaf Whittier


492.  FOLKS NEED A LOT OF LOVING

Folks need a lot of loving in the morning;
  The day is all ahead, with cares beset--
The cares we know, and those that give no warning;
  For love is God's own antidote for fret.

Folks need a heap of loving at the noontime--
  The battle lull, the moment snatched from strife--
Halfway between the waking and the croontime,
  When bickering and worriment are rife.

Folks hunger so for loving at the nighttime,
  When wearily they take them home to rest--
At slumber song and turning-out-the-light time.
  Of all the times for loving, that's the best.

Folks want a lot of loving every minute--
  The sympathy of others and their smile!
Till life's end, from the moment they begin it,
  Folks need a lot of loving all the while.

Strickland Gillilan

## 493. LOVE'S OLD SWEET SONG

Once in the dear dead days beyond recall,
When on the world the mist began to fall,
Out of the dreams that rose in happy throng,
Low in our hearts Love sang an old sweet song;
And in the dusk where fell the firelight gleam,
Softly it wove itself into our dream.

Even today we hear Love's song of yore,
Deep in our hearts it dwells forever more;
Footsteps may falter, weary grow the way,
Still we can hear it at the close of day;
So till the end, when life's dim shadows fall,
Love will be found the sweetest song of all.

Just a song at twilight, when the lights are low,
And the flick'ring shadows softly come and go,
Tho' the heart be weary, sad the day and long,
Still to us at twilight comes Love's old song,
Comes Love's old, sweet song.

G. Clifton Bingham

## 494. LITTLE THINGS OF LIFE

A good-bye kiss is a little thing,
  With your hand on the door to go;
But it takes the venom out of the sting
Of a thoughtless word or a cruel fling
  That you made an hour ago.

A kiss of greeting is sweet and rare,
  After the toil of the day;
But it smooths the furrows out of the care
And lines on the forehead you once called fair,
  In the years that have flown away.

'Tis a little thing to say, "You are kind;
  I love you, my dear," each night;
But it sends a thrill through the heart, I find,
For love is tender, as love is blind,
  As we climb life's rugged height.

We starve each other for love's caress;
  We take, but do not give.
It seems so easy some soul to bless,
But we dole love grudgingly, less and less,
  Till 'tis bitter and hard to live.

Author Unknown

## 495. THE LONG ROAD

Long the road,
  Till Love came down it!
Dark the life,
  Till Love did crown it!
Dark the life,
  And long the road,
Till Love came
  To share the load!
For the touch
  Of Love transfigures
All the road
  And all its rigours.
Life and Death,
Love's touch transfigures.
Life and Death
  And all that lies
In between,
Love sanctifies.
Once the heavenly spark is lighted,
Once in love two hearts united,
Nevermore
  Shall aught that was be
As before.

John Oxenham

496.                    CURFEW MUST NOT RING TONIGHT

Slowly England's sun was setting o'er the hilltops far away,
Filling all the land with beauty at the close of one sad day;
And the last rays kissed the forehead of a man and maiden fair,
He with footsteps slow and weary, she with sunny floating hair;
He with bowed head, sad and thoughtful, she with lips all cold and white,
Struggling to keep back the murmur, "Curfew must not ring tonight!"

"Sexton," Bessie's white lips faltered, pointing to the prison old,
With its turrets tall and gloomy, with its walls, dark, damp and cold--
"I've a lover in the prison, doomed this very night to die
At the ringing of the curfew, and no earthly help is nigh.
Cromwell will not come till sunset"; and her face grew strangely white
As she breathed the husky whisper, "Curfew must not ring tonight!"

"Bessie," calmly spoke the sexton--and his accents pierced her heart
Like the piercing of an arrow, like a deadly poisoned dart--
"Long, long years I've rung the curfew from that gloomy, shadowed tower;
Every evening, just at sunset, it has told the twilight hour;
I have done my duty ever, tried to do it just and right--
Now I'm old I still must do it:  Curfew, girl, must ring tonight!"

Wild her eyes and pale her features, stern and white her thoughtful brow,
And within her secret bosom Bessie made a solemn vow.
She had listened while the judges read, without a tear or sigh,
"At the ringing of the curfew, Basil Underwood must die."
And her breath came fast and faster, and her eyes grew large and bright,
As in undertone she murmured, "Curfew must not ring tonight!"

With quick step she bounded forward, sprang within the old church door,
Left the old man  treading  slowly paths he'd often trod before;
Not one moment paused the maiden, but with eye and cheek aglow
Mounted up the gloomy tower, where the bell swung to and fro
As she climbed the dusty ladder, on which fell no ray of light,
Up and up, her white lips saying, "Curfew shall not ring tonight!"

She has reached the topmost ladder, o'er her hangs the great dark bell:
Awful is the gloom beneath her like the pathway down to Hell;
Lo, the ponderous tongue is swinging. 'Tis the hour of curfew now,
And the sight has chilled her bosom, stopped her breath and paled her brow;
Shall she let it ring? No, never! Flash her eyes with sudden light,
And she springs and grasps it firmly: "Curfew shall not ring tonight!"

Out she swung, far out; the city seemed a speck of light below;
She 'twixt Heaven and earth suspended as the bell swung to and fro;
And the sexton at the bell rope, old and deaf, heard not the bell,
But he thought it still was ringing fair young Basil's funeral knell.
Still the maiden clung more firmly, and, with trembling lips and white,
Said, to hush her heart's wild beating, "Curfew shall not ring tonight!"

It was o'er; the bell ceased swaying, and the maiden stepped once more
Firmly on the dark old ladder, where for hundred years before
Human foot had not been planted; but the brave deed she had done
Should be told long ages after--often as the setting sun

Should illume the sky with beauty, aged sires, with heads of white,
Long should tell the little children, "Curfew did not ring that night."

O'er the distant hills came Cromwell; Bessie sees him, and her brow,
Full of hope and full of gladness, has no anxious traces now.
At his feet she tells her story, shows her hands all bruised and torn;
And her face so sweet and pleading, yet with sorrow pale and worn,
Touched his heart with sudden pity--lit his eye with misty light;
"Go, your lover lives!" said Cromwell; "Curfew shall not ring tonight!"

Rosa Hartwick Thorpe

### 497.  A CHILD'S THOUGHT OF GOD

They say that God lives very high!
  But if you look above the pines
You cannot see our God.  And why?

And if you dig down in the mines
  You never see Him in the gold,
Though from Him all that's glory shines.

God is so good, He wears a fold
  Of Heaven and earth across His face--
Like secrets kept, for love untold.

But still I feel that His embrace
  Slides down by thrills, through all things made,
Through sight and sound of every place:

As if my tender mother laid
  On my shut lids her kisses' pressure,
Half-waking me at night and said,
  "Who kissed you through the dark, dear guesser?"

Elizabeth Barrett Browning

### 498.  THOSE WE LOVE

They say the world is round, and yet
  I often think it's square;
So many little hurts we get
  From corners here and there.
There's one truth in life I've found
  While journeying east and west,
The only folk we really wound
  Are those we love the best.

The choicest garb, the sweetest grace,
  Are oft to strangers shown;
The careless word, the frowning face,
  Are given to our own.

We flatter those we scarcely know,
  We please the fleeting guest,
And deal full many a thoughtless blow
  To those we love the best.

Ella Wheeler Wilcox

# MISCELLANEOUS

### 499.   THE BELLS

Hear the sledges with the bells--
    Silver bells!
What a world of merriment their melody foretells!
   How they tinkle, tinkle, tinkle!
    In the icy air of night!
   While the stars that oversprinkle
   All the heavens seem to twinkle
    With a crystalline delight--
   Keeping time, time, time,
   In a sort of Runic rhyme,
To the tintinnabulation that so musically wells
   From the bells, bells, bells, bells,
      Bells, bells, bells--
   From the jingling and the tinkling of the bells.

   Hear the mellow wedding bells--
    Golden bells!
What a world of happiness their harmony foretells!
   Through the balmy air of night
   How they ring out their delight!
    From the molten-golden notes,
      All in tune,
   What a liquid ditty floats
To the turtle-dove that listens, while she gloats
      On the moon!
   O, from out the sounding cells,
What a gush of euphony voluminously wells!
     How it swells!
     How it dwells
    On the Future! how it tells
    Of the rapture that impels
   To the swinging and the ringing
    Of the bells, bells, bells,
   Of the bells, bells, bells, bells,
      Bells, bells, bells--
To the rhyming and the chiming of the bells.

   Hear the loud alarum bells--
    Brazen bells!
What a tale of terror, now, their turbulency tells!
   In the startled ear of night
   How they scream out their affright!
    Too much horrified to speak,
    They can only shriek, shriek,
      Out of tune,
In the clamorous appealing to the mercy of the fire
In a mad expostulation with the deaf and frantic fire
    Leaping higher, higher, higher,
    With a desperate desire,
   And a resolute endeavor,

Now--now to sit, or never,
By the side of the pale-faced moon.
    O the bells, bells, bells,
    What a tale their terror tells
        Of despair!
    How they clang and clash and roar!
    What a horror they outpour
On the bosom of the palpitating air!
    Yet the ear it fully knows,
        By the twanging,
        And the clanging,
    How the danger ebbs and flows;
    Yet the ear distinctly tells,
        In the jangling,
        And the wrangling,
    How the danger sinks and swells,
By the sinking or the swelling in the anger of the bells--
        Of the bells--
    Of the bells, bells, bells, bells,
        Bells, bells, bells--
In the clamor and the clangor of the bells!

    Hear the tolling of the bells--
        Iron bells!
What a world of solemn thought their monody compels!
    In the silence of the night,
    How we shiver with affright
  At the melancholy menace of their tone!
    For every sound that floats
    From the rust within their throats
        Is a groan.
    And the people--ah, the people--
    They that dwell up in the steeple,
        All alone,
    And who tolling, tolling, tolling,
      In that muffled monotone,
    Feel a glory in so rolling
      On the human heart a stone--
    They are neither man nor woman--
    They are neither brute nor human--
        They are ghouls:
    And their king it is who tolls;
    And he rolls, rolls, rolls,
            Rolls,
        A paean from the bells!
    And his merry bosom swells
        With the paean of the bells!
    And he dances and he yells;
    Keeping time, time, time,
    In a sort of Runic rhyme,
      To the paean of the bells--
        Of the bells:
    Keeping time, time, time,
    In a sort of Runic rhyme,

To the throbbing of the bells--
Of the bells, bells, bells--
To the sobbing of the bells;
Keeping time, time, time,
As he knells, knells, knells,
In a happy Runic rhyme,
To the rolling of the bells--
Of the bells, bells, bells--
To the tolling of the bells--
Of the bells, bells, bells, bells--
Bells, bells, bells--
To the moaning and the groaning of the bells.

Edgar Allan Poe

### 500. MOMENTOUS DAYS

Momentous days are on us!
Our eyes may soon behold
A mighty clash of nations,
Which prophets have foretold:
A clashing and a cleaving
Of unmatched magnitude,
Wrought by some super being
With evil power endued.

Momentous! Yes, momentous!
But shall we be afraid?
The mighty conflict cometh,
Yet may our hearts be stayed:
The Lord from glory cometh--
His coming draweth nigh;
Earth's most colossal conflict--
We'll see yet from on high.

The nations all are arming!
The worst is yet to be!
For Armageddon cometh
Not far from Galilee;
But brothers, Christian brothers,
Fear not of being there;
Before that awful carnage--
Christ cometh to the air.

The days of tribulation
May soon be near at hand;
"Perplexity of nations"
Will sure invade each land;
Yet not for woes and terrors,
And earth's onrushing might
Look we for, but the morning
Of cloudless glory bright.

J. Danson Smith

### 501. A DUMB OLE COUNTRY BOY

I'm just a dumb ole country boy,
That ain't so very smart;
And when I talk I get mixed up,
My gears are hard to start:
It seems I don't have many brains,
Like other folks I know;
And when it comes to s'ciety,
My dumbness there I show.

I found it don't take brains, my friend,
The best in life to gain;
It's not your wealth or what you are;
Prestige you might obtain:
It only takes just simple faith,
Eternal life to find:
No matter who or where you stand,
There's grace for all mankind.

I went down to the jailhouse once
To witness for the Lord:
I told them how the Lord saved me--
They sure looked mighty bored:
They nudged each other and they smiled,
They thought that I was dumb:
But they stayed in and I walked out,
When leavin' time had come.

I'm still a dumb ole country boy,
I hope I'll always be;
Just dumb enough to trust the Lord
For all eternity:
And so I'll just keep travelin' on,
No brains and not too smart:
I'm just a dumb ole country boy,
With Jesus in my heart.

Walt Huntley

502.   JESUS AND PETER

Two sayings of the Holy Scriptures beat
Like pulses in the church's brow and breast;
And by them we find rest in our unrest,
And, heart-deep in salt tears, do yet entreat
God's fellowship, as if on heavenly seat.
The first is "Jesus wept"; whereon is prest
Full many a sobbing face, that drops its best
And sweetest waters on the record sweet.
And one is where the Christ, denied and scorned,
"Looked upon Peter." Oh, to render plain,
By help of having loved a little and mourned,
That look of sovran love and sovran pain,
Which He, who could not sin yet suffered, turned
On him who could reject but not sustain.

The Saviour looked on Peter. Ay, no word,
No gesture of reproach; the heavens serene,
Though heavy with armed justice, did not lean
Their thunders that way; the forsaken Lord
**Looked** only on the traitor. None record
What that look was; none guess; for those who have seen
Wronged lovers loving through a death-pang keen,
Or pale-cheeked martyrs smiling to a sword,
Have missed Jehovah at the judgment call.
And Peter from the height of blasphemy--
"I never knew this man"--did quail and fall,
As knowing straight that God; and turned free,
And went out speechless from the face of all,
And filled the silence, weeping bitterly.

I think that look of Christ might seem to say:
"Thou, Peter! art thou a common stone
Which I at last must break My heart upon,
For all God's charge to His high angels may
Guard My feet better? Did I yesterday
Wash **thy** feet, My beloved, that they should run
Quick to destroy Me 'neath the morning sun?
And do thy kisses, like the rest, betray?
The cock crows coldly. Go, and manifest
A late contrition, but no bootless fear!
For, when thy final need is dreariest,
Thou shalt not be denied, as I am here;
My voice to God and angels shall attest,
**Because I know this man, let him be clear.**

Elizabeth Barrett Browning

## 503. THE SINNER'S RECORD

In a day that is not far
At the blazing judgment bar,
   Even now the awful summons I can hear;
I must meet the mighty God,
I must face His holy Word,
   I must stand before the judgment bar.

I must meet each broken vow
That I hold so lightly now,
   Every heartache I have caused, each sigh, each tear;
Things that time cannot erase,
I must meet them face to face,
   When I stand before the judgment bar.

Every secret lust and thought
There shall be to judgment brought,
   When the Lord in all His glory shall appear;
All the deeds of darkest night
Shall come out to greet the light
   When I stand before the judgment bar.

I must meet my cankered gold,
For whose greed my life was sold,
   It shall mock me in the judgment's lurid glare,
Saying, "Ye have sold for nought,
All the Saviour's blood had bought,
   And you stand before the judgment bar."

Oh, my record will be there,
Be its pages dark or fair,
   When I stand before the judgment bar;
When the books shall open lie,
In the morning by and by,
   Oh, my record! Oh, my record will be there!

J. A. Brown

## 504. WHAT I HAVE SEEN

I have visioned the perfect and true
   In the midst of the false and the base;
I have seen in the visage of hate
   A gleam of the Holy One's face.

In the wild mocking laugh of the lewd
   I have heard the deep sobs of a soul
Crying out for the power that saves
   From the burdens of sorrow and dole.

And the glories eternal I've seen
   In the world's passing pomp and parade;
I've heard the glad songs of the saved
   In the moans of the lost and the strayed.

I've discerned the sweet smile of a friend
   In the sneer of my bitterest foe;
I have seen on the high road of life
   Those who travel the byway of woe.

'Tis a faint glimpse of what might have been,
   And a vision of what may yet be;
'Tis **the image of God** sin defiled,
   That the Spirit has made me to see.

W. B. McCafferty

505. REMORSE

My days are in the yellow leaf;
 The flowers and fruits of love are gone;
The worm, the canker, and the grief,
 Are mine alone!

The fire that in my bosom preys
 Is like to some volcanic isle;

No torch is kindled at its blaze,--
 A funeral pile.

The hope, the fear, the jealous care,
 The exalted portion of the pain
And power of love, I cannot share,
 But wear the chain.

George Gordon, Lord Byron,
1788-1824

506. THE DUEL

The gingham dog and the calico cat
Side by side on the table sat;
'T was half-past twelve, and (what do you think!)
Nor one nor t' other had slept a wink!
 The old Dutch clock and the Chinese plate
 Appeared to know as sure as fate
There was going to be a terrible spat.
 (I wasn't there; I simply state
 What was told to me by the Chinese plate!)

The gingham dog went, "bow-wow-wow!"
And the calico cat replied, "mee-ow!"
The air was littered, an hour or so,
With bits of gingham and calico,
 While the old Dutch clock in the chimney-place
 Up with its hands before its face,
For it always dreaded a family row!
 (Now mind: I'm only telling you
 What the old Dutch clock declares is true!)

The Chinese plate looked very blue,
And wailed, "Oh, dear! what shall we do!"
But the gingham dog and the calico cat
Wallowed this way and tumbled that,
 Employing every tooth and claw
 In the awfullest way you ever saw--
And, oh! how the gingham and calico flew!
 (Don't fancy I exaggerate--
 I got my news from the Chinese plate!)

Next morning, where the two had sat
They found no trace of dog or cat;
And some folks think unto this day
That burglars stole that pair away!
 But the truth about the cat and pup
 Is this: they ate each other up!
Now what do you really think of that!
 (The old Dutch clock it told me so,
 And that is how I came to know.)

Eugene Field

507.    THE MODEL CHURCH

Well, wife, I've found the model church--I worshipped there today!
It made me think of good old times, before my hair was gray.
The meetin'-house was fixed up more than they were years ago,
But then I felt when I went in, it wasn't built for show.

The sexton didn't seat me away back by the door;
He knew that I was old and deaf, as well as old and poor:
He must have been a Christian, for he led me through
The long aisle of that crowded church, to find a place and pew.

I wish you'd heard that singin'--it had the old-time ring;
The preacher said, with trumpet voice, "Let all the people sing!"
The tune was Coronation, and the music upward rolled,
Till I thought I heard the angels all striking their harps of gold.

My deafness seemed to melt away; my spirit caught the fire;
I joined my feeble, trembling voice, with that melodious choir,
And sang as in my youthful days, "Let angels prostrate fall.
Bring forth the royal diadem, and crown Him Lord of all."

I tell you, wife, it did me good to sing that hymn once more;
I felt like some wrecked mariner who gets a glimpse of shore;
I almost wanted to lay down this weather-beaten form,
And anchor in the blessed port forever from the storm.

The preachin'?  Well, I can't just tell all the preacher said;
I know it wasn't written: I know it wasn't read;
He hadn't time to read it, for the lightnin' of his eye
Went flashin' along from pew to pew, nor passed a sinner by.

The sermon wasn't flowery, 'twas simple gospel truth;
It fitted poor old men like me, it fitted hopeful youth.
'Twas full of consolation for weary hearts that bleed;
'Twas full of invitations to Christ, and not to creed.

The preacher made sin hideous in Gentiles and in Jews;
He shot the golden sentences down in the finest pews,
And--though I can't see very well--I saw the falling tear
That told me Hell was some ways off, and Heaven very near.

How swift the golden moments fled within that holy place!
How brightly beamed the light of Heaven from every happy face!
Again I longed for that sweet time when friend shall meet with friend,
"Where congregations ne'er break up, and Sabbaths have no end."

I hope to meet that minister--that congregation, too--
In that dear home beyond the stars that shine from Heaven's blue.
I doubt not I'll remember, beyond life's evening gray,
That happy hour of worship in that model church today.

Dear wife, the fight will soon be fought, the victory be won;
The shining goal is just ahead, the race is nearly run.
O'er the river we are nearin', they are throngin' to the shore,
To shout our safe arrival where the weary weep no more. --John H. Yates

## 508. OL' JONAH

Now de Lawd done tole ol' Jonah,
  "Go to Ninevah" one day,
"An' dis hyah is what yo' tell 'em,
  Ah will tell yo' what yo' say."

Tell 'em Ah done seen de ebil
  An' de wickedness aroun'
So Ah's gwana jedge de city
  Till no ebil can be foun'.

Now ol' Jonah, he done hurried
  Down de road dat's by de sea,
But he wahnt a preachin' nothin',
  He wuz scahd as he could be.

He done tuk a ship to someplace
  Whah he shouldn't orter go,
An' dey hardly got it goin',
  When de win' began to blow--

An' de waves wuz rollin' awful,
  While de watah come on bo'hd,
'N de men who run de riggin'
  'Gan to pray unto de Lawd--

An' de Lawd--He p'ints to Jonah,
  As de one who cause de fuss,
'N ol' Jonah tells de people,
  "Der's no room fo' all ub us.

"So yo' take an' trow me ober,
  An' de stohm will disappeah."
An' dey 'lowed dey'd better try it,
  If de "wanted out ob hyah."

Now when Jonah hit de watah,
  Den de Lawd--He tuk a han',
Kaze He knew jes how He'd work it
  Gittin' Jonah back to lan'.

Fust He made de ocean quiet,
  Den de bigges' fish ob all,
He jes up an' swaller Jonah
  At de place dey let him fall.

Now ol' Jonah is a prayin',
  An' de fish--he head fo' shore,
Kaze he doesn't think he wanta
  Keep ol' Jonah any more.

An' when Jonah's feet is settled
  On de dry groun' lak befo'

De Lawd said, "Haid fo' Ninevah,"
  An' yo' orter see him go!

Den he cried, "De jedgments's comin'"
  N' de people heahd 'im call,
An' repented ob de ebil,
  'N de Lawd fo'give dem all.

                Shel Helsley

## 509. NOT ON SUNDAY NIGHT

I love the church that Jesus bought,
  She is the dark world's light;
I always go on Sunday morn,
  But not on Sunday night.

I love to sing the Gospel songs
  And worship in daylight;
That's why I come on Sunday morn,
  But not on Sunday night.

I love to hear the Gospel horn,
  It gives me such delight;
It thrills me every Sunday morn,
  But not on Sunday night.

I'd go through storm, and rain, or snow,
  Do anything that's right;
To be at church on Sunday morn,
  But not on Sunday night.

I hope the faithful few keep on
  Engaging in the fight;
I'll do my part on Sunday morn,
  But not on Sunday night.

Too bad someday we all must die.
  I hope the morn is bright,
For I want to die on Sunday morn,
  But not on Sunday night.

I know that Christ is coming soon,
  And He will find me right,
If He appears on Sunday morn--
  But--not on Sunday night.

The Holy Spirit sent this poem,
  It set my heart aright;
You'll see me there next Sunday morn
  And also--Sunday night.

                H. E. M. Snyder

## 510.  GIVE THEM THE FLOWERS NOW

Closed eyes can't see the white roses,
  Cold hands can't hold them, you know,
Breath that is stilled cannot gather
  The odors that sweet from them blow.
Death, with a peace beyond dreaming,
  Its children of earth doth endow;
Life is the time we can help them,
  So give them the flowers now!

Here are the struggles and striving,
  Here are the aches and the tears;
Now is the time to be smoothing
  The frowns and the furrows and fears.
What to closed eyes are kind sayings?
  What to hushed heart is deep vow?
Naught can avail after parting,
  So give them the flowers now!
Just a kind word or a greeting.
  Just a warm grasp or a smile--
These are the flowers that will lighten
  The burdens for many a mile.

After the journey is over
  What is the use of them; how
Can they carry them who must be carried?
  Oh, give them the flowers now!
Blooms from the happy heart's garden
  Plucked in the spirit of love;
Blooms that are earthly reflections
  Of flowers that blossom above.
Words cannot tell what a measure
  Of blessing such gifts will allow
To dwell in the lives of many,
  So give them the flowers now!

Leigh M. Hodges

## 511.  SWEET AND LOW

Sweet and low, sweet and low,
  Wind of the western sea,
Blow, blow, breathe and blow,
  Wind of the western sea!
Over the rolling waters go,
Come from the dying moon, and blow,
  Blow him again to me;
While my little one, while my pretty one,
    sleeps.

Sleep and rest, sleep and rest,
  Father will come to thee soon;
Rest, rest, on mother's breast,
  Father will come to his babe in the nest,
Silver sails all out of the west:
  Under the silver moon;
Sleep, my little one, sleep, my pretty one,
  sleep.

Alfred Tennyson

### 512. EVOLUTION!

Three monkeys dining once in a cocoanut tree
Were discussing some things that they heard true to be.
"What do you think? Now, listen you two;
Here, monkeys, is something that cannot be true,

"That humans descend from our noble race!
Why, it's shocking--a terrible disgrace.
Whoever heard of a monkey deserting his wife
And leaving a baby to starve and ruin its life?

"And have you ever known of a mother monk
To leave her darling with strangers to bunk?
Their babies are handed from one to another
And some scarcely know the love of a mother.

"And I've never known a monkey so selfish to be
As to build a fence around a cocoanut tree
So other monkeys can't get a wee taste,
But would let all the cocoanuts there go to waste.

"Why, if I'd put a fence around this cocoanut tree,
Starvation would force you to steal from me.
And here is another thing a monkey won't do:
Seek a cocktail parlor and get on a stew;

"Carouse and go on a whoopee disgracing his life,
Then reel madly home and beat up his wife.
They call this all pleasure and make a big fuss--
They've descended from something, but not from us!"

Author Unknown

### 513. OUR QUEER ENGLISH LANGUAGE

We'll begin with box; the plural is boxes,
    But the plural of ox is oxen, not oxes.
One fowl is a goose, but two are called geese,
    Yet the plural of mouse is not ever meese.
You may find a lone mouse, or a whole nest of mice,
    But the plural of house is still never hice.
If the plural of man is always men
    Why shouldn't the plural of pan be pen?
If I speak of a foot and you show me two feet,
    And I give you a boot, would a pair be called beet?
If one is a tooth, and a whole set are teeth
    Why shouldn't the plural of booth be called beeth?
If a singular this is a plural these
    Should the plural of kiss ever be keese?
We speak of a brother and also of brethren,
    And though we say mother we never say methren.
Then the masculine pronouns are he, his and him,
    But imagine the feminine she, shis and shim.

Alice Hess Beveridge

514.    ABOU BEN ADHEM AND THE ANGEL

Abou Ben Adhem (may his tribe increase)
Awoke one night from a deep dream of peace,
And saw, within the moonlight of the room,
Making it rich, and like a lily in bloom,
An angel writing in a book of gold:--
Exceeding peace had made Ben Adhem bold,
And to the presence in the room he said,
"What writest thou?"  The vision rais'd his head,
And with a look made of all sweet accord,
Answer'd, "The names of those who love the Lord."
"And is mine one?" said Abou.  "Nay, not so,"
Replied the angel.  Abou spoke more low,
But cheerly still; and said:  "I pray thee then
Write me as one that loves his fellow men."

The angel wrote, and vanish'd.  The next night
It came again with a great wakening light,
And show'd the names whom love of God had bless'd
And lo!  Ben Adhem's name led all the rest.    --Leigh Hunt

515.    MY GIT UP IS GONE

How do I know my youth is all spent?
Well, my git up and go has got up and went.
I really don't mind; I can say it and grin
When I think of the places my git up has been.

When I was young, my slippers were blue;
I could go all day long, and half the night too.
Now I am old and my shoes are plain black;
I shuffle to the store--and puff all the way back.

Old age is golden, so it has been said--
But sometimes I wonder, when going to bed,
With my ears in the drawer and my teeth in a cup
And my eyes on the dresser until I get up;

Before going to sleep I say to myself,
"Is there anything more I should lay on the shelf?"
I wake in the morning and dust off my wits;
Glance through the paper and read the Obits.

I know I ain't dead if my name isn't there,
So it's breakfast for me, then the old rocking chair.
And that's how I know I ain't young any more;
The things that were easy, are now a big chore.

Oh, I still git to church, and my Bible I read;
And I still find my chances to do a good deed.
But one thing I'm glad of:  on Heaven's bright shore,
There ain't nobody going to get old any more.

                    Author Unknown

## 516. TEARS, IDLE TEARS

Tears, idle tears, I know not what they mean,
Tears from the depth of some divine despair
Rise in the heart, and gather to the eyes,
In looking on the happy autumn fields,
And thinking of the days that are no more.

Fresh as the first beam glittering on a sail,
That brings our friends up from the
                underworld,
Sad as the last which reddens over one
That sinks with all we love below the verge;
So sad, so fresh, the days that are no more.

Ah, sad and strange as in dark summer
               dawns
The earliest pipe of half-awaken'd birds
To dying ears, when unto dying eyes
The casement slowly grows a glimmering
               square;
So sad, so strange, the days that are
             no more.

Dear as remember'd kisses after death,
And sweet as those by hopeless fancy feign'd
On lips that are for others: deep as love,
Deep as first love, and wild with all regret;
Oh, death in life! the days that are no more.

               Alfred Tennyson

## 517. TOO LATE

Late, late, so late! and dark the night and chill!
Late, late, so late! but we can enter still.
   Too late, too late! ye cannot enter now.

No light had we; for that we do repent,
And learning this, the Bridegroom will relent.
   Too late, too late! ye cannot enter now.

No light! so late! and dark and chill the night!
Oh, let us in, that we may find the light!
   Too late, too late! ye cannot enter now.

Have we not heard the Bridegroom is so sweet?
Oh, let us in, though late, to kiss His feet!
   No, no, too late! ye cannot enter now.

            Alfred Tennyson,
            1809-1892

## 518. THE GOSPEL OF LABOR

But I think the King of that country comes
   out from His tireless host
And walks in this world of the weary, as if
   He loved it the most:
For here in the dusty confusion, with
   eyes that are heavy and dim
He meets again the laboring men who are
   looking and longing for Him.

He cancels the curse of Eden, and brings
   them a blessing instead,
Blessed are they that labor for Jesus par-
   takes of their bread,
He puts His hands to their burdens, He
   enters their homes at night:
Who does his best shall have as his guest
   the Master of life and light.

And courage will come with His presence,
   and patience return at His touch,
And manifold sins be forgiven to those who
   love Him much:
And the cries of envy and anger will
   change to the songs of cheer,
For the toiling age will forget its rage
   when the Prince of Peace draws near.

This is the gospel of labor, ring it, ye bells
   of the kirk, --
The Lord of Love comes down from above
   to live with the men who work,
This is the rose that He planted, here in
   the thorn-cursed soil--
Heaven is blessed with perfect rest, but
   the blessing of earth is work.

            Henry Van Dyke

# MISSIONARY

## 519. YOUR MISSION

Hark, the voice of Jesus crying, --
  "Who will go and work today?
Fields are white and harvest waiting!
  Who will bear the sheaves away?"
Loud and strong the Master calleth,
  Rich reward He offers thee;
Who will answer, gladly saying,
  "Here am I; send me, send me!"

If you cannot cross the ocean,
  And the heathen lands explore;
You can find the heathen nearer,
  You can help them at your door.
If you cannot give your thousands,
  You can give the widow's mite;
And the least you do for Jesus,
  Will be precious in His sight.

If you cannot speak like angels;
  If you cannot preach like Paul;
You can tell the love of Jesus,
  You can say He died for all.
If you cannot rouse the wicked
  With the judgment's dread alarms,
You can lead the little children
  To the Saviour's waiting arms.

If you cannot be the watchman
  Standing high on Zion's wall,
Pointing out the path to Heaven,
  Offering life and peace to all;
With your prayers and with your bounties
  You can do what Heaven demands;
You can be like faithful Aaron,
  Holding up the prophet's hands.

If among the older people,
  You may not be apt to teach;
"Feed my lambs," said Christ, our
        Shepherd,
  "Place the food within their reach,"
And it may be that the children
  You have led with trembling hand,
Will be found among your jewels
  When you reach the better land.

Let none hear you idly saying,
  "There is nothing I can do,"
While the souls of men are dying,
  And the Master calls for you.

Take the task He gives you gladly;
  Let His work your pleasure be;
Answer quickly when He calleth,
  "Here am I; send me, send me!"

Daniel March

## 520. A MISSIONARY CRY

A hundred thousand souls a day,
Are passing one by one away,
  In Christless guilt and gloom.
Without one ray of hope or light,
With future dark as endless night,
  They're passing to their doom.

O Holy Ghost, Thy people move,
Baptize their hearts with faith and love,
  And consecrate their gold.
At Jesus' feet their millions pour,
And all their ranks unite once more,
  As in the days of old.

Armies of pray'r your promise claim,
Prove the full pow'r of Jesus' name,
  And take the victory.
Your conq'ring Captain leads you on,
The glorious fight may still be won,
  This very century.

The Master's coming draweth near,
The Son of man will soon appear,
  His kingdom is at hand.
But ere that glorious day can be,
This Gospel of the kingdom, we
  Must preach in ev'ry land.

Oh, let us then His coming haste,
Oh, let us end this awful waste
  Of souls that never die.
A thousand millions still are lost,
A Saviour's blood has paid the cost,
  Oh, hear their dying cry.

They're passing, passing fast away,
A hundred thousand souls a day,
  In Christless guilt and gloom,
O Church of Christ, what wilt thou say
When in the awful judgment day,
  They charge thee with their doom?

A. B. Simpson

## 521.   AT NIGHT

When noonday's sun is buried low
   Within a casket in the West,
When evening breezes come and go
   Like sighings of an anxious breast,
When blackened shadows slowly creep
   O'er wooded moor and pathless sod,
Then nature lays her down to sleep
   And all are well who trust in God;
Then what of him who, robbed of light,
Trembles and starts with venomed fright,
The wretch who gropes all full of sin,
Tormented by the Hell within,
   Alone upon the road at night;
Whose life is full of theft and lies,
Who totters, falls, and, falling, dies,
Upon the road of sin at night,
Alone upon the road at night?

Yea, what of him whose sun shall set
   Amid the silvery clouds of time,
Who sees the shadows, black as jet,
   Come thick and fast from that dread clime,
Peopled with shrouds, the well-fed tomb,
   The rotting flesh and broken bone;
   Nor hears aught save an endless moan?
Oh, what of him who, robbed of light,
Trembles and starts with venomed fright;
The wretch who gropes, all full of sin,
Tormented by the Hell within,
   Alone upon the road at night?
Who falls and falling ne'er shall rise,
Who dies and dying never dies,
Upon the road at night,
Alone upon the road at night?

                       Selected

## 522.   IN JERUSALEM

We're concerned for the sinner in China,
   The heathen in Mandalay.
But, say, do we care, have we offered a prayer
   For the neighbor just over the way?

We say we would go with the Gospel
   To lighten dark Africa's shore.
Have we spoken a word in the name of the Lord
   To the people who live next door?

That farmer who lives down the highway,
   Who looks so forbidding and grim,
Do we have no "call" to witness at all,
   Or to speak of the Saviour to him?

We'd take the Gospel to savages,
   We'd cross the stormy tide.
But we cannot tell out what the Gospel's about
   To the fellow who works by our side.

We'd tell of our wonderful Saviour
   And His love we have found so sweet
To the Hottentot, but certainly not
   To the friends whom we meet on the street.

Oh, we would be missionaries
   And go out the lost ones to seek.
We will send a preacher to Hindustan,
And we'll give for Testaments for Japan,
   But never a word will we speak.

                Lorie C. Gooding,

## 523.   SEND OUT THE LIGHT!

Thou, whose almighty Word
Chaos and darkness heard
   And took their flight,
Hear us, we humbly pray,
And, where the gospel day
Sheds not its glorious ray,
   Let there be light.

Thou, who didst come to bring
On Thy redeeming wing
   Healing and sight,
Health to the sick in mind,
Sight to the inly blind,
O now to all mankind
   Let there be light.

Spirit of truth and love,
Life-giving, holy Dove,
   Speed forth Thy flight;
Move o'er the water's face,
Bearing the lamp of grace,
And in earth's darkest place
   Let there be light.

Blessed and holy Three,
Glorious Trinity,
   Wisdom, Love, Might,
Boundless as ocean's tide
Rolling in fullest pride,
   Through the world, far and wide,
   Let there be light.

                J. Marriott

## 524. VOICES FROM AFAR

I planned a lavish modern home
Where wealthy friends could call;
But then I heard an orphan say,
"I have no home at all."
I planned to buy a bedroom suite,
So exquisite with charm;
But then I heard a mother pray,
"Lord, keep my baby warm."

"A new expensive dryer
Is what I really need";
I had this thought down in my mind
Until I heard one plead:
"I am a victim of the war,
Oh help me," was her cry;
"You have a nice big clothes line,
I have no clothes to dry."

I wanted, then, a freezer
To store my fancy food,
For mine was now old-fashioned
And not the kind that stood.
Just then across the ocean came
This bitter plaintive cry,
"But I don't have a bite of food,
Please help me or I die."

I bought a car for Christmas,
'Twas for my loved ones dear;
But then I heard an orphan cry,
"I have no loved ones here."
I spent a lot of money
For friends at Christmastime,
But when it came to missions,
I didn't give a dime.

When Christmas was all over,
I reckoned what I'd spent;
It was so vast and large a sum,
I could not but repent;
For it just seemed I heard that morn
A far-off mother say,
"How long ago was Jesus born
To take our sins away?"

Her words began to haunt my heart
For it had grown so cold;
My children had the Gospel light,
But hers were still untold.
I vowed that day that I would give
And work with all my might

To win a lost and dying world
From sin and heathen night.

Fred D. Jarvis
Missionary to Japan

## 525. DO YOU CARE

Do you care for souls, my brother?
  Do you really care?
Souls are dying, dying, dying;
  Ah, they perish everywhere!
The gates of Hell are wide and open;
  Christian, will you work?
Jesus gave His life to save them;
  Christian, will you shirk?

Do you care for souls, my brother?
  Would you give your wealth?
Satan has his minions blinded,
  Steals away their souls by stealth.
Deaf their ears to all God's wooings;
  Christian, will you give?
Send the Word to rouse their slumber
  That the dead in sin may live?

Do you care for souls, my brother?
  Care enough to spend an hour
On your knees in fervent praying?
  Tears and prayer break Satan's power.
Pray the Lord of all the harvest
  He will send His workers; pray
For the children, for the sinners;
  Christian, pray, and pray, and pray!

Do you care for souls, my brother?
  Care enough to rise and go
As the Lord Himself commanded?
  Can't you see the awful flow
Of human souls into perdition?
  Can't you hear their dreadful cry?
Work, and give, and pray; oh, Christian,
  Go! They die, they die, they die!

Grace Howard

# NATURE

## 526. THE BROOK

I come from haunts of coot and hern;
  I make a sudden sally,
And sparkle out among the fern,
  To bicker down a valley.

By thirsty hills I hurry down,
  Or slip between the ridges,
By twenty thorps, a little town,
  And half a hundred bridges.

Till last by Philip's farm I flow
  To join the brimming river,
For men may come and men may go,
  But I go on forever.

I chatter over stony ways,
  In little sharps and trebles,
I bubble into eddying bays,
  I babble on the pebbles.

With many a curve my banks I fret,
  By many a field and fallow,
And many a fairy foreland set
  With willow-weed and mallow.

I chatter, chatter, as I flow
  To join the brimming river,
For men may come and men may go,
  But I go on forever.

I wind about, and in and out,
  With here a blossom sailing,
And here and there a lusty trout,
  And here and there a grayling;

And here and there a foamy flake
  Upon me as I travel,
With many a silvery waterbreak
  Above the golden gravel;

And draw them all along, and flow
  To join the brimming river;
For men may come and men may go,
  But I go on forever.

I steal by lawns and grassy plots,
  I slide by hazel covers;
I move the sweet forget-me-nots
  That grow for happy lovers.

I slip, I slide, I gloom, I glance,
  Among my skimming swallows;
I make the netted sunbeams dance
  Against my sandy shallows.

I murmur under moon and stars
  In brambly wildernesses;
I linger by my shingly bars,
  I loiter round my cresses.

And out again I curve and flow
  To join the brimming river,
For men may come and men may go,
  But I go on forever.

                              Alfred Tennyson

## 527.    ALL THINGS BRIGHT AND BEAUTIFUL

All things bright and beautiful,
  All creatures great and small,
All things wise and wonderful,
  The Lord God made them all.

Each little flower that opens,
  Each little bird that sings,
He made their glowing colours,
  He made their tiny wings.

The purple-headed mountain,
  The river running by,
The sunset, and the morning
  That brightens up the sky,

The cold wind in the winter,
  The pleasant summer sun,
The ripe fruits in the garden,
  He made them every one.

The tall trees in the greenwood,
  The meadows where we play,
The rushes by the water,
  We gather every day.

He gave us eyes to see them,
  And lips that we might tell
How great is God Almighty,
  Who has made all things well.

                     Cecil Frances Alexander,
                              1818-1895

## 528.   JUNE

And what is so rare as a day in June?
 Then, if ever, come perfect days;
Then heaven tries the earth if it be in tune,
 And over it softly her warm ear lays;
Whether we look, or whether we listen,
 We hear life murmur, or see it glisten;
Every clod feels the stir of might,
 An instinct within it that reaches and towers,
And, groping blindly above it for light,
 Climbs to a soul in grasses and flowers;
The flush of life may well be seen
 Thrilling back over hills and valleys;
The cowslip startles in meadows green.

The buttercup catches the sun in its chalice,
And there's never a leaf nor a blade too mean
 To be some happy creature's palace;
The little bird sits at his door in the sun,
 Atilt like a blossom among the leaves,
And lets his illumined being o'errun
 With the deluge of summer it receives.

His mate feels the eggs beneath her wings,
 And the heart in her dumb breast flutters and sings;
He sings to the wide world, and she to her nest--
 In the nice ear of nature, which song is the best?

James Russell Lowell

## 529.   A BALLAD OF TREES AND THE MASTER

Into the woods my Master went,
Clean forspent, forspent.
Into the woods my Master came,
Forspent with love and shame.
But the olives they were not blind to Him;
The little gray leaves were kind to Him;
The thorn-tree had a mind to Him
When into the woods He came.

Out of the woods my Master went,
And He was well content.
Out of the woods my Master came,
Content with death and shame.
When Death and Shame would woo Him last,
From under the trees they drew Him last:
'Twas on a tree they slew Him--last
When out of the woods He came.

Sidney Lanier,
1842-1881

## 530.   TREES

I think that I shall never see
A poem lovely as a tree.

A tree whose hungry mouth is pressed
Against the earth's sweet-flowing breast;

A tree that looks at God all day,
And lifts her leafy arms to pray;

A tree that may in summer wear
A nest of robins in her hair;

Upon whose bosom snow has lain;
Who intimately lives with rain.

Poems are made by fools like me,
But only God can make a tree.

Joyce Kilmer,
1886-1918

## 531. LIKE WHEN HE WAS A BOY

Along about this time o' year
When leaves begin to turn
And everything's all colored up,
It makes a feller yearn
To do the things he used to do
And always did enjoy;
Traipse through fields and woods again,
Like when he was a boy.

There's something 'bout this time o' year,
When there's purple, yeller 'n' red
And you're walkin' 'long an old rail fence
Just lookin' up ahead
Where the colors seem more gorgeous
Sort o' act as a decoy,
To lead a feller on and on,
Like when he was a boy.

To find a brown'd leaf hickory tree
As often he has found,
With nuts a layin' thick as hops
And coverin' up the ground,
A feller'll start to pickin' up
To fill his corduroy
Exactly as he used to do,
Like when he was a boy.

There's something 'bout this time o' year
That makes it really fine
To traipse 'round through the colors
Spread on bushes, trees and vine;
A feller has a feelin'
Of refreshin' overjoy--
Just drinkin' Nature's beauty in,
Like when he was a boy.

Ottis Shirk

## 532. SPACIOUS FIRMAMENT ON HIGH

The spacious firmament on high,
With all the blue eternal sky,
And spangled heavens a shining frame
Their great Original proclaim.
The unwearied sun, from day to day,
Does his Creator's power display,
And publishes to every land
The work of an Almighty hand.

Soon as the evening shades prevail
The moon takes up the wondrous tale

And nightly to the listening earth,
Repeats the story of her birth;
Whilst all the stars that round her burn,
And all the planets in their turn
Confirm the tidings as they roll,
And spread the truth from pole to pole.

What though the solemn silence all
Move round the dark terrestial ball;
What though no real voice nor sound
Amidst their radiant orbs be found?
In reason's ear they all rejoice
And utter forth a glorious voice;
Forever singing, as they shine,
"The hand that made us is divine."

Joseph Addison

*"The heavens declare the glory of God; and the firmament sheweth his handywork."--Ps. 19:1.*

## 533. DAFFODILS

I wandered lonely as a cloud
   That floats on high o'er vales and hills,
When all at once I saw a crowd,
   A host, of golden daffodils;
Beside the lake, beneath the trees,
Fluttering and dancing in the breeze.

Continuous as the stars that shine
   And twinkle on the Milky Way,
They stretched in never-ending line
   Along the margin of a bay;
Ten thousand saw I at a glance,
Tossing their heads in sprightly dance.

The waves beside them danced; but they
   Outdid the sparkling waves in glee;
A poet could not but be gay
   In such a jocund company;
I gazed--and gazed--but little thought
What wealth the show to me had brought.

For oft, when on my couch I lie
   In vacant or in pensive mood,
They flash upon that inward eye
   Which is the bliss of solitude;
And then my heart with pleasure fills,
And dances with the daffodils.

William Wordsworth

534.    THE OLD OAKEN BUCKET

How dear to this heart are the scenes of my childhood,
    When fond recollection presents them to view!
The orchard, the meadow, the deep-tangled wildwood,
    And every loved spot which my infancy knew;
The wide-spreading pond, and the mill that stood by it;
    The bridge and the rock where the cataract fell;
The cot of my father, the dairy-house nigh it,
    And e'en the rude bucket which hung in the well!
The old oaken bucket, the iron-bound bucket,
    The moss-covered bucket which hung in the well.

                                        Samuel Woodworth


535.  I SAW GOD WASH THE WORLD

I saw God wash the world last night
    With His sweet showers on high,
And then, when morning came, I saw
    Him hang it out to dry.

He washed each tiny blade of grass
    And every trembling tree;
He flung His showers against the hill,
    And swept the billowing sea.

The white rose is a cleaner white,
    The red rose is more red,
Since God washed every fragrant face
    And put them all to bed.

There's not a bird, there's not a bee
    That wings along the way
But is a cleaner bird and bee
    Than it was yesterday.

I saw God wash the world last night.
    Ah, would He had washed me
As clean of all my dust and dirt
    As that old white birch tree.

                Wm. L. Stidger,
                    1885-


536.    THE STAR

Twinkle, twinkle, little star,
How I wonder what you are,
Up above the world so high,
Like a diamond in the sky.

When the blazing sun is set,
And the grass with dew is wet,
Then you show your little light,
Twinkle, twinkle, all the night.

Then the traveler in the dark
Thanks you for your tiny spark,
He could not see where to go
If you did not twinkle so.

In the dark blue sky you keep,
And often through my curtains peep,
For you never shut your eye
Till the sun is in the sky.

As your bright and tiny spark
Lights the traveler in the dark,
Though I know not what you are,
Twinkle, twinkle, little star.

                        Jane Taylor

# PATRIOTISM

### 537.    PAUL REVERE'S RIDE

Listen, my children, and you shall hear
Of the midnight ride of Paul Revere,
On the eighteenth of April, in Seventy-five;
Hardly a man is now alive
Who remembers that famous day and year.

He said to his friend, "If the British march
By land or sea from the town tonight,
Hang a lantern aloft in the belfry arch
Of the North Church tower as a signal light--
One, if by land, and two, if by sea;
And I on the opposite shore will be,
Ready to ride and spread the alarm
Through every Middlesex village and farm,
For the country folk to be up and to arm."

Then he said, "Goodnight!" and with muffled oar
Silently rowed to the Charlestown shore,
Just as the moon rose over the bay,
Where swinging wide at her moorings lay
The **Somerset**, British man-of-war;
A phantom ship, with each mast and spar
Across the moon like a prison bar,
And a huge black hulk, that was magnified
By its own reflection in the tide.

Meanwhile, his friend, through alley and street,
Wanders and watches, with eager ears,
Till in the silence around him he hears
The muster of men at the barrack door,
And the measured tread of the grenadiers,
Marching down to their boats on the shore.

Then he climbed to the tower of the Old North Church,
By the wooden stairs, with stealthy tread,
To the belfry-chamber overhead,
And startled the pigeons from their perch
On the somber rafters, that round him made
Masses and moving shapes of shade--
By the trembling ladder, steep and tall,
To the highest window in the wall,
Where he paused to listen and look down
A moment on the roofs of the town,
And the moonlight flowing over all.

Beneath in the churchyard, lay the dead,
In their night-encampment on the hill,
Wrapped in silence so deep and still
That he could hear, like a sentinel's tread,
The watchful night-wing, as it went
Creeping along from tent to tent,

And seeming to whisper, "All is well!"
A moment only he feels the spell
Of the place and the hour, and the secret dread
Of the lonely belfry and the dead;
For suddenly all his thoughts are bent
On a shadowy something far away,
Where the river widens to meet the bay--
A line of black that bends and floats
On the rising tide, like a bridge of boats.

Meanwhile, impatient to mount and ride,
Booted and spurred, with a heavy stride
On the opposite shore walked Paul Revere.
Now he patted his horse's side,
Now gazed at the landscape far and near,
Then, impetuous, stamped the earth,
And turned and tightened his saddle girth;
But mostly he watched with eager search
The belfry tower of the Old North Church,
As it rose above the graves on the hill,
Lonely and spectral and somber and still.

And lo! as he looks, on the belfry's height
A glimmer, and then a gleam of light!
He springs to the saddle, the bridle he turns,
But lingers and gazes, till full on his sight
A second lamp in the belfry burns!

A hurry of hoofs in a village street,
A shape in the moonlight, a bulk in the dark,
And beneath, from the pebbles, in passing, a spark
Struck out by a steed flying fearless and fleet:
That was all! And yet, through the gloom and the light,
The fate of a nation was riding that night;
And the spark struck out by that steed, in his flight,
Kindled the land into flame with its heat.

He has left the village and mounted the steep,
And beneath him, tranquil and broad and deep,
Is the Mystic, meeting the ocean tides;
And under the alders that skirt its edge,
Now soft on the sand, now loud on the ledge,
Is heard the tramp of his steed as he rides.

It was twelve by the village clock,
When he crossed the bridge into Medford town.
He heard the crowing of the cock,
And the barking of the farmer's dog,
And felt the damp of the river fog,
That rises after the sun goes down.
It was one by the village clock,
When he galloped into Lexington.
He saw the gilded weathercock
Swim in the moonlight as he passed,
And the meeting-house windows, blank and bare,

Gaze at him with a spectral glare.
As if they already stood aghast
At the bloody work they would look upon.

It was two by the village clock,
When he came to the bridge in Concord town.
He heard the bleating of the flock,
And the twitter of birds among the trees,
And felt the breath of the morning breeze
Blowing over the meadows brown.
And one was safe and asleep in his bed
Who at the bridge would be first to fall,
Who that day would be lying dead,
Pierced by a British musket-ball?

You know the rest. In the books you have read
How the British Regulars fired and fled--
How the farmers gave them ball for ball,
From behind each fence and farmyard wall,
Chasing the red-coats down the lane,
Then crossing the fields to emerge again
Under the trees at the turn of the road,
And only pausing to fire and load.

So through the night rode Paul Revere;
And so through the night went his cry of alarm
To every Middlesex village and farm--
A cry of defiance and not of fear,
A voice in the darkness, a knock at the door,
And a word that shall echo forevermore!
For, borne on the night-wind of the Past,
Through all our history, to the last,
In the hour of darkness and peril and need,
The people will awaken and listen to hear
The hurrying hoof-beats of that steed,
And the midnight message of Paul Revere.

Henry Wadsworth Longfellow

## 538. HERE COMES THE FLAG!

Here comes the flag,
  Hail it!
Who dares to drag
  Or trail it?
Give it hurrahs--
Three for the stars,
Three for the bars.
  Uncover your head to it!
  The soldiers who tread to it
  Shout at the sight of it,
  The justice and right of it,
  The unsullied white of it,
  The blue and the red of it,
  And tyranny's dread of it!

Here comes the flag!
  Cheer it!
Valley and crag
  Shall hear it.
  Fathers shall bless it,
  Children caress it,
  All shall maintain it,
  No one shall stain it.
Cheers for the sailors that fought on the wave for it,
Cheers for the soldiers that always were brave for it,
Tears for the men that went down to the grave for it.
    Here comes the flag!

Arthur Macy

### 539. I THOUGHT OF FREE

On Independence Day I thought of "Free";
As if the word were new, it came to me.
I thought of those who aren't and those who are;
Some of both are near and some are far.
I thought of those who think of "Free" with me,
They think the most who have no liberty.

On Independence Day, I thought of "Free";
And those who've tasted liberty.
I'd rather say that I have never seen
A ray of light, than say I've never been
Completely free. And yet, that's what they say,
The ones who've never lived in freedom's day.

On Independence Day, I thought of "Free";
And those who are are those who trouble me,
For, right today we see the ones who were
Are not. Unthinking now, they cannot stir
To loose their chains and gain their liberty.
On Independence Day I thought of "Free."

On Independence Day, I thought of "Free."
Determined more to love my liberty,
I shook myself. What happened to the ones
Who had been free could happen to the sons
Of liberty. Responsibility
Cries out to me: "Freedom is not free!"

Bill Harvey

*"And ye shall know the truth, and the truth shall make you free...If the Son therefore shall make you free, ye shall be free indeed."*
*--John 8:32,36.*

### 541. SAIL ON, O SHIP OF STATE!

Thou, too, sail on, O Ship of State!
Sail on, O Union, strong and great!
Humanity with all its fears,
With all its hopes of future years,
Is hanging breathless on thy fate!
We know what Master laid thy keel,
What Workmen wrought thy ribs of steel,
Who made each mast, and sail, and rope,
What anvils rang, what hammers beat,
In what a forge and what a heat
Were shaped the anchors of thy hope!
Fear not each sudden sound and shock,
'Tis of the wave and not the rock;
'Tis but the flapping of the sail,

### 540. A TOAST TO THE FLAG

Here's to the red of it:
There's not a thread of it,
No, nor a shred of it
In all the spread of it
    From foot to head,
But heroes bled for it,
Faced steel and lead for it,
Precious blood shed for it,
    Bathing it Red!

Here's to the white of it:
Thrilled by the sight of it,
Who knows the right of it
But feels the might of it
    Through the day and night?
Womanhood's care for it,
Made manhood dare for it,
Purity's prayer for it
    Keeps it so White!

Here's to the blue of it:
Beauteous view of it,
Heavenly hue of it,
Star-spangled dew of it--
    Constant and true.
States stand supreme for it,
Diadems gleam for it,
Liberty's beam for it
    Brightens the Blue!

Here's to the whole of it:
Stars, stripes and pole of it,
Body and soul of it;
On to the goal of it--
    Carry it through.
Home or abroad for it,
Unsheathe the sword for it,
Fight in accord for it--
    Red, White and Blue!

John Jay Daly

And not a rent made by a gale!
In spite of rock and tempest's roar,
In spite of false lights on the shore,
Sail on, nor fear to breast the sea!
Our hearts, our hopes, are all with thee,
Our hearts, our hopes, our prayers, our tears,
Our faith, triumphant o'er our fears,
Are all with thee,--are all with thee!

Henry Wadsworth Longfellow

## 542. BREATHES THERE THE MAN

Breathes there the man, with soul so dead,
Who never to himself hath said,
   This is my own, my native land!
Whose heart hath ne'er within him burn'd,
As home his footsteps he hath turn'd
   From wandering on a foreign strand?
If such there breathe, go, mark him well;
For him no minstrel raptures swell;
High though his titles, proud his name,
Boundless his wealth as wish can claim,--
Despite those titles, power, and pelf,
The wretch, concentred all in self,
Living, shall forfeit fair renown,
And, doubly dying, shall go down
To the vile dust from whence he sprung,
Unwept, unhonor'd, and unsung.

> From "The Lay of the Last Minstrel,"
> Canto VI
> By Sir Walter Scott, 1771-1832

## 543. A NATION'S STRENGTH

Not gold, but only man can make
   A people great and strong;
Men who, for truth and honor's sake,
   Stand fast and suffer long.

Brave men who work while others sleep,
   Who dare while others fly--
They build a nation's pillars deep
   And lift them to the sky.

> Ralph Waldo Emerson

## 544. THE FLAG GOES BY

   Hats off!
Along the street there comes
A blare of bugles, a ruffle of drums,
A flash of color beneath the sky:
   Hats off!
The flag is passing by!

Blue and crimson and white it shines,
Over the steel-tipped, ordered lines.
   Hats off!
The colors before us fly;
But more than the flag is passing by:
Sea-fights and land-fights, grim and great,
Fought to make and to save the State;
Weary marches and sinking ships;
Cheers of victory on dying lips;

Days of plenty and years of peace;
March of a strong land's swift increase;
Equal justice, right and law,
Stately honor and reverend awe;

Sign of a nation great and strong
To ward her people from foreign wrong;
Pride and glory and honor--all
Live in the colors to stand or fall.

   Hats off!
Along the street there comes
A blare of bugles, a ruffle of drums;
And loyal hearts are beating high:
   Hats off!
The flag is passing by!

> Henry Holcomb Bennett

# PRAISE and THANKSGIVING

### 545.   SONGS IN THE MOUNTAINS

There are songs in the mountains, there are songs in the vale,
Hearts may sing in the daytime, and when night shade prevails.
Oh, then sing when the birds sing or when storm clouds are low,
For the saints can rejoice while God His blessings bestow.

There will come days of sadness, there may come times of need;
The Saviour is with me, He's my Shepherd indeed.
For He bears all my burdens, and He comforts my heart;
He is here when I need Him; He will never depart.

The light songs of the worldlings do not last through the night,
The rejoicings of sinners often change into fright.
But the heartease of Eden, in the soul of God's own,
Is the gift of our Saviour, with His presence made known.

I've a Spirit to comfort, and to teach and to guide,
I've a Father to hear me, let whatever betide.
And my High Priest forever takes my part at the throne,
So I sing on my journey, for I'm never alone.

So I sing, sing, sing! Sing, sing, sing!
For I'm happy in Jesus, there's a song in my soul!

John R. Rice

### 546.   HE IS MINE

He is mine.  The great Creator
Spoke, and worlds came into being;
  Countless stars as yet unnumbered,
  Boundless deeps as yet unfathomed,
  Mighty mountains, rushing rivers--
And He's mine.

He, the mighty God of power,
Yet with tender hands of mercy
  Spun the iridescent moonbeams
  And infinitesimal beings,
  Fashioned filigrees of snowflakes,
And He's mine.

He is mine.  The great Creator
Is my Father, Christ my Saviour.
  And in me the Holy Spirit
  Dwells to be my guide and comfort.
  Not three gods, but One--the Triune,
And He's mine.
Praise God, He's mine.

Maxine Stevens

### 547.  WHAT GLORY GILDS

What glory gilds the sacred page!
  Majestic, like the sun,
It gives a light to every age;
  It gives, but borrows none.

The power that gave it still supplies
  The gracious light and heat;
Its truths upon the nations rise;
  They rise, but never set.

Lord, everlasting thanks be Thine
  For such a bright display,
As makes a world of darkness shine
  With beams of heavenly day.

My soul rejoices to pursue
  The steps of Him I love,
Till glory breaks upon my view
  In brighter worlds above.

Author Unknown

## 548. GOD IS GOOD

Though trials come, though fears assail,
    Through tests scarce understood;
One trust shines clear; it cannot fail--
    My God is right and good.

Though times be dark, the struggle grim,
    And cares rise like a flood;
This sweet assurance holds to Him--
    My God is near and good.

When health gives way, the body breaks,
    When seized by darkest mood;
E'en yet God maketh no mistakes--
    My God is wise and good.

Through nights of pain when doubts rise high,
    Death's shade doth haunt and brood;
My heart is fixed, for He is nigh--
    My faithful God is good.

When fervent prayers unanswered go,
    And Providence seems rude;
To all our plans His will says, No!
    Yes, God is changeless, good.

As long as Heaven and earth do stand,
    So long His oath hath stood;
And though I may not comprehend,
    I know my God is good.

Since His own Son for man God gave
    And Christ died on the rood;
I cannot doubt His power to save--
    I know He's love, He's good.

Come then what may of storm and stress,
    Of strife or pain or blood;
In this fixed trust my heart shall rest--
    My God is God, He's good!

                          Harry J. Hager

## 549. GOD LOVED AND GAVE HIS SON

How often do I wonder
    That Christ should love me so;
But never can I answer
    Why He such love should show;
It passeth understanding,
    Outreaching human thought,
That He, the Lord of glory,
    My soul with blood hath bought.

                          E. G. K. Wesley

## 550. SING UNTO THE LORD

He listened as the pastor spoke,
He bowed his head for prayer;
And when the off'ring plate was passed
He gladly gave his share.

But when a hymn was wont to sing,
He tightly sealed his tongue,
'Til songs of praise that cried for strength
Were weak and feebly sung.

Not just because he failed to sing,
But others joined him, too,
And mocked with hollow silence
The praises of the few.

Forgive us, Lord, who fail to see
The glory of the song,
That nobly lifts the name of Christ
Above all sin and wrong.

And tune our hearts to sing Thy praise
Until each sincere soul
Shall stand condemned within his heart
To shrink back from our goal--

The goal that each heart born anew
May gladly join our song;
Not just within the worship hour,
But through the whole day long.

                          Ronald K. Wells

## 551. FOR THOSE WHO SING

Sometimes I envy you, when lovely songs
Are aching to be sung, and in my heart
A music with its many voices throngs,
Yet, inarticulate, I stand apart.
To lift the voice as sure as any bird
Of clear perfection in each thrilling note,
This must be joy! To bring each
                    shining word
To living beauty, capture the remote
And subtle fire that only singers know!
How may I praise this sweet ability,
Save in my little rhymes that try to show
I recognize what such a gift can be?
Yet God has given me this blessed thing--
To know, at least, the art of listening!

                          Lee Avery

## 552. "MY CUP RUNNETH OVER"

There is always something over
  When we trust our gracious Lord,
Every cup He fills o'erfloweth,
  His great rivers all are broad.
Nothing narrow, nothing stinted,
  Ever issues from His store;
To His own He gives full measure,
  Running over, evermore.

There is always something over
  When we, from the Father's hand,
Take our portion with thanksgiving,
  Praising for the path He planned.
Satisfaction, full and deepening,
  Fills the soul, and lights the eye,
When the heart has trusted Jesus,
  All its need to satisfy.

There is always something over
  When we tell of all His love;
Unplumbed depths still lie beneath us,
  Unscaled heights rise far above:
Human lips can never utter
  All His wondrous tenderness,
We can only praise and wonder,
  And His name forever bless.

        Margaret E. Barber

## 553. "IN EVERY THING GIVE THANKS!"

'Mid sunshine, cloud or stormy days,
When hope abounds or care dismays;
When trials press and toils increase,
Let not thy faith in God decrease--
  "In every thing give thanks."

All things we know shall work for good,
Nor would we change them if we could;
'Tis well if only He commands;
His promises will ever stand--
  "In every thing give thanks."

He satisfies the longing heart,
He thwarts the tempter's cruel dart,
With goodness fills the hungry soul,
And helps us sing when billows roll.
  "In every thing give thanks."

        Selected

## 554. BORN A SAVIOUR

Jesus, a Saviour born
  Without:
Without the inn, refused with scorn.
  Cast out:
Cast out for me, my Saviour King,
  Cast out to bring this lost one in.

Jesus, a Saviour born
  A man:
A man of sorrows, smitten, torn,
  By stripes:
By stripes, O Lord, my soul is healed,
By stripes, Thy stripes, my pardon sealed.

Jesus, a Saviour born
  The Lamb:
The Lamb of God hath bled and borne
  My sins:
My sins the Sacrifice did slay,
My sins the Lamb doth take away.

Jesus, a Saviour born
  To save:
To save at night, at noon, at morn.
  To keep:
To keep from sin, from doubt, from fear,
To keep, for lo! the Keeper's here.

Jesus, a Saviour born
  A King:
A King! exalt His glorious horn
  And sing:
Oh, sing ye Heavens! He burst His grave.
And sing, O earth, He lives to save.

        The late General Bramwell Booth

## 555. CHRIST MAKES THE DIFFERENCE

Heaven above is softer blue,
  Earth beneath is sweeter green,
Something lives in every hue,
  Christless eyes have never seen!

Birds with sweeter songs o'erflow,
  Flowers with newer beauty shine,
Since I know as now I know
  I am His and He is mine!

        Selected

## 556. IN EVERYTHING GIVE THANKS

When clouds of sorrow sweep across my sky of brilliant hue,
When grey and somber, warlike, fierce they hide away the blue,
I am not bidden to despair or mope with clouded brow;
God's Word comes shining--'tis His Sun, my courage to endow,
"In Everything Give Thanks!"

When faced with dire calamity, when driven to despair,
When tempted to cry out, "My God! Thy dealings are unfair!"
He shows me One whose awful grief made Heaven hide its face;
And then His Word comes shining through to give sustaining grace--
"In Everything Give Thanks!"

When bounties rich and plentiful are lavished from His hand,
When all my needs are met by Him on whom my life depends,
'Tis then of all times, I am tempted to forget His Love,
Forget to offer praise to Him, to lift mine eyes above--
"In Everything Give Thanks!"

God grant that I may learn to walk so humbly with my Lord,
So keep in fellowship with Him, abiding in His Word,
That not **one** day but **every** day may be Thanksgiving Day,
That life and lips, and all I am--may all of me, alway,
"In Everything Give Thanks!"

                              Paul Hutchens

## 557. ONCE FOR ALL

*"...we are sanctified through the offering of the body of Jesus Christ once for all."—Heb. 10:10.*

Free from the law, O happy condition,
Jesus hath bled, and there is remission;
Cursed by the law and bruised by the fall,
Grace hath redeemed us once for all.

Now are we free--there's no condemnation,
Jesus provides a perfect salvation;
"Come unto Me," O hear His sweet call,
Come, and He saves us once for all.

"Children of God," O glorious calling,
Surely His grace will keep us from falling;
Passing from death to life at His call,
Blessed salvation once for all.

Once for all, O sinner, receive it;
Once for all, O brother, believe it;
Cling to the cross, the burden will fall,
Christ hath redeemed us once for all.

                    P. P. Bliss

## 558. SAVED, HALLELUJAH!

Once I was lost, but the cross of the Saviour
Loomed as a beacon to dispel despair.
There I saw Jesus, who died in my favor,
Offered forgiveness and Heaven so fair!

Would He receive me, a child of sin's
                darkness?
How could a just God o'er look all my
                wrong?
How could He heal such sin-sickness and
                harken
To cries for mercy I'd needed so long?

Open His arms were, receiving the sinner;
Freely forgiven were all of my sins;
Made me a son of God, new heart He gave me;
Wiped out the past and gave sweet
                peace within.

Saved, hallelujah! I'm born of the Spirit,
Redeemed by the blood of the Saviour
                who died.
Now I am justified, sins all forgiven;
I'm kept by the High Priest ascended on high.

                    John R. Rice

559.    THE OLD-TIME METHODIST
"AMEN CORNER"

You ask me why I look so sad, a sayin' not a word,
Why Beckie! thoughts of long ago, my memory have stirred;
I'm thinkin' of the meetin' house, where preached old Father
    Horner,
But, mostly, I've been thinkin' 'bout that dear old "amen corner."

Them days have long since fled and gone; dear friends have
    passed away;
And even the old meetin' house is goin' to decay;
I look around among the folks if any I may see:
But all are gone, it seems to me, but, Beckie, you and me.

I see the dear old corner yet; 'twas close beside the altar;
Them good old souls whose seats were there, had faith that
    wouldn't falter.
Their hearts were all aglow with love, their shouts would awe the
    scorner,
Like thunder claps their loud "amens" would shake the "amen
    corner."

Indeed, it seemed sometimes we sat by cool Siloam's fountain;
And then again, we seemed to stand on Sinai's awful mountain;
No matter what the text might be, for sinner, saint, or mourner,
There always flamed the Spirit's fire, around the "amen corner."

It was as if the Pentecost, with flaming tongues of fire,
Was still a bringin' Heaven down, and liftin' souls up higher;
And loud as was the earnest voice of dear old Father Horner,
Far louder were the glad amens that shook the "amen corner."

That dear old spot was holy ground, the very gate of Heaven;
The glory cloud seemed restin' there, by mercy's shower riven;
The manna and the smitten rock, our hungry souls sustainin',
Along the road beset with foes, from Egypt up to Canaan.

Sometimes, I well remember yet, things seemed a little dreary;
The meetin's 'peared a little slow, the people dull and weary;
Then victory would seem to be with Satan and the scorner
Until a "hallelujah" broke from out the "amen corner."

Then quick as lightning things would change, the foe would flee
    before us
And shouts of Glory! Praise the Lord! would blend in mighty
    chorus.
I tell you, Beckie, 'tis a truth, it cheered the weakest mourner;
Old Satan never could prevail against the "amen corner."

The tears will dim my failin' eyes, my heart seems almost broken
When now I'm in the meetin' house with not an "amen" spoken.
Our preacher is a learned man, not much like Father Horner,
Who preaches while the people "snore" in that old "amen corner."

They've got a bran' new meetin' house, with cushions for the people
And windows made of painted glass, and on the top a steeple;
An organ does the praisin' now, they've no bench for the mourner,
They've Brussels carpet on the floor, but where's the "amen corner"?

I tell you, Beckie, I believe that's why we keep retreating;
The world and Satan have combined, to give the church a beating;
They say they've found a better way, "religion has no mourner,
And so they've SMASHED the mourner's bench, and KILLED the
  "amen corner."

But wife, there's one thing comforts me, the church will be a standin',
When Satan and his scoffing crew have made a final landin',
The church is built on solid rock, and proof against the scorner,
We'll find the New Jerusalem much like the "amen corner."

        Louis Eisenbeis

## 560. THANKSGIVING

Once again our glad thanksgivings
 Rise before our Father's throne,
As we try to count the blessings
 Of the year so swiftly flown;
As we trace the wondrous workings
 Of His wisdom, power, and love
And unite our "Holy! Holy!"
 With the seraphim above.

As we gather round our firesides
 On this new Thanksgiving Day
Time would fail to count the blessings
 That have followed all our way.
Grace sufficient, help and healing,
 Prayer oft answered at our call;
And the best of all our blessings,
 Christ Himself, our All in all.

He has blessed our favored country
 With a free and bounteous hand;
Peace and plenty in our borders,
 Liberty through all our land.
And although our sins and follies
 Oft provoked Him to His face,
Mercy still restrains His judgments,
 And prolongs our day of grace.

While we love to count the blessings,
 Grateful for the year that's gone,
Faith would sweep a wider vision,
 Hope would gaze yet farther on.
For the signals all around us
 Seem with one accord to say,

"Christ is coming soon to bring us
 Earth's last, best, Thanksgiving Day!"
      A. B. Simpson

## 561. GLORY TO GOD!

Glory be to Him who loved us,
 Washed us from each sinful stain;
Glory be to Him who made us
 Priests and kings with Him to reign;
Glory, worship, laud, and blessing,
 To the Lamb who once was slain.

"Glory, worship, laud, and blessing"--
 Thus the choir triumphant sings;
"Honour, riches, power, dominion"--
 Thus its praise creation brings;
Thou art worthy, Thou art worthy,
 Lord of lords and King of kings.

Glory to the King of angels,
 Glory to the Church's King,
Glory to the King of nations,
 Heaven and earth His praises sing;
Glory ever and for ever
 To the King of Glory bring.

Glory be to Thee, O Father,
 Glory be to Thee, O Son,
Glory be to Thee, O Spirit,
 Glory be to God alone,
As it was, is now, and shall be
 While the endless ages run.
     Horatius Bonar

562.    LET THE JOY BELLS RING!

Let the joy bells ring, my sins are forgiven,
   Let the cup run o'er, my blessings o'erflow!
Let the music sing in praises to Jesus,
   For the riches mine are more than I know.

Sin had led me far, but love overtook me.
   Satan bound me fast, but Grace broke my chains.
All the world's allure never gave what it promised.
   But when Jesus found me, oh, what I gained!

Heaven, ope your doors, I'm coming with Jesus!
   Tell the world goodbye, I'm facing the sky.
Open arms, to greet, all the dear ones departed,
   For when Jesus calls, we'll come with glad cries.

There is room, more room, in heavenly mansions,
   And the way is Christ, He is the one Door.
And He comes to take His own into Heaven,
   Bids us come, and calls us o'er and o'er.

Oh, the joy fills my heart, that He loves me.
   What a treasure is Jesus today!
And I know I am His and He holds me,
   Ever loved, ever kept, ever saved.

            John R. Rice

563.  JESUS WEPT

Jesus wept! those tears are over,
   But His heart is still the same;
Kinsman, Friend, and Elder Brother,
   Is His everlasting name.
Saviour, who can love like Thee,
Gracious One of Bethany?

When the pangs of trial seize us,
   When the waves of sorrow roll,
I will lay my head on Jesus,
   Pillow of the troubled soul.
Surely, none can feel like Thee,
Weeping One of Bethany!

Jesus wept! and still in glory,
   He can mark each mourner's tear;
Living to retrace the story
   Of the hearts He solaced here.
Lord, when I am called to die,
Let me think of Bethany.

Jesus wept! that tear of sorrow
   Is a legacy of love;
Yesterday, today, tomorrow,

He the same doth ever prove.
Thou art all in all to me,
Living One of Bethany!

       Sir Edward Denny

564.   A SONG

It is a little thing--a song;
   And yet it brings the warmth of May,
And helps to make a faint heart strong,
   And gives a joy to each new day.

It is a little thing--a song;
   A lullaby to soothe the young;
A cheerful hum when tasks are long;
   A hymn of hope when hearts are wrung.

It is a little thing--a song;
   Yet Heaven would be a lonely place,
Despite the vastness of its throng,
   Without a choir to praise God's grace.

      Dorothy R. Larson

## 565.   THANKS TO GOD

*"In every thing give thanks: for this is the will of God in Christ Jesus concerning you."*
*—I Thess. 5:18.*

Thanks to God for my Redeemer;
 Thanks for all Thou dost provide;
Thanks for times now but a mem'ry;
 Thanks for Jesus, by my side;
Thanks for pleasant, balmy springtime;
 Thanks for dark and dreary fall,
Thanks for tears by now forgotten;
 Thanks for peace within my soul.

Thanks for prayers that Thou hast answered,
 Thanks for what Thou dost deny!
Thanks for storms that I have weathered,
 Thanks for all Thou dost supply!
Thanks for pain, and thanks for pleasure,
 Thanks for comfort in despair,
Thanks for grace that none can measure,
 Thanks for love beyond compare.

Thanks for roses by the wayside,
 Thanks for thorns their stems contain!
Thanks for home and thanks for fireside,
 Thanks for hope, that sweet refrain.
Thanks for joy and thanks for sorrow,
 Thanks for heavenly peace with Thee,
Thanks for hope in the tomorrow,
 Thanks through all eternity.

J. A. Hultman

## 566.   THE BEST FRIEND OF ALL

*"Unto him that loved us, and washed us from our sins in his own blood."—Rev. 1:5.*

How sweet the sunshine after rain,
And sweet the rest that follows pain;
But sweeter far His face to see,
The Son of God who died for me.

But not until He calls me Home,
No, not till then will I behold
The Saviour who did die for me,
And bore my sins on Calvary.

He suffered, bled and died alone,
Alone, alone for you and me.
Could I for shame reject such love,
A sacrifice from God above?

I do accept His sacrifice,
Will serve Him now forevermore;
For only such a Friend as He
Could pardon, cleanse and make me free.

If you receive His pardoning grace,
You'll meet Him yonder face to face,
And have a home in Heaven above
Where all is joy and peace and love.

Then when around God's throne we meet
And lowly bow at Jesus' feet,
A song of praise we'll ever sing
To Christ, our Saviour, Lord and King.

Ruby McKenzie

## 567.  THE PRAISE OF GOD

Speak, lips of mine!
 And tell abroad
 The praises of my God.
Speak, stammering tongue!
 In gladdest tone,
 Make His high praises known.

Speak, sea and earth!
 Heaven's utmost star,
 Speak from your realms afar!
Take up the note,
 And send it round
 Creation's farthest bound.

Speak, heaven of heavens!
 Wherein our God
 Has made His bright abode.

*"Be careful for nothing; but in every thing by prayer and supplication with thanksgiving let your requests be made known unto God."*
*—Phil. 4:6.*

Speak, angels, speak!
 In songs proclaim
 His everlasting name.

Speak, son of dust!
 Thy flesh He took
 And Heaven for thee forsook.
Speak, child of death!
 Thy death He died,
 Bless thou the Crucified.

Horatius Bonar

## 568. MY REDEEMER LIVES

I know that my Redeemer lives;
What joy the blest assurance gives!
He lives, He lives, who once was dead;
He lives, my everlasting Head!

He lives, to bless me with His love;
He lives, to plead for me above;
He lives, my hungry soul to feed;
He lives, to help in time of need.

He lives, to grant me daily breath;
He lives, and I shall conquer death;
He lives, my mansion to prepare;
He lives, to bring me safely there.

He lives, all glory to His name;
He lives, my Saviour, still the same--
What joy the blest assurance gives,
I know that my Redeemer lives!

                    Samuel Medley


## 569. EVER SAFE!

Safe in Jehovah's keeping,
  Safe in temptation's hour,
Safe in the midst of perils,
  Kept by Almighty power.
Safe when the tempest rages,
  Safe though the night be long;
E'en when my sky is darkest
  God is my strength and song.

          Sir Robert Anderson


## 570. THE BLESSINGS THAT REMAIN

There are loved ones who are missing
  From the fireside and the feast;
There are faces that have vanished,
  There are voices that have ceased;
But we know they passed forever
  From our mortal grief and pain,
And we thank Thee, O our Father,
  For the blessings that remain.

Thanksgiving, oh, thanksgiving,
  That their love once blessed us here,
That so long they walked beside us
  Sharing every smile and tear;
For the joy the past has brought us
  But can never take away,
For the sweet and gracious memories
  Growing dearer every day,

For the faith that keeps us patient
  Looking at the things unseen,
Knowing Spring shall follow Winter
  And the earth again be green,
For the hope of that glad meeting
  Far from mortal grief and pain--
We thank Thee, O our Father--
  For the blessings that remain.

              Annie Johnson Flint


## 571. A CHILD'S GRACE

Some hae meat and canna eat,
  And some wad eat that want it;
But we hae meat and we can eat,
  And sae the Lord be thankit.

                    Robert Burns


## 572. IN THE DEPTHS OF THE SEA

He hath cast in the depth of the fathomless sea,
All my sins and transgressions, tho' many they be,
Both the great and the small, the first and the last:
In the depths of the ocean I know they are cast,
I shall meet them no more for they never shall rise,
For who shall condemn whom God justifies?
So I sing of His mercy so wondrous and free,
He hath cast all my sins in the depths of the sea.

          From Evangelical Christian

# PRAYER

## 573.   THE MERCY SEAT

Jesus, where'er Thy people meet,
There they behold Thy mercy seat;
Where'er they seek Thee, Thou art found,
And every place is hallowed ground.

For Thou, within no walls confined,
Dost dwell with those of humble mind;
Such ever bring Thee where they come,
And, going, take Thee to their home.

Great Shepherd of Thy chosen few,
Thy former mercies here renew;
Here, to our waiting hearts, proclaim
The sweetness of Thy saving name.

Here may we prove the power of prayer
To strengthen faith and sweeten care;
To teach our faint desires to rise,
And bring all Heaven before our eyes.

What various hindrances we meet
In coming to a mercy seat!
Yet who that knows the worth of prayer
But wishes to be often there?

Prayer makes the darkened clouds withdraw;
Prayer climbs the ladder Jacob saw;
Gives exercise to faith and love;
Brings every blessing from above.

Restraining prayer, we cease to fight;
Prayer keeps the Christian's armor bright;
And Satan trembles when he sees
The weakest saint upon his knees.

While Moses stood with arms spread wide,
Success was found on Israel's side;
But when through weariness they failed,
That moment Amalek prevailed.

Have you no words? Ah, think again.
Words flow apace when you complain,
And fill your fellow creature's ear
With the sad tale of all your care.

Were half the breath thus vainly spent
To Heaven in supplication sent,
Our cheerful song would oftener be,
"Hear what the Lord has done for me!"

William Cowper

## 574.   SOMEBODY PRAYED!

The day was long; the burden I had borne
    Seemed heavier than I could longer bear,
And then it lifted--but I did not know
    Some one had knelt in prayer;

Had taken me to God that very hour,
    And asked the easing of the load, and He
In infinite compassion had stooped down
    And taken it from me.

We cannot tell how often as we pray
    For some bewildered one, hurt and
                    distressed,
The answer comes--but many times
                    those hearts
    Find sudden peace and rest.

Someone had prayed; and Faith, a
                    reaching hand,
    Took hold of God, and brought Him
                    down that day!
So many, many hearts have need of prayer--
    Oh, let us pray!

Grace Noll Crowell

## 575.   KEEPING VICTORY

Meet your Saviour in the morning
    In the secret place of prayer,
And obtain the strength and courage
    You shall need for ev'ry care.
Meet your loved ones and your neighbors,
    Meet your friends and meet your foes;
Meet the sinners and the Christians
    With sweet peace that overflows.

Meet your trials and your problems,
    Meet your heartaches and your sighs;
Meet your many disappointments,
    And whatever sorely tries,
With a heart of love and kindness
    And with faith that reaches God,
Knowing that His hand will lead you
    Up the way that saints have trod.

Walter E. Isenhour

## 576. TAKE TIME TO TALK WITH GOD

Take time to talk with God before you hurry  
   To life's appointed tasks. Bring all your care,  
Your disillusionment, your doubt, your worry.  
   And talk it over with the Lord in prayer.  

Take time to talk with God. He stands between you  
   And all the unexpected that can come:  
From every unseen foe His love would screen you,  
   And in its warmth are light and peace and home.  

Take time to talk with God. Be not contriving  
   To push beyond today's uncertain rim.  
Commit it to the Lord. Not all our striving  
   Can do as much as one small word with Him.  

Helen Frazee-Bower

## 577. "THE LORD BLESS THEE..."

With the gladness that knoweth no decay,  
With the riches that cannot pass away,  
With the sunshine that makes an endless day--  
   Thus may He bless thee.  

### "...AND KEEP THEE"

With the all-covering shadow of His wings,  
With the strong love that guards from evil things,  
With the sure power that safe to glory brings--  
   Thus may He keep thee.  

George Henderson

## 578. PRAY ANY TIME

Come at the morning hour;  
   Come, let us kneel and pray;  
Prayer is the Christian pilgrim's staff  
   To walk with God all day.  

At noon, beneath the Rock  
   Of Ages, rest and pray;  
Sweet is the shelter from the sun  
   In weary heat of day.  

At evening, in thy home,  
   Around its altars, pray;  
And finding there the house of God,  
   With Heaven then close the day.  

When midnight veils our eyes,  
   Oh, it is sweet to say,  
"I sleep, but my heart waketh, Lord,  
   With Thee to watch and pray."  

James Montgomery

## 579. PRAY!

Pray! for earth has many a need.  
Pray! for prayer is vital deed.  
Pray! for God in Heaven hears.  
Pray! prayer will move the spheres.  
Pray! for praying leads to peace.  
Pray! for prayer gives release.  
Pray! for prayer is never lost.  
Pray! for prayer well pays its cost.  
Pray! for prayer is always power.  

Pray! for every prayer's a flower.  
Pray! for prayer the Saviour finds.  
Pray! for prayer creation binds.  
Pray! for every prayer is gold.  
Pray! for prayer is joy untold.  
Pray! for praying frees from care.  
Pray! for Jesus joins your prayer.  

Amos R. Wells

### 580.  PRAY!

Pray in the early morning
   For grace throughout the day;
We know not what temptations
   And trials may cross our way.

Pray in the gladsome noontide,
   When the day is at its best;
Pray when the night o'ertakes thee
   To Him who giveth rest.

Pray in the silent midnight,
   If wakeful hours be thine;
Pray for a heart submissive,
   That never will repine.

Pray in the hour of sorrow,
   Pray in the hour of grief;
In coming to the Father,
   Thy soul shall find relief.

Pray when the sun shines brightest,
   Thy path with roses strewn;
Pray that thy heart be ever
   With the Saviour's kept in tune.

Pray when the dark day cometh,
   And clouds hang overhead;
In the secret of His presence
   Thy soul hath nought to dread.

Pray for the Father's guidance
   In all thy works and ways,
So shall thy days be fruitful,
   Thy life be full of praise.

Living in touch with Jesus,
   Keeping our own hearts right,
Others will be attracted
   From darkness into light.

                Mrs. Major Arnold

### 581.  UNANSWERED YET

Unanswered yet? the prayer your lips have pleaded
   In agony of heart these many years?
Does faith begin to fail? Is hope departing?
   And think you all in vain those falling tears?
Say not the Father hath not heard your prayer;
You shall have your desire sometime, somewhere.

Unanswered yet? though when you first presented
   This one petition at the Father's throne
It seems you could not wait the time of asking,
   So urgent was your heart to make it known.
Though years have passed since then, do not despair;
The Lord will answer you sometime, somewhere.

Unanswered yet? Nay, do not say ungranted;
   Perhaps your work is not yet wholly done.
The work began when first your prayer was uttered,
   And God will finish what He has begun.
If you will keep the incense burning there,
His glory you shall see sometime, somewhere.

Unanswered yet? Faith cannot be unanswered,
   Her feet are firmly planted on the Rock;
Amid the wildest storms she stands undaunted,
   Nor quails before the loudest thunder shock.
She knows Omnipotence has heard her prayer,
And cries, "It shall be done"--sometime, somewhere.

            Ophelia G. Browning

### 582. A CHORISTER'S PRAYER

I can't be just a pathway so that Thy words may tread--
For the path beneath the passerby is only something dead.
I can't be just a mirror, Lord, from which Thy psalms may shine--
Reflection is the only way a mirror can design.
I can't be just an echo which is softly heard,
For echoes tell just one small part, on which the words are strung,
For every word is born again and lives as it is sung.
Make me a child of God, that when I sing Thy song
Thy words become my very own and then I will be strong.
My voice is just a part of me, but all of me is Thine--
May I forget my glory, Lord, and make Thy glory shine!

*Author Unknown*

### 583. PRAYER

Prayer is the mightiest force that men can wield;
A power to which Omnipotence doth yield;
A privilege unparalleled, a way
Whereby the Almighty Father can display
His interest in His children's need and care.
Jehovah's storehouse is unlocked by prayer,
And faith doth turn the key. Oh, would that men
Made full proof of this wondrous means, for then
Would mightier blessings on the church be showered,
Her witness owned, her ministers empowered,
And souls ingathered. Then the Gospel's sound
Would soon be heard to earth's remotest bound.

*Anonymous*

### 584. WITH US!

In the silence of my chamber
  I may with my Saviour share
All my worries and my troubles,
  As I talk with Him in prayer.
When I kneel before my Master,
  I can feel His presence there,
And the load of care and sorrow
  Seems much easier to bear.

In the silence of my chamber
  I find peace, and lose despair,
For the glory of the Saviour
  Comes to me by way of prayer:
I can feel sweet peace descending
  Like a shower from above,
And my heart grows calm and tender
  In the blessing of His love.

*Selected*

### 585. PRAYER WITHOUT WORDS

Sometimes I do not pray in words--
I take my heart in my own hands
And hold it up before the Lord.
I am so glad He understands.

Sometimes I do not pray in words.
My spirit bows before His feet,
And with His hands upon my head
We hold communion silent, sweet.

Sometimes I do not pray in words.
For I am tired and long for rest.
My weary heart finds all it needs
Upon the Saviour's gentle breast.

*Martha Snell Nicholson*

## 586. AN HOUR WITH THEE

My heart is tired, so tired tonight;
    How endless seems the strife--
Day after day the restlessness
    Of all this weary life!
I come to lay the burden down
    That so oppresseth me,
And shutting all the world without
    To spend an hour with Thee,
        Dear Lord,
To spend an hour with Thee.

I would forget a little while
    The bitterness of tears,
The anxious thought that crowds my life
    That buried hopes in years;
Fraught with woman's weary toil
    My patient care must be.
A tired child I come tonight
    To spend an hour with Thee,
        Dear Lord,
One little hour with Thee.

A foolish, wayward child, I know,
    So often wandering;
A weak, complaining child--but, Oh!
    Forgive my murmuring,
And fold me to thy loving breast--
    Thou who hast died for me,
And let me feel 'tis peace to rest
    A little hour with Thee,
        Dear Lord,
One little hour with Thee.

The busy world goes on and on,
    I cannot heed it now,
Thy sacred hand is laid upon
    My aching, throbbing brow.
Life's toil will soon be past, and then,
    From all its sorrow free,
How sweet to think that I shall spend
    Eternity with Thee.
        Dear Lord,
Eternity with Thee!

Mary Wheaton Lyon

## 587. AT PRAYER MEETING

There were only two or three of us
    Who came to the place of prayer--
Came in the teeth of a driving storm;
    But for that we did not care.
Since after our hymns of praise had risen,
    And our earnest prayers were said,
The Master Himself was present there
    And gave us the living bread.

We knew His look in our leader's face
    So rapt and glad and free:
We felt His touch when our heads were bowed,
    We heard His "Come to Me."
Nobody saw Him lift the latch,
    And none unbarred the door;
But "peace" was His token to every heart,
    And how could we ask for more?

Each of us felt the load of sin
    From the weary shoulders fall:
Each of us dropped the load of care,
    And the grief that's like a pall;
And o'er our spirits a blessed calm
    Swept in from the jasper sea,
And strength was ours for toil and strife
    In the days that were thence to be.

It was only a handful gathered in
    To the little place of prayer;
Outside were struggle and pain and sin,
    But the Lord Himself was there;
He came to redeem the pledge He gave--
    Wherever His loved ones be
To stand Himself in the midst of them
    Though they count but two or three.

And forth we fared in the bitter rain
    And our hearts had grown so warm,
It seemed like the pelting of summer flowers
    And not the crash of storm;
" 'Twas a time of the dearest privilege
    Of the Lord's right hand," we said,
As we thought how Jesus Himself had come
    To feed us with living bread.

Margaret Sangster

## 588. TOO FAST

Slow me down, Lawd,
    I'se goin' too fast.
I can't see my brother
    When he's walkin' past.

I miss a lot of good things
    Day by day;
Don't know a blessing
    When it comes my way.

589.  ASK, SEEK, KNOCK

Is there anything too great for God to do?
  Is there ought beyond His pow'r?
He commanded us to open wide our mouth;
  We should ask our needs this hour!

Do you think He does not love enough to give
  All His children want and need?
His beloved Son He gave to save our souls;
  He would give all else indeed!

When we read the Book of God, we see His grace
  In His promises all through.
Every word reveals that God does answer pray'r;
  We should claim each promise true.

We may ask "in Jesus' name," or "ask in faith,"
  Pray united or alone;
We may pray with trembling faith, but pray we should;
  We should plead 'til it is done!

We should ask and seek
  Keep knocking at the door at Jesus' feet;
We have not our need
  Because we do not plead with Jesus!

John R. Rice

590.  THE HOUR OF PRAYER

My God, is any hour so sweet
  From blush of morn to evening star
As that which calls me to Thy feet,
  The hour of prayer?

Blest is that tranquil hour of morn,
  And blest that solemn hour of eve,
When, on the wings of prayer up-borne,
  The world I leave.

No words can tell what sweet relief
  Here for my every want I find;
What strength for warfare, balm for grief,
  What peace of mind.

Hushed is each doubt, gone every fear;
  My spirit seems in Heaven to stay,
And e'en the penitential tear
  Is wiped away.

Lord, till I reach that blissful shore,
  No privilege so dear shall be
As thus my inmost soul to pour
  In prayer to Thee.

Charlotte Elliott

591.  MY DAILY PRAYER

If I can do some good today,
If I can serve along life's way,
If I can something helpful say,
  Lord, show me how.

If I can right a human wrong,
If I can help to make one strong,
If I can cheer with smile or song,
  Lord, show me how.

If I can aid one in distress,
If I can make a burden less,
If I can spread more happiness,
  Lord, show me how.

If I can do a kindly deed,
If I can help someone in need,
If I can sow a fruitful seed,
  Lord, show me how.

If I can feed a hungry heart,
If I can give a better start,
If I can fill a nobler part,
  Lord, show me how.

Grenville Kleiser

592.  HE ANSWERS PRAYER

I believe God answers prayer,
Answers always, everywhere;
I may cast my anxious care,
Burdens I could never bear,
On the God who heareth prayer.
Never need my soul despair
Since He bids me boldly dare
To the secret place repair,
There to prove He answers prayer.

Selected

### 593. GOD'S VARIED ANSWERS

God answers prayer! the prayer of His dear children!
    He's sure to answer, if they keep His will.
He answers prayer! Yes,--prayer concerning all things!
    There's nothing overmuch for His great skill.

God answers prayer! Not always **when** we ask Him;
    It may seem good to Him that we should wait.
How long? Ah well, 'tis only He that knoweth;
    But sure, His answer will not be too late.

God answers prayer! Not always **as we want Him**;
    He does not always answer prayer with "Yes";
He sometimes answers "No!" because He loves us,
    And sees the thing we ask could never bless.

And God would have us learn to sweetly trust Him,--
    To chiefly want **His will**--not our request;
To know, whate'er may be His settled answer,
    His will is highest, holiest, and best.

Mourn not, then, soul, if God's unerring wisdom
    Should answer thy strong pleading with His "No!"
And afterward, perhaps up in the Glory,--
    It will be clear just why He willed it so.

Whate'er His "No!" may be,--whate'er it cost thee,
    Accept, submissively, His will as best,--
And thou shalt hear, more constantly, heart-music,--
    Enjoy a deeper, fuller, sweeter rest.

                        J. Danson Smith

### 594. GOD KNOWS THE ANSWER

I question not God's means or ways,
Or how He uses time or days,
To answer every call or prayer,
I know He will, somehow, somewhere.

I question not the time or place
When I shall feel His love and grace;
I only know that I believe,
And richest blessings shall receive.

I cannot doubt that He'll attend
My every call, and that He'll send
A ministering angel fair,
In answer to my faithful prayer.

                F. B. Whitney

### 595. WHO PRAYED?

Did you think of us this morning
    As you breathed a word of prayer?
Did you ask for strength to help us
    All our heavy burdens bear?

Someone prayed, and strength was given
    For the long and weary road,
Someone prayed and faith grew stronger
    As we bent beneath our load.

Someone prayed--the way grew brighter,
    And we walked all unafraid.
In our heart a song of gladness--
    Tell me, was it **you** who prayed?

                Selected

### 596.    HE PRAYED

*(Based on the Prayer Life of Jesus)*

| | |
|---|---|
| He prayed as He stood in Jordan | |
| To begin a mission of love; | Luke 3:21 |
| He prayed before the break of morn, | |
| For guidance from above. | Mark 1:35 |
| He prayed all night before He called | |
| The twelve to follow Him; | Luke 6:12 |
| He prayed beyond the close of day | |
| In twilight shadows dim. | Matt. 14:23 |
| | |
| He prayed for human confidence-- | |
| For faith to be made bold; | Luke 9:18 |
| He prayed till Heaven glorified | |
| His person and His goal. | Luke 9:29 |
| He prayed with joy at their return | |
| With hearts inspired and blest; | Luke 10:21 |
| He prayed in tears to raise the dead | |
| And shamed the doubting guest. | John 11:41 |
| | |
| He prayed and taught them how to pray | |
| With words to guide the way; | Luke 11:1 |
| He prayed from His own troubled soul | |
| And cried, "What can I say?" | John 12:27 |
| He prayed twice on His knees, | |
| And then fell on His face; | Luke 22:41 |
| He prayed till sweat became as drops of blood | |
| While drinking sin's disgrace. | Luke 22:44 |
| | |
| He prayed for those about Him then, | |
| For all as yet unborn; | John 17 |
| He prayed for one who stood in fear | |
| Beside the fire of scorn. | Luke 22:32 |
| He prayed, "Father, forgive them, | |
| They know not what they do." | Luke 23:34 |
| He prayed at Calvary's darkest hour, | |
| "O Father, where are You?" | Mark 15:34 |
| He prayed at last with dying breath, | |
| And bowed His head in peace; | |
| "Into Thy hands I commend my spirit"; | |
| And this earthly prayer life ceased. | Luke 23:46 |

J. Tillman Lake

### 597.    PRAYER

I know not by what methods rare,
But this I know, God answers prayer.
I know not when He sends the word
That tells us fervent prayer is heard.
I know it cometh soon or late:
Therefore we need to pray and wait.

I know not if the blessing sought
Will come in just the guise I thought.
I leave my prayers with Him alone
Whose will is wiser than my own.

Eliza M. Hickok

## 598. SAVIOUR, LIKE A SHEPHERD LEAD US

Saviour, like a shepherd lead us,
  Much we need Thy tender care;
In Thy pleasant pastures feed us,
  For our use Thy folds prepare:
Blessed Jesus, blessed Jesus,
  Thou hast bought us, Thine we are.

We are Thine, do Thou befriend us,
  Be the Guardian of our way;
Keep Thy flock, from sin defend us;
  Seek us when we go astray:
Blessed Jesus, blessed Jesus,
  Hear Thy children when they pray.

Thou hast promised to receive us,
  Poor and sinful though we be;
Thou hast mercy to relieve us,
  Grace to cleanse and power to free:
Blessed Jesus, blessed Jesus,
  Early let us turn to Thee.

Early let us seek Thy favor;
  Early let us do Thy will;
Blessed Lord and only Saviour,
  With Thy love our bosoms fill:
Blessed Jesus, blessed Jesus,
  Thou hast loved us, love us still.

Anonymous

## 599. O GOD, OUR HELP IN AGES PAST

O God, our help in ages past,
  Our hope for years to come,
Our shelter from the stormy blast,
  And our eternal home!

Under the shadow of Thy throne,
  Still may we dwell secure;
Sufficient is Thine arm alone,
  And our defense is sure.

Before the hills in order stood,
  Or earth received her frame,
From everlasting Thou art God
  To endless years the same.

O God, our help in ages past,
  Our hope for years to come;
Be Thou our guide while life shall last,
  And our eternal home.

Isaac Watts

## 600. I WANT MY FRIENDS TO PRAY FOR ME

I need the prayers of those I love
  While traveling on life's rugged way,
That I may true and faithful be,
  And live for Jesus every day.

I want my friends to pray for me,
  To bear my tempted soul above;
To intercede to God for me,
  I need the pray'rs of those I love.

I need the pray'rs of those I love,
  To help me in each trying hour,
To bear my tempted soul to Him,
  That He may keep me by His pow'r.

I want my friends to pray for me,
  To hold me up on wings of faith,
That I may walk the narrow way,
  Kept by our Father's glorious grace.

James D. Vaughan

## 601. SOMEONE PRAYED

The weary ones had rest, the sad had joy
  That day, and wondered "how?"
A plowman singing at his work had prayed,
  "Lord, help them now."

Away in foreign lands, they wondered "how"
  Their simple word had power.
At home, the gleaners, two or three had met
  To pray an hour.

Yes, we are always wondering "how?"
  Because we do not see
Someone, unknown perhaps, and far away
  On bended knee.

Selected

## 602. GRASS ON THE PRAYER PATH

From the converts of Uganda
Comes to us a story grander,
In the lesson that it teaches,
Than a sermon often preaches.

For they tell what sore temptation
Come to them; what need of patience,
And a need, all else outweighing,
Of a place of private praying.

So each convert chose a corner,
Far away from eye of scorner,
In the jungle, where he could
Pray to God in solitude.

And so often went thither,
That the grass would fade and wither,
Where he trod; and you could trace,
By the paths, each prayer place.

If they hear the evil tiding
That a brother is backsliding,
And that some are even saying,
"He no longer cares for praying;"

Then they say to one another,
Very soft and gently, "Brother,
You'll forgive us now for showing
On your path the grass is growing."

And the erring one, relenting,
Soon is bitterly repenting:
"Ah, how sad I am at knowing
On my path the grass is growing."

"But it shall be so no longer;
Prayer I need to make me stronger
On my path so oft' I'm going
Soon no grass will there be growing."

Author Unknown

## 603. THE SECRET PLACE

God met me there, in secret place this
morning,
   And I'm so glad that Jesus bids me pray!
A stranger there? Ah no, God is my Father!
   And I'm at home when'er I seek His face.

In secret prayer, He bids unload my burdens,
   And ask that He would give my heart's desire,
My daily bread, my need of grace and comfort,
   And wisdom give, and strength that will
                     not tire.

And when my sin and failure leave me shaken,
   And I am shamed to find I've gone astray,
I boldly come confessing all, intreating
   In Jesus' name, forgiveness, as I pray.

The secret place is where I wait for power.
   To tell the lost ones of His saving way.
And as I plead and tarry there before Him,
   God breathes His Spirit on me from above.

Oh, when I pray I talk with God my Father
   And there I ask Him all I need that hour.
Oh, blessed place and time of secret pleading
   For cleansing and His Holy Spirit power.

John R. Rice

## 604. I AM ONLY...

I am only a spark; make me a fire.
I am only a string; make me a lyre.
I am only a drop; make me a fountain.
I am only an ant hill; make me a mountain.
I am only a feather; make me a wing.
I am only a serf; make me a king.
I am only a link; make me a chain.
I am only a sprinkle; make me a rain.

Author Unknown

## 605. PROOF

If radio's slim fingers can pluck a melody
From night--and toss it over a continent or sea;
If the petalled white notes of a violin
Are blown across the mountains or the city's din;
If songs, like crimson roses, are culled from thin blue air--
Why should mortals wonder if God hears prayer?

Ethel Romig Fuller

### 606. A LITTLE TALK WITH JESUS

While fighting for my Saviour here,
  The tempter tries me hard;
He uses all his mighty pow'r,
  My progress to retard.
He's up to ev'ry move,
  But yet through all to prove
A little talk with Jesus makes it right, all right.

Though dark the night and clouds look black
  And stormy overhead,
And woes of almost ev'ry kind
  Across my path are spread;
How soon I conquer all
  As to the Lord I call--
A little talk with Jesus makes it right, all right.

When those who once were dearest friends
  Begin to persecute,
And more, who once professed to love,
  Have silent grown and mute;
I tell Him all my grief,
  He quickly sends relief--
A little talk with Jesus makes it right, all right.

And thus, by frequent little talks,
  I gain the victory,
And march along with cheerful song,
  Enjoying liberty.
With Jesus as my Friend,
  I'll prove until the end--
A little talk with Jesus makes it right, all right.

A little talk with Jesus makes it right, all right;
  A little talk with Jesus makes it right, all right;
In cares of ev'ry kind,
  Praise God, I always find
A little talk with Jesus makes it right, all right.

                              Anonymous

# SALVATION

### 607. OUT OF THE DEPTHS

Lost! Lost! Lost!
The cry went up from a sea--
The waves were wild with an awful wrath,
Not a light shone down on the lone ship's path;
The clouds hung low:
Lost! Lost! Lost!
Rose wild from the hearts of the tempest-tossed.

Lost! Lost! Lost!
The cry floated over the waves--
Far over the pitiless waves;
It smote on the dark and it rended the clouds:
The billows below them were weaving white shrouds
Out of the foam of the surge,
And the wind-voices chanted a dirge:
Lost! Lost! Lost!
Wailed wilder the lips of the tempest-tossed.

Lost! Lost! Lost!
Not the sign of a hope was nigh,
In the sea, in the air or the sky;
And the lifted faces were wan and white,
There was nothing without them but storm and night,
And nothing within but fear;
But far to a Father's ear,
Lost! Lost! Lost!
Floated the wail of the tempest-tossed.

Lost! Lost! Lost!
Out of the depths of the sea--
Out of the night and the sea;
And the waves and the winds of the storm were hushed
And the sky with the gleams of the stars was flushed.
Saved! Saved! Saved!
And a calm and a joyous cry
Floated up through the starry sky,
In the dark--in the storm--"Our Father" is nigh.

Father Ryan (a Catholic Priest)

### 608. SALVATION

Not what these hands have done
Can save this guilty soul;
Not what this toiling flesh has borne
Can make my spirit whole.

Not what I feel or do
Can give me peace with God;

Not all my prayers, my sighs, my tears
Can bear my awful load.

Thy work alone, O Christ,
Can ease this weight of sin;
Thy blood alone, O Lamb of God,
Can give me peace within.

Horatius Bonar

## 609. NOTHING TO PAY

Nothing to pay! the debt is so great.
What will you do with the awful weight?
How shall the way of escape be made?
Nothing to pay--yet it must be paid!
  Hear the voice of Jesus say;
"Verily thou hast nothing to pay!
All has been put to My account.
I have paid the full amount."

Nothing to pay; yes, nothing to pay!
Jesus has cleared all the debt away--
Blotted it out with His bleeding hand!
Free and forgiven, and loved, you stand.
  Hear the voice of Jesus say,
"Verily thou hast nothing to pay!
Paid is the debt, and the debtor free!
Now I ask thee, lovest thou Me?"

Author Unknown

## 610. COME, YE SINNERS

Come, ye sinners, poor and needy,
Weak and wounded, sick and sore;
Jesus, ready stands to save you,
Full of pity, love and power:
He is able, He is able,
He is willing: doubt no more.

Now, ye needy, come and welcome;
God's free bounty glorify;
True belief and true repentance,
Ev'ry grace that brings you nigh,
Without money, without money,
Come to Jesus Christ and buy.

Let not conscience make you linger,
Nor of fitness fondly dream;
All the fitness He requireth
Is to feel your need of Him:
This He gives you, this He gives you;
'Tis the Spirit's glimm'ring beam.

Come, ye weary, heavy-laden,
Bruised and mangled by the fall;
If you tarry till you're better,
You will never come at all;
Not the righteous, not the righteous,
Sinners Jesus came to call.

William J. Kirkpatrick

## 611. PRECIOUS BLOOD

Precious, precious blood of Jesus,
  Shed on Calvary;
Shed for rebels, shed for sinners,
  Shed for thee.

Precious, precious blood of Jesus,
  Let it make thee whole;
Let it flow in mighty cleansing
  O'er thy soul.

Though thy sins are red like crimson,
  Deep in scarlet glow,
Jesus' blood shall wash thee
  White as snow.

Precious blood whose full atonement
  Makes us nigh to God:
Precious blood, our way of glory,
  Praise and laud.

F. R. Havergal

## 612. THE PRODIGAL COMES HOME

I left my Father away from my home,
To the far country I eagerly roamed;
Wild were the nights and so hectic my days.
Then came the famine to stop my wild ways.

Sin lured so brightly and promised so much,
Oh, but how false to all who believe such!
Sin never blesses and sin never pays!
Heartbreak awaits at the end of that way.

Wild my companions; drank deep of the cup,
Money flowed freely, I scarce could keep up.
When I spent all and no longer could pay,
Gone were the friends of my prodigal days.

Then came the hogpen, when fain I would dine
On the scarce crumbs of a life such as mine.
No one would give me and no one did care.
Then came repentance from out my despair.

Back from the hogpen of sin to my Father.
Back for forgiveness--"I've sinned so,"
    I cried.
He came to meet me, His arms went
        around me,
White robe upon me, I'm safe home tonight.

John R. Rice

## 613.    A LITTLE PILGRIM
### OR JESUS PAID THE FARE

One summer evening, ere the sun went down,
When city men were hastening from the town,
To reach their homes--some near at hand, some far,
By snorting train, by omnibus or car,
To be beyond the reach of city's din,
A street car stopped, a little girl got in:
A cheery looking girl, scarce four years old;
Although not shy, her manners were not bold;
But all alone!  one scarce could understand.

She held a bundle in her little hand--
A tiny handkerchief with corners tied,
But which did not some bread and butter hide;
A satin scarf, so natty and so neat,
Was o'er her shoulders thrown.  She took her seat,
And laid her bundle underneath her arm,
And smiling prettily, but yet so calm,
To the conductor said, "May I sit here?"
He answered instantly, "Oh yes, my dear."
And there she seemed inclined to make her stay,
While once again the car went on its way.

The tall conductor--over six feet high,
Now scanned the travelers with a business eye;
But in that eye was something kind and mild,
That took the notice of the little child.

A little after, and the man went round,
And soon was heard the old familiar sound
Of gathering fares and clipping tickets too-
The car was full and he had much to do.

"Your fare, my little girl," at length he said.
She looked a moment, shook her little head,
"I have no pennies; don't you know," said she,
"My fare is paid, and Jesus paid for me?"

He looked bewildered--all the people smiled:
"I didn't know; and who is Jesus, child?"
"Why, don't you know He once for sinners died.
For little children, and for men beside,
To make us good, and wash us from our sin;
Is this His railway I am traveling in?"

"Don't think it is!  I want your fare, you know."

"I told you Jesus paid it long ago;
My mother told me just before she died
That Jesus paid when He was crucified;
That at the cross His railway did begin,
Which took poor sinners from a world of sin;
My mother said His Home was grand and fair,
I want to go and see my mother there--

I want to go to Heaven, where Jesus lives,
Won't you go too?  My mother said He gives
A loving welcome--shall we not be late?
I want to go before He shuts the gate;
And He bids little children come to Him."

The poor conductor's eyes felt rather dim,
He knew not why--he fumbled at his coat,
And felt a substance rising in his throat.
The people listened to the little child,
Some were in tears--the roughest even smiled,
And some one whispered as they looked amazed:
"Out of the mouth of babes the Lord is praised."

"I am a pilgrim," said the little thing:
"I'm going home.  My mother used to sing
To me of Jesus and His Father's love;
Told me to meet her in His home above.
And so today when aunt went out to tea,
And looking out I could not father see,
I got my bundle--this my little kit,
(I am so hungry--I'd like to have a bit!)
And got my hat, and then I left my home,
A little pilgrim up to Heaven to roam;
And then your nice car stopped, and I could see
You looked so kind--I saw you beckon me,
I thought you must belong to Jesus' train.
And are you going home to Heaven again?"


The poor conductor only shook his head;
Tears in his eyes--the power of speech had fled.
Had conscience by her prattle roused his fears,
And struck upon the fountain of his tears;
And made his thoughts in sad confusion whirl?

At last he said, "I had a little girl,
I loved her much; she was my little pet,
And with great fondness I remember yet
How much she loved me.  But one day she died."

"She's gone to Heaven," the little girl replied;
"She's gone to Jesus--Jesus paid her fare.
O dear conductor, won't you meet her there?"

The poor conductor now broke fairly down:
He could have borne the harshest look or frown,
But no one laughed; and many sitting by
Beheld the scene with sympathetic eye.

He kissed the child, for she his heart had won.
"I am so sleepy," said the little one,
"If you will let me, I'll lie here and wait
Until your street car comes to Jesus' gate;

Be sure you wake me up, and pull my frock,
And at the gate give just one little knock,
And you'll see Jesus there!"
          The strong man wept...

I could but think as from the car I stept,
How oft a little one has found the road,
The narrow pathway to that blest abode:
Through faith in Christ had read its title clear,
While learned men remain in doubt and fear.
A little child!  the Lord oft uses such
The stoutest heart to break, or bend, or touch;
Then by His Spirit bids the conflict cease,
And once forever enter into peace.

And now to all the happy news we bear:
That Jesus paid our fare.

                    Author Unknown

### 614.  PARDON

Now, oh joy! my sins are pardoned!
  Now I can and do believe!
All I have, and am, and shall be,
  To my precious Lord I give;
He roused my deadly slumbers,
  He dispersed my soul's dark night;
Whispered peace, and drew me to Him,
  Made Himself my chief delight.

Let the babe forget its mother,
  Let the bridegroom slight his bride;
True to Him, I'll love none other,
  Cleaving closely to His side.
Jesus, hear my soul's confession;
  Weak am I, but strength is Thine;
On Thine arms for strength and succor,
  Calmly may my soul recline!

                Albert Midlane

### 615.  HIGHWAY

By lonely trails that pioneers
  Blazed for the coming people's feet,
We trace the path of living truth
  From wilderness to city street,
And find the footprints of the Man
  Who bore love's cross out to a hill,
And built life's highway through to God
  Where all who seek may find it still.

            Albert Leonard Murray

### 616.  WHAT MUST I DO TO BE SAVED?

Nothing, either great or small,
  Nothing, sinner, no;
Jesus did it, did it all,
  Long, long ago.

When He from His lofty throne
  Stooped to do and die,
Everything was fully done;
  Hearken to His cry--

"It is finished!"  Yes, indeed!
  Finished every jot.
Sinner, this is all you need;
  Tell me is it not?

Weary, working, burdened one,
  Wherefore toil you so?
Cease your doing; all was done
  Long, long ago.

Till to Jesus' work you cling,
  By a simple faith,
"Doing" is a deadly thing--
  "Doing" ends in death.

Cast your deadly "doing" down--
  Down at Jesus' feet;
Stand "in Him," in Him alone,
  Gloriously "complete!"

                    Author Unknown

## 617. NOT 'TRY' BUT 'TRUST'

Not saved are we by trying;
    From self can come no aid;
'Tis on the blood relying,
    Once for our ransom paid.
'Tis looking unto Jesus,
    The Holy One and Just;
'Tis His great work that saves us--
    It is not 'try' but 'trust'!

No deeds of ours are needed
    To make Christ's merit more:
No frames of mind or feelings
    Can add to His great store;
'Tis simply to receive Him,
    The Holy One and Just;
'Tis only to believe Him--
    It is not 'try' but 'trust'!

Author Unknown

## 618. UNCLE REMUS'S REVIVAL HYMN

*Atlanta Constitution*

Oh! whar shall we go w'en de great day comes,
Wid de blowin' uv de trumpets an' de bangin' uv de drums?
How many po' sinners'll be cotched out late,
An' fine no latch to the goldin gate?
        No use fer to wait 'twell to-morrer--
        De sun mus'n't set on yo' sorrer.
        Sin's ez sharp ez a bamboo brier--
        O Lord! fetch the mo'ners up higher!

W'en de nashuns uv de earf is a stannin' all aroun',
Who's a gwine ter be choosen fer ter war de Glory crown?
Who's a gwine fer ter stan' stiff-kneed an' bol',
An' answer to dere name at de callin' uv de roll?
        You better come now ef you comin'--
        Ole Satan is loose an's a bummin'--
        De weels uv destrucshun is a hummin'--
        Oh, come along sinner, ef you comin'.

De song uv salvation is a mighty sweet song,
An' de Pairadise win' blo' fur an' blo' strong;
An' Aberham's buzzum is saf' an' it's wide,
An' dat's de place where de sinner orter hide.
        No use ter be stoppin' an' a lookin',
        Ef you fool wid Satan you'll git took in,
        You'll hang on de edge an' git shook in,
        Ef you keep on a stoppin' an' a lookin'.

De time is right now an' dis here's de place--
Let de salvashun sun shine squar' in yo' face,
Fight de battles uv de Lord, fight soon an' fight late,
An' you'll allers fine a latch on de goldin gate.
        No use fer ter wait 'twell to-morrer--
        De sun mus'n't set on yo' sorrer.
        Sin's ez sharp ez a bamboo brier--
        Ax de Lord fer ter fetch you up higher.

Joel Chandler Harris

## 619. THE INNOCENT FOR THE GUILTY

My sins laid open to the rod,
   The back which from the law was free;
And the eternal Son of God
   Received the stripes once due to me.

Nor beam was in His eye, nor mote;
   Nor laid to Him was any blame:
And yet His cheeks for me were smote--
   The cheeks that never blushed for shame.

I pierced those sacred hands and feet
   That never touched or walked in sin;
I broke the heart that only beat
   The souls of sinful men to win.

That sponge of vinegar and gall
   Was placed by me upon His tongue;
And when derision mocked His call,
   I stood that mocking crowd among.

And yet His blood was shed for me,
   To be of sin the double cure;
And balm there flows from Calv'ry's tree
   That heals my guilt and makes me pure.

            Author Unknown

## 620. COME AND TAKE SALVATION

The Spirit and bride say come to the Saviour,
O thirsty one, come and drink of His favor.
"Whosoever will" has God's invitation
To freely come take this blessed salvation.

The burden of sin, the conscience accusing
Will, lifted and cleansed, be just when you
            choose Him.
For Jesus has paid the price of your sinning,
Salvation for you His precious blood winning.

Believe on the Son, have life everlasting;
The fountain e'er flows, its water ne'er wasting.
Just trusting in Christ means no condemnation.
All praises to Him for such a salvation.

Why longer delay, defer such a blessing?
Why trifle with sin, why risk Heaven missing?
He stands at the door, oh, open to Jesus,
And praise God, He will in Christ's name
            receive us.

Oh, come and take salvation,
Full pardon and forgiveness;
Oh, come, from Christ take eternal life
And a home above.

            John R. Rice

## 621. MY TESTIMONY

Not the good that I have done,
Not the race that I have run,
But because of His dear Son,
I'm sealed unto redemption.

Not of what I give or take,
Not of habits I forsake,
But for His dear name's sake,
I'm sealed unto redemption.

Not because of righteous stand,
Not for keeping His command,
But I'm covered by His hand,
I'm sealed unto redemption.

Not by gifts so great or small,
Not of wrong I can forestall,
But because He gave His all,
I'm sealed unto redemption.

Not by deeds: I can't atone,
For this guilty heart of stone,
By His grace, and His alone,
I'm sealed unto redemption.

            Dale Hatcliff

## 622. ALL PAID!

Complete atonement Thou hast made,
And to the utmost farthing paid,
Whate'er Thy people owed;
How, then, can wrath on me take place,
Now standing in God's righteousness,
And sprinkled by the blood?

Since Thou hast my discharge procured,
And freely in my place endured
The whole of wrath divine,
Payment God will not twice demand,
First at my bleeding Surety's hand,
And then again at mine.

            Author Unknown

### 623. THEN JESUS CAME

BARTIMAEUS-- Mark 10:46
One sat alone beside the highway begging,
    His eyes were blind, the light he could not see;
He clutched his rags and shivered in the shadows,
    Then Jesus came and bade his darkness flee.

THE GADARENE DEMONIAC--Mark 5:1-8
From home and friends the evil spirits drove him,
    Among the tombs he dwelt in misery;
He cut himself as demon powers possessed him,
    Then Jesus came and set the captive free.

LAZARUS--John 11:1-44
Their hearts were sad as in the tomb they laid him,
    For death had come and taken him away;
Their night was dark and bitter tears were falling,
    Then Jesus came and night was turned to day.

SINNERS TODAY
So men today have found the Saviour able,
    They could not conquer passion, lust, and sin;
Their broken hearts had left them sad and lonely,
    Then Jesus came and dwelt Himself within.

When Jesus comes the tempter's power is broken;
    When Jesus comes the tears are wiped away.
He takes the gloom and fills the life with glory,
    For all is changed when Jesus comes to stay.

                    Oswald J. Smith

### 624. LEST HE WAIT OUTSIDE

No cradle waited for Him at His birth;
    Haste!  Clear your heart today!
Still homeless in the wilderness of earth,
    Make room for Him to stay.

The life is desolate that does not know
    The presence of this Guest;
The mind unsatisfied, although it go
    On far and varied quest.

Make shelter ready, lest He wait outside
    Who could transform your walls.
Unlatch the cautious door and fling it wide
    The instant Heaven calls!

                    Elinor Lennen

### 625. LORD, KEEP ME TRUE

For years and years I walked in sin,
    I had no peace without, within;
'Til one day Jesus came along,
    And put within my heart a song.
And now I praise Him day by day
    As I walk along the narrow way.

Methinks I hear Him say to me,
    "Come, My son, and you shall see
The glories and the mansions bright,
    Where comes no sickness and no night."
My heart did burn and stir anew;
    My prayer right there was
        "Lord, keep me true."

                    Selected

## 626. THE THREE BIDDERS

**The Conversion of Lady Ann Erskine**

(A True Incident in the Life of Rowland Hill.)

Will you listen, kind friends, for a moment,
　While a story to you I unfold;
A marvelous tale of a wonderful sale
　Of a noble lady of old:--
How hand and heart, at an auction mart,
　Both soul and body, she was sold!

'Twas in the broad "king's highway,"
　Near a century ago,
That a preacher stood--though of noble blood--
　Telling the fallen and low
Of a Saviour's love, and a Home above,
　And a peace that they all might know.

All crowded around to listen:
　They wept at the wondrous love,
That could put away sin and welcome them in
　His spotless mansion above:--
While slow through the crowd, a lady proud,
　Her gilded chariot drove.

"Make room," cried the haughty outrider,
　"You are closing the king's highway;
My lady is late, and their Majesties wait;
　Give way, good people, I pray."
The preacher heard and his soul was stirred,
　And he cried to the rider, "Nay."

Then--bending his gaze on the lady,
　And marking her soft eye fall--
"And now in His name, a sale I proclaim
　And bids for this fair lady call.
Who will purchase the whole--her body and soul,
　Coronet, jewels and all?

"I see already three bidders--
　THE WORLD steps up as the first:
'I will give her my treasures, and all the pleasures
　For which my votaries thirst;
She shall dance each day more joyous and gay,
　With a quiet grave at the worst.'

"But out spoke THE DEVIL, boldly:
　'The kingdoms of earth are mine.
Fair lady, thy name, with an envied fame,
　On their brightest tablets shall shine;
Only give me thy soul, and I give thee the whole
　Their glory and wealth to be thine.'

"And, pray, what hast **Thou** to offer,
　Thou MAN OF SORROWS unknown?
And He gently said: 'My blood I have shed

To purchase her for Mine own;
To conquer the grave, and her soul to save,
   I trod the winepress alone.

" 'I will give her My cross of suffering,
   My cup of sorrow to share;
But with endless love, in My Home above,
   All shall be righted there:
She shall walk in light, in a robe of white,
   And a radiant crown shall wear.' "

"Thou hast heard the terms, fair lady,
   That each hath offered for thee.
Which wilt thou choose, and which wilt thou lose,
   This life, or the life to be?
The fable was mine, but the choice is yet thine.
   Which of the three shall it be?"

"Pardon, good people," she whispered,
   As she rose from her cushioned seat;--
Full well, they say, as the crowd made way
   You could hear her pulses beat;
And each head was bare, as the lady fair
   Knelt at the preacher's feet.

She took from her hand the jewels,
   The coronet from her brow;
"Lord Jesus," she said, as she bowed her head,
   "The highest bidder art Thou;
Thou gav'st for my sake, Thy life, and I take
   Thine offer--and take it now.

"I know the World and her pleasures,
   At best they weary and cloy;
And the Tempter is bold, but his honors and gold
   Prove ever a fatal decoy;
I long for Thy rest--Thy bid is the best,
   Lord Jesus I accept it with joy!"

"Amen," said the noble preacher;
   And the people wept aloud.
Years have rolled on--and they all have gone,
   Who formed that awe-struck crowd.
Lady and throng have been swept along,
   As on the wind a morning cloud.

But the Saviour has claimed His purchase;
   And around His radiant seat,
A mightier throng, in an endless song,
   The wondrous story repeat;
And a form more fair, is bending there,
   Laying her crown at His feet.

                    Author Unknown

## 627. FOUND WANTING?

At the feast of Belshazzar and a thousand of his lords,
While they drank from golden vessels as the Book of Truth records;
In the night, as they revelled, in the royal palace hall,
They were seized with consternation, 'twas the Hand upon the wall.
So our deeds are recorded--there's a Hand that's writing now;
Sinner, give your heart to Jesus, to His royal mandates bow;
For the day is approaching; it must come to one and all,
When the sinner's condemnation will be written on the wall.
    'Tis the hand of God on the wall!
      Shall the record be "Found wanting"
      Or shall it be "Found trusting"
    While that Hand is writing on the wall?

Author Unknown

## 628. WRITTEN; KNOW; HAVE

This piece of paper in your hand
Declares to you that, on demand,
You twenty shillings shall receive:
This simple promise you believe,
It sets your mind as much at rest,
As though the money you possessed.
So Christ who died, but now doth live,
Doth unto you this promise give--
That if on Him you will believe,
Eternal life you shall receive.
Upon the first you calmly rest;
Which is the safer? Which the best?
The Bank may break, Heaven never can;
'Tis safer trusting God than man.

(Written on the back of a Bank of Ireland note.)

## 629. RESOLVED!

"...and if I perish, I perish."—Esther 4:16b.

I'll to His gracious feet approach
  Whose sceptre mercy gives.
Perhaps He may command me "Touch!"
  And then the suppliant lives.

I can but perish if I go;
  I am resolved to try,
For if I stay away, I know
  I must forever die.

But, should I die with mercies sought,
  When I the King have tried,
That were to die, delightful thought!
  As sinner never died.

Author Unknown

## 630. THE LOST SHEEP

In the wilderness bare, Jesus found me.
  Oh, what grace He did show me that day!
Like a lost sheep, I strayed, but He found me
  As He followed my wandering way.

In the night on His shoulders He had me,
  And He came down the stern mountainside,
For He loved this poor lost straying sinner,
  And for me on the cross He had died.

Now my heart is a-joy, and I'm singing,
  As I tell Jesus did this for me.

And I want all the lost and the straying
  Just to learn what salvation can be!

All the years by my side--never leaves me.
  He reproves, but He loves and forgives.
Ever peace in my heart with the Saviour
  And forever in Heaven I'll live.

Ah poor sinner, He loves you, He seeks you!
  And He offers to save your doomed soul.
If repenting, you trust Him to save you,
  In a moment He'll make you whole.

John R. Rice

631. TRY JESUS

Are you feeling down and out?
    Try Jesus;
Heavy-laden with fear and doubt?
    Try Jesus;
Ne'er you mind uproar and din,
He can wash away your sin
And will show you how to win--
    Try Jesus.

In your cell so dark and still,
    Try Jesus;
If your life's a fight uphill,
    Try Jesus;
Even though you're low and sad
And the world should call you bad,
There is joy that can be had--
    Try Jesus.

Prison bars cannot withhold,
    Try Jesus;
Dingy cells no longer cold,
    Try Jesus;
There's a Light for you to see,
A man for you to be--
He will save and set you free--
    Try Jesus.

Parole your all to Him,
    Try Jesus;
He will fill you to the brim,
    Try Jesus;
Full of joy and hope and peace,
Radiant love to never cease,
And eternal, blessed lease--
    Try Jesus.

Author Unknown

632. REDEMPTION THROUGH CHRIST

Weary of earth, and laden with my sin
I look at Heaven, and long to enter in,
But there no evil thing may find a home,
And yet I hear a voice that bids me "Come."

So vile I am, how dare I hope to stand
In the pure glory of that holy land?
Before the whiteness of that throne appear?
Yet there are hands stretched out to draw me near!

The while I fain would tread the heavenly way,
Evil is ever with me, day by day;
Yet on mine ears the gracious tidings fall,
"Repent, confess; thou shalt be loosed from all."

It is the voice of Jesus that I hear;
His are the hands stretched out to draw me near,
And His the blood that can for all atone,
And set me faultless there before the throne.

'Twas He who found me on the deadly wild,
And made me heir of Heaven, the Father's child,
And day by day, whereby my soul may live,
Gives me His grace of pardon, and will give.

Yes, Thou wilt answer for me, righteous Lord:
Thine all the merits, mine the great reward;
Thine the sharp thorns, and mine the golden crown;
Mine the life won, and Thine the life laid down.

Author Unknown

### 633. OH, TURN YOUR HEART!

Why is your heart so wayward?
  Why does your stubborn will
Turn still away from Jesus?
  Why go on sinning still?

Babies all trust their mothers;
  Sick trust the doctors, too.
Sweethearts rely on lovers;
  Why not the Saviour true?

What is the sin, entrancing?
  What worldly bauble dear,
To keep the heart from Jesus
  Rejecting Heav'n so near?

Who has complained of Jesus?
  Who ever found Him less--
Less than the world's famed pleasure,
  Less than the world's unrest?

End of the road is coming,
  Then will close mercy's call.

Open doors still unheeded
  Will at last close for all.

Oh, turn your heart to Jesus,
  Flee to the mercy seat!
Jesus will not refuse you,
  Kneeling at His dear feet.

John R. Rice

### 634. WASHED IN THE BLOOD

My robes were once all stained with sin,
I knew not how to make them clean
Until a voice said, sweet and low,
"Go wash, I will make them white as snow."

That promise, "whosoever will,"
Included me, includes me still.
I came, and ever since I know
His blood has made me white as snow.

I have washed my robes in Jesus' blood
And He has made them white as snow.

Author Unknown

### 635. COME AND DRINK

Come and drink from out the fount of living waters;
Come into the day and leave the night of sorrow;
Come, let Jesus guarantee a new tomorrow;
  Come, forgiveness find in Jesus' loving arms.

How uneasy is the heart without a Saviour;
Oh, the tho't of meeting God without His favor,
Fear of death when life is fleeting like a vapor.
  Only Jesus gives eternal life and joy.

Sin deceitful, pleasure fleeting, plans all failing--
Where is comfort, rest, and peace for hearts so aching?
Jesus offers mercy freely without waiting.
  Here the penitent finds everlasting life.

Now I claim the offered boon of sins forgiven;
Now I trust in Christ for life e'erlasting given.
Now the blood that pour'd out from His side spear-riven
  Is my hope, my claim, and all my peace with God.

Jesus, I am coming.
I'm so tired of sin and straying;
Take me in Your arms forgiving;
  Dear Lord Jesus, save me now!

John R. Rice

## 636. ARE ALL THE CHILDREN IN?

Are all the children in?  The night is falling,
  And storm clouds gather in the threatening
        West;
The lowing cattle seek a friendly shelter;
  The bird flies to her nest;
The thunder crashes; wilder grows the
        tempest,
  And darkness settles o'er the fearful din.
Come, shut the door, and gather round the
        hearthstone--
  Are all the children in?

Are all the children in?  The night is falling,
  When gilded sin doth walk about the street.
Oh, at last it biteth like a serpent!
  Poisoned are stolen sweets.
O mothers! guard the feet of inexperience,
  Too prone to wander in the paths of sin!
Oh, shut the door of love against temptation!
  Are all the children in?

Are all the children in?  The night is falling,
  The night of death is hastening on apace;
The Lord is calling: "Enter thou thy chamber,
  And tarry there a space."
And when He comes, the King in all His glory,
  Who died the shameful death our hearts
        to win,
Oh, may the gates of Heaven shut about us,
  With all the children in.

                    Elizabeth Rosser

## 638. I WAS A WANDERING SHEEP

I was a wandering sheep,
  I did not love the fold,
I did not love my Shepherd's voice,
  I would not be controlled;
I was a wayward child,
  I did not love my home,
I did not love my Father's voice,
  I loved afar to roam.

The Shepherd sought His sheep,
  The Father sought His child;
They followed me o'er vale and hill,
  O'er deserts waste and wild;
They found me nigh to death,
  Famished, and faint, and lone;
They bound me with the bands of love,
  They saved the wandering one.

## 637. OPEN YOUR HEART'S DOOR

Jesus is here, Jesus is here,
Here on the doorstep He's waiting so near;
Not far away, but ready today,
Your poor lost soul this moment to save.

Whosoe'er will, whosoe'er will
May take the water of life to your fill.
Jesus has paid, His life down He laid,
For all your sins, atonement He made.

"Don't turn away, don't turn away
From the soft warning," your conscience
        would say.
God's broken laws, your sin and your fall--
Oh, do not grieve God's Spirit who calls.

Jesus, come in, Jesus, come in;
Oh, lift the burden, forgive all my sin.
Conquer, O Mild One, my heart so wild;
Take now and cleanse and make me
        God's child.

Open your heart's door to Jesus,
He's standing near waiting to hear
Your heart's confession
And He'll take possession,
So open your heart's door and let Him
        come in.

                    John R. Rice

*"For by grace are ye saved through faith;
and that not of yourselves:  it is the gift
of God:  Not of works, lest any man should
boast."--Eph. 2:8,9.*

I was a wandering sheep,
  I would not be controlled;
But now I love the Shepherd's voice,
  I love, I love the fold!
I was a wayward child;
  I once preferred to roam;
But now I love my Father's voice,
  I love, I love His home!

                    Horatius Bonar

639.    STILL UNSAVED?

STILL UNSAVED???
After all the Spirit's pleading,
After all God's tender leading,
After all of Calvary's cross
To redeem your soul from loss:
While His love and grace abound,
Can it be that you are found
    Still unsaved?  Still unsaved?

STILL UNSAVED???
Will you still refuse His pardon?
Still in sin your conscience harden?
Still reject till death o'ertake you?
Then when every hope forsakes you,
Dare you face your God at last,
When your every chance is passed,
    Still unsaved?  Still unsaved?

STILL UNSAVED???
Sinner, stop and look before you,
See the storm-clouds gathering o'er you;
Ere they burst in judgment on you
And in endless woe o'erwhelm you,
To the cross of Jesus fly,
Lest forever you will cry--
    Still unsaved.  Still unsaved.

                    Author Unknown

640.    ONE THING I KNOW

Oh yes, I know my sins are forgiven,
Oh yes, I know I love the Lord;
I'm under the blood, there's no condemnation,
All praise to God that one thing I know.

And this I know, all things work together
For good to those who love the Lord;
I know not what may come tomorrow;
But praise His name, that one thing I know.

Oh yes, I know my Redeemer liveth,
And Christ will come to claim His own;
The day, the hour impends, each moment;
I know not when, but I know He'll come.

I know not now all that Jesus doeth,
Nor understand I all His plans;
But I shall know all when one day He cometh;
Then hand in hand we'll speak face to face.

One thing I know since Jesus came in;
One thing I know, my sins are forgiv'n;
Sinner condem'd and fit but to die,
Eternal Hell mine if Christ passed me by;--
One thing I know since Jesus came in
Is that Jesus has saved my soul.

                    John R. Rice

641.    WILL GOD'S PATIENCE
        HOLD OUT FOR YOU?

The patience of Job is a story old,
    We marvel at this good man.
Yet infinitely greater God's patience is
    Toward those who reject His plan.
He yearns and He pleads and He waits to save
    The many--not just the few--
But some day His patience will have expired--
    Say--will it hold out for you?

God's mercy and love are wonderful,
    So tender that heart divine.
'Tis not in His plan that a single soul
    In Hell should be cast to pine.
This human family He yearns to save;
    He's calling, my friend, to you.
But we know that some day He will call no more--
    Will His patience hold out for you?

God's Spirit, He says, will not always strive
    On earth in the hearts of men.
How grateful, my friend, you should be today
    That you still hear His pleadings then.
Some day, oh how sad, you will know no more
    That patience and love so true.
O sinner, today make your peace with Him,
    While His patience holds out for you!

                    Edythe Johnson

(Written March 22, 1944, after hearing
Dr. Rice speak on "When God's Patience
Runs Out.")

# SECOND COMING

## 642. COMING TODAY?

Coming today? Today? Yes,
  Jesus may come today.
Watch for the Lord's returning;
  Watch as we work and pray.
Oh, what a grand awak'ning
  When shall arise the dead;
And what a blest reunion
  When He comes, as He said!

Saints from the North, South, East, West,
  Come to the wedding grand;
There with the shining Bridegroom,
  Saved ones from ev'ry land.
How we'll rejoice and sing then
  And our rewards receive,
And ever be with Jesus
  Him on whom we believe.

Then will the King come leading
  Armies of Heaven strong,
On a white horse returning
  To sit on David's throne.
Bringing His saints to serve Him
  And to enjoy His peace;
Over the whole world reigning,
  Making all wars to cease.

Then will our wrongs be righted;
  Then will be dried our tears!
Then all our sins be conquered;
  Still will be all our fears.
Eyes of the blind be opened,
  Ears of the deaf shall hear;
Sorrow and sighing ended
  Throughout the endless years.

When He comes, Hail, Hail, Hail Him!
  Jesus may come today,
Then what a shout of triumph,
  Up and with Him away.
Rending the sky, wide, high, all,
  All the redeemed we'll see,
So we will go to Heaven,
  Ever with Christ to be!

                              John R. Rice

## 643. THE LORD'S RETURN-- OUR ATTITUDE

Not only looking, but longing,
Lord Jesus returning to greet,
A chaplet of glory to gather
And cast it with joy at His feet.

Not only waiting, but watching,
Wistfully scanning the skies,
Anticipating the daybreak
When the world's true Sun shall arise.

Not only planning, but ploughing,
Planting the seed of the Word,
Occupying His vineyard
Till we give an account to our Lord.

Not only dreaming, but doing,
Dangers and fears we disdain:
Burning hearts glowing within us
At the thought of His coming again.

                              W. A. Phipson

## 644. THE PRINCE OF PEACE

Hark! the glad sound! the Saviour comes,
  The Saviour promised long:
Let every heart prepare a throne,
  And every voice a song.

He comes, the prisoners to release
  In Satan's bondage held;
The gates of brass before Him burst,
  The iron fetters yield.

He comes, from the thick films of vice
  To clear the mental ray,
And on the eyeballs of the blind
  To pour celestial day.

He comes, the broken heart to bind,
  The bleeding soul to cure,
And, with the treasures of His grace,
  To enrich the humble poor.

Our glad hosannas, Prince of Peace,
  Thy welcome shall proclaim,
And Heaven's eternal arches ring
  With Thy beloved name.

                              Philip Doddridge

### 645. CAUGHT UP TOGETHER

I sing hallelujah that Jesus is coming,
    And oh, what a raising of life from the dead;
The graves bursting open to give up God's children,
    Those bodies long moldered in grave's dusty bed.

We wait for the coming of Jesus our Saviour,
    Expecting the rapture, caught up in the clouds;
The world has its sorrows, we'll leave them so gladly,
    We'll wipe all our tears when the trumpet calls loud.

We'll rise incorruptible when sounds the trumpet;
    O Grave, where the victory long you have known?
All changed then the living, and all go together,
    And oh, what a gath'ring to Christ of His own.

Come up all ye saints of the past to that meeting,
    From Abel to Moses, from David to Paul;
Come up, all ye martyrs, soul winners, Christ lovers,
    All under the blood of our Saviour, come all.

Caught up to greet Him together, together,
    Caught up with Jesus and never to part;
Changed in a moment to be with my Saviour,
    Caught up together and never to part.

                            John R. Rice

### 646. THE TRUEST FRIEND

Never was a mother with a love so true,
Never friend or brother who so faithful proved.
Father ne'er provided half so bounteously;
All your dreams surpassing will the Saviour be.

He who made the worlds and set them in the sky,
Now will hear the penitent and heed their cry.
He who knows our weakness will forgive our sin;
When we cry for mercy He will come within.

When the world brings sorrow, He will still be near.
Age be not a foe, nor sickness bring sad tears.
And should friends forsake, or loved ones far be gone,
He will fill the lack for all who lean more strong.

Loving, keeping, giving all the happy years.
Jesus makes it Heaven in this vale of tears.
But He's coming for me and will cleave the sky
With the saints forever where we'll never die!

                            John R. Rice

### 647. WHAT A GATH'RING THAT WILL BE

At the sounding of the trumpet, when the saints are gather'd home,
  We will greet each other by the crystal sea,
With the friends and all the lov'd ones there awaiting us to come,
  What a gath'ring of the faithful that will be!

When the angel of the Lord proclaims that time shall be no more,
  We shall gather, and the saved and ransom'd see,
Then to meet again together, on the bright celestial shore,
  What a gath'ring of the faithful that will be!

At the great and final judgment, when the hidden comes to light,
  When the Lord in all His glory we shall see;
At the bidding of our Saviour, "Come, ye blessed, to My right,"
  What a gath'ring of the faithful that will be!

When the golden harps are sounding, and the angel bands proclaim,
  In triumphant strains the glorious jubilee;
Then to meet and join to sing the song of Moses and the Lamb,
  What a gath'ring of the faithful that will be!

What a gath'ring, gath'ring,
  At the sounding of the glorious jubilee!
What a gath'ring, gath'ring,
  What a gath'ring of the faithful that will be!

J. H. Kurzenknabe

### 648. WHEN JESUS COMES TO REIGN

Sorrow and sighing shall flee away,
  When Jesus comes to reign.
Eyes of the blind will be opened then;
  Tongue of the dumb shall sing.

Raptured with Christ, then a honeymoon
  With Him in Gloryland.
With Him to earth, when the angels bring
  Israel to Holy Land.

Lame men shall leap as an hart, for then
  All sickness gone, all sore.
Deserts will bloom and the thorns, and briars
  Shall curse the earth no more!

Kingdoms shall fall, and old Satan's rule
  Shall end with all its tears.
Righteousness fill all the earth, and peace
  Reign for a thousand years.

We pray, dear Lord, may Thy kingdom come,
  On earth Thy will be done.
But we have now all Thy peace and joy
  And in our hearts Thy throne.

Sorrow and sighing shall flee away!
Flee away that glory day!
Garden of Eden restored that day!
  When Jesus comes to reign.

John R. Rice

### 649. LOOKING FOR HIS BLEST APPEARING

There's a longing for my Saviour
  That I cannot hide away;
There's a yearning wish to see Him,
  That will never pass away
Till the day, when looking for Him
  To descend from out the sky,
He will come in all His beauty;
  Take me to His home on High.
Then my longing and my yearning
  Will be over, for I'll be
Dwelling ever in His presence
  Throughout all eternity.

Eva Gray

### 650. JESUS IS COMING

Come, dear Lord Jesus, for long we've been watching;
  God's children are homesick for Heaven our home.
Come then, Lord Jesus, come quickly and take us;
  The wedding feast waits when the Bridegroom shall come.

Midnight approaches, wise virgins are ready;
  With oil in our lamp, may our wicks be trimm'd too.
"Ho! comes the Bridegroom, go ye out to meet Him!"
  Oh, glad blest announcement we hope to hear soon.

Night when we sleep He may take one and leave one,
  Or day those we work with be left when we're gone.
Witness today then, and turn men to Jesus,
  Soon passes the season for winning our own.

Glad resurrection, O happy reunion
  When we shall be chang'd in a moment of time;
Meet all our loved ones, redeemed of all ages.
  And, oh, what glad greetings for mine and for thine!

Jesus is coming, is coming, is coming!
  It may be tomorrow, it may be today.
May be the trumpet sound, may be the angel shout,
  Then, "Come up higher," the Saviour will say!

John R. Rice

### 651. OUR GREAT KING-PRIEST

Blest day! When Christ on earth shall reign,
Hold sway o'er all of earth's domain,
And scatter poverty and pain,
  From our tomorrow;
With vision we foresee the day,
When men will gladly Christ obey,
And He will drive their clouds away
  All free from sorrow.

Sing on! And crown eternal bliss,
For righteousness and peace shall kiss;
Thy frets and worries now dismiss,
  Rest comes tomorrow;

The King, all hearts will satisfy.
No more of anguish or of sigh,
Behold, He cometh from on high,
  Why troubles borrow?

Christ reigns! There comes sweet jubilee
The world His glory yet shall see,
And from all bondage be set free,
  When comes the morrow;
"Behold, I come," I hear Him say,
So, quickly come, O Lord, I pray;
Come rule and reign, and hold Thou sway,
  End all our sorrow.

R. E. Neighbour

# SERVICE and SOUL WINNING

## 652.   ANOTHER YEAR

Another year!
How swiftly do they pass
Into the yesterdays.
No need to try to bring them back,
Or grieve o'er much the bitter lack
Of growth in virtue's ways.

Another year!
The Past--beyond recall--
Has brought its lessons stern.
And on before us lies the way
To greater things--a brighter day,
If we did aptly learn.

Another year!
With pages white and clean.
Each day a record page
On which to write a deed well done,
Some battle fought, and vict'ry won,
And growth in grace, with age.

Another year!
In which to strive and win;
In which to live anew.
"Forgetting that which is behind"--
Saving the lesson brought to mind--
That we may better do.

Another year!
With much to dare and do--
If Jesus tarries still:
Great mountainpeaks ahead to climb;
Dear souls to win, while there is time;
And conquest, if we will.

Another year!
What shall it mean to me--
The days and weeks before?
Perhaps some glist'ing tears to shed,
A cross to bear, as on I'm led;
The Father knows what more.

Another year!
I cannot see the path,
But I shall take the way.
When its tomorrows all shall flee
Into the yesterdays, I'll be
Near the "Perfect Day."

Unknown

## 653.   O LORD, SEND A REVIVAL

Of self I am weary,
  My sin I abhor,
I long to be holy
  And pure to the core;
Oh why do I labor
  On husks to be fed,
Or spend my poor money
  For what is not bread?

Thy church, O my Saviour,
  Thy body and bride,
The saints Thou hast ransomed,
  For whom Thou hast died--
How cold are we growing
  In service and pray'r!
Our love needs rekindling,
  Our altars repair.

The world, in its sorrow,
  The world needeth Thee;
Revive Thy disciples,
  Beginning in me!
Endue us with boldness
  Thy grace to proclaim;
Oh help us with power
  To speak in Thy name!

Thy glorious coming--
  We long for the day!
But are we preparing
  The holy highway?
Our hand seemeth weakened,
  And feeble the knee;
Oh send a revival,
  Beginning in me!

James M. Gray

## 654.   OUR NEED

It is not a grand church organ,
It is not a new church bell,
It is not a set of cushions,
Or a marble font will tell.
It is none of these **things**, my brother,
That we are in need of most;
But the old Saint Paul religion
And the power of the Holy Ghost.

J. Danson Smith

## 655. NOBODY TOLD ME OF JESUS

Would you care if some friend you have met
    day by day
Should never be told about Jesus?
Are you willing that he in the judgment shall
    say;
"No one ever told me of Jesus?"

Care you not if one soul of the children of men
Should never be brought unto Jesus?
Or would say in that day when He cometh
    again,
"No one ever told me of Jesus?"

Would you care if your crown should be
    starlessly dim,
Because you led no one to Jesus?
Make it true that some heart shall not answer
    to Him:
"No one ever told me of Jesus."

Then be silent no longer! but earnestly pray
For grace to be telling of Jesus,
So that no one can say on that great judgment
    day,
"No one ever told me of Jesus."

                    Mrs. Frank A. Breck

## 656. THE WORLD'S BIBLE

Christ has no hands but our hands
    To do His work today,
He has no feet but our feet
    To lead men in His way,
He has no tongue but our tongues
    To tell men how He died,
He has no help but our help
    To bring them to His side.

We are the only Bible
    The careless world will read,
We are the sinner's gospel,
    We are the scoffer's creed,
We are the Lord's last message,
    Given in deed and word.
What if the type is crooked?
    What if the print is blurred?

What if our hands are busy
    With other work than His?
What if our feet are walking
    Where sin's allurement is?

What if our tongues are speaking
    Of things His lips would spurn?
How can we hope to help Him
    And hasten His return?

                    Annie Johnson Flint

## 657. THEY'RE FALLING INTO HELL!

They're falling into Hell!
The millions all around us are!
No more to see the light again,
Their life now spent, the Judgment Bar
Is theirs to meet, their works in vain!

They're falling into Hell!
Is my heart stirred, or don't I care!
The ones with whom I've lived and played
Have now passed on to deep despair.
O that I had with them wept and prayed!

They're falling into Hell!
Is it real, or just could be?
For if 'tis real I'm sure not moved,
And in my life one cannot see
Concern for souls, from self removed.

They're falling into Hell!
Lord show it to me plain!
For this Thy Word declares.
Forever lost! eternal, endless pain!
For all those caught by Satan's snares!

They're falling into Hell!
The barricade I should have built
Is nowhere to be found!
And on they rush like diamonds spilt
To sink in miry ground!

They're falling into Hell!
Yes, some are at the brink!
Have I warned? O help me plead
'Ere they begin to sink!
For them to save Christ died and bled.
They're falling into Hell!

                    Jim Norton

*"They that sow in tears shall reap in joy. He that goeth forth and weepeth, bearing precious seed, shall doubtless come again with rejoicing bringing his sheaves with him."--Ps. 126:5,6.*

658.    OCCUPIED

Martha in the kitchen, serving with her hands;
Occupied for Jesus, with her pots and pans.
Loving Him, yet fevered, burdened to the brim,--
Careful, troubled Martha, occupied for Him.

Mary on the footstool, eyes upon her Lord;
Occupied with Jesus, drinking in His word.
This the one thing needful, all else strangely dim:
Loving, resting Mary, occupied with Him.

So may we, like Mary, choose the better part:
Resting in His presence--hands and feet and heart;
Drinking in His wisdom, strengthened with His grace;
Waiting for the summons, eyes upon His face.

When it comes, we're ready, spirit, will, and nerve;
Mary's heart to worship, Martha's hands to serve;
This the rightful order, as our lamps we trim,--
Occupied with Jesus, then occupied for Him!

Lois Reynolds Carpenter

659.    WORKING AND WAITING

A husbandman who many years
Had ploughed his field and sown in tears
Grew weary with his doubts and fears:
"I toil in vain! these rocks and sands
Will yield no harvest to my hands;
The best seeds rot in barren lands.
My drooping vine is whithering;  '
No promised grapes its blossoms bring;
No birds among the branches sing;
My flock is dying on the plain;
The heavens are brass--they yield no rain;
The earth is iron,--I toil in vain!"

While yet he spake, a breath had stirred
His drooping vine, like wing of bird,
And from its leaves a voice he heard:
"The germs and fruits of life must be
Forever hid in mystery,
Yet none can toil in vain for Me.
A mightier hand, more skilled than thine,
Must hang the clusters on the vine,
And make the fields with harvest shine.
Man can but work; God can create:
But they who work, and watch, and wait,
Have their reward, though it come late.
Look up to Heaven! behold, and hear
The clouds and thunderings in thy ear--
An answer to thy doubts and fear."

He looked, and lo! a cloud-draped car,
With trailing smoke and flames afar,
Was rushing from a distant star;
And every thirsty flock and plain
Was rising up to meet the rain,
That came to clothe the fields with grain;
And on the clouds he saw again,
The covenant of God with men,
Rewritten with His rainbow pen:
"Seedtime and harvest shall not fail,
And though the gates of Hell assail,
My truth and promise shall prevail!"

Anonymous

660.    MAKE USE OF ME

Make use of me, my God!
  Let me not be forgot;
A broken vessel cast aside,
  One whom Thou needest not.

All things do serve Thee here,
  All creatures, great and small;
Make use of me, of me, my God--
  The meanest of them all.

Horatius Bonar

### 661. ARE YOUR HANDS CLEAN?

Once in my boyhood days long dead,
I watched a supper table being spread
By busy hands, and eagerly I said,
Wishing to help, "Please may I bring
        the bread?"
Gently, reprovingly, a kind voice said,
  "Are your hands clean?"
  Abashed I hung my head.

Oft when I see the multitude unfed
And waiting, hungering for the Living Bread,
My heart and hands are eager to be sped
To bring the Manna that they might be fed,
But one Voice says, even as a voice once said,
  "Are your hands clean?"
  I only bow my head.

Author Unknown

### 662. THE MINISTER'S WIFE

You may sing of your heroes of war and of peace,
Your soldiers of fortune or strife;
When the tumult shall die, and the shouting shall cease,
Let me sing of the minister's wife.

You may laud to the skies all the learned and wise,
The servants with dignities rife;
My heart says amen, but I take up my pen
In praise of the minister's wife.

Oh, the minister's wife is a cook and a clerk;
A dressmaker, mother, and nurse;
A wonderful teacher, a maid-of-all-work,
And a player and singer, of course!

She must listen, with nerves that are raw to the quick
To heartaches and troubles galore;
She must welcome the stranger, and visit the sick,
Wearing dresses her sister once wore.

She must work with the Aid, and the junior Hi-Y;
She must help with the Sunday school stunts;
Be a leader in missions, or tell us all why;
And not miss a prayer meeting once!

She must comfort her husband when Monday's are blue
And smooth out his trials--and coats;
Be ready to move every twelvemonth or two
When he shepherds new sheep, (and new goats).

And whether the weather be cloudy or bright;
In season or out--all the while,
If her heart it be heavy, or if it be light--
She must smile, smile, smile!

Oh, sing of the noble, the great, and the good,
Whom you meet in the course of your life;
I take up the strain, be it here understood,
In praise of the minister's wife!

Author Unknown

## 663. YOUR MISSION

If you cannot on the ocean
  Sail among the swiftest fleet,
Rocking on the highest billows,
  Laughing at the storms you meet,
You can stand among the sailors,
  Anchored yet within the bay;
You can lend a hand to help them
  As they launch their boats away.

If you are too weak to journey
  Up the mountain, steep and high,
You can stand within the valley
  While the multitudes go by;
You can chant in happy measure
  As they slowly pass along--
Though they may forget the singer,
  They will not forget the song.

If you have not gold and silver
  Ever ready at command;
If you cannot toward the needy
  Reach an ever-helping hand,
You can succor the afflicted,
  O'er the erring you can weep;
With the Saviour's true disciples
  You a tireless watch may keep.

If you cannot in the harvest
  Garner up the richest sheaves,
Many a grain, both ripe and golden,
  Oft the careless reaper leaves;
Go and gleam among the briers
  Growing rank against the wall,
For it may be that their shadow,
  Hides the heaviest wheat of all.

If you cannot in the conflict
  Prove yourself a soldier true;
If where fire and smoke are thickest
  There's no work for you to do;
When the battlefield is silent,
  You can go with careful tread--
You can bear away the wounded,
  You can cover up the dead.

Do not, then, stand idly waiting
  For some greater work to do;
Fortune is a lazy goddess--
  She will never come to you.
Go and toil in any vineyard;
  Do not fear to do or dare--
If you want a field of labor
  You can find it anywhere.

Ellen M. H. Gates

## 664. YOU CAN

If you cannot cross the ocean
  And the heathen lands explore,
You can find the heathen nearer,
  You can help them at your door.

If you cannot give your thousands,
  You can give the widow's mite,
And the least you do for Jesus
  Will be precious in His sight.

With your prayer and with your bounty
  You can do what God demands;
You can be like faithful Aaron,
  Holding up the prophet's hands.

Selected

## 665. OPEN MY EYES

Open my eyes, that I may see
This one and that one needing thee:
Hearts that are dumb, unsatisfied;
Lives that are dark, for whom Christ died.

Open my eyes in sympathy
Clear into man's deep soul to see;
Wise with Thy wisdom to discern,
And with Thy heart of love to yearn.

Open my eyes in power, I pray
Give me the strength to speak today,
Some one to bring, dear Lord, to Thee;
Use me, O Lord, use even me.

Betty Scott Stam

## 666. GOD PAYS HIS WORKERS

Who does God's work will get God's pay,
However long may seem the day,
However weary be the way.
He does not pay as others pay,
In gold or land or raiment gay,
In goods that perish and decay.
But God's high wisdom knows the way:
And that is sure, let come what may,
Who does God's work will get God's pay.

Dennis McCarthy

## 667. WHAT IF?

What if your own were starving,
  Fainting with famine pain,
And yet you knew where golden grew
  Rich fruit and ripened grain?
    Would you hear their wail
    As a thrice-told tale,
  And turn to your feast again?

What if your own were thirsting
  And never a drop could gain,
And you could tell where a sparkling well
  Poured forth melodious rain?
    Would you turn aside,
    While they gasped and died,
  And leave them to their pain?

What if your own were darkened,
  Without one cheering ray,
And you alone could show where shone
  The pure, sweet light of day?
    Would you leave them there
    In their dark despair,
  And sing on your sunlit way?

What if your own were wand'ring
  Far in a trackless maze,
And you could show them where to go
  Along your pleasant ways?
    Would your heart be light,
    Till the pathway right
  Was plain before their gaze?

What if your own were prisoned
  Far in a hostile land,
And the only key to set them free
  Held in your safe command?
    Would you breathe free air,
    While they stifled there,
  And wait, and hold your hand?

Yet, what else are you doing,
  O ye by Christ made free,
If you'll not tell what you know so well,
  To those across the sea,
    Who have never heard
    One tender word
  Of the Lamb of Calvary?

"They're not our own," you answer,
  "They're neither kith nor kin."
They are God's own:  His love alone
  Can save them from their sin;
    They are Christ's own:

He left His throne
And died their souls to win.

L. G. M'Vean

## 668. HOW SHALL WE GIVE?

Give as the morning that flows out of Heaven;
Give as the waves when their channel is riven;
Give as the free air and sunshine are given;
  Lavishly, joyfully, utterly give.

Not the waste drops from thy cup overflowing;
Not a faint spark from thy heart ever glowing;
Not a pale bud from thy June roses blowing;
  Give as God gave, who gave thee to live.

Give as the heart gives whose fetters are
                breaking,
Life, Love and Hope, all thy dreams and
                thy waking,
Soon at life's river thy soul fever slaking,
  Thou shalt know God and the gifts that
                He gave.

Rose Terry Cook

## 669. HELP IN SIMPLE DUTY

I do not ask for mighty words
  To leave the crowd impressed,
But grant my life may ring so true
  My neighbor shall be blessed.
I do not ask for influence
  To sway the multitude;
Give me a "word in season" for
  The soul in solitude.

I do not ask to win the great--
  God grant they may be saved!--
Give me the broken sinner, Lord,
  By Satan long enslaved.
Though words of wisdom and of power
  Rise easily to some,
Give me a simple message Lord,
  That bids the sinner come.

Barbara Cornet Ryberg

670.  SOULS ARE DYING

One lost sheep, the Shepherd sought me, leaving ninety-nine
Safe and shelter'd, but He yearned for this poor soul of mine.
Oh, He found me, then He laid me on His shoulders strong,
Now He grieves o'er all the straying, dying throng.

Souls are dying, millions dying, dying one by one;
Aliens, strangers, blinded, sinning, without Christ the Son.
Sons of Adam, born of woman, born with hearts of sin.
Only Jesus' blood can save them, trusting Him.

Once I had a friend and loved him, hoped to see him saved,
Waited long, alas I waited till he slipped away.
Death had claimed him, unforgiven, while I vainly sought
A convenient time to win him, Christ had bought.

Souls are dying, brother, do you care?
Souls undone, away from God, my brother, do you care?
Souls are dying, brother, do you care?
    Souls are dying.

John R. Rice

671.  THE BUSY MAN

If you want to get a favor done
  By some obliging friend,
And want a promise safe and sure
  On which you may depend,
Don't go to him who always has
  Much leisure time to plan,
But if you want your favor done,
  Just ask the busy man.

The man of leisure never has
  A moment he can spare;
He's busy "putting off" until
  His friends are in despair;
But he whose every waking hour
  Is crowded full of work,
Forgets the art of wasting time--
  He cannot stop to shirk.

So when you want a favor done,
  And want it right away,
Go to the man who constantly
  Works twenty hours a day.
He'll find a moment, sure, somewhere
  That has not other use,
And fix you while the idle man
  Is framing an excuse.

Selected

672.  SPEAK OUT FOR JESUS

You talk about your business,
Your bonds and stocks and gold;
And in all worldly matters
You are so brave and bold.
But why are you so silent
About salvation's plan?
Why don't you speak for Jesus,
And speak out like a man?

You talk about the weather,
And the crops of corn and wheat;
You speak of friends and neighbors
That pass along the street;
You call yourself a Christian,
And like the Gospel plan--
Then why not speak for Jesus,
And speak out like a man?

Are you ashamed of Jesus
And the story of the cross,
That you lower His pure Banner
And let it suffer loss?
Have you forgot His suffering?
Did He die for you in vain?
If not, then live and speak for Jesus,
**And praise HIS precious name.**

Forrest L. Eonte

## 673.   JONAH AND THE WHALE

Listen, my friends, I'll tell you a tale
How Jonah the prophet got caught by a whale.
That fish caught Jonah, and bless your dear soul
It not only caught him, but swallowed him whole.

Now part of my story is awfully sad--
'Twas about a great city that had gone to the bad.
When God saw these people with such wicked ways
He said, "I can't stand them more than forty more days."

So He spoke to old Jonah and said, "You go cry
Against all those people, and tell them that I
Give them forty days only to get settled down--
And if they don't heed you I'll tear up the town."

When Jonah heard God speak, he answered Him "No,
It's against my religion, and I just won't go;
Those Nineveh people mean nothing to me--
And besides, I'm against foreign missions, you see."

So he went down to Joppa.  In that city he found
A ship bound for Tarsus, paid the fare and went down;
Found a comfortable spot there and fell fast asleep.
But soon came a storm raging on the great deep.

Then Jonah confessed it was due to his sin.
So the crew tossed him out, and the fish took him in.
Said the fish, "See here, Jonah, now don't you forget,
I was sent here to bring you in out of the wet."

On a bed of green sea weeds the fish tried to rest,
But Jonah was tough and just would not digest.
That fish became nervous and sorely afraid,
As he rumbled inside while the old prophet prayed.

He blinked his big eyelids and wiggled his tail,
And made for the shore to deliver his male.
Then coming near to shore he looked all around,
And coughed up old Jonah right out on the ground.

Jonah first thanked the Lord for His mercy and grace,
Then turned and looked that fish square in the face.
"Old fellow," he said, "after three days you've found
When you tackle a good man, he's hard to keep down."

Jonah thought how much better his preaching would be
Since from Whale Seminary he had his degree.
Although the old prophet was several days late,
He preached from the time that he entered the gate;

'Til the whole population repented and prayed
And the stern hand of justice and vengeance was stayed.
Now this is the lesson:  God's Word cannot fail.
When you think of backsliding--look out for the whale. --Anonymous

## 674. LORD, SEND THE FIRE!

Thou Christ of burning, cleansing flame
  Send the fire, send the fire, send the fire!
Thy blood-bought gift today we claim,
  Send the fire, send the fire, send the fire!
Look down and see this waiting host,
Send us the promised Holy Ghost,
We want another Pentecost,
  Send the fire, send the fire, send the fire!

God of Elijah, hear our cry,
  Send the fire, send the fire, send the fire!
He'll make us fit to live or die,
  Send the fire, send the fire, send the fire!
To burn every trace of sin,
To bring the light and glory in,
The revolution now begin,
  Send the fire, send the fire, send the fire!

'Tis fire we want, for fire we plead,
  Send the fire, send the fire, send the fire!
The fire will meet our every need,
  Send the fire, send the fire, send the fire!
For strength to ever do the right,
For grace to conquer in the fight,
For power to walk the world in white,
  Send the fire, send the fire, send the fire!

To make our weak hearts strong and brave,
  Send the fire, send the fire, send the fire!
To live a dying world to save,
  Send the fire, send the fire, send the fire!
Oh, see us on Thy altar lay
Our lives, our all this very day--
To crown the offering now we pray,
  Send the fire, send the fire, send the fire!

Author Unknown

## 675. NEW YEAR'S PRAYER

Lord, give me this new year a burning zeal
For souls immortal; make me plead for such
With earnestness intense, love strong as death;
And faith God-given. Will the world cry "mad"?
I would be mad. Such madness be my joy,
For thrice it blesses--first my own cold heart,
Then glorifies my God, and straightway plucks
My sin-stained brother from the jaws of death.

Author Unknown

## 676. "TRACKS"

"Well, Ben, how did you like that Tract
  I gave to you one day?"
The country parson asked his man
  Who kept the weeds away.

"Ah, Massa, it was jes' for me,
  It sure did me some good;
I couldn't tell why call 'em 'Tracks'
  But now I'm sure I could.

"For when I read that little book
  It track me everywhere;
It track me down the cellar-steps,
  It track me up the stair.

"It track me right out to de barn--
  'Nen to de house it comes;
It track me all aroun' de farm--
  At las'--it track me 'home.'

"It track me till I 'fessed my sins--
  Took dat I stole right back;
It done has tracked me to de Lawd--
  God bless yo' fer dat Track!

"I jes' abouten wore it out--
  But did yo' wan' 't back?
It's trackin' Mandy! An' I knows
  Jes' why you call it 'Track.'"

Effie O. Foss

## 677. ENTIRELY HIS

There is a joy in serving Christ
  Which nothing else can give,
And richest blessings crown the life
  When for the Lord we live.
Our "loaves and fishes" brought to Him
  He breaks and multiplies
To feed the hungry souls of men
  With bread that satisfies.
How good to be an instrument
  Of grace that He can use
At any time, in any place,
  However He may choose.
A vessel purified and filled
  With living water sweet,
A harp divinely tuned and thrilled
  A Heaven's mercy seat!

Ida A. Guirey

678. "ARE YOU GOING?"

It was
Sunday morning
At the breakfast
Table,
And my host asked
Mrs. Host--
Meaning his wife--
If she was
Going to church.

And I thought
That was funny--
If that's the
Right word.
Strange is better

Maybe--
Or tragic--
Or unfortunate.

I couldn't see why
It should be a
Matter for debate;
Because she was
In good health,
And they were
Members of the
Church.

Your children don't
Ask if they are
Going to school
Today.
They know they are--

If they aren't sick
Or can't make
You think they are.

I was wondering
Why going to church
Isn't taken for
Granted,
And how many
Fires would get
Put out
If only the
Chief got there,
And the volunteers
Came when they
Felt like it.

Author Unknown

679.    SO LITTLE TIME

So little time!  The harvest will be over.
    Our reaping done, we reapers taken Home.
Report our work to Jesus, Lord of harvest,
    And hope He'll smile and that He'll say, "Well done!"

How many times I should have strongly pleaded;
    How often did I feel to strictly warn.
The Spirit moved, oh had I pled for Jesus!
    The grain is fallen, lost ones not reborn.

Despite the heat, the ceaseless toil, the hardship,
    The broken heart o'er those we cannot win;
Misunderstood because we're oft peculiar,
    Still no regrets we'll have but for our sin.

A day of pleasure, or a feast of friendship;
    A house or car or garments fair or fame,
Will all be trash, when souls are brought to Heaven.
    And then how sad to face the slackers' blame!

The harvest white, with reapers few is wasting
    And many souls will die and never know
The love of Christ, the joy of sins forgiven.
    Oh let us weep and love and pray and go!

Today we reap, or miss our golden harvest!
    Today is given us lost souls to win.
Oh then to save some dear ones from the burning.
    Today we'll go to bring some sinner in.

John R. Rice

## 680. PREACH CHRIST, O MEN!

Preach Christ, O men--His blood, His saving power!
Never the need was greater in an hour
Than in this hour! Cry out His blessed name.
O preachers, teachers, set the world aflame
For Christ, that those who walk earth's darkened roads
May feel His hand beneath their heavy loads;
May come to know Him as their Saviour, Friend,
Who will walk with them until the journey's end.

Preach Christ, O men! Their hunger is so great!
The days are swift--there is no time to wait.
You hold the bread of life within your hands,
And the living water for their thirst. The lands
Of earth cry out for what you have to give:
The living Christ--preach Him, that they may live.

Grace Noll Crowell

## 681. TIME TO REAP

Now is the time to rise and reap,
  The fields are harvest white;
This is the hour, I now repeat,
  To spread the Gospel light.

This is the hour to give and work
  Until the war is won;
Oh, let us not our duty shirk
  Before the work is done.

The entire world is Christ's domain,
  Yet heathen millions wait;
Let's quickly reap that golden grain
  Before it is too late.

We must not let that harvest field
  Grow ripe, then rot and die;
Oh, let us then the sickle wield,
  We dare not pass them by.

Our hearts must heed their strong appeals,
  Perhaps our worst defect,
Is damning souls while we just sit,
  It's murder by neglect.

It's time to call a halt, dear friend,
  It's time to pray and weep;
The sheaves must quickly be brought in;
  It's time for us to reap!

Fred D. Jarvis

## 682. SOULS WE MUST WIN

Look on the harvest now waiting;
  Behold the fields that are white--
Souls to be won for the Saviour,
  Heaven is waiting so bright.

Win them, and shine as the stars bright.
  Win them for Jesus' dear sake.
Oh, in eternity's mansions
  We will rejoice in His praise.

See all the price for their pardon;
  See all the blood of the cross,
Wrought for the sinner, atonement.
  Jesus has paid all it cost.

Tenderly plead with the straying;
  Solemnly warn of their sin;
Tell them of mercy God offers;
  Bid them believe and come in!

Oh, not alone do we witness,
  But with God's Word do we plead.
Go with His Spirit convicting,
  And where He guides us and leads.

Souls we must win for the Saviour;
  Souls we must win for the sky.
Teach them to turn and trust Jesus,
  Who for their rescue did die.

John R. Rice

## 683. HERE AM I

Let none hear you idly saying,
  "There is nothing I can do,"
While the souls of men are dying,
  And the Master calls for you.
Take the task He gives you gladly,
  Let His work your pleasure be;
Answer quickly when He calleth,
  "Here am I; send me, send me!"

J. Danson Smith

## 684. AT PEACE BUT NOT AT EASE

*"We have peace with God through our Lord
Jesus Christ."—Rom. 5:1.*

At peace am I
Freed from my sin, its guilt, its power;
Now I may look into the face of God
And sing each hour!
He bids me cast on Him each care
That would perplex,
Nor fear the snares that Satan lays
My soul to vex.
I gladly grasp His gift,
The holy Son,
Whose love assumed my debt,
My ransom won.
For there upon the cross, in anguish sore,
He shed His blood--
To be my Perfect Sacrifice,
My King--my God!

*"Woe to them that are at ease in Zion!"—Amos 6:1.*

But not at ease, am I
Who now can joy, who now can see;
Each hour I dedicate to Him
Who set me free.
While others stagger 'neath their load
Of care, of sin,
I must arise from sloth and sleep
These souls to win!
I have a story now to tell
At home--afar:
My tongue must spread abroad
Where'er men are--
That God would reconciled be
To every soul!
I must invite them all to come
To be made whole!

A. P. N.

## 685. A LITTLE WHILE

A little while to sow in tears and weakness
  The precious seed along the vernal plain,
Till into life the tender blade expanding
  Fresh promise gives of summer's
        ripening grain.

A little while of patient, earnest labor,
  For His dear sake, our best and
        truest Friend;
A little while to wait for His appearing,
  And then the joy that nevermore shall end.

A little while to bear the cross for Jesus
  And meet the foes that once He overcame;
To stand unmoved, the sword of
        truth uplifting,
  And through its power to conquer in
        His name.

Fanny Crosby

## 686. HAVE I DONE MY BEST FOR JESUS?

I wonder, have I giv'n my best to Jesus
  Who died upon the cruel tree?
To think of His great sacrifice at Calv'ry,
  I know my Lord expects the best from me.

How many are the lost that I have lifted?
  How many are the chained I've helped
        to free?
I wonder, have I done my best for Jesus,
  When He has done so much for me?

The hours that I have wasted are so many,
  The hours I've spent for Christ so few.
Because of all my lack of love for Jesus,
  I wonder if His heart is breaking too?

I wonder have I cared enough for others,
  Or have I let them die alone?
I might have helped a wand'rer to the Saviour;
  The seed of precious life I might
        have sown.

No longer will I stay within the valley,
  I'll climb to mountain heights above;
The world is dying now for the want
        of someone
  To tell them of the Saviour's
        matchless love.

Ensign Edwin Young

## 687. OH, BRING YOUR LOVED ONES

How can I meet Him without my loved ones;
How can I smile and know they are lost;
When I see Jesus up in the glory
Without the souls He bought at such cost?

Time now for warning, time now
for pleading,
Time now to weep, to cling to the cross.
Too late in Heaven to win our loved ones;
Too late to pray, to weep o'er the lost.

Solemn accounting, facing our Saviour.
Rewards receiving--suffering loss!
Judgment seat, facing Jesus in Heaven;
Wood, hay and stubble, burning as dross.

How poor investment, in land or business;
What cheap returns, we'll have for
our pains!
But how the wise will shine in their glory,
When souls appear, what eternal gain!

How glad the greeting, praises and singing
When we meet Jesus, with all our own!
Then will our labor seem but a trifle,
And all our tears and toiling be done!

Oh, bring your loved ones, bring them
to Jesus!
Bring ev'ry brother and sister to Him!
When come the reapers home with
the harvest,
May all our dear ones be safe gathered in!

John R. Rice

## 688. SERVICE--WHERE?

"Father, where shall I work today?"
And my love flowed warm and free.
Then He pointed me out a tiny spot,
And said, "Tend that for Me."
I answered quickly, "Oh, no, not that.
Why no one would ever see,
No matter how well my work was done,
Not that little place for me!"
And the word He spoke, it was not stern,
He answered me tenderly,
"Ah, little one, search that heart of thine:
Art thou working for them or Me?
Nazareth was a little place,
And so was Galilee."

Author Unknown

## 689. PRAYER FOR AN OFFICE

What a frail, poor company we are, dear Lord! How
weak we are to be serving Thee!
Things go wrong with our heads,
Things go wrong with our hearts,
And things go wrong with our bodies.

Take our heads, O Lord, and use them. Clear them
of their biases, their mistaken ideas, their poor
judgment. Give us Thy wisdom for our heads.

Take our hearts, O Lord--they need Thee most of all.
We forget to love others, we fail to love Thee--the issues
of our hearts are not the clean and shining life issues Thou
canst give. Give us Thy love for our hearts.

Take our bodies, O Lord. They are so weak, so full of
aches and pains. This frail encasing of our endeavor
must serve Thee, too, so make them well and use them
for Thee. Give us Thy strength for our bodies.

Grace Rice MacMullen

690.   "THE COLD ONES"

There are ninety and nine that safely lie in the shelter of the fold,
But millions are left outside to die, for the ninety and nine are cold--
      Away in sin's delusive snare,
      Hastening to death and dark despair
      Hastening to death, and none to care--
For the ninety and nine are cold.

"Lord, Thou hast here Thy well-fed sheep:  are they not enough for Thee?"
But the Shepherd made answer, "Millions sleep on the brink of eternity.
      And these My sheep within the fold
      Care not for the dying in sin's stronghold,
      Care not for the dying outside the fold
On the brink of eternity."

But none of the ransomed ever knew how the heart of the Shepherd did yearn:
Nor the travail of soul that He passes through for His sheep without concern.
      For no other way had He to reach
      The millions of earth, His way to teach,
      The millions of earth except through each
Of His sheep without concern.

"Lord, whence are the marks in Thy hands and side and whence the scars of Thy feet?"
"They were made for those for whom I died, both saved and wandering sheep."
      "Lord, when wilt Thou come and claim Thine own?"
      "Not till the wandering the way are shown,
      Not till the wandering My Word have known,
My wandering, dying sheep."

Ah!  Ninety and nine, dost thou hear His voice; forth then to the work so great;
Beyond life's span there is no choice for those outside the gate,
      If they're brought at all, it must be NOW,
      Then ninety and nine, don't question how,
      O, sheep of Mine, go quickly thou,
Else for them--and you--too late.

But all through the churches, apostate riven, and up from the world's sleep,
There'll arise a cry to the gates of Heaven, "Rejoice, I am finding My sheep."
      And the angels shall echo around the throne,
      "Rejoice, for the dying the way are shown."
His wandering, perishing sheep.

               Author Unknown

# SIN--CLEANSING

## 691.  LIQUOR IS TO BLAME

A mother has a broken heart,
　Her eyes are dim with tears;
Untimely wrinkles on her face
　Reveal her dread and fears;
For as the years have come and gone
　Her husband's made a sot,
And gives small comfort to her life,
　But troubles, Oh, a lot;
　　Then add to this the shame--
　　But liquor is to blame!

Her home is wretched, Oh, indeed--
　A place of poor abode,
Where poverty and want and woe
　Have made a great inroad!
The children hear no father pray,
　Whose voice is harsh and stern,
And ofttimes hear him speak the words
　That cut and sting and burn--
　　With this he is aflame,
　　But liquor is to blame.

Then in the country where he lives,
　(Oh, pause a while and think!)
He's helped to injure other homes
　By causing them to drink.
And from these homes perhaps there's gone
　Some ruined, blighted youth
Who'll never know God's saving grace,
　Nor His uplifting truth,
　　Nor have a noble name--
　　But liquor is to blame.

Oh, cursed liquor! Why not hate
　This blight of humankind,
That's killed its millions through the years
　And wrecked them, soul and mind?
Just think of what some might have been
　In godliness and love,
And how they might have led the way
　To Heaven sweet above;
　　But oh, the awful game,
　　And liquor is to blame!

Walter E. Isenhour

## 692.    IF YOU LINGER TOO LONG

If the Saviour has called you to return from your wand'ring;
　If the Spirit has pleaded that you turn from your sin;
If the knock at your heart's door so insistent continues,
　Oh, refuse Him no longer; let Him quickly come in!

You have waited and linger'd still refusing the Saviour,
　All His warnings so patient, all His pleading so kind;
Thus you ate fruit forbidden, you believed Satan's promise;
　Thus your heart has been harden'd; sin has darkened your mind.

Not a day more convenient ever comes while you linger
　Nor does sin lose attraction while you walk on that way;
Only Hell draws still nearer, grinning Death sly approaching;
　Oh, awake from your stupor; oh, repent while 'tis day!

You have waited so flippant, and refused Him so lightly,
　You have sinned long and dreadful--and your heart is so wrong;
Oh, if God grows impatient, the sweet Spirit offended,
　If no longer He calls you, doom is yours when He's gone.

Then how sad facing judgment, you'll recall with no mercy
　That you tarried and linger'd till the Spirit was gone;
What reproaches and mourning, if when death finds you hopeless,
　You have tarried and linger'd and have waited too long!

John R. Rice

## 693. THE BARTENDER

A vendor of liquid woe,
 White-aproned thief,
Selling for base gain
The mixed curse of Cain
 And gall of grief!

Armed with writs to sell
 Law-licensed wrong,
Brew of the lowest Hell,
An ill no tongue can tell
 Bitter and strong!

He slays boys and men
 On life's highway,
That prayers and loving pen
Cannot bring back again
 And turn night to day!

Great God, palsy the hand
 And benumb the throat
That curses this land
Wide and rich and grand
 By voice and vote!

Frank Earl Herrick

## 694. WRAPPED IN SELF

Wrapped in himself he comes to church,
Takes off his overcoat and hat,
And, going to his pew, sits down,
Pulling his problems tighter around his
 shoulder,
Crawling...cold...deeper into himself
As the hymns, the anthems, the prayers,
And the sermon pour over him.

Then, wrapped in himself, his overcoat
 and hat,
He goes away again,
Wondering vaguely where God was during
 the service
And how he missed Him,
As though he expected to find God in his
 pocket,
Or gazing out between the hands of his watch,
Or rolled up in the service leaflet.

Without God in his pocket
Or in his soul, he goes away...
Wrapped in himself.

Bob Carlin

## 695. CHOOSING YOUR HELL

Forever round the mercy seat
 The guiding lights of love shall burn;
But what if, habit bound, thy feet
 Shall lack the will to turn!
What if thine eyes refuse to see,
 Thine ear the call of mercy fail,
And thou eternal captive be,
 Thyself, thine own dark jail?

O doom beyond the saddest guess
 As the long years of God unroll,
To make thy sordid sinfulness
 The prison of thy soul!
Thy selfishness a gnawing worm,
 Thy hopelessness an eating fire,
What Hell, to pull and twist and squirm
 Forever deeper in the mire.

Anonymous

*". . .where sin abounded, grace did much more abound."--Rom. 5:20.*

## 696. THE ROBBER

What! rob a poor man of his beer,
 And give him good victuals instead!
Your heart's very hard, sir, I fear,
 Or at least you are soft in the head.

What! rob a poor man of his mug,
 And give him a house of his own;
With a kitchen and parlor so snug!
 'Tis enough to draw tears from a stone.

What! rob a poor man of his glass,
 And teach him to read and write!
What! save him from being an ass!
 'Tis nothing but malice and spite.

What! rob a poor man of his ale,
 And prevent him from beating his wife,
From being locked up in jail,
 With penal employment for life!

What! rob a poor man of his beer
 And keep him from starving his child!
It makes me feel awfully queer,
 And I'll thank you to draw it more mild.

Author Unknown

## 697. REMEMBERED NO MORE

If sin be remembered and cometh to judgment
  Oh sad the day, God's judgment day.
But Christ met that judgment for penitent sinners;
  Their sins are all taken away!

Now I am washed whiter than snow, and forgiven.
  How much I gain, eternal gain.
My sins are all pardoned and cancelled and covered,
  And never remembered again.

His law in my heart is now written; I love Him.
  Oh, Him to please, nor e'er displease!
My conscience is purged and the shadow of judgment
  Is gone now forever!  I'm free!

So great a salvation, so wondrous a Saviour!
  His blood all pays, through endless days.
So I must urge others to put trust in Jesus,
  And His name forever I'll praise!

No more, no more, remembered no more,
My sins are all paid for in Christ's body borne.
Jesus has died for them, God has forgotten them.
Who shall condemn when the slate is all clean then?
No more! no more! remembered no more,
My sins are remembered no more.

                        John R. Rice

## 698.  WHAT WOULD YOU DO THEN?

If you knew that your boy with eyes so blue--
With manly tread and heart so true,
Should enter yonder bar-room bright
And stain his soul in one wild night,
  What would you do then; what would you do?

If you knew that your girl with silken hair--
With winsome way and face so fair,
By felon drink at last were seen
To follow the steps of Magdalene,
  What would you do then; what would you do?

If you knew that your wife through
              weary years,
Should drown her grief in bitter tears,
Because her boy of tender care
Was lured to death by liquor's snare;
  What would you do then; what would you do?

But you know, somebody's boy must lie
In drunken stupor and must die;

Some girl go wrong in tender years--
Somebody's wife must sob in tears.
  What will you do then, what will you do?

                        Alex Cairns

## 699.  SIN'S WILES

Sin is composed of naught but subtle wiles,
It fawns and flatters and betrays by smiles.
'Tis like the panther, or the crocodile--
It seems to love, and promises no wile.
It hides its sting, seems harmless as a dove;
It hugs the soul, and hates when it vows
              most love.
It secretly ensnares the soul it kills,
It plays the tyrant most by gilded pills.
          *       *       *
No thief so vile nor treacherous as sin
Whom fools do hug and take much pleasure in.

                        B. Keach

700.   THE DRINKING HOUSE OVER THE WAY

The room was so cold and cheerless and bare,
  With its rickety table and one broken chair,
With its curtainless window with hardly a pane
  To keep out the snow, the wind and the rain.
A cradle stood empty, pushed up to the wall,
  And somehow that seemed the saddest of all.

In the rusty old stove the fire was dead.
  There was snow on the floor at the foot of the bed
And there, all alone, a pale woman was lying,
  You need not look twice to see she was dying,
Dying of want, of hunger and cold.
  Shall I tell you her story--the story she told:

"No, Ma'am, I'm no better; my cough is so bad;
  It's wearing me out, tho', and that makes me glad,
For it's wearisome living when one's all alone,
  And Heaven, they tell me, is just like a home.
Yes, Ma'am, I've a husband, he's somewhere about,
  I hoped he'd come in 'fore the fire went out;
But I guess he has gone where he's likely to stay,
  I mean to the DRINKING HOUSE over the way.

It was not always so, and I hope you won't think
  Too hard of him, lady, it's only the drink.
I know he's kindhearted, for, oh! how he cried
  For our poor little baby the morning he died.
You see he took sudden, and grew very bad,
  And we had no doctor--my poor little lad--
For his father had gone, never meaning to stay
  I am sure, to the DRINKING HOUSE over the way.

And when he came back, 'twas far in the night,
  And I was so tired and sick with fright,
Of staying so long with my baby alone,
  And it cutting my heart with its pitiful moan.
He was cross with the drink; poor fellow, I know
  It was that, not his baby that bothered him so;
But he swore at the child, as panting it lay,
  And went back to the DRINKING HOUSE over the way.

I heard the gate slam, and my heart seemed to freeze
  Like ice in my bosom, and there on my knees
By the side of the cradle all shivering I stayed,
  I wanted my mother.  I cried and I prayed.
The clock, it struck two, ere my baby was still,
  And my thoughts went back to my home on the hill,
Where my happy girlhood had spent its short day,
  Far, far from the DRINKING HOUSE over the way.

Could I be a girl, I, the heart-broken wife,
  There watching alone while the dear little life

Was going so fast that I had to bend low
  To hear if it breathed, 'twas so faint and so slow.
Yes, it was easy, his dying, he just grew more white
  And his eyes opened wider to look for the light,
As his father came in 'twas just break of day--
  Came in from the DRINKING HOUSE over the way.

Yes, ma'am, he was sober, at least mostly I think,
  He often stayed that way to wear off the drink.
And I know he was sorry for what he had done,
  For he set a great store by our first little one.
And straight did he come to the cradle-bed, where
  Our baby lay dead, so pretty and fair.
I wondered that I could have wished him to stay
  When there was a DRINKING HOUSE over the way.

He stood quiet a while, did not understand,
  You see, till he touched the cold little hand.
Oh! then came the tears, and he shook like a leaf,
  And he said 'twas the drinking that made all the grief.
The neighbors were kind and the minister came,
  And he talked of my seeing my baby again,
And of the bright angels--I wondered if they
  Could see in the DRINKING HOUSE over the way.

And I thought when my baby was put in the ground,
  And the men with their spades were shaping the mound,
If somebody only would help me to save
  My husband who stood by the side of the grave.
If only it were not so handy to drink--
  The men that make laws, ma'am, sure didn't think
Of hearts they would break, of the souls they would slay,
  When they licensed the DRINKING HOUSE over the way.

I've been sick since, and it cannot be long,
  Be pitiful, lady, to him when I'm gone.
He wants to do right, but you never can think
  How weak a man grows when he's fond of drink.
And it's tempting him here and it's tempting him there--
  Four places I've counted in this very square,
Where a man can get whiskey by night and by day,
  Not to mention the DRINKING HOUSE over the way.

There's a verse in the Bible the minister read,
  No drunkard shall enter the kingdom, it said.
And he is my husband, and I love him so,
  And where I am going I want him to go.
Our baby and I will both want him there--
  Don't you think the dear Saviour will answer our prayer?
And please, when I'm gone, ask someone to pray
  For him at the DRINKING HOUSE over the way.

                              Author Unknown

701.      MY SINS GONE!

I will cast all thy sins in the depths of the sea,
All thy sins and transgressions, whatever they be;
Though they mount up to Heaven, though they go down to Hell,
I have buried them there, and above them shall swell,
All my waves of forgiveness so boundless and free,
I have cast all thy sins in the depths of the sea.

I have buried them there far away from the shore,
Where they never may rise up to trouble thee more;
Where no far-reaching tide, with its pitiless sweep,
May stir the dark waves of forgetfulness deep.
I have buried them there where no mortal can see,
I have cast all thy sins in the depths of the sea.

Author Unknown

702.  SIN

Sin is the living worm, the lasting fire;
Hell soon would lose its heat could sin expire.
Better sinless in Hell than to be where
Heaven is and to be found a sinner there.

One sinless with infernals might do well,
But sin would make of Heaven a very Hell.
Fools make a mock of sin, will not believe
It carries such a dagger in its sleeve.

How can it be, say they, that such a thing
So full of sweetness ere should wear a sting?
They know not that it is the very spell
Of sin to make men laugh themselves to Hell.

John Bunyan

703.  BREAKING OUR JINX

If our people would save all the cash
They are spending for liquor and trash,
   And would come to their senses,
   We'd be meeting expenses,
And have plenty for clothing and hash.

If the effort that's turned into smoke
Could be saved, we need never be broke;
   Our onerous "beefers,"
   And poorest reliefers,
Would find all their troubles a joke.

All our substance will surely be lost,
If for liquor 'tis carelessly tossed;
   For the habit of drinking
   Is the cause of our sinking,
And our youth has been paying the cost.

All we spend for our smokes and our drinks
Would pay all our debtors, methinks,
   Not a soul should begrudge it,
   For 'twould balance our budget,
'Tis the sure way of breaking our jinx.

Harriet A. Waldman

704.  CONSCIENCE AND REMORSE

"Good-bye," I said to my conscience--
   "Good-bye for aye and aye,"
And I put her hands off harshly,
   And turned my face away;
And conscience smitten sorely
   Returned not from that day.

But a time came when my spirit
   Grew weary of its pace;
And I cried: "Come back, my conscience;
   I long to see thy face."
But conscience cried: "I cannot;
   Remorse sits in my place."

Paul Laurence Dunbar
1872-1906

## 705. IF BEER IS SUCH A TEMPERANCE DRINK...

The many claims for beer, I think
  Might need no explanation
If surgeons guzzled it before
  A major operation.

If beer is just as advertised,
  I earnestly would crave
To know why barbers don't indulge
  Before they give a shave.

If beer's a drink for learned men,
  Why doesn't some judge quench
His thirst by having mugs of beer
  Convenient at his bench?

If beer's as healthful as I'm told,
  How strange when he indulges,
A man so frequently acquires
  Those funny-looking bulges.

If beer is really good for one
  Why do the beer-and-winers
Insist that they will not permit
  The sale of it to minors?

If beer is all it's claimed to be,
  Why don't athletes of fame
All get together 'round the keg
  Before a Big League game?

If beer is such a "temperance drink"
  Which causes "needless fears,"
Why is it railroads fail to hire
  The beery engineers?

If beer produces steady men,
  Why is it they affix
Such signs to Safety Bulletins
  As--"Booze and Work Don't Mix."

Florence M. Stellwagen

~⌣~

Vice is a monster of so frightful mien,
As to be hated needs but to be seen;
Yet seen too oft, familiar with her face,
We first endure, then pity, then embrace.

Pope

## 706. THE DEBT

This is the debt I pay
Just for one riotous day,--
Years of regret and grief,
Sorrow without relief.

Pay it I will to the end--
Until the grave, my friend,
Gives me a true release,
Gives me the clasp of peace.

Slight was the thing I bought,
Small was the debt, I thought,
Poor was the loan at best--
God!  but the interest!

Paul Laurence Dunbar
1872-1906

## 707. "NOBODY'S BUSINESS"

It's nobody's business what I drink;
I care not what my neighbors think
Or how many laws they choose to pass,
I'll tell the world I'll have my glass!
Here's one man's freedom cannot be curbed
My right to drink is undisturbed.

So he drank in spite of law or man,
Then got into his old tin can,
Stepped on the gas and let it go
Down the highway to and fro.
He took the curves at fifty miles
With bleary eyes and drunken smiles.

Not long till a car he tried to pass;
There was a crash, a scream and
                breaking glass.
The other car was upside down
About two miles from the nearest town.
The man was clear but his wife was caught
And he needed the help of that drunken sot
Who sat in a maudlin, drunken daze,
And heard the scream and saw the blaze,
But was too far gone to save a life
By helping the car from off the wife.

The car was burned, and the mother died,
While a husband wept and a baby cried
And a drunk sat by--and still some think
It's nobody's business what they drink.

Selected

## 708.  URIAH

I am Uriah, the Hittite.
David's subject, Joab's soldier, Bathsheba's
Lord.  She waits as I help seige Rabbah's
City walls.  She waits for me to come
And wash my feet, and eat and sleep at home;
But, with these other comrades in the fray,
I've made a vow and sworn this day
To dwell in tents until the battle's done,
When clash and din have ceased and vict'ry's won.
The mighty ark doth dwell within a tent,
And so shall I.  I'm sure that word was sent
To David in Jerusalem how goes
The battle.  With the ark of God, these foes
Will know defeat and then I'll wash my feet
And eat and sleep at home and know the sweet
And gentle kisses of a wife who waits
To see me march into the city gates.
Silence, silly heart!  No time to think
Of anything but battle, nor to shrink
From duty.  What is next?  Why can't we win?
Are we so long at war because of the sin
Of someone here or in Jerusalem?
My lord, the king is sure to find them...
Whoever they might be...our God will show
Them to my king and surely let him know
Who would this evil do.  To wait and not
To fight is hardest of the soldier's lot.

Behold...Joab comes to see me now.
Perhaps I'll find when we'll attack, and how.
"Ah, Joab, Captain for David, our liege!
How goes the war...how longer now the siege?"
"Uriah, friend!"  Joab doth retort,
"Our lord the king doth ask that you report
To him at once.  You are a lucky one,
Uriah!  All the way, the runners run
To tell me this., Who knows...perhaps the king
Doth have a plan and he will have you bring
It back to me.  Please give him my regards
And say we hope to capture Rabbah's lords
And bring them soon to him and tell him how
We hope to see him soon, Uriah.  Now...
You must be going.  Take this word:  I send
My best to our dear ones.  Good-by, my friend!"

### The Warrior Back to Jerusalem

Now...to Jerusalem, to see my king
And give him such report as I should bring.
I trust he's doing well.  Perhaps he knows
Why we have not won and our foes
Are able still to hold our hosts at bay.

I wonder what King David has to say?
My heart leaps! I see the massive walls
Of yon Jerusalem, and soon, its halls
Shall know my feet and I shall then repeat
The tidings of my lord Joab and greet
My king!

"Uriah!" Now, my King David speaks my name
And kisses me. My lord doth look the same
As he did long before I left my wife
To serve him in the Ammon strife.
"Long live my lord the king! I bring thee word
Of Joab. He is doing well, my lord!"
David worries now and doth send all
His servants from the palace hall.
He must have something urgent now to say
And have me take a message back this day
To Joab!

King David asks me things he surely knows:
About the people, war, and of our foes.
He seems so nervous. This is something new.
"Uriah! There is something you must do!"
"Of course, my lord! I'll do it if I can,"
I say to him. Perhaps he has a plan.
"You must go down unto your house and stay
Awhile and take your rest," I hear him say.
Now, this is strange. Does he know of danger
To my home? Yes...this is strange and stranger
Still. There is a battle to be won,
And doth my lord bring me away to run
Down to my house and take my ease, instead?
But, I shall keep my vow and take my bread
Elsewhere...Yea, right here, with the servants of
My lord! I will not see those whom I love
Until I know that Rabbah's walls are down!
I keep my oath in spite of David's crown!

My lord looks better; far more rested than
He looked yesterday. Perhaps I can
Return to Rabbah soon. "Uriah!" Now,
He sounds a bit provoked; "Uriah! How
Is it you would not go down and sleep
At home?" "I've made a vow that I must keep.
The ark and Israel and Judah abide
In tents and would thou have me now reside
In pleasant rooms, in warm and cozy halls
While comrades fight to capture Rabbah's walls?
My lord, I cannot easily forget
The vow I made!" Now, David seems to fret...
So unlike him. What has my king to gain
By insisting that I not refrain
From going to my house and Bathsheba?
What gain to yonder host and walled Rabbah?

Ah, Jerusalem! How pleasant are
Thy cobbled streets; indeed, worth fighting for.
City of a glorious destiny!
Honored with the name of Deity!
How wise to keep the battle far away
From these fair streets and let the children's gay
And lilting laughter make the day sound bright;
Keep it far away: the battle fright.

### Uriah Made Drunk With King David's Wine

"Uriah!" said my king, "You soon shall go
To battle once again and face the foe;
And so, since you're reluctant to partake
Of comforts for thy vow, then; for my sake
Would you now drink the wine I pour for thee?
I offer thee my hospitality!"
"Of course, my lord; at thy command," I said.
My vow keeps me from going to my bed,
But I shall drink with thee. Wilt thou propose
A toast? To whom or what to drink? To those
Who battle while we drink and take our rest...
Who feel a weariness and battle-pressed?"
We drink and I'm well drunk on regal wine.
I find a servant's couch and I recline.

A servant wakens me: "Uriah! My lord
Is calling now for thee." So at his word
I enter in and wait for him to say
What he would have to say. "Uriah, this day,
Thou shalt go to Joab in the field
And take to him these orders which are sealed."
His words are curt and crisp. I refrain
From asking what these orders might contain.
Maybe in these orders there's a way
To gain the vict'ry 'fore another day.

"Joab! Valiant friend, how goes the war?"
"Uriah, noble friend, the same; but far
Too long we've been in siege arrayed and we
Should long ago have won the victory!
But, tell me. What about my lord, the king?
And, what of home? Now, tell me ev'rything!"
"Of course, my Captain, and yet, first I have
The orders sealed for you that David gave."
Joab takes the orders, breaks the seal
And reads them to himself. Somehow I feel
He isn't reading what he thought to find;
He reads again, like something's on his mind.
He reads and looks at me and reads some more,
Then looks at me again, just as before.
"Uriah...go to thy tent and take thy rest;
Tomorrow, thou shalt have thy valiant test!"

### Uriah Dies as David Planned

So, in my tent, I ponder what will be,

Remembering what Joab said to me.
But, what will be will be. I've made my vow
And face whatever fate awaits me now.
O Lord, Jehovah, I am not afraid!
But, let there be, when history is made,
A line or two that says I did my part,
And never ran, but had a warrior's heart.

'Tis early day and deathly cold to me.
Before me, Rabbah's mighty walls I see;
And, in the near-light of the coming dawn
I see the archers with their arrows drawn,
And citizens, with all that's heavy poised
To drop on us. Their courage, greatly noised,
Is daring us to scale the massive wall
Where, on its crest, they wait with sword and maul.
Joab honors me and I'm assigned
With valiant men to charge a hill that's lined
With Ammonites before the city gates,
And not a man among us hesitates,
But, forward, fending arrows with our shields
An enemy gives ground and finally yields.
Forward, ever forward I keep going.
All around my feet the blood is flowing:
Blood of Ammonite and Israelite.
Blood of all! I'm tired. The pain is slight.
An arrow's found its mark from Rabbah's wall!
My shield is holding me and I can't fall.
I heard my comrades' names and heard the sign
As they withdrew. I heard their names, not mine!
Oh! Who has sinned that we have not taken Rabbah?
Oh Joab! My King David! Bathsheba!
I die!

Bill Harvey

### 709. WANTED--100,000 BOYS
*(To replace the hundred thousand drunkards
that will die this year.)*

Wanted, some boys who have minds bright and clear,
To stand at my counter as drinkers of beer,
To fill up the ranks without further delay,
Of the army of drunkards, passing away.
A hundred thousand a year, this will only supply
The loss of the trade from the drunkards that die.
Send those who can toil, or have wealth to bestow,
For profits are small on old drunkards, you know.
Let them come from the shop, the school, or the home,
We will welcome them all; care not if they roam.
If fathers and mothers keep running the mill
They must furnish boys or the wheel will stand still.

Author Unknown

710.     YOU'D NEVER DRINK
         IF YOU STOPPED TO THINK

You'd never drink
If you'd stop to think
Of the drunkard's face--
The vice and disgrace
Written there.

You'd never drink
If you'd stop to think
Of your loved one's shame
Who must bear your name
Everywhere.

Would you ever drink
If you'd stop and think
Of the bloated face
Which will soon deface
Manhood fair?

Could you stoop to drink
If you'd stop to think
Of honor at stake
And the hearts that must ache--
Your shame share?

But you never think,
You who love to drink,
Of your defamed name
And your loved one's shame--
Shame, their share.

No, you never think,
When you crave a drink,
Of eyes, skin and face
Nor loved one's disgrace--
Drink doesn't care.

                Mrs. H. A. McCamy


712.   IF NOT SATAN, WHO?

Who is mixing the fatal draught
  That palsies heart and brain?
And loads the bier of each passing year
  With ten hundred thousand slain?
Who blights the youth of the land today
  With the fiery breath of Hell?
If the Devil isn't, and never was,
  Won't somebody rise and tell?

Who dogs the footsteps of the saints?
  Who digs the pits for his feet?

711.  STRANGE FIRE

*"And...the sons...offered strange
fire...which he commanded them
not."—Lev. 10:1.*

Strange fire before My altar
  Which I commanded not,
As to annul what's written
  By tittle and with jot.

Strange feet as so to hasten
  Unto the sacred place,
Which walk in ways forbidden
  That savor not of grace.

Strange lips to call Me Father,
  As though My love to woo,
As seemeth it delighteth
  My holy will to do.

Strange so a gift to offer,
  Yet hold in high disdain,
A broken, contrite spirit,
  As to My mercy gain.

Strange wish for My atonement
  A substitute instead,
Unclean the hands that handle
  And break My holy bread.

Strange words of worldly wisdom
  Embrace their heresy
To preach another gospel
  As that it came from Me.

Strange lips proclaim My glory,
  Unclean to bear My praise,
Who come to bow before Me,
  But keep not to My ways.

Strange fire before My altar,
  And shall My hand not slay?
But see thou rend no garment
  For such as shun My way.

                J. Paul Sutton


Who sows his tares in the field of time
  Wherever God sows His wheat?
The Devil is voted not to be,
  And of course it must be true,
But who is doing the kind of work
  The Devil alone can do?

                Author Unknown

713.   VISION OF BELSHAZZAR

*(Read Daniel, Chapter 5)*

The king was on his throne,
   The satraps thronged the hall:
A thousand bright lamps shone
   O'er that high festival.
A thousand cups of gold,
   In Judah deemed divine--
Jehovah's vessels hold
   The godless heathen's wine!

In that same hour and hall,
   The fingers of a hand
Came forth against the wall,
   And wrote as if on sand:
The fingers of a man;--
   A solitary hand
Along the letters ran,
   And traced them like a wand.

The monarch saw and shook,
   And bade no more rejoice;
All bloodless waxed his look,
   And tremulous his voice.
"Let the men of lore appear,
   The wisest of the earth,
And expound the words of fear,
   Which mar our royal mirth."

Chaldea's seers are good,
   But here they have no skill;
And the unknown letters stood
   Untold and awful still.
And Babel's men of age
   Are wise and deep in lore;
But now they were not sage,
   They saw--but knew no more.

A captive in the land,
   A stranger and a youth,
He heard the king's command,
   He saw that writing's truth.
The lamps around were bright,
   The prophecy in view;
He read it on that night--
   The morrow proved it true.

"Belshazzar's grave is made,
   His kingdom passed away,
He, in the balance weighed,
   Is light and worthless clay;
The shroud his robe of state,
   His canopy the stone;

The Mede is at his gate!
   The Persian on his throne!"

                    Lord Byron

*"...and sin, when it is finished, bringeth
forth death."--James 1:15.*

714.   BOLT THAT DOOR!

Each sin has its door of entrance.
Keep--that--door--closed!
Bolt it tight!
Just outside, the wild beast crouches
In the night.
Pin the bolt with a prayer,
God will fix it there.

                    John Oxenham

715. ALL THAT I WAS, MY SIN, MY GUILT

All that I was, my sin, my guilt,
   My death, was all my own;
All that I am, I owe to Thee,
   My gracious God, alone.

The evil of my former state
   Was mine, and only mine;
The good in which I now rejoice
   Is Thine, and only Thine.

The darkness of my former state,
   The bondage, all was mine;
The light of life in which I walk,
   The liberty, is Thine.

Thy grace first made me feel my sin,
   It taught me to believe;
Then in believing, peace I found,
   And now I live, I live.

All that I am, e'en here on earth,
   All that I hope to be
When Jesus comes and glory dawns,
   I owe it, Lord, to Thee.

                    Horatius Bonar

716. TOM GRAY'S DREAM

Tom Gray lay down on the barroom floor,
Having drunk so much he could drink no more;
So he fell asleep with a troubled brain,
To dream that he rode on a Hell-bound train.

The engine with blood was red and damp,
And brilliantly lit by a brimstone lamp;
An imp, for fuel, was shoveling bones,
While the furnace rang with a thousand groans.
The boiler was filled with lager beer;
And the Devil himself was the engineer.

The passengers made such a motley crew--
Church member, atheist, Gentile and Jew;
Rich men in broadcloth and beggars in rags,
Handsome young ladies and withered old hags;
Yellow and black men, red, brown and white,
And all chained together--a horrible sight.
While the train dashed on at an awful pace,
And a hot wind scorched them on hands and face.

Wilder and wilder the country grew,
As faster and faster the engine flew;
Louder and louder the thunder crashed,
And brighter and brighter the lightning flashed.
Hotter and hotter the air became,
Till the clothes were burnt from each quivering frame.

Then in the distance there rose such a yell,
Ha! Ha! croaked the Devil, we're nearing Hell.
Then oh, how the passengers shrieked with pain,
And begged of the Devil to stop the train!
But he capered about and sang with glee,
And laughed and joked at their agony.

My faithful friends, you have done my work,
And the Devil can never a pay-day shirk.
You have bullied the weak, you have robbed the poor,
And a starving brother turned from your door;
You have laid up gold where the canker rusts,
And given free vent to your fleshly lusts;
You have justice scorned and corruption sown,
And trampled the laws of nature down;

You have drank and rioted, murdered and lied,
And mocked at God in your Hell-born pride.
You have paid full fare, so I'll carry you through,
For it's only right you should get your due;
Why, the laborer always expects his hire,
So I'll land you safe in the Lake of Fire,
Where your flesh shall roast in the flames that roar,
And my imps torment you more and more.

Then Tom awoke with an agonized cry,
His clothes soaked with sweat, his hair standing high,
And he prayed as he never had prayed before,
To be saved from drink and the Devil's power;
And his prayers and his cries were not made in vain,
For he never more rode on the Hell-bound train.

Author Unknown


717.    OUR WISE INSANITY

Who made him the product of futility and despair, a stuttering bum who
    grieves not and thinks not,
But only desperately clutches for the liquor which has made him a ruin?
Who caused him to stagger and stammer and leer, doomed in the jaws of
    a deadly dope?
Who made him a drunken lunatic?  Who blasted out the beauty of that
    God-given brain?
Who fusilladed the fears and compressed deep-seated futility in the
    heart of that child?
Who is to blame for the sunken eyes of that mother brimmed full of bit-
    terness?
Who is accountable when the teenager takes a gun and blasts the beast
    who is beating his mom?
When will we conclude this farce of profit from erosion?  This babble of
    gain from Hell-bound debauchees?

Is it the right method we practice?  Is our way a credit to freedom or
    enslavement?
Millions pour in from our colossal liquor corporations but have we
    counted the cost of the coffers tainted dollars?
With ten dollars gain we have a wobbling man whose faculties are crazed
    and decency gone!
For twenty dollars we have gained a bombastic brute mingling curses
    with indistinguishable babble;
One thousand dollars and the foundations of homes have rotted away!
On the auction block of enslavement there are four million for whom we
    have dug gutters!
And while they wallow in the vomit of their degradation we glibly boast
    about the billions in our treasuries!

And we so quickly forget the hot rod rammed down a baby's throat by a
    whiskey-beserk dad,
Yet this is multiplied millions of times!  And we choose not to see that
    tender lad as tears trickle from his heart!
These tragedies are hidden in the shadows of our tremendous whiskey
    scheme boiling from blind mentalities;
And we cry out for the rehabilitation of wrecks whom we have made by
    the legalization of booze in beautiful bottles!
O, my God!  Is this intelligence or stupidity?  May Wisdom return to her
    throne, and Reason rise again from the ruin of liquored looseness;
Let us stop this stampede of heart-rending waste for the dung of dirty
    dollars!

Russell V. Jensen

## 718. THE PRICE OF A DRINK

"Ten cents a glass!" Does any one think
That that is really the price of a drink?
"Ten cents a glass," I heard you say,
"Why, that isn't very much to pay!"
Ah, no, indeed, 'tis a very small sum
You are passing over 'twixt finger and thumb;
And if that were all that you gave away,
It wouldn't be very much to pay.

The price of a drink! Let him decide
Who has lost his courage and lost his pride,
And lies a groveling heap of clay,
Not far removed from a beast today.
The price of a drink! Let that one tell
Who sleeps tonight in a murderer's cell,
And feels within him the fires of Hell.
Honor and virtue, love and truth,
All the glory and pride of youth,
Hopes of manhood, and wreath of fame,
High endeavor and noble aim--
These are the treasures thrown away
At the price of a drink, from day to day.

"Ten cents a glass!" How Satan laughed,
As over the bar the young man quaffed
The beaded liquor, for the demon knew
The terrible work that drink would do!
And before morning the victim lay
With his life blood swiftly ebbing away;
And that was the price he paid, alas!
For the pleasure of taking a social glass.

The price of a drink! If you want to know
What some are willing to pay for it, go
Through that wretched tenement over there,
With dingy windows and broken stair,
Where foul disease, like a vampire, crawls
With outstretched wings o'er the moldy walls.

There poverty dwells with her hungry brood,
Wild-eyed as demons for lack of food;
There shame, in a corner, crouches low;
There violence deals its cruel blow;
The innocent ones are thus accursed
To pay the price of another's thirst.

"Ten cents a glass!" Oh, if that were all,
The sacrifice would, indeed, be small!
But the money's worth is the least amount
We pay, and whoever will keep account
Will learn the terrible waste and blight
That follows the ruinous appetite.
"Ten cents a glass!" Does any one think
That that is really the price of a drink?

Josephine Pollard

## 719. THE EVOLUTIONIST

I know a man out our way
That always spouts off and has his say
'Bout evolution, and all that trash;
He says he's kin to my jackass:
    Well, he ain't no kin to me.

He says his family had to climb
Out of a puddle of mud and slime;
They was just insects at the time:
    Well, they ain't no kin to me.

He says they lived in a coconut tree
A long time ago, and then, says he,
They picked lice off from each other's head,
And ate 'em, after they'd squashed 'em dead:
    Well, they ain't no kin to me.

He says his family used to live
Out in the mountains, in a cave;
They'd fight with clubs and stones an' staves:
    Well, they ain't no kin to me.

He says they'd drag a girl by the hair
An' take her back to the cave man's lair;
An' he says the girl, she didn't care;
    Well, they ain't no kin to me.

'Cause I'm from the people the good
                    Lord made,
The people that Jesus came to save;
The monkey-man heads but for the grave:
    He ain't no kin to me.

Some day he'll stand before our God,
And wish he hadn't talked so loud;
And Jesus will look at him an' say,
"Don't let him in; take him away:
    He ain't no kin to Me."

L. O. Engelmann

## 720. PREVENTION

'Twas a dangerous cliff, as they freely confessed,
  Though to walk near its crest was so pleasant;
For over its terrible edge there had slipped
  A duke and full many a peasant;
So the people said something would have to be done,
  But their projects did not at all tally.
Some said, "Put a fence round the edge of the cliff";
  Some, "An ambulance down in the valley."

But the cry for the ambulance carried the day,
  For it spread through the neighboring city;
A fence may be useful or not, it is true;
  But each heart became brimful of pity
For those who slipped over the dangerous cliff,
  And the dwellers in highway and alley
Gave pounds or gave pence, not to put up a fence,
  But an ambulance down in the valley.

"For the cliff is all right if you're careful," they said,
  "And if folks even slip and are dropping,
It isn't the slipping that hurts them so much
  As the shock down below when they're stopping."
So day after day as these mishaps occurred,
  Quick forth would the rescuers sally,
To pick up the victims who fell off the cliff,
  With their ambulance down in the valley.

Then an old sage remarked: "It's a marvel to me
  That people give far more attention
To repairing results than to stopping the cause
  When they'd much better aim at prevention.
Let us stop at its source all this mischief," cried he,
  "Come, neighbors and friends, let us rally;
If the cliff we will fence, we might almost dispense
  With the ambulance down in the valley."

Better guide well the young than reclaim them when old,
  For the voice of true wisdom is calling:
"To rescue the fallen is good, but 'tis best
  To prevent other people from falling."
Better close up the source of temptation and crime,
  Than deliver from dungeon or galley;
Better put a strong fence round the top of the cliff,
  Than an ambulance down in the valley.

                                        Joseph Malin

## 721. A HYMN TO GOD THE FATHER

Wilt Thou forgive that sin where I begun,
  Which was my sin, though it were done
      before?
Wilt Thou forgive that sin, through which
      I run
  And do run still, though still I do deplore?
When Thou hast done, Thou hast not done;
  For I have more.

Wilt Thou forgive that sin which I have won
  Others to sin, and made my sins their
      door?
Wilt Thou forgive that sin which I did shun
  A year or two, but wallow'd in, a score?
When Thou hast done, Thou hast not done;
  For I have more.

I have a sin of fear, that when I've spun
  My last thread, I shall perish on the shore;
But swear by Thyself, that at my death
      Thy Son
  Shall shine, as He shines now and
      heretofore:
And having done that, Thou hast done;
  I fear no more.

John Donne

## 722. DAD'S CIGAR

Twinkle, twinkle little star
On the end of Dad's cigar,
Filling all the air with smoke
Till we have to cough and choke.

One time I heard my daddy say
He's going to Heaven some sweet day.
But tell me, will the angels care
If Daddy smokes cigars up there?

And really what will Daddy do
When he wants to smoke or take a chew?
I've thought about it quite a bit--
No ash trays there; no place to spit.

I think it really is too bad
I'm feeling sorry for my dad;
I'm just afraid he'll have to wait
And stay outside the Pearly Gate.

There's just one other place I know,
And that's where sinners have to go;
That hot place is sure no joke--
But that's the only place to smoke!

Lillie Buffum

## 723. I'D SUPPORT THE LIQUOR TRAFFIC

If it weren't for
    Children abused,
    Decency refused,
    Wrong excused,
    Satan amused,
    Lives misused,
    Minds confused,
I'd support the liquor traffic.

If it weren't for
    Dishonesty,
    Brutality,
    Infidelity,
    Immaturity,
    Impurity,
    Immorality,
    Nonspirituality,
I'd support the liquor traffic.

If it weren't for
    Truth compromised,
    Good ostracized,
    Evil exercized,
    God criticized,
    Children terrorized,
    Homes jeopardized,
    Wrong legalized,
I'd support the liquor traffic.

If it weren't for
    The drunken sot,
    The hungry tot,
    The Devil's knot,
    The mind's rot,
    The widow's lot,
    The damning spot,
    The final plot,
I'd support the liquor traffic.

Bill Harvey

# SPECIAL OCCASIONS

## 724. NEW YEAR WISHES

What shall I wish thee, dear friend,
   As you enter another year?
A life all free from sorrow,
   With never a pain or fear?

A path all strewn with roses
   With never a prickly thorn,
With all of joy to gladden
   And naught to make thee mourn?

Nay, then thou'lt lose the blessing
   That comes with sorrow's hour,
Thou then wouldst lose the comfort
   Of Christ's own mighty power.

Oft in the deepest trial
   The richest blessings come,
And pain but leads us upward
   Toward our heavenly home.

So I will leave thy future
   In His all-loving hand,
With Him will leave the mysteries
   We cannot understand.

Content that He will lead thee
   The way that's always right,
The roughest path but brings thee
   To His own glory light.

I know that He will give thee
   His own deep joy and rest,
I know that He will send thee
   All that is wise and best.

So I will only wish thee
   Just His own perfect will,
His own great love and blessing
   Thine inmost soul to fill.

Yet "more and more" of glory
   Until the goal is won,
And in His Royal Presence
   Eternity's begun.

               E. M. U.

## 725. NEW YEAR'S WISH

All that is beautiful, all that is best--
Joy of activity, calmness of rest,
Health for life's pilgrimage,
Strength for its strife,
Sunshine to brighten the pathway of life;
Courage to trust, tho' the skies be o'ercast,
Hope for the future born out of the past,
Love that is tender and friends who are true;
This is my New Year's wish for you.

               Author Unknown

## 726. NEW TIME

Time is a treasure;
   How shall we use it?
We can make useful,
   Or can abuse it!
Only the Giver
   Can make our hearts wise,
Teaching us daily
   The New Time to prize.

Time is a treasure,
   So view it, my soul!
Keep all its spending
   'Neath watchful control;
Employ each moment
   In God's holy fear,
And He will ensure thee
   A Happy New Year.

               Author Unknown

## 727. A PROSPEROUS NEW YEAR

The new year lies before me,
   A spotless, shining thing,
Bright as the promises of God,
   Fresh as the breath of spring.

A year to fill with lovely thoughts,
   And kindly, helpful deeds,
Losing all consciousness of self,
   In prayer for others' needs.

               Sybil Leonard Armes

## 728. AT THIS NEW YEAR

At this new year
The page is clear.
The sheet is white.
Then what I write
Must be with care.

When once it's marred
And by sin scarred,
'Tis too late then
To moan for sin
And call life hard.

Words are a seed.
Then what I read
I must take care,
And what I hear
I must take heed.

I will delight
To do the right,
And thus fulfill
Thy perfect will
With all my might.

I dare not see
What ought not be,
Or live one hour
Without Thy power
And grace on me.

I must not play
When I should pray.
I must not sleep
When I should weep
For souls astray.

Since Christ is near
I must not fear,
But fight all Hell
Good News to tell
That all might hear.

The snow white sheet
I must keep neat
That all may see
Thyself in me,
Bowed at Thy feet.

O Lord, help me
Like Thee to be,
And in Thy light
The page keep white,
Lord--all for Thee.

Fred D. Jarvis

"Blessed be the Lord, who daily loadeth us
with benefits. . ."--Ps. 68:19.

## 729. A PRAYER FOR THE NEW YEAR

Lord, I would ask for a holy year,
  Spent in Thy perfect will:
Help me to walk in Thy very steps;
  Help me to please Thee still.

Lord, I would ask for a busy year,
  Filled up with service true;
Doing with all Thy Spirit's might;
  All that I find to do.

Lord, I would ask for a dying world;
  Stretch forth Thy mighty hand,
Scatter Thy Word--Thy power display
  This year in every land.

Lord, I would ask for a year of hope,
  Looking for Thee to come,
And hastening on that year of years
  That brings us Christ and Home.

A. B. Simpson

## 730. THIS DAY OF ALL THE YEAR

O Night of Glory, when the star
  Lit all the Orient sky,
When hill and valley, near and far,
  Rang back the angel's cry,
When men saw Heaven's bright portals ope
  With sounds of holy cheer--
O Night of glory! Night of hope!
  O Night of all the year.

To Him this day our prayers arise,
  Each soul its tribute pays:
The precious myrrh of sacrifice,
  The incense sweet of praise,
The glowing gold of sacred love
  That knows no stain of fear,
These gifts we bring to Christ above
  This Day of all the year.

Give us the calm and tranquil soul,
  The loving, open heart,
The life that sways to Thy control
  And dwells in Thee apart;
The peace that makes life's thorny way
  Seem beautiful and clear:
Grant us these boons on this Thy day,
  This Day of all the year.

Author Unknown

## 731. HAPPY NEW YEAR

New mercies, new blessings, new light on the way,
New courage, new hope, and strength for each day,
New notes of thanksgiving, new chords of delight,
New praise in the morning, new songs in the night,
New wine in thy chalice, new altars to raise,
New fruits for thy Master, new garments for praise,
New gifts from His treasures, new smiles from His face,
New streams from the fountain of infinite grace,
New stars for thy crown, and new tokens of love,
New gleams of the glory that waits thee above,
New light of His countenance, full and unpriced,
All this to be the joy of thy new life in Christ.

Frances Ridley Havergal

*"I will arise and go to my father, and will say*
*unto him, Father, I have sinned against heaven,*
*and before thee."--Luke 15:18.*

## 732. HAPPY NEW YEAR

I do not know, I cannot see
What God's kind hand prepares for me,
Nor can my glance pierce through the haze
Which covers all my future ways;
But yet I know that o'er it all
Rules He who notes the sparrow's fall.

I know the Hand that hath me fed
And through the year my feet hath led;
I know the everlasting arm
That hath upheld and kept from harm.
I trust Him as my God and Guide
And know that He will still provide.

So at the opening of the year,
I banish care and doubt and fear,
And clasping His kind hand, essay
To walk with God from day to day,
Trusting in Him who hath me fed,
Walking with Him who hath me led.

Farewell, Old Year, with goodness crowned.
A hand divine hath set thy bound.
Welcome the New Year, which shall bring
Fresh blessings from my God and King.
The Old we leave without a tear,
The New we hail without a fear.

Author Unknown

## 733. ANOTHER YEAR

Another year is dawning!
    Dear Master, let it be
In working or in waiting
    Another year with Thee.

Another year of leaning
    Upon Thy loving breast,
Of ever-deepening trustfulness,
    Of quiet, happy rest.

Another year of mercies,
    Of faithfulness and grace;
Another year of gladness
    In the shining of Thy face.

Another year of progress;
    Another year of praise;
Another year of proving
    Thy presence "all the days."

Another year of service,
    Of witness for Thy love;
Another year of training
    For holier work above.

Another year is dawning!
    Dear Master, let it be
On earth, or else in Heaven,
    Another year for Thee!

Frances R. Havergal

734. A PSALM FOR NEW YEAR'S EVE

A Friend stands at the door;
    In either tight-closed hand
Hiding rich gifts, three hundred and threescore;
    Waiting to strew them daily o'er the land,
Even as seed the sower,
    Each drops he, treads it in and passes by:
    It cannot be made fruitful till it die.


O good New Year, we clasp
    This warm shut hand of thine,
Losing forever, with half sigh, half grasp,
    That which from ours falls like dead fingers' twine:
Ay, whether fierce its grasp
    Has been, or gentle, having been, we know
    That it was blessed: let the old year go.


O New Year, teach us faith!
    The road of life is hard:
When our feet bleed and scourging winds us scathe,
    Point thou to Him whose visage was more marred
Than any man's: who saith,
    "Make straight paths for your feet," and to the opprest,
    "Come ye to Me, and I will give you rest."


Yet hang some lamp-like hope
    Above this unknown way,
Kind year, to give our spirits freer scope
    And our hands strength to work while it is day.
But if that way must slope
    Tombward, oh, bring before our fading eyes
    The lamp of life, the hope that never dies.


Comfort our souls with love--
    Love of all human kind;
Love special, close, in which like sheltered dove
    Each weary heart its own safe next may find;
And love that turns above
    Adorningly; contented to resign
    All loves, if need be, for the love divine.


Friend, come thou like a friend,
    And whether bright thy face,
Or dim with clouds we cannot comprehend,
    We'll hold out patient hands, each in his place,
And trust Thee to the end,
    Knowing Thou leadest onwards to those spheres
    Where there are neither days nor months nor years.

The Author of "John Halifax, Gentlemen" 1855

## 735.  ONE DAY AT A TIME

One day at a time, with its failures and fears,
With its hurts and mistakes, with its weakness and tears,
With its portion of pain and its burden of care;
One day at a time we must meet and must bear.

One day at a time to be patient and strong;
To be calm under trial and sweet under wrong;
Then its toiling shall pass and its sorrow shall cease;
It shall darken and die, and the night shall bring peace.

One day at a time--but the day is so long,
And the heart is not brave and the soul is not strong.
O Thou pitiful Christ, be Thou near all the way;
Give courage and patience and strength for the day.

Swift cometh His answer, so clear and so sweet;
"Yea, I will be with thee, thy troubles to meet;
I will not forget thee, nor fail thee, nor grieve;
I will not forsake thee; I never will leave."

Not yesterday's load we are called on to bear,
Nor the morrow's uncertain and shadowy care;
Why should we look forward or back with dismay?
Our needs, as our mercies, are but for the day.

One day at a time, and the day is His day;
He hath numbered its hours, though they haste or delay.
His grace is sufficient; we walk not alone;
As the day, so the strength that He giveth His own.

                              Annie Johnson Flint

## 736.  FACING A NEW YEAR

Standing at the portal of the opening year,
Words of comfort meet us, hushing every fear;
Spoken through the silence by our Father's voice,
Tender, strong, and faithful, making us rejoice.
Onward then, and fear not, children of the day!
For His Word shall never, never pass away!

For the year before us, oh, what rich supplies!
For the poor and needy living streams shall rise;
For the sad and sinful shall His grace abound;
For the faint and feeble, perfect strength be found.
Onward then, and fear not, children of the day!
For His Word shall never, never pass away.

                              Frances Ridley Havergal

### 737. THE RESURRECTION

Dark was the night and hearts were dark with sorrow,
  No gleam of hope could pierce the awful gloom;
No word of cheer or promised bright tomorrow,
  All, all seemed hidden in the silent tomb.

Their Lord their Light by Roman soldiers taken,
  Nailed to the cross had suffered there in shame,
Died all alone by followers forsaken,
  Mocked and derided for His kingly claim.

Love had prepared sweet spices for anointing;
  At early morn they came to seek Him there;
Angels they saw who joyously were pointing,
  Saying, "Behold the place; He is not here!

"There is the grave, o'er Death He is victorious,
  See where He lay, He's risen as He said,
Wondrous in power, in majesty most glorious.
  Why seek the living among the silent dead?"

Shout all ye lands and hail Him King of Glory;
  Victor o'er Death your Saviour loud proclaim;
O'er all the earth go tell the wondrous story;
  Shout glad hosannas to His glorious name.

Hail Him your Lord all powerful to deliver;
  All ye His saints His praises gladly sing;
Sing of His grace and boundless love forever,
  Mighty to save, our Saviour, Priest and King.

J. H. Turnbull

### 738. EASTER

THE LORD IS RISEN, the resurrection morning
  Has dawned, and from my troubled heart has fled
The fear of death, and now in place of mourning
  Joy, sweetest joy and peace are mine instead.

THE LORD IS RISEN, the reign of sin has ended,
  He holds the key of death, and from its sway
My soul is freed, for now in Him ascended
  Life, everlasting life is mine today.

THE LORD IS RISEN, He Satan's power has broken,
  And from the foe, my ransomed soul is free;
THE LORD IS RISEN, and by His wondrous token
  I too shall rise His glorious face to see.

Marion E. C. Netherton

739. A ROMAN SOLDIER'S STORY

I loved Him not--and yet, I could not hate Him.
   I was A ROMAN...He was but a Jew.
Yet, there He hung, and agonized for others.
   Was ever love of MAN so pure and true?

Upon the cross between two thieves they hung Him.
   (And now, my stylus falters as I write--
For I must stand and see His awful anguish;
   Must watch the daytime turn to darkest night).

One thief cried out, "If Thou be Lord, then save us!"
   The other looked at Him with glazing eyes,
And said, "Remember me, Lord, in Thy kingdom."
   Christ said, "Today, thou'lt be in Paradise."

The hours dragged on; yet there He hung suspended
   'Twixt Heaven and earth. Ah, 'twas an awful sight!
I'd seen such sights before--I was a soldier--
   Yet ne'er before did day become as night.

For three long hours the darkness lay around us;
   The rocks were rent and lightning flashed around.
One called, "The veil is rent within the Temple!"
   And saints rose from their graves within the ground.

I dared not look.... The sky grew darker, darker--
   Until it seemed like midnight all around.
And then I cried out, "Stop my ears, O Father!"
   For I had heard His blood drip to the ground.

They said to me, "Go pierce His side, proud Roman."
   But ah...my spear hung heavy at my side--
For, once more He had cried out to His Father.
   I would that in His place I might have died!

I could not thrust...and so they called another.
   The blood and water poured out from His side.
The people smote their breasts and left Golgotha.
   I knew then that it was THE CHRIST who died.

His seamless coat lay folded on the ground there.
   (They said the lot had fallen unto me.)
With reverent, trembling hands I touched its border,
   Then placed it where no human eye could see.

The day grew old. The thieves' legs had been broken;
   And men came now to take our Lord away.
More worthy lips than mine shall tell the story
   Of how Christ rose that Resurrection Day.

                    Mrs. Leo R. Goodwin

740. EASTER MORNING...

As dawn crept o'er the garden fair,
  Around the vault where Jesus lay,
The heavy-hearted women came,
  Their last sad solemn dues to pay
To Him who through the gladsome years
  Their hearts and souls so strangely stirred,
Who healed their hurts, who stilled their fears,
  Who spake the True and Living Word.

A glance within the opened tomb,
  The message of the angel given,
On joyous eager feet they run
  To tell the news:  The Lord is risen;
The promise made has been fulfilled;
  Within the tomb He may not stay;
But bursting from the bonds of death
  Comes forth this first glad Easter Day.

With joyful hearts repeat the news
  To men bowed down with grief and pain:
O'er sin and death the victory's won;
  The Lord returns with us to reign.
Triumphant o'er the powers of Hell,
  The gates of life He opens wide.
Rejoice!  Rejoice!  Exalt His name!
  The risen Lord be glorified!

E. R. Bingham

741. HE LIVES...

Blest morning! whose first dawning ray
Beheld the Son of God
Arise triumphant from the grave,
And leave His dark abode.

Wrapt in the silence of the tomb
The Great Redeemer lay,
Till the revolving skies had brought
The third, the appointed day.

Hell and the grave combined their force
To hold our Lord in vain;
Sudden the Conqueror arose,
And burst their feeble chain.

Salvation and immortal praise
To our victorious King!
Let Heaven and earth, and rocks and seas,
With glad hosannas ring.

To Father, Son, and Holy Ghost,
To God whom we adore,
Be glory, as it was, and is,
And shall be evermore.  Amen.

Isaac Watts

742.                    THANKSGIVING

I've been countin' up my blessin's, I've been summin' up my woes,
But I ain't got the conclusion some would naturally suppose:
Why, I quit a-countin' troubles 'fore I had a half a score,
While the more I count my blessin's, I keep a findin' more and more.
There's been things that wan't exactly as I thought they'd ought to be,
An' I've often growled at Providence for not a-pettin' me!
But I hadn't stopped to reckon what the other side had been--
How much o' good an' blessin' had been thickly crowded in.
Fer there's been a rift o' sunshine after every shower o' tears,
An' I found a load o' laughter scattered all along the years.
If the thorns have pricked me sometimes, I've good reason to suppose
Love has hid 'em often from me, 'neath the rapture of the rose!
So I'm goin' to still be thankful fer the sunshine an' the rain,
Fer the joy that's made me happy; fer the purgin' done by pain;
Fer the love o' little children; fer the friends that have been true;
Fer the guidin' hand that's led me every threatenin' danger through!

L. A. Tubbs

# INDEX OF AUTHORS

## INDEX OF AUTHORS

# INDEX OF TITLES

# INDEX OF FIRST LINES

Be brave, dear friend! God still has use for you--J. Danson Smith, 223
Be comforted! In God thy comfort lies--J. Danson Smith, 253
Beautiful toiler, thy work all done--Lathrop, 265
Beautiful Zion, built above--Gill, 300
Because He set before me--Jorg, 100
Behind him lay the gray Azores--Joaquin Miller, 47
Behold a stranger at the door--O'Kane, 96
Beloved! I cannot wear for thee--C. C. White, 264
Blessed inspired Word of God--John R. Rice, 4
Blessings on thee, little man--Whittier, 471
Blest are the pure in heart--Unknown, 199
Blest day! When Christ on earth shall reign--Neighbour, 651
Blest morning! whose first dawning ray--Watts, 741
Born without a bed in a stable--John R. Rice, 61
Breathe on me, Breath of God--Hatch, 432
Breathes there the man, with soul so dead--Scott, 542
Bring me men to match my mountains--Sam Walter Foss, 14
But I think the King of that country comes--van Dyke, 518
By faith and not by sight--Clarkson, 382
By lonely trails that pioneers--Murray, 615


Chosen men of God had spoken--Helsley, 92
Christ for sickness, Christ for health--H. W. S., 98
Christ has no hands but our hands--Flint, 656
Christ is near for all who seek--John R. Rice, 378
Christian, when thy way seems darkest--Unknown, 228
Closed eyes can't see the white roses--Hodges, 510
Come and drink from out the fount of living waters--John R. Rice, 635
Come at the morning hour--Montgomery, 578
Come, dear Lord Jesus, for long we've been watching--John R. Rice, 650
Come, Holy Spirit, heavenly Dove--Watts, 435
Come share the road with me, my own--Oxenham, 422
Come, ye sinners, poor and needy--Kirkpatrick, 610
Coming today? Today? Yes--John R. Rice, 642
Complete atonement Thou hast made--Unknown, 622
Courage, brother! do not stumble--M'Leod, 365
Creep into thy narrow bed--Matthew Arnold, 24


Dark was the night and hearts were dark with sorrow--Turnbull, 737
Dear Friend, whose presence in the house--Clarke, 477
Death be not proud, though some have called thee--Donne, 296
Dey say Dod made the babies--Lillie Buffum, 484
Did you ever pass a youngster, who had been an' stubbed his toe--Unknown, 232
Did you give him a lift? He's a brother of man--Gawell, 414
Did you tackle that trouble that came your way--E. V. Cooke, 54
Did you think of us this morning--Selected, 595
Do not ask me not to speak--Nicholson, 298
Do you care for souls, my brother--Howard, 525
Don't go to the theatre, concert, or ball--Anonymous, 449
Don't tell me what you will do--Selected, 41
Down in the little back garden--Unknown, 452
Draw up the papers, lawyer, and make 'em good and stout--Carleton, 472
Dream not too much of what you'll do tomorrow--Anonymous, 39

## INDEX OF FIRST LINES

# Notes: